Windows Programming with Borland C++

Jeff Mackay

Windcrest®/ McGraw-Hill

New York   San Francisco   Washington, D.C.   Auckland   Bogotá
Caracas   Lisbon   London   Madrid   Mexico City   Milan
Montreal   New Delhi   San Juan   Singapore
Sydney   Tokyo   Toronto

NOTICES

Borland®	Borland, International
dBase™	
Paradox™	
Intel®	Intel Corporation
Microsoft®	Microsoft Corporation
MS-DOS®	
NT™	
Win32™	
Windows NT™	

FIRST EDITION
SECOND PRINTING

©1993 by **Windcrest**, an imprint of McGraw-Hill, Inc.
The name "Windcrest" is a registered trademark of McGraw-Hill, Inc.

Printed in the United States of America. All rights reserved. The publisher takes no responsibility for the use of any materials or methods described in this book, nor for the products thereof.

Library of Congress Cataloging-in-Publication Data
Mackay, Jeff
    Windows programming with Borland C++ / by Jeff Mackay
      p.   cm
    Includes index.
    ISBN 0-8306-4319-2 (paper)
      1. C++ (Computer program language) 2. Borland C++ 3. Microsoft Windows (Computer file) I. Title
QA76.73.C15M32   1993
005.4'3--dc20   92-40040
                                                                                                 CIP

Acquisitions editor: Brad Schepp
Editorial team: Bob Ostrander, Executive Editor
                  John C. Baker, Book Editor
                  Len Dorfman, Consulting Editor
                  Jodi L. Tyler, Indexer
Production team: Katherine G. Brown, Director
                    Ollie Harmon, Coding
                    Susan E. Hansford, Coding
                    Brenda S. Wilhide, Layout
                    Wendy Small, Layout
                    Wanda Ditch, Layout
                    Lorie L. White, Proofreading
Design team: Jaclyn J. Boone, Designer
               Brian Allison, Associate Designer   WU1
Cover design and illustration: Sandra Blair Design, Harrisburg, Pa.   4340

Contents

Acknowledgments viii
Introduction ix
   Using this book x
   What's next x

1 Object-oriented Windows programs 1

Object-oriented systems 1
The Windows object model 2
   Graphical objects 2
   Window objects 3
   Events & messages 4
   Is Windows object-oriented? 4
   Object-oriented Windows programming with C++ 5
Why use C++ 5
   A better C 5
   Object-oriented extensions 6
   Class libraries 6
   Application frameworks 7
   Converting Windows programs to C++ 8
The Vista Application Framework 8
   Application and support classes 8
   Window classes 9
   Graphic classes 10
   Communicator classes 11
What's next 11

2 Windows applications 13

A traditional Windows program 14
   The program 14
   The main driver: WinMain 17
   Program initialization 18
   Creating window classes 19
   Creating & displaying a window 19
   Messages & the message loop 20
   The window procedure 20
   Cleaning up 21
   Windows naming conventions 21
   Stricter coding practices 22
   New data types 22
A Vista windows application 23
   The program 25
   Creating an applicationobject 25
   Creating a window class 26

    Creating action methods 26
    Using graphical drawing objects 27
    Vista naming conventions 29
  What's next 29

3   *Building programs* 31
  The Windows development cycle 31
    Creating C++ source files 32
    Creating resource scripts 33
    Creating a module definition file 35
    Creating help files 35
    Creating a project 36
  Building WinVista and WinApp 36
  Debuggging your program 36
    Using Turbo Debugger 37
    Using WInspector 37
    Drastic measures 38
  What's next 38

4   *Applications & events* 39
  Vista applications & the VAppl class 39
    Interface, implementation, & access control 40
    Inheritance & initialization 44
    Program cleanup 45
    Running the program 45
    Overloaded operators 45
  Sizer: using the Application class 46
    Retrieving windows state information 46
    Maintaining configuration data 46
  Communicating with Windows: the VEvent class 48
    Windows messages 48
    The VEvent class 53
    Event portability 53
  MSGLIST: responding to events 55
    Initializing the event dispatcher 59
    Initializing the window 60
    Painting the window 60
    Responding to mouse events 62
  What's next 64

5   *Vista window objects* 65
  VWindow: the base window class 65
    The window procedure 65

      Dispatching messages   68
      Two-step initialization   70
      The VWindow class hierarchy   70
   FileView: a file viewer   70
      Designing FileView   70
      The FileView class   71
      The Viewer class   75
      The FileBuffer and TextLine classes   79
   Scrolling the window   82
   Moving C programs to Vista   87
   What's next   88

6 *Getting input with menus & accelerators*   89

   Windows menus   89
      Pull-down menus   90
      Cascading menus   91
      Pop-up menus   93
   Using Vista menu objects   94
      Adding a menu to a window object   97
      Reacting to user commands   97
   Creating dynamic menus with the VMenu class   98
   Creating a floating menu   104
   Using accelerators   109
   Moving C programs to Vista   113
   What's next   113

7 *Dialog & message boxes*   115

   Vista dialog boxes   115
   Message boxes   115
   Windows common dialogs   117
      Opening files with the VFileOpenDialog class   126
      Managing the printer   127
      Selecting a font with the VFontDialog class   130
      Setting colors with the VColorDialog class   130
      Search for text with the VfindDialog class   132
   What's next   134

8 *Child window control objects*   135

   Child window controls   135
   Attaching data objects to a dialog box   137
   Data validation with controls   150
      Character-level validation   150
      Field-level validation   151

Custom controls 151
Using global window messages 152
Moving C programs to Vista 153
What's next 153

9 MDI window objects 155

The Multiple Document Interface 155
Vista MDI classes 156
    Managing child windows 156
    Swapping menus 163
    Object dependencies 169
Unconventional MDI windows 170
    Drag-and-drop operations 176
    Simulating a program manager icon 177
An MDI FileView 179
Moving MDI programs from C to Vista 194
What's next 195

10 Graphical objects 197

The Windows graphics model 197
    Device contexts 198
    Drawing tools 199
    Graphics primitives 199
    Win32 improvements 199
Vista graphics objects 200
    Device objects 200
    Graphics tool objects 202
    High-level graphics objects 204
    Printing with objects 208
What's next 210

11 Memory management & dynamic link libraries 211

The Windows 3.x memory architecture 212
Memory & the Windows operating modes 212
    Memory segment attributes 212
    Standard mode 214
    386-enhanced mode 215
    Program organization 216
    The Windows 3.x memory management API 218
The Win32 memory architecture 218
Memory management with objects 219
The default new & delete operators 219
    The VAllocator class 221

The VHandle class   223
  Template classes   225
    Overloading pointer dereferences   227
    Extending the VHandle classes   228
  Using dynamic link libraries   231
    LibMain and WEP   231
    Windows NT dynamic link libraries   232
    Exporting & importing functions   233
    Special requirements for objects   233
  What's next   235

12 Clipboard, DDE, & OLE objects   237
  Windows interprocess communication   237
  The clipboard   238
    The VClipboard class   238
    The VClipItem class   239
    An example applications: CLIP   240
  Dynamic data exchange   247
    DDEML basics   248
    Vista DDE Classes   251
    The VDdeObject class   252
    The VDdeServer class   253
    Data management callbacks   255
    The VDde Client & conversation class   260
  Object Linking and Embedding   265
    Why use OLE?   267
    What is OLE?   269
    OLE server applications   270
    OLE client applications   271
    Vista OLE classes   273
    Event dispatching   273
    Building and OLE server   274
    Building and OLE client   284
    Debugging OLE applications   294
  Wrapping up   295

Appendix: 297
  The Vista library   297

Bibliography   543
Index   545
About the author   551

Acknowledgments

This book wouldn't have been possible without the assistance and support of many people. I did the initial work on the book while consulting at Candler Hospital in Savannah, Georgia. Thanks to Bert Hopkins, Carol Moseley, Mike Howard, Trudy Pranulis, Gifford Usher, Cindi Hobbs, Rachel All, and the entire CIS staff at Candler. Without their support and encouragement, this book never would have materialized. Yes, Bert, I still owe you one.

I also received a lot of support from everyone at CASEWORKS, Inc. Thanks to Joe Richburg, Joe Trino, Al Nickles, Perry Bynum, Tareef Saeb, Lin LiHui, and William Holden. Last, but definitely not least, thanks to my whole family, especially Mom, Dad, and Mi Suk. Most of all, thanks to Linda and Danny for being so patient. Now maybe we'll have time to go to the park.

Introduction

Starting with Release 3.0, the popularity of Microsoft Windows exploded. Users began to expect the convenience and power provided by Windows, and developers responded. Over 5000 Windows applications were written by the time Microsoft released Windows 3.1. Future releases of Windows promise more features and an even larger market.

While developers worked on the existing base of Windows applications, vendors introduced Windows-compatible C^{++} compilers. The C^{++} language improves on C by providing object-oriented extensions similar to those provided by the Windows environment itself. If you've written a Windows application, you probably plan to convert it to C^{++} or at least plan to use C^{++} for future development.

You probably have heard that good C programs also are good C^{++} programs. This is true; most example applications you'll find in Windows programming manuals will compile under C^{++} as well as they will under C. However, just because a program compiles cleanly doesn't mean it's a C^{++} program. To make it a C^{++} program, you need to use the object-oriented features provided by the language. Writing a C^{++} program without classes is like driving down the highway at 35 miles per hour in a Porsche. You can do it, but why would you want to?

This book is about object-oriented programming for Windows using the Borland C^{++} development tools. It focuses on exploiting object-oriented features within Windows programs using the Vista class library. This book is not just a collection of source code; each chapter gives background on the design behind the examples, covering new topics in both C^{++} and Windows in each chapter. It also presents step-by-step guidelines on converting existing C programs to use the Vista library.

This book covers some basic topics like window and menu management, and then moves on to more advanced topics: graphics, memory management and dynamic link libraries. It also covers the newest features of Windows: Windows NT and the Win32 library; the Dynamic Data Exchange Manager Library (DDEML); and Object Linking and Embedding (OLE). By the time you finish this book, you'll be able to build your own Windows applications using the latest techniques and offering the modern features common to the most sophisticated Windows programs.

Using this book

To get the most out of this book, you should be familiar with both Windows and C++. While you don't need to be an expert on C++ or a Windows guru, some exposure to both will be helpful. This is not an introduction to either topic, it is instead a guide to using the two together. You can use the following books for additional information:

> Stroustrup, Bjarne. 1991. *The C++ Programming Language*, Second Edition. Reading, MA.:Addison-Wesley.
>
> Petzold, Charles. 1992. *Programming Windows*. Third Edition. Redmond, WA.:Microsoft Press.
>
> Borland International. 1992. *Windows API*, Volume 1-3, Scotts Valley, CA.:Borland International.

I try to explain new topics whenever they arise, but many are far beyond the scope of this book. The previous books are recognized as the definitive sources for their subject areas. The bibliography lists a number of other books on both topics that might be helpful.

Windows programmers need some heavy hardware horsepower. A minimal configuration for a Windows user is an 80386SX machine with 2Mb of memory and a 40Mb hard drive. For programming, you'll need at least 4Mb of memory, a larger disk drive, and a faster processor.

You also will need a Windows C++ compiler. The Vista library and sample applications you'll find in this book were developed using Borland C++. However, portability was one of my goals when designing the library, so the examples should compile under the Microsoft and Zortech C++ compilers with few changes.

What's next

The chapters in this book are grouped together by the general subject. The first group covers designing and building Windows applications. Chapter 1 introduces the concepts I'll use throughout the rest of the book. Chapter 2 contrasts a traditional Windows application with a Vista application. Chapter 3 covers using the Borland C++ and Turbo C++ for Windows tools to build a Vista application.

The second group covers basic Windows programming concepts. It starts with chapter 4, examining the Vista application and event classes and their use within an application. Chapter 5 discusses the use of window objects, which are the basic building blocks for a Windows application. Chapter 6 covers menus and accelerators, which are the major source of command input for a Windows program. Chapter 7 discusses dialog boxes, message boxes, and menus. Chapter 8 examines the use of child window controls and custom dialog boxes, and chapter 9 looks at the Windows Multiple Document Interface.

The third group examines some more advanced Windows programming topics. Chapter 10 takes a whirlwind tour through Windows graphics programming. Chapter 11 looks at Windows memory management and dynamic link libraries. Finally, chapter 12 examines the three major methods of interprocess communication: the clipboard, dynamic data exchange, and object linking and embedding.

As this book is going to press, the Windows NT operating system has not yet been released. I am currently working on porting the Vista Application Framework and sample applications to the new environment. The porting effort was suprisingly simple, and few changes have been required. Because of production requirements, the examples in the book do not reflect my latest efforts; however, the files on the companion disk have been ported with an early version of Borland C++ for Windows NT.

Windows NT

1 Object-oriented Windows programs

There has always been a relationship between graphical user interfaces (GUIs) and object-oriented programming. The first GUI served as the interface for an object-oriented Smalltalk development system at Xerox's Palo Alto Research Center. The original GUI developers recognized that graphical environments provided an ideal setting for object-oriented programming.

When other vendors, including Microsoft, began developing their own graphical environments, they built them using procedural languages like C and Pascal. Object-oriented languages hadn't matured enough or generated enough of a following for successful commercial systems. As a result, most Windows programs were written using the C language.

This chapter discusses the object-oriented principles that make the C++ language ideal for Windows programming. First, I'll discuss what an object-oriented system really is. Then, I'll look at the object model used by the Windows environment itself. Finally, I'll look at some useful C++ properties that I'll use to enhance the Windows object model.

Object-oriented systems

Over the past few years, the term "object-oriented has become almost cliche. Software publishers all promote their products as being object-oriented and the media extols the benefits of object-oriented technology, but few agree on what the term "object-oriented really means. So, before I go any further, I'll define some terms.

An *object-oriented system* or *language* uses the object as a basic component. In his book *Object-Oriented Design With Applications*, Grady Booch defines an object simply as "something you can do things to. Further, "an object has state, behavior, and identity. In other words, an object is data and the operations that act on that data all unified into a single package. An object without operations is just data, while an object without data is just a collection of procedures.

According to Booch, to classify a system or language as object-oriented, it must exhibit three characteristics:

- It must provide direct support for *objects* and *instances*. An instance is just a synonym for an object. An object's data should be hidden from general use, and its behavior controlled by a specific set of operations.
- Object are categorized into *classes*. Objects of a single class share data and behavior. The object-oriented concept of a class is similar to a data type in a procedural environment.
- Object classes are related to each other via *inheritance*, or the ability to share behavior or data among a hierarchy of classes.

Bjarne Stroustrup, the original designer of the C++ language, adds a fourth requirement for object-oriented programming languages that we can extend to include environments like Windows. An object-oriented language or environment must make it convenient to use objects. If it takes too much work to exploit objects, the environment is not object-oriented. For example, traditional programming languages like C, Pascal, or COBOL allow you to build objects, but they don't provide direct support for inheritance. So, although you can coerce programs to use objects with these languages, they aren't object-oriented.

The Windows object model

Because you now are clear on the meaning of an object and know what the term "object-oriented means, I'll look at some of the major components of the Windows environment and see how they implement their own objects.

Graphical objects

Windows uses some limited object-oriented concepts in its graphics library, the Graphics Device Interface (GDI). All graphics operations are performed on a device context, which represents a physical device like a video display or printer. A device context, which actually is a data structure maintained by the GDI, contains state information in much the same way a C++ class contains data members. You retrieve and modify that information with a set of procedures just as you modify an object's member data using member functions.

The GDI also provides a set of tools used to draw graphics into a device context. The device context keeps track of which tools—pens, brushes, palettes, and fonts—are in use at any given time. Each type of tool uses a separate set of functions to control different drawing attributes. The GDI's use of the device context and drawing tools simplifies graphics operations. Instead of requiring you to specify every attribute each time you draw, the device context remembers the attributes you previously set and applies them to subsequent drawing requests.

The concepts behind the GDI's graphics model employ some object-oriented principles: the device context can be viewed as an object and the GDI functions the operations for that object. Unfortunately, the interface is entirely procedural. Several hundred procedures exist to manage device contexts and drawing tools and to draw graphical elements. In the second group, I'll extend the GDI's graphics model by using objects provided by the Vista library to build on the GDI.

Window objects

The central theme in Windows is, as its name suggests, the window. Each window is an object with its own data and a single procedure that defines the behavior of that object. Individual windows are grouped together by type into classes, just like classes in C^{++}. The window class implements the common attributes and behavior of one type of window. For example, all pushbutton controls belong to a single window class, as do list box, scrollbar, and other controls, as well as dialog boxes and Multiple Document Interface (MDI) windows.

One of the attributes contained in the window class is the address of a window procedure, which carries out the behavior of the class. The window procedure responds to messages sent to it when events occur that may affect the window. All applications share the window procedure, so that whenever a window receives an event, instances of the class act on the message in the same way. This arrangement adds to the consistency of the Windows environment. A button in one application acts just like a button in another program. Likewise, dialog boxes, scrollbars, edit controls, and list boxes all share a common window procedure and therefore share similar behavior among dissimilar programs.

The window procedure is the Windows equivalent to a C^{++} member function, but with a twist. A C^{++} member function normally is very limited in scope, only handling a small aspect of an object's behavior. A window procedure, on the other hand, is responsible for carrying out all aspects of a window's behavior. Instead of handling a single operation, it acts as a traffic cop, routing message traffic in the correct direction.

Windows supports a limited form of inheritance through subclassing and superclassing window classes. By overriding or augmenting the window procedure for a window, you can specify a new behavior for that window. For example, by subclassing the edit control, you can create a text field that only accepts numeric data from the user. In keeping with object-oriented principles, a window subclass reuses the code implementing the behavior of its parent class.

While subclassing might appear to be inheritance, it isn't. When you create a window and subclass it, you change the behavior of only a single window. Superclassing, on the other hand, modifies the behavior of an existing window class to produce a new class. This can be considered true inheritance.

Events & messages

Another area within Windows that has object-oriented roots is its communication scheme. Windows uses an event-driven style of communication that is very similar to that used by many object-oriented languages. It passes messages to a window whenever an event occurs that might require the window's attention. When the window receives a message, it determines what, if anything, it will do with it.

This same message-passing communication scheme is used to communicate between windows in an application and between multiple applications. To change the appearance of a child window control, pass it a message. To obtain the text in an edit control, pass it a message. To get the selection in a list box, pass it a message. The two Windows interprocess communication protocols, Dynamic Data Exchange (DDE) and Object Linking and Embedding (OLE), also are implemented with messages.

The message-passing communication scheme used by Windows implements a distinctly object-oriented characteristic: polymorphism. *Polymorphism* refers to the ability of different types of objects to respond to the same operation in a unique way. All windows receive the same standard messages from the system, but instances of different window classes exhibit different behavior when they receive those messages.

For example, Windows sends a WM_PAINT message to all windows to tell them they need to display themselves. Each window then makes the necessary GDI function calls to draw itself. Windows doesn't differentiate between window classes when it sends this message: it treats application windows, pop-up windows, and child window controls in the same way. The windows receive identical messages but take different actions based on their internal state.

Is Windows object-oriented?

After looking at the graphics, window management, and communication models used by Windows, you can make your own decision as to whether or not it's object-oriented. At first glance, it might seem to be. Windows are objects that belong to classes that support inheritance. The objects support communication through message-passing and implement a form of polymorphism.

If you step back and look at the system in its entirety, however, you'll find some inconsistencies. Although windows themselves are objects, the entire application programming interface (API) used to create and manage those windows is procedural. There isn't an easy way to create and manage the window objects. The huge procedural library used by the GDI adds to this inconsistency.

So, although Windows isn't strictly object-oriented, it definitely leans toward using objects. One of the most difficult tasks in object-oriented programming is finding the objects to model within your program. Windows makes this much simpler by laying out a well-defined hierarchy of window classes. In the next section, I'll discuss how you can use C++ to build on the Windows object model and build Windows programs using true object-oriented techniques.

Object-oriented Windows programming with C++

Windows programs have traditionally been developed using the C language. C gives programmers the flexibility they need to deal with a dynamic environment like Windows. It also provides the efficiency needed to build responsive programs in a very demanding graphical environment. Nonetheless, a couple of object-oriented languages, namely Actor and Smalltalk, have stubbornly held on to their own share of the Windows development market. With the recent introduction of Windows C++ compilers like Borland C++, the language rapidly is becoming the most popular object-oriented language with Windows programmers.

Why use C++

Windows applications can benefit from C++ in the same ways DOS applications can. Bjarne Stroustrup designed the C++ language to make it easier to write good programs. Designed as an extension of the C language, C++ provides features that make programs more reliable and easier to develop.

A better C

C++ "inherits" most of the features of the C language. It uses the same arithmetic, control statements, and input/output functions. Good C programs—those that don't exploit pointer arithmetic and other C features that make it a lower-level language—also are C++ programs. Most well-written Windows programs will compile under Borland C++ without major modifications.

Besides supporting most the features offered by C, C++ adds new features that improve on the C language.

Strict type checking C++ prevents many programming errors by testing the data types of arguments to functions. By requiring function prototypes, the compiler knows the number and type of arguments expected by a function and the type returned by a function. If you make a mistake when you call a function, the compiler lets you know it at compile time.

Reference variables C++ uses reference variables as aliases for other variables. By using references, you can pass a variable by address and access it without dereferencing a pointer. Unlike pointers, reference variables must be initialized to point to a valid variable. They can eliminate many of the pointer errors common to C programs. I'll use reference variables extensively to try to reduce those problems in your own programs.

Constants True constant variables, as implemented by C++, reduce the need for a preprocessor. Instead of defining constants using preprocessor commands, C++ programs use constant variables that allow the compiler to perform type checking on constant arguments. The const keyword also is used to identify variables that can't be changed, even when passed to different functions.

Function & operator overloading In C++, two functions can share the same name as long as they take a different number or type of argument. Function overloading allows you to define generic functions that can perform the same operation with differing arguments. C++ also allows operators to be overloaded, giving a user-defined type the same language support as a predefined type.

Object-oriented extensions The stricter type checking and other features that C++ adds to the C language can benefit any program. However, the most important extensions that C++ provides are those that provide support for objects. When you write a program with the object-oriented features of C++, you don't concentrate on the procedures needed to implement the program. Instead, you focus on objects and their relationship with other objects within the program.

To build a C++ program, you decide which objects you will provide, express the relationships between different objects, and specify the operations that act on those objects. The data abstraction and inheritance mechanisms provided by C++ allow you to define new data types (classes) that behave just like predefined types. These new data types let you write programs that look more natural and are easier to maintain. They also allow you to build components that provide generic solutions to common programming problems.

So, what does all this mean to a Windows programmer? Instead of focusing on Windows requirements in every program you build, you create those programs with objects that take care of the details for you. With C++, you concentrate on the operations your programs were intended to provide in the first place. Rather than writing code to perform low-level window management, build some reusable classes that you can share between multiple applications.

Class libraries To make the task of creating reusable classes easier, the examples throughout this book are built using objects from the Vista Application Framework class library. A class library like Vista furnishes a set of tools that provide a solution to a number of problems. It differs from a library for a procedural language, like a screen management or communication library (or the Windows API), which provides only a set of functions. You call the functions in the library to perform specific operations. A class library, on the other hand, supplies a set of generic objects that you use as a starting point for more specialized objects in your programs.

The typical class library gives you a hierarchy of objects that you can build on to produce a complete application. For example, a container class library like the one provided with Borland C++ provides generic "container objects like bags, sets, queues, and binary trees. Instead of reinventing the wheel every time you need to use one of these objects in a program, you can reuse the object provided by the class library. You use these classes as a foundation and build a framework around them to construct a complete application.

Building a good class library requires careful design and organization. When you write a program, you can make assumptions about how different components will be used. A class library designer can't make those assumptions. Because the classes in the library are meant to be used by a number of programs, their flexibility, consistency, and extensibility are very important.

Application frameworks

An *application framework* is like a class library on steroids. It provides a framework for you to use to wrap around your application code, giving you everything that you need to build an application. Unlike classes in a special-purpose class library, the classes in an application framework offer a very wide interface—you can build a complete application using only the components provided by the framework.

Building an application using only those objects in an application framework won't serve any useful purpose. Making the program useful is your job. When you use an application framework, you don't need to make allowances for special requirements imposed by the environment your application runs under. Instead, derive new class definitions from those provided by the framework. Your classes need to implement only the behavior that makes your application unique.

An application framework is especially useful in the Windows environment. Let the framework classes worry about handling messages, accessing high and low words, exporting functions, and all the other details required to build a Windows program. You can concentrate on the behavior of those objects that solve the problem your application originally was intended to solve. As an added benefit, an application framework can make your program more portable to other environments.

Several application frameworks and class libraries are available for Windows programs, including Borland's ObjectWindows, the Microsoft Foundation Classes, the Zinc Interface Library, XVT, CommonView, C++/Views, and others. The examples in this book are based on the Vista library but easily could be converted to another.

Converting Windows programs to C++

C++ provides the ideal avenue for converting your procedural Windows program to a more object-oriented style. Using C++, you have two alternatives in converting your program. The first is to completely redesign the application using any of the latest object-oriented design and analysis methodologies. If your application is due an overhaul, this might be the best approach.

The second approach—the one taken in this book—is to convert the application one step at a time. Because C++ is an extension of C, you can mix and match C and C++ code in the same program. The ability to do this makes C++ a very attractive language to many developers. To convert your application to use the Vista library:

- Add an application object to the program. Convert the program's initialization and termination actions into member functions belonging to that object.
- Migrate the code for creating windows and dialogs into code creating objects as the next step.
- Split your message-handling switch statement into action methods in another step.
- Modify your drawing operations to use graphical objects as the final step.

Instead of having to start from scratch, you can migrate your C programs to C++ at your own speed, taking advantage of the new features of C++ without losing the simplicity and speed of C. I'll discuss conversion techniques throughout the rest of this book.

The Vista Application Framework

I'll build the examples in this book using the Vista Application Framework. The Vista library includes a set of classes that provide a higher level of abstraction than that provided by Windows. It consists of a hierarchy of classes, with most directly mapping into objects you can see on the screen. The framework itself is divided into several areas.

Application & support classes

Vista provides a set of high-level application classes and several lower-level support classes that hide some of the details of Windows programming. TABLE 1-1 lists the application and support classes.

Table 1-1
Vista application and support classes.

Class	Description
VAppl	The top-level object. Controls a Vista application.
VEvent	The source of all communication with Vista window classes, the VEvent class is equivalent to a Windows message.
VString	String class. Operations provided to support strings, string resources, and DDE strings.
VAllocator	Fixed-size memory allocation class.
VHandle	Abstract handle class.
VGlobal	Handle class for objects represented by global memory handles.
VLocal	Handle class for objects represented by local memory handles.
VArray	Array template class.
VDynArray	Dynamic array template class.
VList	Linked list template class.
VDblList	Doubly-linked list template class.

Window classes

The window classes wrap around the predefined window classes supplied by Windows. They add consistency to the Windows programming environment by providing useful methods that perform common operations. They provide convenient access to the entire Windows API without duplicating its operations and don't require any extensions to the C++ language. TABLE 1-2 lists the window classes.

Table 1-2
Vista window classes.

Class	Description
VWindow	The root of the hierarchy for all window-based classes. VWindow provides basic functions common to all windows.
VControl	An abstract class that serves as a base class for all control classes. Inherits data and operations from VWindow.
VLabel	Displays a string as a label in a window. Represents a Windows static text control.
VButton	Abstract class that provides common operations for different styles of button objects.
VPushbutton	A pushbutton control object that allows the user to perform an action. Inherits from VButton.
VRadioButton	A radio button control used to present one of a number of exclusive choices. Inherits from VButton.
VCheckBox	A checkbox control used to allow the user to choose from. Inherits from VButton.
VListBox	A listbox control that allows the user to choose from a scrolling list of items. Also serves as a base class for the VOptionList. Inherits from VControl.
VComboBox	A specialized listbox control object that represents a Windows combo box control. Inherits from VListBox.

Table 1-2 Continued.

Class	Description
VScrollbar	A scrollbar control that allows the user to scroll through the contents of a window. Inherits from VControl.
VEditable	An abstract class that provides common operations for the edit control objects. Inherits from VControl.
VText	A simple multi-line edit control. Inherits from VEditable.
VTextField	A single-line edit control used for data entry. Inherits from VEditable.
VMenu	A base class that manages interaction with a menu.
VPopupMenu	A class to represent Windows pop-up (floating) menus and pull-down menus.
VSystemMenu	A class used to manage a program's system menu.
VMdiParent	Manages multiple MDI child windows. Inherits from VWindow.
VMdiChild	A child of an MdiParent. Inherits from VWindow.
VDialog	A generic dialog box class. Inherits from VWindow.
VFileDialog	Interface for the standard Windows FILEOPEN dialog box.
VColorDialog	Interacts with the Windows color chooser dialog box.
VPrintDialog	Interface for the standard Windows print and print setup dialog boxes.

Graphics classes

In addition to classes that provide abstractions for windows, Vista provides a small set of graphics classes that you can use to develop custom controls or graphical applications. As with the window classes, Vista graphic classes provide convenient access to the Windows API. TABLE 1-3 lists the graphics classes.

Table 1-3 Vista graphics classes.

Class	Description
VDevice	Base class for all device interaction. Used for drawing objects on the screen or printer.
VMemoryDevice	Device class for manipulating bitmaps. Inherits from VDevice.
VPrinterDevice	Device class for printing graphics and text. Inherits from VDevice.
VDisplayDevice	Device class for displaying graphics on a window. Inherits from VDevice.
VShape	An abstract graphical shape class.
VLine	Represents a graphical line. Derived from VShape.
VRectangle	Draws a rectangle on a device. Derived from VShape.
VArc	Represents an arc. Derived from VShape.
VGraphicsText	Draws text on a device. Provides more control over text output than a static control.
VTool	Abstract graphics drawing tool class.
VBrush	Represents a brush used to fill objects. Derived from VTool.
VPen	A pen object used to draw lines and text. Derived from VTool.
VFont	Represents the text font used by a VGraphicsText object. Derived from VTool.

Communicator classes

The communicator classes provide a way to communicate between applications in the Windows environment. They cover everything from the clipboard to Dynamic Data Exchange and Object Linking and Embedding. TABLE 1-4 lists the communicator classes.

Table 1-4 Vista communicator classes.

Class	Description
VClipboard	Manages interaction with the clipboard.
VDdeClient	A class to manage the client operations in a DDE conversation. Uses DDEML functions.
VDdeServer	Manages operations required for a DDE server. Uses DDEML functions.
VOleClient	A class to manage operations for OLE clients.
VOleServer	Manages operations required by an OLE server.

What's next

In this chapter, I looked at the object-oriented features of Windows and C^{++}. I also discussed converting existing Windows programs to use C^{++} and saw the layout of the classes comprising the Vista Application Framework. In the next chapter, you'll see how to combine these concepts to create a Windows application; first in C, and then in C^{++} using Vista.

2 Windows applications

A Windows application serves the same purpose as a text-based DOS application. It provides you with a solution to a problem or a tool to make a task easier. However, a Windows program usually presents a better appearance and provides more features than its DOS counterpart.

Windows broadens the support that DOS provides for applications. DOS applications run alone; the program takes control of the entire computer. Windows allows multiple programs to run side-by-side with a non-preemptive multitasking architecture, sharing the computer's resources. Windows/New Technology (Windows NT) widens that support even further as it takes the place of DOS as an operating system. It provides preemptive scheduling and other features of a modern multitasking operating system while retaining a high level of compatibility with programs written for previous versions of Windows.

To take advantage of the sophisticated features offered by Windows, your program needs to follow many rules. A Windows program relies on the system for much of its control and virtually all of its interaction with the user. This dependence forces Windows programs to take on a rigid structure. Thus, the code driving most Windows applications looks very similar.

This chapter guides you through building a simple Windows application. First, I'll build an application with C or, more accurately, the C subset of C++. This sample program, WinApp, does nothing more than display a string in a window. However, it will familiarize you with some Windows concepts and the effort required to write a Windows program.

Then, I'll convert that program to use Vista classes using the approach covered in chapter 1. I'll use this second program as a template for other sample programs in the book.

A traditional Windows program

Borland C++ allows you to use either C or C++ syntax (or a combination of the two) to build Windows programs. In this section, I'll build a simple Windows program written in C. I'll also look at some new requirements for the Win32 environment. If you already have written Windows programs with C and are familiar with Win32, you might want to skip to the next section.

All Windows programs are structured in a common format. They perform the following basic steps:

- Initialize the application.
- Create a top-level window.
- Dispatch messages.
- Respond to incoming messages with a Window procedure.
- Clean up the application when it terminates, if necessary.

The program

Listing 2-1 contains the complete listing for our first sample application, WinApp. As you can see in FIG. 2-1, the program just displays a greeting, but it also includes all the familiar window management components you'll find on any other Windows program.

Listing 2-1
WINAPP.C: an example Windows program written in C.

```c
/* ---------------------------------------------------------
   WinApp.c

        A sample Windows program written in C

   Copyright (C) 1992, by Jeff Mackay - TAB BOOKS
***
   --------------------------------------------------------- */

#include <windows.h>

/*
** Constant and Macro Definitions
*/
static char szAppName[] = "Windows Application";
static char szClassName[] = "VWinApp";

/*
** Function Prototypes
*/
LPARAM CALLBACK _export WndProc(HWND, UINT, WPARAM, LPARAM);
static int InitProgram(HINSTANCE, HINSTANCE, int)
```

```c
/*
** WinMain is the main driver.  It takes the place of the
** standard C 'main()' function
*/
int PASCAL WinMain(HINSTANCE hInstance,
                   HINSTANCE hPrevInstance,
                   LPCSTR    lpszCmdLine,
                   int       nCmdShow)
{
    MSG msg;

    InitProgram(hInstance,
                hPrevInstance,
                nCmdShow);

    /*
    ** Enter a loop to retrieve messages from Windows,
    ** translate them, and dispatch them.
    */
    while(GetMessage(&msg, NULL, NULL, NULL))
    {
        TranslateMessage(&msg);
        DispatchMessage(&msg);
    }
    return msg.wParam;
}


static int InitProgram(HINSTANCE hInstance, HINSTANCE hPrevInstance
                       int nCmdShow)
{
    if (hPrevInstance)
    {
        WNDCLASS wc;

        wc.style         = CS_HREDRAW | CS_VREDRAW;
        wc.lpfnWndProc   = WndProc;
        wc.cbClsExtra    = 0;
        wc.cbWndExtra    = 0;
        wc.hInstance     = hInstance;
        wc.hIcon         = LoadIcon(NULL, IDI_APPLICATION);
        wc.hCursor       = LoadCursor(NULL, IDC_ARROW);
        wc.hbrBackground = COLOR_WINDOW + 1;
        wc.lpszMenuName  = NULL;
        wc.lpszClassName = szClassName;
        return RegisterClass(&wc);
    }

    HWND hWnd;

    hWnd = CreateWindow(szClassName,
```

A traditional Windows program

Listing 2-1
Continued.

```
                            szAppName,
                            WS_OVERLAPPEDWINDOW,
                            CW_USEDEFAULT,
                            CW_USEDEFAULT,
                            CW_USEDEFAULT,
                            CW_USEDEFAULT,
                            NULL,
                            NULL,
                            hInstance,
                            NULL);
    if (!hWnd)
        return(FALSE);

    ShowWindow(hWnd, nCmdShow);
    UpdateWindow(hWnd);
    return (TRUE);
}


LRESULT CALLBACK _export WndProc(HWND hWnd,
                                 UINT message,
                                 WPARAM wParam,
                                 LPARAM lParam)
{
    static RECT rect;
    static char szGreeting[] = 'Hello, World!';
    PAINTSTRUCT ps;
    HDC         hdc;

    switch(message)
    {
        case WM_PAINT:
            hdc = BeginPaint(hWnd, &ps);
            DrawText(hdc, szGreeting, -1, &rect,
                    DT_CENTER |
                    DT_VCENTER |
                    DT_SINGLELINE);
            EndPaint(hWnd, &ps);
            return 0;

        case WM_SIZE:
            GetClientRect(hWnd, &rect);
            return 0;

        case WM_DESTROY:
            PostQuitMessage(0);
            return 0;
    }
    return DefWindowProc(hWnd, message,
                        wParam, lParam);
}
```

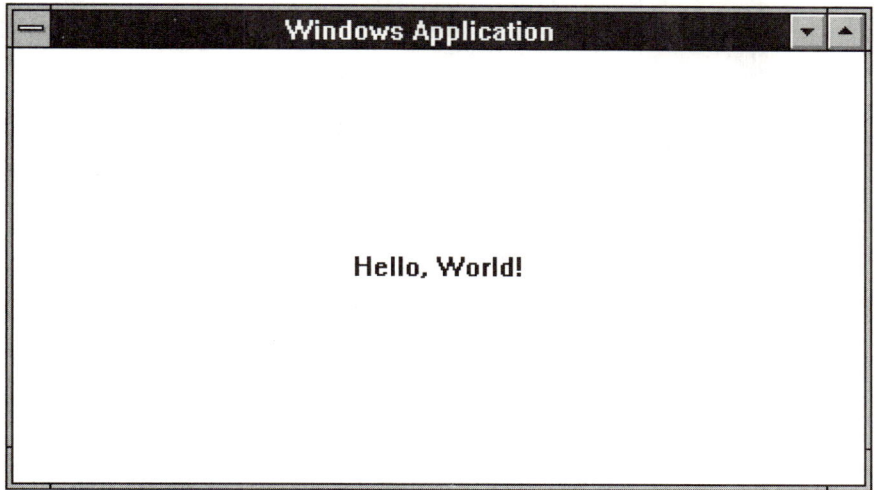

2-1
Output from the WinApp sample application.

You can adjust the window's size, shrink it to an icon, maximize it to fill the whole screen, or move it to a different location on the screen. Providing these operations doesn't require any specific effort on your part—Windows provides them to any application—but it almost justifies the amount of work you need to do just to display a window on the screen. Let's look at the sample program.

A function you'll find in every Windows program is WinMain. Like any other C program, Windows programs require the main driver to start and control an application. WinMain serves the same purpose as a traditional C program's main function. When you run the program, it appears to start executing at the first line of the main driver.

However, the program actually executes some initial startup code before executing the driver. In a C program, the startup code opens standard files and accesses the program's command line and environment. In a C^{++} program, the startup code also creates any global objects by calling their constructors. The Windows startup code in a Windows program performs the standard language-specific initialization, then registers the application as a Windows task. It then calls the driver, WinMain. The function header for WinMain looks like this:

```
int PASCAL WinMain( HINSTANCE hInstance,
            HINSTANCE hPrevInstance,
            LPSTR lpszCmdLine,
            int nCmdShow)
```

WinMain takes four arguments. The hInstance argument identifies the program's instance identifier or handle. The instance handle is a unique number that Windows assigns to every active task. It identifies the program and shows ownership for resources used by the program.

The main driver: WinMain

A traditional Windows program 17

The second argument, `hPrevInstance`, is an instance handle for another active instance of the same program. In the Windows 3.*x* environment, multiple copies of a program can run simultaneously. Each copy is known as an instance of the program. Programs use the `hPrevInstance` handle to share resources between each running copy of the program. Under Win32, this parameter is always NULL.

The `lpszCmdLine` argument contains the command line that you used to activate the program. The contents are similar to the `argv` argument passed to main. However, Windows passes the command line as a single string (without the program name) instead of as an array of strings.

The final argument, `nCmdShow`, is a flag that instructs the program how to display its main window when it starts. A program usually displays its window at full size, but the user can request Windows start the program as an icon. The `nCmdShow` flag tells the program how the user wants its window to look when it first starts.

Program initialization

Written to be compatible with the Win32 environment, WinApp initializes itself with a single function: InitProgram. If you've developed programs for previous versions of Windows, it might seem that WinApp is missing half of its initialization code.

Earlier Windows applications performed initialization in two steps. The first, application initialization, was performed for only the first instance of a program. It usually registered window classes and allocated resources shared between all instances of the program. The second step, instance initialization, initialized the program's unshared resources and was performed for every instance of the program.

This two-step initialization scheme originally was created to optimize the sharing of resources between multiple programs. However, aside from creating shared window classes, few programs needed it. It was used most often to limit the number of times a user could simultaneously run a program.

Win32 doesn't support this method of sharing resources. Because programs run as separate tasks in their own protected address space, they can't access resources in another task's data segments. Therefore, initialization can be handled in a single step. Each task needs to create its own window classes, GDI objects, and windows.

If your program needs to support both Windows 3.*x* and Win32 and needs to share resources between multiple instances, you'll have to make allowances for the differing initialization techniques with conditional compilation or some other means.

Creating window classes

As I mentioned earlier, one of the steps in initializing a program's resources is registering its window classes. Windows groups windows that behave in a similar fashion into window classes. You can look at a window class as a template for creating a window, just as you could consider a C++ class a template for creating an object. Every window displayed on the screen is a member of some window class.

To register a window class, the program calls the RegisterWindow API routine:

```
ATOM RegisterClass(LPWNDCLASS lpWndClass);
```

RegisterWindow takes a pointer to a WNDCLASS structure, which contains the properties of the window class, such as its name and the address of its window procedure. Visual properties for a window class, also contained in the WNDCLASS structure, include the class's icon, cursor, and background color. Whenever a program creates a window or instance of this window class, it inherits the properties of the window class. RegisterClass returns an ATOM that uniquely identifies the window class.

Creating & displaying a window

The second step in preparing a program to run is to create and display its main window. A window class describes the generic properties of a window—those common to all instances of the class. When it creates a window, the program describes it further by specifying additional properties. The program passes these properties to the CreateWindow routine:

```
HWND CreateWindow(LPCSTR lpClassName,
          LPCSTR lpWindowName,
          DWORD dwStyle, int x, int y, int nWidth,
          int nHeight, HWND hWndParent, HMENU hMenu,
          HANDLE hInstance, LPSTR lpParam);
```

CreateWindow returns a window handle (similar to the instance handle) that the program uses to identify the window. The program saves this window handle because it needs to pass it as an argument to any routine that operates on the window. Internally, CreateWindow creates a data structure (accessible only by Windows) that describes a window—it doesn't draw the window on the screen. Displaying a window involves two other API routines: ShowWindow and UpdateWindow:

```
BOOL ShowWindow(HWND hWnd, int nCmdShow);
void UpdateWindow(HWND hWnd);
```

ShowWindow initially displays the window on the screen. The `nCmdShow` argument tells Windows which state to use when drawing the window: normal, minimized, or maximized. WinApp just passes the `nCmdShow` flag passed to WinMain to ShowWindow, although it could pass flags telling Windows to display the window maximized or minimized. ShowWindow then tells Windows to draw the window and the standard "window dressing" components it uses. When ShowWindow finishes, Windows displays the window, empty, on the screen.

A traditional Windows program

The UpdateWindow routine tells the window to draw its contents on the screen by sending it a WM_PAINT message. When the window receives the message, it responds by drawing its contents.

Messages & the message loop

The CreateWindow, ShowWindow, and UpdateWindow routines all communicate with the windows they operate on by passing messages to them. A message informs a window that an event has occurred that might require its attention. The window then takes some action in response to the event.

Messages can originate from several sources. Windows generates messages to inform windows of user activity like clicking or moving the mouse or pressing a key on the keyboard. Windows also can generate events on its own. For example, when the user exits from the Program Manager, Windows sends a message to each active program's main window telling it that it's about to die. Messages also can originate from within your own program or from another program. The Windows model for inter-process communication, Dynamic Data Exchange (DDE), uses messages to pass data between applications.

To organize all the messages generated from these diverse sources, Windows maintains a message queue for every active task. Each program checks the queue for messages and, when one is available, processes it. A typical message loop (like the one in WinApp) looks like this:

```
MSG msg;
while (GetMessage(&msg, NULL, 0, 0))
{
 TranslateMessage(&msg);
 DispatchMessage(&msg);
}
```

The GetMessage routine retrieves messages from the application's queue. If the queue contains any messages, GetMessage fills the MSG structure with data describing the message. Otherwise, GetMessage suspends the program and yields control back to the system until the queue receives a message.

TranslateMessage converts keyboard messages, generated whenever the user presses or releases a key, into simpler character messages. Finally, DispatchMessage, directs the message to the target window's window procedure.

The window procedure

A *window class* describes properties common to all instances of a single type of window. One of these attributes is the window procedure, which implements the behavior of a window by responding to messages. For example, a push-button used in one Windows application behaves just like a push-button in other Windows programs because the same procedure deals with the messages directed to both windows.

Whenever the program receives a message directed to a window, DispatchMessage calls the window's window procedure. The function header for the window procedure looks like this:

```
LRESULT FAR PASCAL _export WindowProc(HWND hWnd,
                                      UINT message,
                                      WPARAM wParam,
                                      LPARAM lParam)
```

The `hWnd` argument identifies the window targeted by the message. The `message` argument identifies the message. The `wParam` and `lParam` contain parameters that contain optional information about the message. The `_export` keyword identifies the function to the linker as being exported. This is a requirement for all window procedures that we'll discuss in the next chapter.

The window procedure contains a switch statement to process each message it's interested in, with each case handling a separate message. The message handling switch statement can grow very large and hard to maintain and debug on more complicated programs.

The final task in a Windows application is to clean up the resources used by the program. Like initialization, WinApp's cleanup is handled by a single operation: CleanupApplication.

Cleaning up

Clean-up operations in a Windows program are even more important than those in a DOS program. When a program exits, DOS automatically takes care of closing its files and releasing memory. Windows does this whenever possible, but it delegates much of the clean-up responsibility to the program. Win32 does a much better job of cleaning up after a Windows program, but it still is a good idea to always release all resources you use within the program.

Notice the nonstandard data types used in LISTING 2-1. Windows uses type definitions and macros extensively to ease memory management and portability. They hide some complexity of the different memory management schemes used on the 80x86 processor. For example, all addresses passed to Windows API functions must be far addresses. So, to pass a string to Windows, you would need to declare the variable like this:

Windows naming conventions

```
char far *string;
```

This declaration is good for a DOS-based Windows program, but the far keyword isn't necessary—and might not be supported—on other platforms. Instead, Windows programs use the LPSTR (long pointer to string) data type:

```
LPSTR string;
```

Not only is LPSTR easier to type (and, arguably, to remember), the typedef also makes it easier to port Windows programs to an environment like Windows NT that doesn't need far addresses.

Traditional Windows programs also use a naming convention known as Hungarian notation (after Charles Simonyi, a Microsoft developer of Hungarian descent). Variables named using Hungarian notation include a prefix that identifies its data type or usage. Hungarian notation can come in useful in a C program because by looking at a variable name, you know the variable's data type and its purpose.

Stricter coding practices

Windows 3.0 offered major improvements over previous versions. However, the environment itself was not as stable as it could have been. Applications too often ended with the dreaded Unrecoverable Application Error (UAE). Many of these UAE's were caused by invalid or improper arguments to API functions. The large number of UAE's had a negative impact on Windows' reputation and caused many users to stick with DOS.

To remedy this, Microsoft made several improvements in Windows 3.1. Windows 3.1 performs better memory management, checks the validity of arguments to API functions, and introduces a stricter coding style that takes advantage of the features of modern C compilers. It consists of new typedefs for Windows data types and full prototypes for all API functions.

The major difference you'll see with strict code is the new type definitions. Taking advantage of the strict coding style is simple. Just #define STRICT before including the WINDOWS.H header file. By using strict coding, it is much more difficult to pass improper arguments to API functions. It also is more in keeping with the spirit of C++ programs. So, I'll follow Borland's recommendations and use strict coding throughout this book.

New data types

In addition to strict coding, Windows 3.1 introduced several new data types that are meant to ease porting to Win32. If you've written Windows programs for previous versions of Windows, you'll notice several unfamiliar data types in WinApp. For example, in Windows 3.0 a window procedure was declared like this:

```
long FAR PASCAL _export WindowProc(HWND hWnd,
                                   WORD message,
                                   WORD wParam,
                                   LONG lParam)
```

In Windows 3.1, the function changes to:

```
LRESULT FAR PASCAL _export WindowProc(HWND hWnd,
                                      UINT message,
                                      WPARAM wParam,
                                      LPARAM lParam)
```

The reason for the change is portability. In Windows 3.x, handles are 16 bits wide and can fit into a WORD variable. In Win32, handles expand to 32 bits and need a LONG variable. To accommodate this change, the wParam argument is expanded from a word to a double word. To allow a larger number of unique message identifiers, the message argument also was widened to 32 bits.

Instead of forcing developers to maintain two versions of a program—one supporting Windows 3.x and one Win32—Windows 3.1 uses new typedefs for the nonportable arguments. The new typedefs are aliased to 16-bit variables in Windows 3.1 and 32-bit in Win32. TABLE 2-1 lists the most commonly used new data types for Windows 3.1.

Table 2-1 New STRICT data types in Windows 3.1.

Windows 3.1 type	Windows 3.0 type	Purpose
UINT	WORD	Message identifiers, other generic uses.
WPARAM	WORD	First parameter to a window procedure.
LPARAM	LONG	Second parameter to a window procedure.
LRESULT	LONG	Value returned by a window procedure.
Handle Types	HANDLE	Handles to specific objects that now use their own data types.

A Vista windows application

The WinApp program I developed in the previous section shows you the complexity of even a simple Windows program. Every Windows program uses the same components in some way. They all have a WinMain, a message loop, and a window procedure for every type of window used by the application. The objects comprising the Vista library offer a higher level of abstraction than the Windows API provides. By taking advantage of the class library, you can focus more on function than form when writing your programs.

In this section, I'll develop a Vista application, WinVista, that serves the same purpose as WinApp. It doesn't do anything useful either, but it provides a good introduction to programming with Vista.

The code for WinVista is illustrated in LISTING 2-2. You'll notice that the program uses several classes that are developed later in the book. Look at appendix B for full documentation for the base classes used in WinVista; the disk that accompanies this book contains the code implementing those classes.

Listing 2-2
WINVISTA.CPP: source code for the first example.

```
/* -----------------------------------------------------------
   WinVista.cpp

   A sample Vista application

   Copyright (C) 1992, by Jeff Mackay - TAB BOOKS

   ----------------------------------------------------------- */
```

Listing 2-2
Continued.

```cpp
#include <vista.h>>
#include <vgrdev.h>
#include <vgrobj.h>

/*
** Application class definition
*/
class WinVistaAppl : public VAppl
{
    public:
        WinVistaAppl(HINSTANCE instance, HINSTANCE prevInstance,
                    LPSTR cmdLine, int cmdShow);
        virtual void InitWindow(void);
};

/*
** Main window class definition
*/
class MainWindow : public VWindow
{
    public:
        MainWindow(void);
        virtual Boolean PaintAction(VEventRef event);
};

/*
** Application class member functions
*/

WinVistaAppl::WinVistaAppl(HINSTANCE instance,
                            HINSTANCE prevInstance,
                            LPSTR cmdLine, int cmdShow)
    : VAppl('WinVista', instance, prevInstance, cmdLine, cmdShow)
{
}

void WinVistaAppl::InitWindow(void)
{
    main_window = new MainWindow();
}

/*
** Main window class member functions
*/
MainWindow::MainWindow(void)
    : VWindow(NULL, "Sample Vista Application")
{
}

Boolean MainWindow::PaintAction(VEventRef event)
{
```

```
    VPaintDevice dev(*this);
    RECT rect;

    VGraphicsText text("Hello, Windows!",
                      DT_SINGLELINE | DT_CENTER | DT_VCENTER,
                      GetDimensions(rect));
    dev << text;
    UNREFERENCED_PARAMETER(event);
    return True;
}

/*
** Main driver
*/
int PASCAL WinMain(HINSTANCE instance, HINSTANCE prevInstance,
                   LPSTR cmdLine, int cmdShow)
{
    WinVistaAppl appl(instance, prevInstance, cmdLine, cmdShow);

    appl.Run();
    return appl.GetStatus();
}
```

The program

I'll follow the porting guidelines in chapter 1 to transform WinApp into WinVista. Before doing any actual conversion, replace the line that includes the Windows header file with directives to include the main Vista header file and header files for base classes used by the program:

```
#include <vista.h>
#include <vgrdev.h>
#include <vgrobj.h>
```

The VISTA.H header file defines common constants and types required by all the Vista classes. It also includes the WINDOWS.H file and the VAPPL.H and VWINDOW.H files necessary for all Vista programs. The other header files—VGRDEV.H and VGRTEXT.H—contain the interface (class definition) for other base classes used in the program.

Creating an application object

The first step in converting the program is to add an application class, which is derived from the VAppl class. The VAppl class handles many of the implementation details of a Windows application. It handles program initialization and cleanup, drives the message loop, and furnishes operations to manage the program's main window. Because the VAppl class does so much work on its own, your own application classes only need to specify the methods that make them unique.

For the WinVistaApp class, this means overriding the InitWindow method. As I mentioned earlier, the VAppl class handles program initialization. Part of the initialization process is to create a main window, and Vista does this with the application's InitWindow member function. In WinVistaAppl, initialization means simply creating a new main window class.

```
void WinVistaAppl::InitApplication(void)
{
    window = new MainWindow(...)
}
```

The only other member function implemented by the WinVistaAppl is its constructor. In C++, the constructor for a class is called whenever you create an instance of that class. It normally initializes data members and performs other setup actions. Because the WinVistaAppl class doesn't define any of its own data members or need to do any other initialization, the class's constructor simply passes its arguments to its superclass's constructor:

```
WinVistaApp::WinVistaApp(VString name, HANDLE instance,
                         HANDLE prevInstance,
                         LPSTR cmdLine, int showFlag) :
  VAppl(name, instance, prevInstance, cmdLine, showFlag)
{
}
```

Creating a window class

After implementing the behavior of the application object, the next step in porting to Vista is to define new window objects. Because it uses only one type of window, WinVista defines the MainWindow class, which specifies the behavior of the main window for the application. The VWindow class, the superclass for MainWindow, provides an abstraction for a window. It encapsulates the data and operations common for all windows.

Just like the WinVistaAppl class, the MainWindow class is very simple. It doesn't need to define any new data elements and only a couple of member functions. The class's constructor looks very similar to that of the WinVistaAppl class:

```
MainWindow::MainWindow(VWindowPtr parent, VString title)
  : VWindow(parent,title)
{
}
```

It allows the VWindow class's constructor to assign default values to all of its data members.

Creating action methods

The other function defined in the MainWindow class is called an action method. An *action method* takes the place of a case statement branch in a window procedure. Instead of using a large case statement with many branches to handle the messages directed to a window, a Vista window object uses action routines to respond to messages. A VWindow object's action methods together implement a window's behavior.

The Vista library translates messages received from Windows into VEvent objects. The VEvent class combines the data from messages with the operations that act on messages. Whenever a message is received, Vista classes translate it into a VEvent object and route it to the appropriate action method. The action method in turn reacts to the event, and returns a Boolean value that specifies whether or not the event was filtered. If the method returns False, Vista forwards the event to the default window procedure. If it returns True, Vista retrieves and processes the next event in its queue, bypassing the default window procedure.

The VWindow class provides several built-in Action methods for the most common events. If your window needs to react to an event in a different way, you can override the default methods by including an new member function in your class definition. If your window needs to respond to events that don't have action methods specified, you can add them in the InitActions member function.

The MainWindow class uses a single action method: PaintAction, which is one of the default action methods provided by the VWindow class. This method draws the greeting on the program's window in the same way that WinApp does:

```
Boolean MainWindow::PaintAction(VEventRef event)
{
 static char greetingString[] = "Hello, World!";
 PAINTSTRUCT ps;
 RECT rect
 HDC hdc = BeginPaint(*this, &ps);
 DrawText(hdc, greetingString, -1, GetDimensions(rect),
       DT_CENTER | DT_VCENTER | DT_SINGLELINE);
 EndPaint(*this, &ps);
 return True;
}
```

Using graphical drawing objects

The final step in porting a program to Vista is to convert GDI function calls into Vista graphics objects. This step is optional; you can leave your GDI code alone if you wish. However, using graphics objects might clarify your code:

```
Boolean PaintAction(VEventRef event)
{
    VPaintDevice device(*this);
    RECT rect;

    VGraphicsString string("Hello, World!",
                      GetDimensions(rect),
                   DT_CENTER | DT_VCENTER |
```

```
                    DT_SINGLELINE);
    device << string;
    return(True);
}
```

Compare this PaintAction method with the version using GDI calls. The GDI code retrieves a device context with BeginPaint, gets the dimensions of the window's client area with GetClientRect, draws the string with DrawText, and frees the device context with EndPaint.

The Vista version uses two objects: a VDisplayDevice and a VGraphicsString. Vista borrows a concept from the standard C^{++} streams library and overloads the left-shift ("<") operator to mean "put to." So, to draw a string on a window, create a VDisplayDevice object, create a VGraphicsString object, and put the string object to the device object. Don't worry about freeing the device object. Its destructor, called automatically when the object goes out of scope, does that for you.

When you run WinVista, it looks and acts just like WinApp (FIG. 2-2). The difference between the two programs is in your ability to extend them later on. While you can add features to a program written in C, it often is a difficult undertaking. You need to determine where to add code in the window procedure's switch statement. Adding those changes to the wrong switch case can cause the program's behavior to change in areas that are seemingly unrelated.

On the other hand, making a change to an object is simpler. Just add a new action method, or change an existing one. As long as you follow some simple rules, the object will always respond consistently.

2-2
Output from the WinVista sample application.

Vista naming conventions

When I designed the Vista library, I decided not to use Hungarian notation. Because C++ uses strong type checking, it verifies the data type of variables passed as arguments to a function at compile time. When you combine the strict type checking of C++ with the strict definitions in the Windows 3.1 header files, using Hungarian notation is overkill. The compiler will tell you if a variable you pass to a function is of the wrong data type. You don't need to give variable names a special prefix to help you remember their data type.

Instead of Hungarian notation, I used some simple rules:

- Function names start with a capital letter. Each word within the function name also is capitalized:

```
void SetWinPointer(void)
int  GetWinState(void)
```

- Classes and typedef names defined by Vista are prefixed by the letter *V*. All words are capitalized:

```
VAppl
VWindow
```

- Local variable names begin with a lowercase letter, but all words other than the first start with a capital letter:

```
int windowCounter
VWindow *window
```

- Class data members are in all lowercase, with words separated by an underscore:

```
Code:window
background_color
```

- Macro names are in all capitalized letters, with words separated by an underscore:

```
TEST_MACRO(x)
```

These rules aren't complicated, and they provide some consistency within the library and the sample applications. I recommend you choose and stick to a similar naming convention for your own programs.

What's next

In this chapter, I first looked at a sample Windows program using the C language. Then, I converted that sample to use Vista objects to get a good look at the use of the class library. In the next chapter, I'll look at the process of producing an executable program from that code using the Borland C++ development tools.

3 Building programs

Building a Windows application can be a complicated endeavor. Borland's development environment can simplify the process, but you need to understand each of the steps necessary to build your program and how all the pieces fit together. In this chapter, I'll discuss each of the components of a Windows program, then cover the tools provided with Borland C++ for Windows to process each component.

When you develop a Windows program with Borland C++, there are several distinct steps you need to take:

1. Create and modify C++ source files (.CPP and .H files).
2. Create and modify resource scripts for any menus, dialog boxes, icons, or other resources used by the program using either a text editor or the resource workshop.
3. Create a module definition file for the program.
4. Create help source and project files for the program.
5. Add each of the files to a project.
6. Use the Borland C++ Integrated Development Environment (IDE) to build the project.
7. Debug the program and go back to step 1.

Each step involves one or more source files. You can see that a Windows program requires more files than you might be accustomed to. Let's look at each step in detail.

The Windows development cycle

Creating C++ source files

As with any other type of program, the first step in creating a Windows program is to edit the main source files. With a C++ program, this normally consists of a .CPP file containing the code implementing one or more classes and a header or .H file that contains class interfaces.

To make the editing process more productive, Borland C++ or BCW moves the integrated development environment to a new level. Running under Windows in either standard or enhanced-386 mode, BCW lets you edit, compile, link, and run your programs while in Windows. It offers an interface built using the standard multi-document interface that lets you view or edit multiple files in separate windows at the same time. Because it is a Windows program, if you know how to use other Windows applications, you also know how to use BCW.

Borland C++ 3.1 (FIG. 3-1) makes editing these source files a true pleasure. Besides offering the rudimentary features found in any text editor, it uses color to highlight the different types of text found in a C++ program. You can configure the editor to use different colors for comments, reserved words, constants, strings, and even illegal characters.

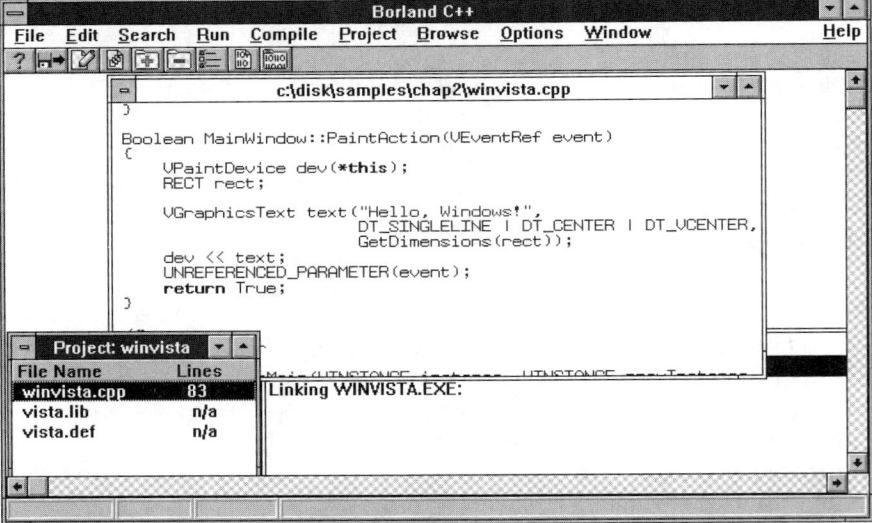

3-1
The Borland C++ Windows-hosted integrated development environment (IDE).

Another feature offered by the Borland C++ IDE is the object browser (FIG. 3-2). Instead of using the traditional text-based tools to search for object and function definitions, use the object browser. It gives you a graphical representation of the class hierarchy contained in your program. When you click on a class, the browser zooms in to show you its methods and data members. When you click on a method, the browser opens the file containing the method in an editor window and positions it to the line defining the method.

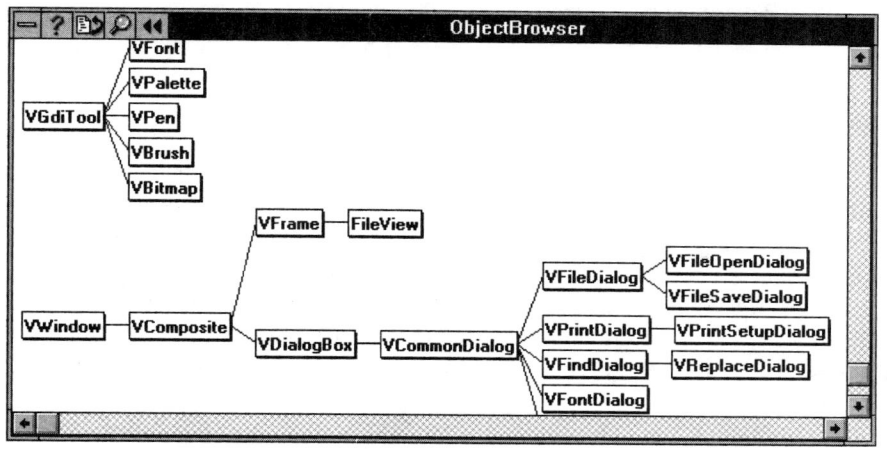

3-2
The Borland C++ Object Browser.

Windows programs use resource scripts to define the resources that either make up the appearance of an application or are language-dependent. Resource scripts typically contain definitions for dialog boxes, controls, menus, icons, accelerators, and strings. Listing 3-1 contains an example resource script.

Creating resource scripts

```
#include "dlgwind.h"

DialogMenu MENU
BEGIN
        POPUP "&File"
        BEGIN
        MENUITEM "&New", IDM_NEW
        MENUITEM "&Open...", IDM_OPEN
        MENUITEM "&Print...", IDM_PRINT
        MENUITEM "Printer &setup...", IDM_PRINTERSETUP
        MENUITEM SEPARATOR
                MENUITEM "E&xit\tF3", IDM_EXIT
        END

    POPUP "&Edit"
    BEGIN
        MENUITEM "&Search...", IDM_SEARCH
    END

    POPUP "&Options"      BEGIN
        MENUITEM "&Font...", IDM_FONT
        MENUITEM SEPARATOR
        MENUITEM "&Background...", IDM_BACKGROUND
        MENUITEM "&Foreground...", IDM_FOREGROUND
    END
```

Listing 3-1
A simple resource script.

Listing 3-1
Continued.

```
                    POPUP "&Help"
                    BEGIN
                            MENUITEM "&About...\tCtrl+A", IDM_ABOUT
                    END
END
```

Although they are optional, almost all Windows programs use resource scripts because they offer two important advantages. First, it is more efficient to load resources from a resource script than to create and manage them using API functions. Second, resource scripts aid in foreign language translation. Instead of modifying source code when translating a program's interface into a foreign language, translators simply edit the program's resource script.

For Borland C++ programmers, there is a third advantage to using resource scripts: the Resource Workshop (FIG. 3-3). While you can create a resource script using any text editor, the workshop makes the task much easier. It combines several tools—a dialog editor, menu editor, bitmap editor, and icon editor—into a single integrated environment. The workshop can read and write resources from and to resource scripts, binary resource files, dynamic link libraries, and executable programs.

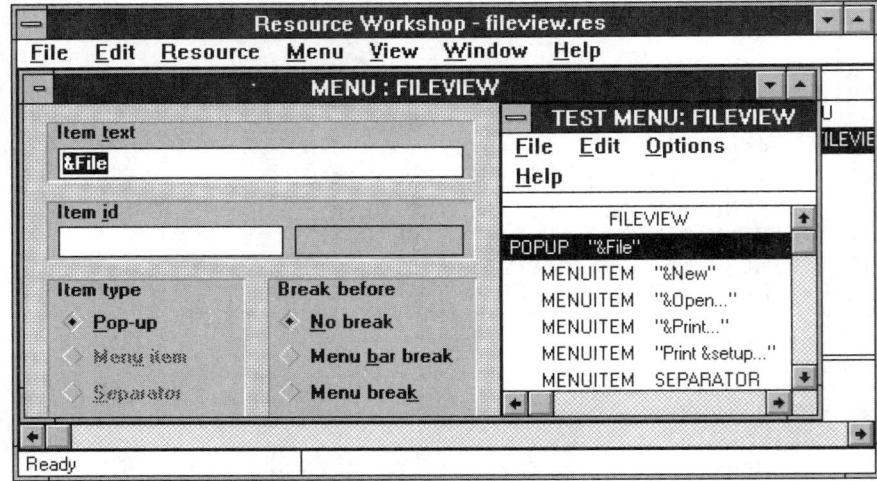

3-3
Borland's Resource Workshop.

Borland C++ provides three command-line tools to compile a resource script into a binary format and add it to a program. The first, BRCC, compiles the resource script into a binary resource (.RES) file. The second, RLINK, adds the binary resource file to a program or DLL. The third, RC, is licensed from Microsoft. It performs either task depending on the switches used to invoke it.

Fortunately, the IDE's project manager understands resources and resource files and takes care of calling the appropriate tool whenever necessary. To add resources to your program, create the resource script and add it to your project file using the IDE. When you make the program, the project manager will add the resources to the program's executable file.

Creating a module definition file

Windows programs necessarily are more complex than DOS programs and offer many more options as to how programs are organized. The linker requires more information to create a Windows program than it does to create one for MS-DOS. The module definition file passes this information to the linker. It includes information on the attributes of segments within the program, functions imported and exported by the program, and other information necessary for the linker to produce a Windows executable. Listing 3-2 contains an example module definition file.

```
EXETYPE WINDOWS
CODE PRELOAD MOVEABLE DISCARDABLE
DATA PRELOAD MOVEABLE MULTIPLE
HEAPSIZE 4096
STACKSIZE 5120
```

Listing 3-2
A simple module definition file.

Fortunately, the Borland C++ linker provides reasonable defaults for most of the values found in a module definition file. If you don't mind the warning generated when linking your program, you often can get by without using one. Another alternative is to use the module definition file provided with the Vista library. Adding it to your project will eliminate the warning message generated by the linker about a missing module definition file.

Creating help files

Windows provides a hypertext help system that you can access from within your programs. You can generate the same type of help system included with other applications like BCW: multiple fonts and text colors, graphics, context-sensitive topics, and hyperlinks between topics.

Two types of files are necessary to build a help system. First, you'll need to create the source for the help system using a word processor that supports footnotes, such as Microsoft Word for Windows. You also will need to create help project files using a text editor that ties the different source files and help topics together. Then, compile these files with the help compiler (HC) included with BCW. For more information on help systems and the help compiler, refer to the *Borland C++ Tools and Utilities Guide*.

Creating a project

To keep track of all these source files, use the BCW Project Manager. The project manager offers all the features of a command-line program make utility, but with the easy-to-use graphical interface built into BCW. It performs automatic dependency checks, tracking changes to the entire hierarchy of files including in a project. If you make a change in one header file, the project manager will recompile any source module using that header file.

Using the project manager is simple: create a project, add files to it, and make it. The Project menu contains commands that allow you to manage your project files. You also can find buttons on the speedbar that serve as shortcuts for the project commands. For more information on the Project Manager, see the *Borland C++ User's Guide*.

Building WinVista & WinApp

Building the sample applications presented in the last chapter with the IDE is simple. Create a project file for each program, add the program's source file to the project, add the Vista library file (VISTA.LIB) to the project, and select `Make` from the Compile menu. The project manager will invoke the proper utilities to compile and link the programs.

You also can use the project files included on the companion disks. Note that, because the project manager includes the relative paths of all files in the project, including header files, you might need to update directory information before you can make the project. Select `Directories` from the Options menu and enter the correct paths for the Borland C++ and Vista include and library files.

One final note about building programs with the project manager. The IDE allows you to set compiler optimization flags. One of these flags `Object Data Calling`, changes the way the arguments are passed to object member functions. If you select this option, you also will need to rebuild the Vista libraries with the same option set.

Debugging your program

Borland C++ includes Turbo Debugger for Windows (BCW). A full-featured source-level debugger, BCW can be a great help in tracking down the most difficult bugs. To access BCW from within the IDE, choose the `Debugger` option from the Run menu. You then can use all the features of the debugger to run your program.

BCW runs in two modes. The interface for the debugger itself is text-based and runs in full-screen mode. While you run your program, it swaps the display back to graphics mode whenever necessary for program input or output. Although it handles the display-swapping very smoothly, BCW also will use a debugging terminal if one is available. It also can run across a serial communications line with the debugger on one machine and your program on another.

Because Windows programs—unlike their DOS counterparts—are event-driven, you'll need to take a different approach to debugging. Windows drives your program, so you can't just step through it line-by-line to come across your error like you can with most DOS programs. With a Vista program, you'll be able to immediately step through only two or three lines before Windows takes control. To complicate things further, `cout` (the C++ equivalent of `stdout`) doesn't work for a Windows program, so you can't use `printf` or the C++ stream operators to display information about the program.

Using Turbo Debugger

This section lists some tips on debugging your programs. Debugging a Windows program often can take longer than it took to write it in the first place. So, I've written some tips to make your debugging a little easier.

Use preventive coding practices to keep your debugging to a minimum. The Vista classes take advantage of the strict type-checking in Windows 3.1, which can prevent many bugs from occurring. In keeping with this theme, cast variables from one type to another only when absolutely necessary. Use the VASSERT macro to validate conditions in your programs. It will display a message box informing you of failed assertions and exit before they wreak more havoc.

If you still encounter errors, set breakpoints on suspect methods. For example, if your program blows up before it displays its main window, set a breakpoint on your application object's InitMainWindow method. You then can step through to see where the error is occurring.

Setting breakpoints can save you quite a bit of time in tracking down bugs; however, if you don't know which method is causing the problem, you need to use another technique. Use the "View Windows Message" dialog box to set a breakpoint on all messages directed to the VWindow::WindowProc window procedure (choose `Windows Message` from the View menu). This function is the window procedure for all Vista frame and MDI child windows. The debugger then will break every time your window receives a message. From there, you should be able to narrow the message search and track down the method causing the problem.

If you still can't catch the error, trying viewing the stack after the error occurs (choose `Stack` from the View menu). Don't be surprised to find that the stack is 10 or 20 levels deep before it hits your error. The unlabeled lines in the stack display are Windows API or system functions. The labeled lines are from your program. The top-most labeled line probably is the routine causing the error.

Using WInspector

If your program fails outside the debugger, use WInspector to get more information. WInspector is a utility included with BCW that displays information about the state of the system at the time a program crashes. WInspector also can interpret the program's stack to give you an idea of where the problem originated.

Although WInspector will display information about any program on your system that crashes, it is most helpful with applications built using Borland

C++. To get WInspector to display full information about the state of your program at the time it crashes, use the TMAPSYM utility to create a map symbol file for the program. WInspector then will display all functions and the value of their arguments at the time the program crashed. This can be especially useful when you're trying to debug timing-related errors that disappear when you use the debugger.

Drastic measures If all else fails, you can use a few other techniques to track down bugs. Strategically placed message boxes and beeps can help you track the flow of events and data through your program. Using a debugging console along with calls to the OutputDebugString API function, also can help. Sometimes, there's just no substitute for sitting down with printed listings for an old-fashioned desk-check session.

What's next In this chapter, I covered some of the tools included in the Borland C++ package. I looked at the development cycle for Windows programs and discussed some methods for debugging Windows programs. In the next chapter, I'll delve deeper into Windows programs with the Vista library by looking at Vista's application and event classes.

4 Applications & events

In chapter 2, I looked at a simple Vista application. I used an application object to drive the program and a window class to manage its main window. I also briefly looked at how Windows communicates with a program using messages. In this chapter, I'll take a closer look at the application and event classes. I'll use these classes to examine the design of the Vista library and see how an application framework operates and how you can take advantage of it within your own programs.

Vista applications & the VAppl class

The VAppl class takes on the responsibility of running a Windows application. As you saw in chapter 2, it handles program initialization and cleanup and drives the Windows message loop. While it takes care of many details necessary for any Windows program, the operations it provides serve as a bare minimum. Like many other classes in an application framework, it serves as a starting point for your own application class. You create a *derived class* to implement an object with its own distinct behavior.

For example, the InitWindow member function creates the program's main window. The default function provided by VAppl simply creates a VWindow object, which does nothing but display a window with a caption and other window decoration elements—you can't do anything else with it.

To gain more functionality, in WinVista, I derive the WinVistaAppl class from VAppl:

```
class WinVistaAppl: public VAppl
{
    ...
    void InitWindow(void);
};
```

The WinVistaAppl class is called a *derived class* or *subclass*, while the VAppl class is called the *base class* or *superclass*. My subclass creates my own type of VWindow object: a MainWindow. It retains the data and operations of its base class, with the exception of the InitWindow member function.

Rather than duplicate the operations of the base class, I used inheritance to refine them. A WinVistaAppl object can do anything a VAppl class can do, but it changes the way the main window is initialized. The VAppl class, like other Vista classes, was designed with this sort of reuse in mind.

Interface, implementation, & access control

The VAppl class is divided into two components: its interface and its implementation. The class's interface is composed of its class declaration and is contained in the header file VAppl.h (LISTING 4-1). A class's interface is its visible portion, you can use it to get an idea of the operations the class supports.

Listing 4-1
SIZER.CPP: source code for the Sizer program.

```
/* -----------------------------------------------------------------
   Sizer.cpp

   A sample Vista application

   Copyright (C) 1992, by Jeff Mackay - TAB BOOKS

   -----------------------------------------------------------------*/

#include <vista.h>>
#include <vgrdev.h>
#include <vgrobj.h>
#include <stdlib.h>

/*
** Application class definition
*/

STDCLASS(SizerAppl);

class _CLASSTYPE SizerAppl : public VAppl
{
```

```cpp
    public:
        SizerAppl(HINSTANCE instance, HINSTANCE prevInstance,
                    LPSTR cmdLine, int cmdShow);
        virtual void InitWindow(void);
        virtual void InitConfig(void);
        virtual void CleanupConfig(void);
        void SetStartup(RECTRef rect, int state);

    private:
        RECT rect;
        char *section;
        char *ini_name;
};

/*
** Main window class definition
*/
STDCLASS(MainWindow);

class _CLASSTYPE MainWindow : public VFrame
{
    public:
        MainWindow(void);
        virtual Boolean PaintAction(VEventRef event);
        virtual Boolean DestroyAction(VEventRef event);
};

Boolean MainWindow::DestroyAction(VEventRef event)
{
    WINDOWPLACEMENT wp;
    memset(&wp, 0, sizeof(wp));
    wp.length = sizeof(wp);
    GetWindowPlacement(*this, &wp);
    ((SizerApplRef)appl).SetStartup(wp.rcNormalPosition,
                wp.showCmd);
    VFrame::DestroyAction(event);
    return True;
}


/*
** Application class member functions
*/

SizerAppl::SizerAppl(HINSTANCE instance,
                        HINSTANCE prevInstance,
                        LPSTR cmdLine, int cmdShow)
    : VAppl("Sizer", instance, prevInstance, cmdLine, cmdShow)
{
    section  = "Placement";
    ini_name = "sizer.ini";
```

Listing 4-1
Continued.

```
}

void SizerAppl::InitWindow(void)
{
    main_window = new MainWindow();
    main_window->SetDimensions(rect);
}

void SizerAppl::InitConfig(void)
{
    rect.top = GetPrivateProfileInt(section, "top",
                                    0, ini_name);
    rect.left = GetPrivateProfileInt(section, "left",
                                    0, ini_name);
    rect.right = GetPrivateProfileInt(section, "right",
                                    CW_USEDEFAULT, ini_name);
    rect.bottom = GetPrivateProfileInt(section, "bottom",
                                    CW_USEDEFAULT, ini_name);
    win_state = GetPrivateProfileInt(section, "state",
                                    SW_SHOWNORMAL, ini_name);
}

void SizerAppl::CleanupConfig(void)
{
    TCHAR string[10];

    WritePrivateProfileString(section, "top",
                              itoa(rect.top, string, 10),
                              ini_name);
    WritePrivateProfileString(section, "left",
                              itoa(rect.left, string, 10),
                              ini_name);
    WritePrivateProfileString(section, "bottom",
                              itoa(rect.bottom, string, 10),
                              ini_name);
    WritePrivateProfileString(section, "right",
                              itoa(rect.right, string, 10),
                              ini_name);
    WritePrivateProfileString(section, "state",
                              itoa(win_state, string, 10),
                              ini_name);
}

void SizerAppl::SetStartup(RECTRef curRect, int curState)
{
    rect = curRect;
    win_state = curState;
}

/*
** Main window class member functions
*/
```

Applications & events

```
MainWindow::MainWindow(void)
    : VFrame(NULL, "Sample Vista Application")
{
}

Boolean MainWindow::PaintAction(VEventRef event)
{
    VPaintDevice dev(*this);
    RECT rect;

    VGraphicsText text("Hello, Windows!",
                       DT_SINGLELINE | DT_CENTER | DT_VCENTER,
                       GetDimensions(rect));
    dev << text;
    UNREFERENCED_PARAMETER(event);
    return True;
}

/*
** Main driver
*/
int PASCAL WinMain(HINSTANCE instance, HINSTANCE prevInstance,
                   LPSTR cmdLine, int cmdShow)
{
    SizerAppl appl(instance, prevInstance, cmdLine, cmdShow);

    appl.Run();
    return appl.GetStatus();
}
```

The class's implementation is contained in its source file, VAppl.cpp. The implementation is the private part of the class that carries out its behavior.

The separation of a class's interface from its implementation enforces encapsulation. By hiding the implementation, you can fully utilize a class without relying on its internal details. The implemenation can change without requiring change to programs that use that class.

One of the greatest benefits of encapsulation or information hiding is portability. Application frameworks use information hiding to implement portability between different systems. For example, if the underlying window system changes from Windows 3.1 to Windows NT or OS/2 Presentation Manager, only the implementation of classes in the framework changes. Programs using only the class's public interface need only minor changes (or no changes) to run in the new environment.

C++ provides a second method of information hiding called *member access control*. Members can be accessed at three levels: public, protected, or private. Public members can be accessed by any client. Protected members can be accessed only by the class and its subclasses. Private members are accessible only by the class itself.

Vista classes use all three levels of access control. All data members are either private or protected, allowing access only to the class and subclasses. Member functions can be private, protected, or public depending on their intended use.

When you develop your own classes, you'll want to provide the same protection to your class members, especially data. You can start by applying private protection to everything and only promoting to protected when necessary. Combining access control with encapsulation can aid in both portability and reliability. You control who can modify an object's data; therefore, you know where to look when something goes wrong.

Inheritance & initialization

The VAppl class provides three methods that perform program initialization. The InitApplication function drives the initialization and is the first function called by the Run method. It first calls InitConfig, which should initialize any configuration information the program needs, such as variables in a Windows .INI file. Then, it calls InitWindow, which initializes the program's main window object.

The initialization functions are declared as virtual functions. Virtual functions are meant to be overridden by derived classes. Then, when a base class calls a virtual function, it calls your overridden function rather than the original. So, when I derived my own InitWindow function, VAppl's Run method called my derived function rather than its own.

You might wonder why the initialization methods are called outside of the class's constructor. Because the constructor is supposed to initialize the object automatically, why call the initialization functions from the Run method? The problem is with the way C++ calls functions from constructors.

When C++ constructs an object, it calls base-class constructors first, then the object's constructor. When the base-class constructor calls a function, C++ invokes the function active for the base class, even if the function is virtual. This makes it appear that even virtual functions are nonvirtual. The same principle applies to nonvirtual functions overridden by subclasses.

So, consider what would happen if I called InitWindow from the VAppl class constructor. When I create the object, the VAppl constructor is invoked. It would in turn call the VAppl class's InitWindow function, which would create its VWindow object as the main window for the program. The derived class's InitWindow function would never be called.

The reason for this behavior is solid. A virtual function in a derived class might depend on data initialized in that class's constructor. If the language called a virtual function in a derived class, that function could access uninitialized data. Who knows what would happen next?

Program cleanup

Program cleanup also is handled by the VAppl class. Like the initialization methods, the cleanup methods are called by the Run method. You can override the cleanup methods or take care of cleanup in your class destructor.

The cleanup methods are called from the Run method for the same reason as the initialization routines. Virtual functions called by a destructor act as if they aren't virtual. If the VAppl destructor called the virtual cleanup methods, only the methods defined in the VAppl class would be called. Your cleanup functions would never be called and your resources never released.

Again, C^{++} has a solid reason for treating virtual functions this way. The subclass's virtual function might depend on data already destroyed by its destructor.

Running the program

Now, that I've looked at the initialization and cleanup services provided by the VAppl class, I can focus on its main operation: Run. This method calls initialization methods, the event loop, and the cleanup methods. In effect, the Run method runs the entire program. One of the more important operations of the Run method is the event loop, but I'll wait until the next section to discuss that.

Overloaded operators

The final significant operation in the VAppl class is its cast operator. C^{++} allows classes to override the language's operators to make the class act just as if it were a built-in data type. The VAppl class overrides a single operator: a cast operator:

```
operator HINSTANCE(void) const
{
    return instance;
}
```

The function is called whenever a VAppl object is cast into an instance handle. This simple function plays an important part in making Vista compatible with the Windows API. It allows you to use a VAppl object with any function requiring an instance handle as an argument. It provides a convenient means of accessing Windows API functions.

Using cast operators in this manner has a more subtle benefit: as far as Vista programs are concerned, a VAppl object is an HINSTANCE. This is an example of one of the goals of object-oriented design: modeling a solution that is as close as possible to the problem domain. For a Windows application framework like Vista, the problem domain is the Windows API. Because one of the design goals for Vista was to provide easy access to the API functions, the cast operator is an ideal solution.

There is a drawback to Vista's approach. Strictly speaking, a cast operator shouldn't be used for a typedef. However, because Turbo C^{++} allows it (many C^{++} compilers do), I decided to use it. However, if the ANSI standard dictates that this practice is illegal (or if Borland changes the compiler), there is a simple solution. Windows 3.1 uses a macro to define an HINSTANCE as a pointer to a constant structure of type HINSTANCE__. It would be a simple matter to change the cast operator to return the pointer instead of the typedef, without having to change programs that use the operator. However, because the typedef makes for easier reading, I'll leave it alone as long as I can.

Sizer: using the Application class

Listing 4-1 contains the code for the second example program: Sizer. This program uses the initialization and cleanup routines to save configuration information: the position, size, and state of the main window. Each time you run the program, it restores the state it was in the last time you ran it.

Retrieving windows state information

Sizer retrieves the main window's state and positioning information in the main window's DestroyAction method, which is called just before the window is destroyed:

```
Boolean MainWindow::DestroyAction(VEventRef event)
{
    WINDOWPLACEMENT wp;
    memset(&wp, 0, sizeof(wp));
    wp.length = sizeof(wp);
    GetWindowPlacement(*this, &wp);
((SizerApplRef)appl).SetStartup(wp.rcNormalPosition,
      wp.showCmd);
    VFrame::DestroyAction(event);
    return True;
}
```

The DestroyAction method uses the GetWindowPlacement function to retrieve the details. New to Windows 3.1, GetWindowPlacement is a very useful routine that manages and retrieves the placement of a window. It is the best way to retrieve and set the coordinates, size, and state of a window, regardless of its current state.

Maintaining configuration data

The program uses two Windows API private profile functions to store the window state information in a private configuration file in the SizerAppl object's InitConfig and CleanupConfig methods:

```
void SizerAppl::InitConfig(void)
{
```

```
    rect.top = GetPrivateProfileInt(section, "top",
                                    0, ini_name);
    rect.left = GetPrivateProfileInt(section, "left",
                                    0, ini_name);
    rect.right = GetPrivateProfileInt(section, "right",
                                    CW_USEDEFAULT, ini_name);
    rect.bottom = GetPrivateProfileInt(section,
                                    "bottom",
                                    CW_USEDEFAULT,
                                    ini_name);
    win_state = GetPrivateProfileInt(section, "state",
                                    SW_SHOWNORMAL,
                                    ini_name);
}

void SizerAppl::CleanupConfig(void)
{
    TCHAR string[10];
    WritePrivateProfileString(section, "top",
                              itoa(rect.top, string,
                              10),
                              ini_name);
    WritePrivateProfileString(section, "left",
                              itoa(rect.left, string,
                              10),
                              ini_name);
    WritePrivateProfileString(section, "bottom",
                              itoa(rect.bottom, string,
                              10),
                              ini_name);
    WritePrivateProfileString(section, "right",
                              itoa(rect.right, string,
                              10),
                              ini_name);
    WritePrivateProfileString(section, "state",
                              itoa(win_state, string,
                              10),
                              ini_name);
}
```

Windows programs use initialization (.INI) files to store user preferences and system configuration details. The file contains any number of sections, with multiple entries each storing a specific value. The initialization file for Sizer looks like this:

```
[Placement]
top=242
left=64
bottom=528
right=721
state=1
```

It's a very good idea to allow the profile functions to manage your program's initialization file. In the network configurations provided by Windows 3.1 and Windows for Workgroups, system files are stored in common directories on a server. Most programs also will reside in their own directory on the server. For security reasons, most sites maintain access controls that allow read-only access to shared files and directories. Users won't have write permissions on common directories, so the profile functions access initialization files in a user's private Windows directory.

WindowsNT complicates matters further by maintaining a binary registration database instead of initializations files. The profile functions offer a simplified interface to storing information on a per-user basis in the registration database. The bottom line is that you must use the Windows profile functions to maintain your program's configuration information.

Communicating with Windows: the VEvent class

In the discussion of the VAppl class, I left out an important detail: the event loop. In this section, I'll look at Windows messages and their relationship with a Windows program. I then will examine the VAppl class's event loop and Vista's mechanism for dealing with events, the VEvent class.

Windows messages

As you saw in chapter 2, messages play an important part in any Windows program. The message itself is a defined as a structure:

```
typedef struct tagMSG
{
    HWND hwnd
    UINT message;
    WPARAM wParam;LPARAM lParam;
    DWORD time;
    POINT pt;
} MSG;
```

The `hwnd` member identifies the window the message is directed to. The `message` member identifies the message itself. `wParam` and `lParam` contain additional, optional information about the message. The `time` and `pt` members, used infrequently, contain the system time and mouse pointer position at the time the event occurred.

A program's message loop retrieves a message from its queue and passes it back to Windows to dispatch it to the correct window procedure. The window procedure then examines the message identifier and maybe the `wParam` or `lParam` values to determine what it needs to do in response to the message.

The `wParam` and `lParam` values differ from message to message. When Microsoft first designed Windows, CPUs were relatively slow and memory scarce. Instead of placing message information into a separate data structure (requiring additional memory), Windows split that information into a 16-bit parameter (wParam) and a 32-bit parameter (lParam) that normally contained two other 16-bit items. This provided flexibility without the storage overhead required by passing a data structure with every message.

Unfortunately, the values contained in wParam and lParam might not be consistent between Windows 3.1 and Win32. One of the biggest changes in the Win32 environment is the widening of handles from 16 bits to 32 bits. This widening has side effects that affect the parameters of several messages.

For example, consider the WM_COMMAND message sent by child window controls to notify their parent window of user actions. Under Windows 3.1, the message placed the child's window identifier in wParam and packed its window handle and a notification code into lParam:

```
switch (message)
{
    ...
    case WM_COMMAND:
        int window_id = wParam;
        HWND hwnd =     (HWND) LOWORD(lParam);
        int notify_code = HIWORD(lParam);
    ...
}
```

Under Win32, parameters were moved around. The window identifier and notification code are packed into wParam, and the window handle is in lParam. The code changes to:

```
switch (message)
{
    ...
    case WM_COMMAND:
        short window_id =   LOWORD(wParam);
        short notify_code = HIWORD(wParam);
        HWND hwnd =         (HWND) (UINT) lParam;
}
```

The conversion of message-handling code is the biggest obstacle to overcome in porting a Windows 3.1 application to Win32. Why did Microsoft take this approach, instead of changing the API to increase consistency? Because one of their goals in creating Windows NT was to make it as easy as possible to port old applications to the new environment. More changes to the API would mean more changes to applications and probably would hinder migration. This approach takes advantage of the 32-bit architecture while requiring only minimal changes to existing applications.

Windows message processing Besides communicating event information to programs, messages perform another important role under Windows 3.1. They control the system's nonpreemptive multitasking. Only one application at a time can process messages; other programs are suspended until the active application yields control back to Windows.

The message loop, therefore, serves two purposes. First, it retrieves and dispatches messages from its message queue. Second, it allows Windows to transfer control to other applications when the program's message queue is empty.

Figure 4-1 illustrates the message-processing scheme of Windows 3.1. The system first inserts messages into a system-wide queue. It then removes messages directed to the active task and places them in its queue. When that task has no more messages to process, Windows transfers control to the next task and goes through the same sequence of events.

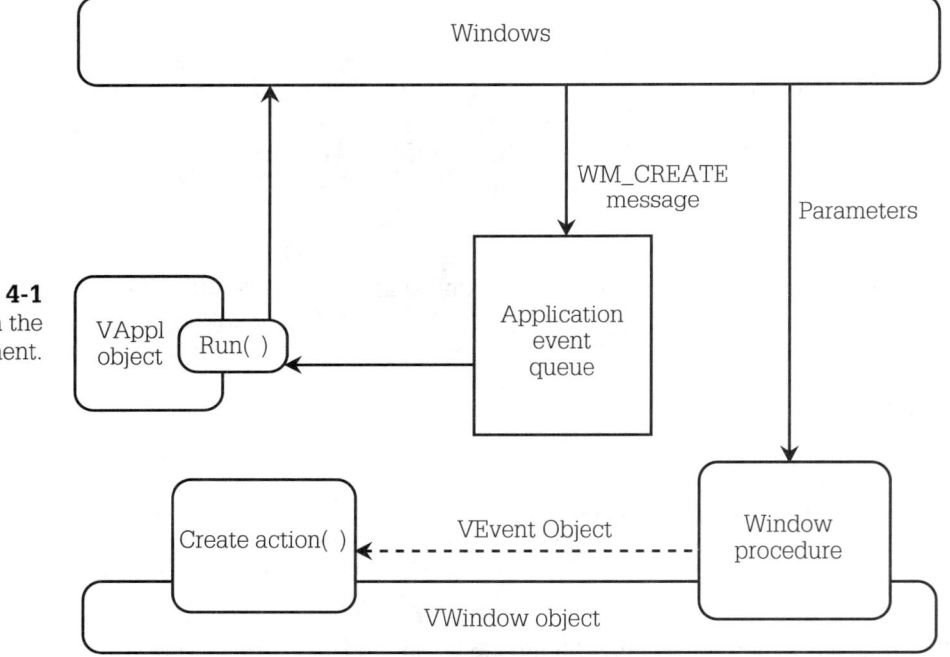

4-1
Message processing in the Windows environment.

This cooperative multitasking scheme can lead to problems. If the active program is slow to respond to messages, it can affect the performance of other applications. Even worse, if the active application hangs in a loop and never yields control, the system also can appear to hang up.

Windows NT, unlike Windows 3.1, uses a preemptive multitasking scheme. Each thread of control gets use of the processor for a specific period of time, regardless of whether it is processing a message or not. Windows still maintains a message queue, but it also includes its own message-passing thread with an elevated priority whose sole responsibility is to pass messages to client tasks (FIG. 4-3).

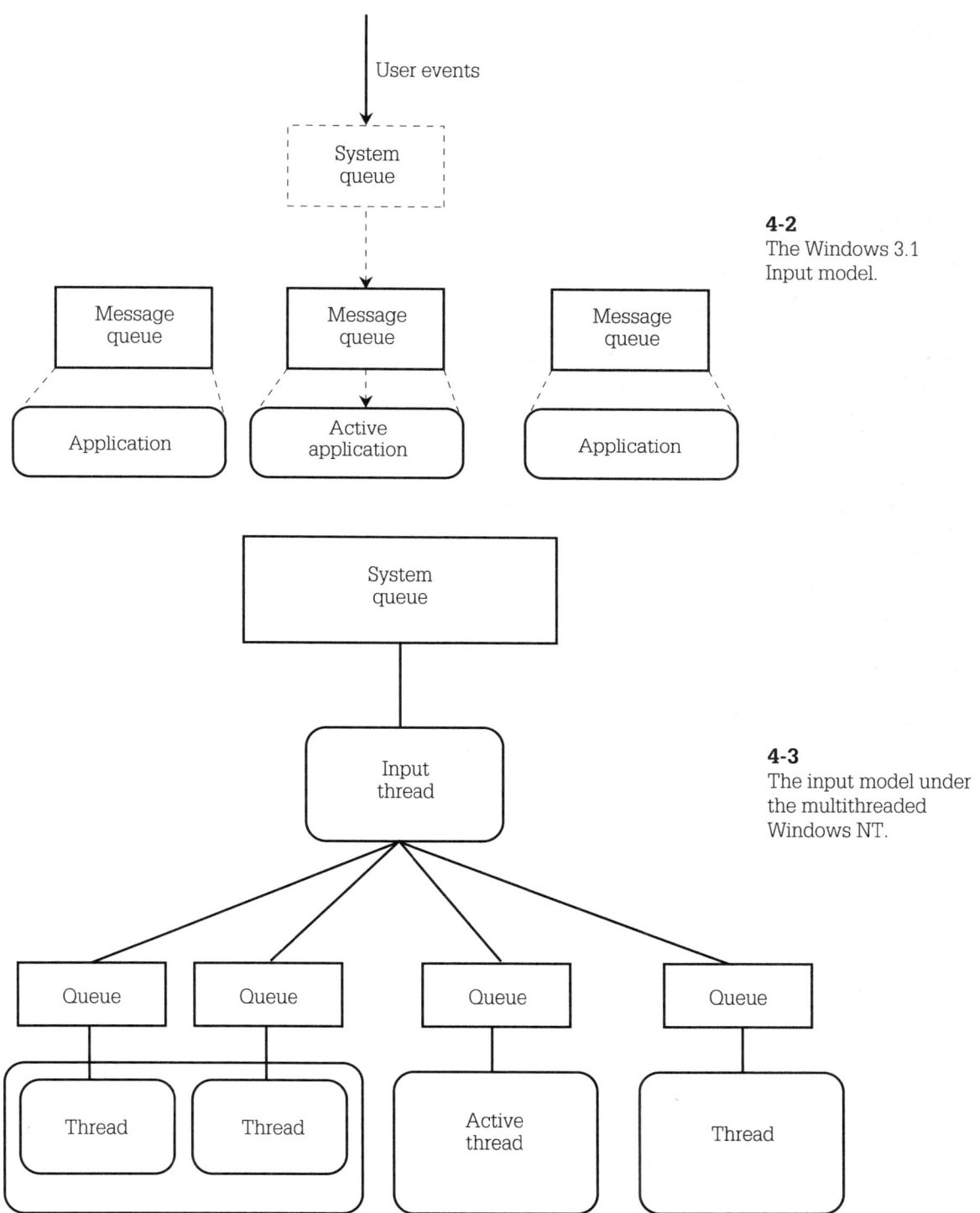

4-2
The Windows 3.1 Input model.

4-3
The input model under the multithreaded Windows NT.

Under the NT multiprocessing model, several applications can process messages at the same time. If one task hangs itself up in a loop, other tasks can continue running. Overall, the system appears to perform much better.

Communicating with messages Windows supplies two different functions that allow windows to communicate with messages. The first, PostMessage, is used when the sender doesn't care what action is taken in response to the message. Most of the standard system messages take this form. For example, whenever a window is moved or resized, Windows posts a WM_WINDOWPOSCHANGED message to the window's message queue. The system doesn't need any response to the event, it is only notifying the window that the event occurred. The PostMessage function returns control immediately after the message is posted to a queue.

The second function, SendMessage, bypasses other messages in an application's queue and sends a message directly to a window procedure. The function is useful when you need to get information from a window. For example, to query the selected (highlighted) item in a list box, use SendMessage. The list box control's window procedure responds by returning the index of the selected item. When you send a message to a window rather than post it, you interrupt normal message traffic to get an immediate response. SendMessage doesn't return until the target window procedure responds to the message.

Use SendMessage only when necessary. If overused, SendMessage can affect performance because it doesn't allow processing of posted messages. The performance of applications running under Windows 3.1 depends a great deal on the use of PostMessage whenever possible. This dependence decreases under Windows NT, but it still is a good idea to use SendMessage only when you require an immediate response to a message.

Vista message processing Because message-processing takes up a vast majority of the processing in a Windows program, flexible and efficient message-handling was one of the design goals for the Vista library. The first component in Vista's message-handling scheme is the EventLoop member function of the VAppl class:

```
VStatus VAppl::EventLoop(void)
{
    MSG msg;
    while (GetMessage(&msg, NULL, 0, 0))
    {
       if (!ConvertKeyMessage(msg))
       {
            TranslateMessage(&msg);
            DispatchMessage(&msg);
       }
    }
```

```
        return (VStatus) msg.wParam;
}
```

This message loop doesn't look much different than it would in a C program. Other than the call to the VAppl member function ConvertKeyMessage (that performs special processing on accelerators and the tab and arrow keys), it is a standard message loop. The message structure is retrieved from the message queue and passed immediately back to Windows, which dispatches the message to the proper window procedure.

The VEvent class

The VEvent class combines the content of a Windows MSG structure with the operations that act on it. It provides operations to access event information, as well as a replacement for the API SendEvent and PostEvent functions.

To send a message to a window, you have a number of choices. The first is to use the native Windows SendMessage function:

```
SendMessage(*window, VM_SOMEMESSAGE, 0, 0);
```

This is a quick and easy way to communicate with another window. The VEvent class offers an alternative:

```
VWindow *win;
...
VEvent *event(*win, VM_SOMEMESSAGE, 0, 0);
event.Send();
```

The VEvent constructor uses default arguments for the `wParam` and `lParam` values, so the call to create the event object can be simplified to:

```
VEvent *event(*win, VM_SOMEMESSAGE);
```

In this example, both `wParam` and `lParam` are initialized to default values of 0. Either example is equivalent to using the SendMessage API function to send a message to a window, but they add an object-oriented flavor to the process. Instead of using a procedural approach, you can use the VEvent class to treat the event as an object. You can choose either technique, it's only a matter of personal preference, although using the VEvent object does have advantages.

Event portability

One of the most significant changes between Windows 3.1 and Win32 is in the content of message parameters. Many messages include handles as arguments. Because Win32 expands the size of a handle from 16 to 32 bits, some of these arguments were moved from the second parameter to the first.

The VEvent class eases your move from Windows 3.1 to Win32. There are two basic approaches to providing event portability:
- Provide wrapper classes for each available message type.
- Restrict access to a subset of the available messages.

Neither approach is ideal. The first option results in a large number of classes that duplicate existing functionality. The second limits the use of features offered by the Windows API.

So, to help you increase the portability of your event-handling code, here are some guidelines:

- Use default mechanisms for responding to events. The WM_COMMAND message, probably the most widely used message in any Windows program, is one of those messages that had to change. However, Vista allows you to respond to WM_COMMAND messages using action methods—you normally don't have to access the message's parameters.
- Use member functions provided by window classes instead of sending events. Vista classes are designed to minimize dependencies on the underlying window environment.
- Rely on the content of an event (wParam and lParam) only when absolutely necessary.
- If you must access parameters for nonportable events (TABLE 4-1), use macros to extract information. When you move from Windows 3.1 to Win32, only the macros need to change.

Table 4-1 Events that are modified in Win32.

Message	Windows 3.1	Win32
WM_ACTIVATE	wParam: state lParam: min, hwnd	wParam: state, min lParam: hwnd
WM_CHARTOITEM	wParam: char lParam: pos, hwnd	wParam: char, pos lParam: hwnd
WM_COMMAND	wParam: id lParam: hwnd, cmd	wParam: id, cmd lParam: hwnd
WM_CTLCOLOR*	wParam: hdc lParam: hwnd, type	See Note
WM_MENUSELECT	wParam: cmd lParam: flags, hMenu	wParam: cmd, flags lParam: hMenu
WM_MDIACTIVATE (to child)	wParam: activate lParam: dHwnd, aHwnd	wParam: dHwnd lParam: aHwnd
WM_MDISETMENU	wParam: 0 lParam: hFrame, hWin	wParam: hFrame lParam: hWin
WM_MENUCHAR	wParam: char lParam: hMenu, fMenu	wParam: char, fMenu lParam: hMenu

WM_PARENTNOTIFY (create/destroy)	wParam: msg lParam: id, hwnd	wParam: msg, id lParam: hwnd
WM_VKEYTOITEM	wParam: code lParam: item, hwnd	wParam: code, item lParam: hwnd
EM_GETSEL	wParam: 0 lParam: 0	wParam: start (or 0) lParam: end (or 0)
EM_LINESCROLL	wParam: 0 lParam: vert, horiz	wParam: horiz lParam: vert
EM_SETSEL	wParam: 0 lParam: start, end	wParam: start lParam: end
WM_HSCROLL WM_VSCROLL	wParam: code lParam: pos, hwnd	wParam: code, pos lParam: hwnd

Note: The WM_CTLCOLOR message is obsolete in Win32. It was replaced by specific WM_CTLCOLOR messages for each type of control.

By following these guidelines, you can limit the amount of effort needed to port your application from Windows 3.1 to Win32. If you follow the first two suggestions and use the class member functions provided by Vista, your program probably won't need any modification at all.

MSGLIST: responding to events

The sample program, MSGLIST, in LISTING 4-2 illustrates some of the ways a Vista program can respond to events. It displays information about mouse events it receives, recording its X and Y positions at the time each event occurs. I'll dissect it in this section to see how the program works.

Listing 4-2
MSGWIND.CPP: illustrates responding to messages.

```
/* --------------------------------------------------------
   msgwind.cpp

      An example that illustrates using events.

   Copyright (C) 1992, by Jeff Mackay - TAB Books
-------------------------------  */
#pragma hdrfile "vista.sym"
#include <vista.h>
#pragma hdrstop
#include "vgrdev.h"
#include "vgditool.h"
#include "msgwind.h"

class MessageWindow  : public VFrame
```

Listing 4-2
Continued.

```cpp
{
public:

    MessageWindow(void);

protected:
    void InitActions(void);
    Boolean MinMaxAction(VEventRef event);
    Boolean MouseAction(VEventRef event);
    Boolean ClearAction(VEventRef event);
    Boolean CreateAction(VEventRef event);
    Boolean PaintAction(VEventRef event);
    Boolean SizeAction(VEventRef event);

private:
    Boolean dragging;
    int char_width;
    int char_height;
    int line;
    int tabs[3];
};


MessageWindow::MessageWindow(void) : VFrame(0, "Using Message Boxes")
{
    dragging = False;
    char_width = 0;
    char_height = 0;
    line = 0;
    tabs[0] = tabs[1] = tabs[2] = 0;
}


void MessageWindow::InitActions(void)
{
    VFrame::InitActions();
    AddAction((VAction)&MessageWindow::MinMaxAction,
                    WM_GETMINMAXINFO);
    AddAction((VAction)&MessageWindow::MouseAction,
                    WM_LBUTTONDOWN);
    AddAction((VAction)&MessageWindow::MouseAction,
                    WM_LBUTTONUP);
    AddAction((VAction)&MessageWindow::MouseAction,
                    WM_MOUSEMOVE);
    AddAction((VAction)&MessageWindow::ClearAction,
                    WM_RBUTTONDOWN);
}
```

```cpp
Boolean MessageWindow::CreateAction(VEventRef event)
{
        TEXTMETRIC tm;
        VDisplayDevice dev(*this);
        GetTextMetrics(dev, &tm);
        char_width = tm.tmAveCharWidth;
        char_height = tm.tmHeight + tm.tmExternalLeading;
        VFrame::CreateAction(event);
        return True;
}


Boolean MessageWindow::PaintAction(VEventRef event)
{
    strstream strm;

    strm << "Event";
    strm << "\tX Pos ";
    strm << "\tY Pos " << ends;
    VPaintDevice dev(*this);
        TabbedTextOut(dev, char_width, char_height,
            strm.str(), strlen(strm.str()), 2, tabs, 0);
    line = 3;
    dragging = False;
    strm.rdbuf()->freeze(0);    // thaw the buffer
    UNREFERENCED_PARAMETER(event);
    return False;
}



Boolean MessageWindow::SizeAction(VEventRef event)
{
    VFrame::SizeAction(event);
    tabs[0] = width / 2;
    tabs[1] = tabs[0] + (tabs[0]/2);
    return True;
}


Boolean MessageWindow::MinMaxAction(VEventRef event)
{
    MINMAXINFO FAR *minMax = (MINMAXINFO FAR *) event.GetLParam();
    minMax->ptMinTrackSize.x = 50 * char_width;
    return False;
}

Boolean MessageWindow::ClearAction(VEventRef event)
{
    Invalidate();
    UNREFERENCED_PARAMETER(event);
```

Listing 4-2
Continued.

```cpp
        return True;
}

Boolean MessageWindow::MouseAction(VEventRef event)
{
    ostrstream strm;

    switch(event.GetId())
    {
        case WM_LBUTTONDOWN:
            strm << "WM_LBUTTONDOWN";
            SetCapture(*this);
            dragging = True;
            break;
        case WM_LBUTTONUP:
            strm << "WM_LBUTTONUP";
            ReleaseCapture();
            dragging = False;
            break;
        case WM_MOUSEMOVE:
            if (!dragging)
                return False;
            strm << "WM_MOUSEMOVE";
            break;
        default:
            break;
    }
    strm << "\t" << LOWORD(event.GetLParam());
    strm << "\t" << HIWORD(event.GetLParam()) << ends;
    VDisplayDevice dev(*this);
        TabbedTextOut(dev, char_width, char_height * line++,
            strm.str(), strlen(strm.str()), 2, tabs, 0);
    strm.rdbuf()->freeze(0);
    return True;
}

class MessageApp : public VAppl
{
public:
        MessageApp(HINSTANCE inst, HINSTANCE prevInst,
                                LPSTR cmdLine, int cmdShow);
        MessageApp(void);
        void InitWindow(void);
};

MessageApp::MessageApp(HINSTANCE inst, HINSTANCE prevInst,
                                LPSTR cmdLine, int
cmdShow)
    : VAppl("MsgWind", inst, prevInst, cmdLine, cmdShow)
{
}
```

58 *Applications & events*

```
MessageApp::MessageApp(void)
{
}

void MessageApp::InitWindow(void)
{
        main_window = new MessageWindow();
}


int PASCAL WinMain(HINSTANCE hInstance, HINSTANCE hPrevInstance,
                                        LPSTR lpszCmdLine, int nCmdShow)
{
        MessageApp mainApp(hInstance,hPrevInstance,

                                                        lpszCmdLine
                                                        ,nCmdShow);

        return mainApp.Run();
}
```

The first key to responding to an event in a Vista program is to initialize its event dispatcher in the window object's InitActions member function:

Initializing the event dispatcher

```
void MessageWindow::InitActions(void)
{
    VFrame::InitActions();

    dispatcher.AddAction((VAction)&MessageWindow::MinMaxAction,
                    WM_GETMINMAXINFO);

    dispatcher.AddAction((VAction)&MessageWindow::MouseAction,
                    WM_LBUTTONDOWN);

    dispatcher.AddAction((VAction)&MessageWindow::MouseAction,
                    WM_LBUTTONUP);

    dispatcher.AddAction((VAction)&MessageWindow::MouseAction,
                    WM_MOUSEMOVE);

    dispatcher.AddAction((VAction)&MessageWindow::ClearAction,
                    WM_RBUTTONDOWN);
}
```

This function simply adds an entry to the dispatcher's event list for each message type the object wants to respond to. It passes the address of an action methods and a message identifier to the dispatcher's AddAction

MSGLIST: responding to events

member function. When the program receives a message directed to a window object, it converts the message into an event and passes it to the window's dispatcher. The dispatcher then determines which member function, if any, is interested in the event.

The first statement in the previous InitActions function calls the window object's superclass InitActions member function. All Vista window objects have some number of default actions; to "inherit" them, derived objects need to chain to the superclass method before adding their own actions. When developing your own objects, if you see that your window isn't acting as it should, make sure you chained to the object's superclass InitActions method.

Most action methods deal with a single type of event; however, that isn't always the case. For example, the MouseAction method is passed to the dispatcher for WM_LBUTTONDOWN, WM_LBUTTONUP, and WM_MOUSEMOVE events. Because the action taken for each is almost identical, a unique action method for each event type would be redundant. Vista allows an action method to handle any number of event types. An event also can be directed to any one of several action methods, depending on the content of the event. You'll see an example of this when I start working with child window controls in chapter 7.

Initializing the window

The CreateAction method handles initializing variables used by other action methods. It's called in response to a WM_CREATE event passed by Windows after the window is created:

```
Boolean MessageWindow::CreateAction(VEventRef event)
{
    TEXTMETRIC tm;
    VDisplayDevice dev(*this);
    GetTextMetrics(dev, &tm);
    char_width = tm.tmAveCharWidth;
    char_height = tm.tmHeight + tm.tmExternalLeading;
    VFrame::CreateAction(event);
    return True;
}
```

For the MessageWindow, the CreateAction method saves the dimensions (`char_width` and `char_height`) of the average character for the window's default font. These dimensions are used by other action methods to display text on the window.

Notice that the CreateAction method isn't passed to the dispatcher in InitActions because it's a default action method inherited from the VWindow class. Although you could add it to the dispatcher's list, doing so would be redundant. Because it's a virtual method, the dispatcher calls this method rather than the VWindow method. CreateAction does chain to the superclass method to allow it to implement the default behavior.

Like all other action methods, CreateAction returns a Boolean value that specifies whether or not it filtered the event. If it returns False, the event will be passed to the object's DefaultProc method. This method usually just passes the event on to the DefWindowProc API function that implements the standard behavior of all windows.

Painting the window

The PaintAction method, another default action inherited from the VWindow class, is called whenever contents of the window need to be displayed:

```
Boolean MessageWindow::PaintAction(VEventRef event)
{
    strstream strm;
    strm << "Event";
    strm << "\tX Pos ";
    strm << "\tY Pos " << ends;
    VPaintDevice dev(*this);
    TabbedTextOut(dev, char_width, char_height,
        strm.str(), strlen(strm.str()),
        2, tabs, 0);
    line = 3;
    dragging = False;
    strm.rdbuf()->freeze(0); // thaw the buffer
    UNREFERENCED_PARAMETER(event);
    return False;
}
```

Because most of the work in displaying message details is done by the MouseAction method, this routine just displays a header. However, it does demonstrate two important details.

First, it uses standard C++ stream output instead of the normal Windows wsprintf function. Although it probably would have been simpler to use wsprintf in this example, the stream objects offer a type-safe way to format data and are used throughout the book. This method uses a particularly useful feature of the strstream class: dynamic allocation. Rather than defining a buffer of some predetermined size, it allows the strstream object to allocate memory as it needs it when elements are inserted into the stream.

Second, the header string is displayed using the TabbedTextOut API function, which is used to display tabular data. The window displays its data in three columns—the x coordinates for the first and second tab stops are set whenever the window is resized in the SizeAction method:

```
Boolean MessageWindow::SizeAction(VEventRef event)
{
    VFrame::SizeAction(event);
    tabs[0] = width / 2;
    tabs[1] = tabs[0] + (tabs[0]/2);
    return True;
}
```

Using this method gives you a clean display with consistent spacing between columns. However, it does introduce a problem. If the user resizes the window so that tab stops collide with text already displayed, the display isn't so clean. To get around this problem, the object restricts the minimize size of the window:

```
Boolean MessageWindow::MinMaxAction(VEventRef event)
{
    MINMAXINFO FAR *minMax =
                (MINMAXINFO FAR *) event.GetLParam();
    minMax->ptMinTrackSize.x = 50 * char_width;
    minMax->ptMinTrackSize.y = 6 * char_height;
    return False;
}
```

The WM_GETMINMAXINFO event that triggers this method is delivered after the window has been created and initially displayed, but before the WM_SIZE message. It is meant for situations like this: limiting the minimum or maximum size of a window because of limitations in the algorithms used to display data in a window.

Responding to mouse events

The last methods that play a visible role in your program respond to mouse events. ClearAction erases the message list from the window when the user clicks the right mouse button:

```
Boolean MessageWindow::ClearAction(VEventRef event)
{
    Invalidate();
    UNREFERENCED_PARAMETER(event);
    return True;
}
```

The Invalidate member function, provided by the VWindow class, erases a window and readies it for more output.

MouseAction displays details about events received when the user clicks, drags, and releases the left mouse button:

```
Boolean MessageWindow::MouseAction(VEventRef event)
{
    ostrstream strm;

    switch(event.GetId())
    {
        case WM_LBUTTONDOWN:
            strm << "WM_LBUTTONDOWN";
            SetCapture(*this);
            dragging = True;
            break;
        case WM_LBUTTONUP:
            strm << "WM_LBUTTONUP";
```

Applications & events

```
            ReleaseCapture();
            dragging = False;
            break;
        case WM_MOUSEMOVE:
            if (!dragging)
                return False;
            strm << "WM_MOUSEMOVE";
            break;
        default:
            break;
    }
    strm << "\t" << LOWORD(event.GetLParam());
    strm << "\t" << HIWORD(event.GetLParam()) << ends;
    VDisplayDevice dev(*this);
    TabbedTextOut(dev, char_width,
                  char_height * line++,
                  strm.str(), strlen(strm.str()),
                  2, tabs, 0);
    strm.rdbuf()->freeze(0);
    return True;
}
```

Like PaintAction, MouseAction uses standard C++ stream objects to create the strings it displays. It also uses the TabbedTextOut API function to display data in columns.

MouseAction displays only WM_MOUSEMOVE events it receives while the left mouse button is down. It sets the dragging flag to True when it receives a

Event	X Pos	Y Pos
WM_LBUTTONDOWN	24	43
WM_MOUSEMOVE	30	45
WM_LBUTTONUP	30	45
WM_LBUTTONDOWN	293	197
WM_MOUSEMOVE	287	197
WM_MOUSEMOVE	267	181
WM_MOUSEMOVE	243	173
WM_MOUSEMOVE	227	165
WM_MOUSEMOVE	226	157
WM_LBUTTONUP	226	157

4-4
Output from the MsgWind example program.

WM_LBUTTONDOWN event and resets it back to False when it receives a WM_LBUTTONUP event.

The function also uses the SetCapture and ReleaseCapture to maintain consistency of the dragging flag. If the object didn't capture the mouse, it wouldn't receive a WM_LBUTTONUP event if the cursor is outside the window's client area. Then, whenever the mouse is moved over the client area of the window (even if the mouse button is up), the MouseAction function would display the event details because the dragging flag still would be set to True. Figure 4-4 shows output from the MsgWind example program.

What's next In this chapter, I looked at Vista's application class VAppl and the event class VEvent. I examined the use of initialization files in Windows programs as an integral part of an application object. I also discussed event processing and saw examples of using events in the MSGLIST sample program. In the next chapter, I'll look at the VWindow class, and start building some more useful sample programs.

5 Vista window objects

In chapter 4, I looked at the application and event classes and showed how they drove an application. While both classes serve vital roles in a Vista application, they only support other objects in the program. They need something to act on: instances of the VWindow class and its descendants. In this chapter, I'll take a closer look at the Vista window objects highlighted in FIG. 5-1.

When you look at a Windows program, virtually everything you see on the screen is displayed within a window. Application windows, dialog boxes, icons, and controls are all based on a single object: the window. Vista mimics the Windows object model within its own class hierarchy.

The VWindow class forms the root of the window class hierarchy. It implements much of the behavior necessary for C^{++} objects to exist in the Windows environment. Before I build any applications using the VWindow class, let's look at one of the most important responsibilities of the VWindow class: reacting to events.

The heart of a window's behavior is in its window procedure. The window procedure is responsible for reacting to the multitude of messages it can receive. In a C program, a window procedure normally consists of a huge

VWindow: the base window class

The window procedure

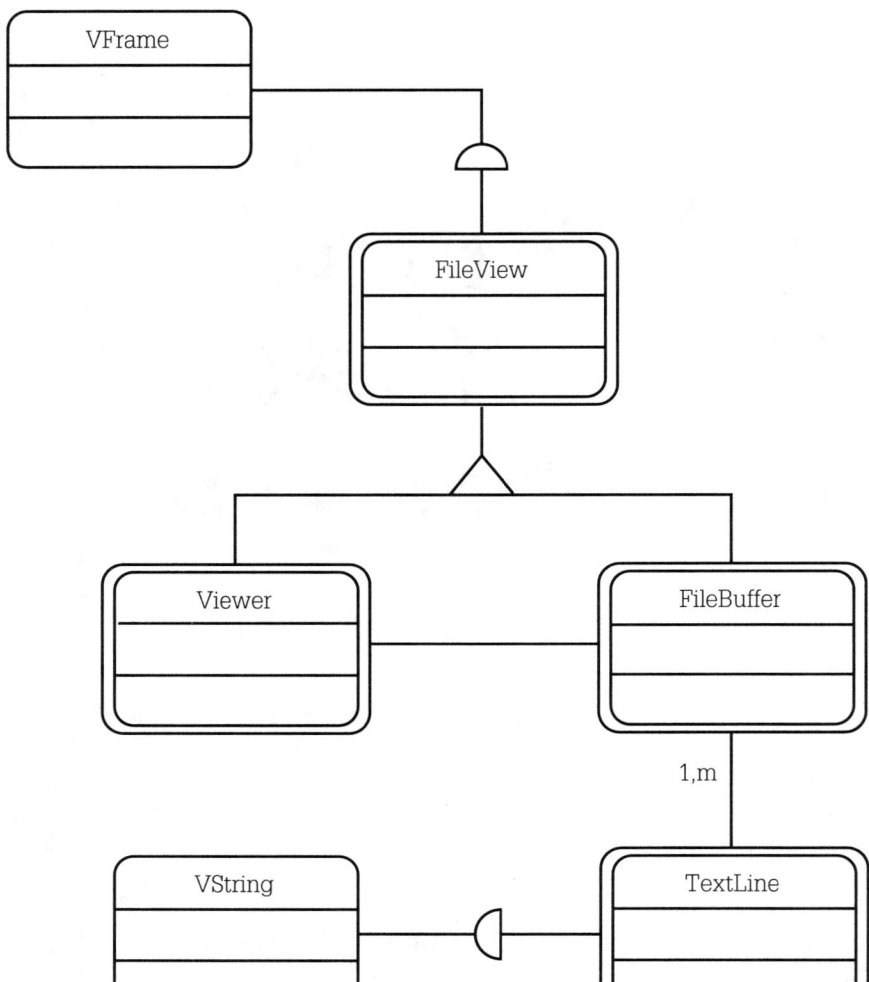

5-1
Design of the FileView program using object-oriented diagramming.

switch statement, with branches handling all the messages the window is interested in. Each window in a program normally uses its own window procedure, often duplicating code to handle common events in each window procedure.

Vista takes a different approach to communicating with Windows. It employs a single window procedure for all of its windows:

```
class VWindow
    {
    ...
    static LRESULT CALLBACK _export
```

```
     VWindow::VWindowProc(...);
       ...
     }
LRESULT CALLBACK _export VWindow::WindowProc(HWND hWnd,
                                  UINT id,
                                  WPARAM wParam,
                                  LPARAM lParam)
{
  VWindowPtr window = GetWinPointer(hWnd);
  if (!window)
  {
       window = _VCreateWindow;
       window->handle = hWnd;
       window->SetWinPointer();
  }

  VEvent event(*window, id, wParam, lParam);
  Boolean filtered = (*window)(event);
  if (!filtered)
       return window->DefaultProc(event);
  else
       return event.GetResponse();
}
```

The procedure itself isn't very interesting—it only deals with extracting an object pointer from the window and routing events to their correct action method. However, it does illustrate another C++ feature: static member functions.

Normal class member functions receive a hidden parameter, the `this` pointer, which points to the object the function is to operate on. For example:

```
class X
{
 int member_var;
 void func() { member_var = 1; } //this->member_var = 1
};
```

Because `func` receives the hidden `this` pointer, it can directly access an object's member variables. Static member functions, on the other hand, don't receive the hidden this pointer:

```
class X
{
    int member_var;
    static void func() { member_var = 1; } //error-no this
pointer
};
```

The static function belongs to the class and actually has access to its member data, but it isn't invoked on a specific instance of the class.

VWindow: the base window class

Therefore, it can't access member data in the same way a nonstatic member function can.

So, what's the purpose of static functions? First, they can be useful when you need to build (or find) an object when one isn't available. This is the purpose of the GetWinPointer function, also a static member function of the VWindow class. It retrieves the this pointer from the window's property list (SetWinPointer, another static member function, stores it there).

They also can act as a sort of intermediary between a C^{++} program and its underlying system. This is the role that VWindow's window procedure plays. Recall from chapter 4 that the window procedure isn't directly invoked by the program; Windows calls it. The system has no knowledge of classes and instances, but it does know about window handles. Action methods know about VWindow objects, but they can't translate an HWND directly into a VWindow object.

This is where VWindow's window procedure steps in. First, it uses GetWinPointer and SetWinPointer to manage the mapping between handles and VWindow objects. Then, it creates a VEvent object from the message it receives. Finally, it uses the VWindow object's controller to dispatch the event to the correct member function.

Dispatching messages

In chapter 4, you got a glimpse of how Vista programs respond to events received from Windows. The VWindow class's window procedure provides the first part of the interface between a Vista program and Windows: it maps windows into objects and translates messages into events. It delegates the second half of that interface, routing messages to the correct action method, to the VDispatcher class.

The VDispatcher object contains a list of structures that maps events to member functions (action methods) of the VWindow class and its descendants. When the window procedure receives a message, it translates it into an event and passes the event to the dispatcher.

The dispatcher uses the event as an index into its list to find the action routine that will handle the event. No, that isn't a misprint. It uses the entire event object, not just the event's ID, as an index into its list. Recall the discussion of operator overloading in chapter 4. With C^{++}, you can overload any operator provided by the language, including the function call () and subscript [] operators. For example:

```
VAction VDispatcher::operator [](const VEventRef event)
const
{

    VActionItemPtr item;
    if (event.GetId() == WM_COMMAND)
```

```
        item = Find(event.GetId(), event.GetWParam(),
            HIWORD(event.GetLParam()));
    else
        item = Find(event.GetId());
    if (item == 0)
        return 0;
    return item->action;
}
```

For most events, using only the message identifier as an index into the list is sufficient. Window objects use a single member function to handle one or more event types, and the mapping between events and action methods is one-to-one.

However, WM_COMMAND events require further examination. Windows uses the WM_COMMAND message to pass information between menus and child window controls and their parent windows. For example, when the user clicks a pushbutton control, the control sends a WM_COMMAND message to its parent to notify it of the user's action. The parent examines the parameters of the message to determine which control sent the message.

In a C program, the window program normally uses a second switch statement to deal with WM_COMMAND messages. For Vista window objects, it is the responsibility of the dispatcher's index operator. When acting on a WM_COMMAND event, the function uses the event's parameters as well as its message identifier to map the event to an action method. It implements a one-to-many mapping between WM_COMMAND events and action methods. You can define a WM_COMMAND action method to handle all WM_COMMAND events, or you can use many WM_COMMAND action methods, each reacting to an event from one or more controls or menu items.

Each window object has its own dispatcher, which usually is initialized by the InitActions member function:

```
void MyWindow::InitActions(void)
{
    VFrame::InitActions();
    dispatcher.AddAction(&MyWindow::ExitCommand, WM_COMMAND,
                            IDM_EXIT);
    dispatcher.AddAction(&MyWindow::ClickedCommand, WM_COMMAND,
                            DEFAULT_CTLID, BN_CLICKED);
}
```

The previous function first calls VFrame's InitActions method to inherit the default behavior of a VFrame object. Then, it adds an action to handle WM_COMMAND events received from a menu item with an identifier of

IDM_EXIT. The last statement adds an action to handle BN_CLICKED notification messages from all child window controls.

Two-step initialization

Like the VAppl class, the VWindow object uses a two-step initialization scheme. First, attributes for the window are stored in its constructor. Then, a window is associated with the object in its Create method. This scheme allows you to create window objects at the start of the program and display them only when necessary.

The VWindow class hierarchy

All Vista window objects descend from the VWindow class. However, it provides only the basic data and operations common to all windows. Two important subclasses are the VComposite and VFrame classes.

The VComposite class provides operations that allow a window object to act as a container for other windows. It manages the dynamic hierarchy of windows that you can find in any Windows program. Its subclasses include the VFrame and VDialog classes, which both manage child windows differently.

A VFrame window is a special type of VComposite window. In addition to supporting multiple child windows, a VFrame window manages optional horizontal and vertical scrollbars and a menu. It normally is used as an independent window in an application, either as the program's top-level window or as an MDI child window.

Now, that I've examined the most important operations provided by the VWindow class, let's build a useful example.

FileView: a file viewer

To get a better understanding of the events and their relationship to a window, I'll build the first version of a substantial application: FileView, a Windows file viewer. However, before I look into the code for the program, let's step back and discuss the design first.

Designing FileView

An important step in any development project, the design stage takes on even more significance with object-oriented software. Mistakes in the design of an object that are caught late in the implementation phase can be very costly. Taking a little time up front to predict the potential usage of an object can mean the difference between success and failure of a project.

One of the aims of an object-oriented language like C^{++} is to maximize the reuse of software components. Reuse probably is the most substantial benefit of object-oriented programming: you don't have to redesign a wheel every time you need to use one. So, with reuse in mind, let's look at how you'll implement the FileView program.

The first step in designing an object-oriented program is to find the objects the program will use. Although this can be a very difficult task sometimes, in this case it's simple: you need an object that displays the content of a file. You know what your object is going to be, but you obviously haven't analyzed the problem enough to begin implementing the file viewer object yet.

The next step is to determine what operations the object will provide. The file viewer object needs to perform several operations. First, it needs to be able to open, read, and close a file. Second, it must display the content of the file. Third, it should retain the content of the file so that it doesn't have to open and read the file every time the window is resized or restored from an icon. Finally, because the file might contain more lines than the object can display at one time, it needs to maintain some notion of a current position in the file.

Now that you know what operations it needs to perform, you can move to the final step: determining the information needed to provide those operations. For the file viewer, you'll need to keep track of the window, the file itself, the text contained in the file, and the current position viewed in the file.

Now that you've found your object, specified its operations, and determined its data requirements, you can begin its implementation. Instead of attempting to implement all the operations of the file viewer object in a single class, you can split it into several objects, each taking on its own responsibilities. Figure 5-1 contains a simple model of the file viewer object. It uses the simple notation introduced in two books by Peter Coad and Edward Yourdon: *Object-Oriented Analysis* and *Object-Oriented Design*.

The FileView object is a type of VFrame object; the subtype relationship is expressed with a semi-circle on the line connecting the two classes. It contains two objects: a Viewer and a FileBuffer. This relationship is denoted by a triangle on the connector between the classes. The FileBuffer is a container for any number of TextLine objects, which are derived from the VString class. Let's look at each new class in detail.

The FileView class (LISTING 5-1) manages the display of a file. Its main responsibility is to react to events it receives from Windows.

The FileView class

Listing 5-1
FILEVIEW.CPP: Source code for the FileView object.

```cpp
/* --------------------------------------------------------------
   fileview.cpp

       Implementation of the FileView class.

   Copyright (C) 1992, by Jeff Mackay - TAB Books

   -------------------------------------------------------- */
#include <dir.h>
#include <fstream.h>
#include <vappl.h>
#include "fileview.h"

FileView::FileView(VFramePtr par, charPtr title)
  : VFrame(par, title), viewer(*this)
{
    buffer = 0;
}

FileView::FileView(void)
{
    delete buffer;
}


Boolean FileView::PaintAction(VEventRef event)
{
    if (buffer == 0)
        return False;

    VPaintDevice dev(*this);
    RECT exposeRect = dev.GetExposeRect();
    viewer.DrawOn(dev, exposeRect);
    UNREFERENCED_PARAMETER(event);
    return False;
}

Boolean FileView::CreateAction(VEventRef event)
{
    VFrame::CreateAction(event);
    VDisplayDevice dev(*this);
    viewer.Init(dev);
    return True;
}

Boolean FileView::SizeAction(VEventRef event)
{
    VFrame::SizeAction(event);
    if (buffer == 0)
        return False;
    RECT rect;
```

```
    GetDimensions(rect);
    viewer.Resize(rect);
    return True;
}


void FileView::SetBuffer(const charPtr name)
{
    TCHAR fileName[MAXPATH+1];
    wsprintf(fileName, "%s", name);
    ifstream strm(fileName);

    delete buffer;
    buffer = new FileBuffer(strm);
    buffer->SetFileName(name);

    RECT rect;
    GetDimensions(rect);
    viewer.Resize(rect);
    SetCaption(fileName);
}

void FileView::SetCaption(const charPtr string)
{
    VString newCaption;
    if (string && lstrlen(string) > 0)
    {
        newCaption = appl.GetAppName();
        newCaption += " - [";
        newCaption += string;
        newCaption += "]";
        VFrame::SetCaption(newCaption);
    }
}

const FileBufferPtr FileView::GetBuffer(void) const
{
    return buffer;
}
```

The CreateAction function is called in response to a WM_CREATE event:

```
Boolean FileView::CreateAction(VEventRef event)
{
    VFrame::CreateAction(event);
    VDisplayDevice dev(*this);
    viewer.Init(dev);
    return True;
}
```

It chains back to the VFrame's CreateAction method, then creates a device and passes it to the viewer so that it can initialize itself with information it will use to display text.

The PaintAction function is called in response to a WM_PAINT event. It calls on the viewer to display the content of the file on the device associated with the window:

```
Boolean FileView::PaintAction(VEventRef event)
{
    if (buffer == 0)
        return False;

    VPaintDevice dev(*this);
    RECT exposeRect = dev.GetExposeRect();
    viewer.DrawOn(dev, exposeRect);
    UNREFERENCED_PARAMETER(event);
    return True;
}
```

It first checks to make sure it has a buffer associated with it. If not, there is no reason to proceed and it returns False. Then, it creates a device object and retrieves a rectangle that contains the expose region.

A window can be partially obscured by another window, like a dialog box or a smaller application. When the obscuring window is hidden, Windows sends a WM_PAINT event to the obscured window so that it can reconstruct and display its contents. The expose region points to the portion of the window that needs to be refreshed. PaintAction passes the expose rectangle to the viewer so that it can determine what text to display.

The SizeAction method, called in response to a WM_SIZE event, tells the viewer to resize itself:

```
Boolean FileView::SizeAction(VEventRef event)
{
    VFrame::SizeAction(event);
    if (buffer == 0)
        return False;
    RECT rect;
    GetDimensions(rect);
    viewer.Resize(rect);
    return True;
}
```

SizeAction first calls its superclass's method so that it can keep track of the window's size. Then, like the PaintAction method, it checks to see if a buffer is associated with this object. If not, it doesn't need to do anything and returns False. Otherwise, it passes the dimensions of the window to the viewer and lets it determine where to display lines of text.

The FileView class uses the SetBuffer function to initialize its buffer from the name of a file:

```
void FileView::SetBuffer(const charPtr name)
{
    TCHAR fileName[MAXPATH+1];
    wsprintf(fileName, "%s", name);
    ifstream strm(fileName);

    delete buffer;
    buffer = new FileBuffer(strm, name);

    RECT rect;
    GetDimensions(rect);
    viewer.Resize(rect);
    SetCaption(fileName);
}
```

It first creates a standard C++ input file stream using the file name parameter. Then, it passes that stream, along with the file name, to a new FileBuffer object. After it creates the file buffer, it passes the FileView window's dimensions to the viewer so that it can resize and associate itself with the new buffer. Finally, it sets the window's title bar to reflect the name of the file being displayed.

The Viewer class

The Viewer object (LISTING 5-2) takes care of displaying a portion of the file being viewed. You can think of it as a "window" into the file that can move up or down to display pieces of a file that is too large to display in a window at one time.

Listing 5-2
VIEWER.CPP: Source code for the Viewer object.

```
/* ----------------------------------------------------------
   Viewer.cpp

      Implementation of the Viewer class.

   Copyright (C) 1992, by Jeff Mackay - TAB Books

---------------------------------------------------------- */
#include <dir.h>
#include <fstream.h>
#include <vappl.h>
#include "fileview.h"

/* ----------------------------------------------------------
constructor:

initializes instance variables
---------------------------------------------------------- */
Viewer::Viewer(class FileView _FAR &par)
    : VDynArray<ViewerLine>(), parent(par)
```

Listing 5-2
Continued.

```
    {
        char_width = 0;
        char_height = 0;
        x_offset = 0;
        last_line = 0;
    }

/* ------------------------------------------------------------------
Init:

Calculates the character height and width
------------------------------------------------------------------ */
void Viewer::Init(VDeviceRef dev)
{
    TEXTMETRIC tm;
    GetTextMetrics(dev, &tm);
    char_width = tm.tmAveCharWidth;
    char_height = tm.tmHeight + tm.tmExternalLeading;
}


/* ------------------------------------------------------------------
DrawOn:

Draws each line it the viewer array.
------------------------------------------------------------------*/
void Viewer::DrawOn(VDeviceRef dev, RECT _FAR &exposeRect)
{
    int top = exposeRect.top;
    int bottom = exposeRect.bottom;
    for(int i=0; data[i].line != 0 && data[i].coord  < top; i++)
        ;

    for(; data[i].line != 0 && data[i].coord <= bottom; i++)
    {
        data[i].line->DrawOn(dev, x_offset,
                          data[i].coord);
    }
}

/* ------------------------------------------------------------------
Resize:

Draws each line it the viewer array.
------------------------------------------------------------------ */
void Viewer::Resize(RECT _FAR &windowSize)
{
    if (char_height == 0)    // don't allow divide-by-zero errors
        return;

    last_line = (windowSize.bottom - windowSize.top) / char_height;
```

```
        FileBufferIter iter(*parent.GetBuffer());

    // reset the viewer array
    for (int i=0; i<last_line; i++)
    {
        data[i].coord = (i*char_height) + char_height;
        TextLinePtr _FAR *x = iter();
        if (x != 0)
            data[i].line = *x;
        else
            data[i].line = 0;
    }
}
```

It maintains an array of structures that track the vertical position of each line being displayed. The Viewer is derived from one of the Vista library's template container classes, the VDynArray. The VDynArray template class implements a dynamic array of any data type that can resize itself as necessary. The data type of the objects in the array is passed as a parameter at runtime:

```
class Viewer : public VDynArray<ViewerLine>
{
// ...
};
```

This declaration makes the Viewer class a dynamic array of ViewerLine structures. Because it is a descendant of the VDynArray class, the Viewer class doesn't need to implement the operations to manage the array. It adds only the operations necessary to implement its unique behavior.

The first of those methods is its initialization function, Init, which is in response to the parent window's WM_CREATE event. It retrieves the size of characters in font for the window:

```
void Viewer::Init(VDeviceRef dev)
{
    TEXTMETRIC tm;
    GetTextMetrics(dev, &tm);
    char_width = tm.tmAveCharWidth;
    char_height = tm.tmHeight + tm.tmExternalLeading;
}
```

Another important method is the Resize function. It performs several operations all at once:

```
void Viewer::Resize(RECT _FAR &winSize)
{
    if (char_height == 0)
        return;
    last_line = (winSize.bottom - winSize.top) /
                char_height;
```

```
            FileBufferIter iter(*parent.GetBuffer());

        // reset the viewer array
        for (int i=0; i<last_line; i++)
        {
            data[i].coord = (i*char_height) + char_height;
            TextLinePtr _FAR *x = iter();
            if (x != 0)
                data[i].line = *x;
            else
                data[i].line = 0;
        }
```

First, it checks the average character size for the window's font. If it is zero, this function is being called before the window is created, so there isn't any reason to continue. Otherwise, it calculates the number of lines that can be displayed in the window and sets each entry in its array. If you want some experience in debugging a Vista program, comment the first two lines in the function and run the program in the debugger. See if you can catch it before it crashes.

The last method I'll cover here is the DrawOn function. It loops through the array and tells each TextLine object to draw itself:

```
void Viewer::DrawOn(VDeviceRef dev,
                    RECTRef exposeRect)
{
    int top = exposeRect.top;
    int bottom = exposeRect.bottom;
    for(int i=0;
            data[i].line != 0 && data[i].coord <= top;
            i++)
        ;

    for(; data[i].line != 0 && data[i].coord <= bottom;
            i++)
    {
        data[i].line->DrawOn(dev, x_offset,
                                  data[i].coord);
    }
}
```

First, it finds the first line that lies within the expose rectangle I discussed in the last section. Then, it passes the proper y coordinate to the TextLine that will be displayed on each line. Instead of specifically drawing each object, it allows the objects to draw themselves.

The last two classes I'll discuss here are the FileBuffer (LISTING 5-3) and TextLine (LISTING 5-4) classes. The FileBuffer is an array of TextLines that together hold the content of the file to be displayed. They are closely related, because the FileBuffer is composed of multiple TextLine objects. The best example of their cooperation is in their overloaded "put to" operators:

The FileBuffer and TextLine classes

```
istream _FAR &operator >>(istream &s,
                          FileBufferRef buffer)
{
    TextLinePtr line;

    int i = 0;
    for (i=0; s.good(); i++)
    {
        line = &buffer[i];
        s >> (*line);
        if (s.good())
        {
            buffer.max_line_len = max(buffer.max_line_len,
                                      line->Length());
        }
    }
    return s;
}

istream _FAR &operator >>(istream &s,
                          TextLineRef line)
{
    ostrstream input;
    TCHAR fchar;
    while(s.get(fchar) && fchar != TEXT('\n'))
    {
        input.put(fchar);
    }
    fchar = TEXT('\0');
    input.put(fchar);
    line.ptr = input.str();
    line.len = input.pcount()-sizeof(TCHAR);
    return s;
}

/* ----------------------------------------------
   filebuf.cpp

   Implementation of the FileBuffer class.

   Copyright (C) 1992, by Jeff Mackay - TAB Books
-------------------------------------------------*/
#include "fileview.h"
```

Listing 5-3
FILEBUF.CPP

Listing 5-3
Continued.

```
FileBuffer::FileBuffer(void)
    : VDblList<TextLinePtr>()
{
}


FileBuffer::FileBuffer(istream _FAR &strm, charPtr name)
    : VDblList<TextLinePtr>(), file_name(name)
{
    strm >> (*this);
}


FileBuffer::FileBuffer(void)
{
}


void FileBuffer::SetFileName(const charPtr name)
{
    file_name = name;
}


const charPtr FileBuffer::GetFileName(void) const
{
    return file_name;
}


istream _FAR &operator >>(istream _FAR &s, FileBufferRef buffer)
{
    TextLine *line;

    line = new TextLine;
    while (s.good() && line)
    {
        s >> (*line);
        if (s.good())
            buffer.Append(line);
        line = new TextLine;
    }
    delete line;   // last line isn't used
    return s;
}


/* -----------------------------------------------------------------
   textline.cpp
```

```
    Implementation of the TextLine class.

    Copyright (C) 1992, by Jeff Mackay - TAB Books
-------------------------------------------------------- */
#include "fileview.h"


istream _FAR &operator >>(istream _FAR &s, TextLineRef line)
{
    ostrstream input;
    TCHAR fchar;

    while(s.get(fchar) && fchar != TEXT('\n'))
    {
        input.put(fchar);
    }
    fchar = TEXT('\0');
    input.put(fchar);
    line.ptr    = input.str();
    line.len    = input.pcount()-sizeof(TCHAR); // skip
newline
    return s;
}


void TextLine::DrawOn(VDeviceRef dev, int char_offset, int
        y_coord, int margin)
{
    if (len > 0)
    {
        TabbedTextOut(dev, margin, y_coord, ptr+char_offset,
                    len, 0, 0, 0);
    }
}

TextLine::TextLine(void)
{
    delete ptr;
    ptr = 0;
}
```

Listing 5-4
TEXTLINE.CPP

The >> operator is a standard overloaded stream "put-to" operator. It loads some part of a stream (C++'s term for a file or other sequence of bytes) into an object. The FileBuffer's operator continuously loops through the stream, passing each line to a newly created TextLine object.

The TextLine's >> operator is more interesting. It creates a dynamic output stream and reads each character in the input stream into it. When it encounters a newline character, it terminates the output stream with a null character and saves the output streams buffer as its own. Because the output stream and its buffer are dynamic, lines in the file can be any length.

Scrolling the window

If you were to build the program now, it would be able to display the first page of a file, but nothing else. To allow you to page through the file, you need to add scrolling operations. The VFrame class provides support for scrolling the contents of its window, with the cooperation of the VScroll class. Together they allow the reader access to objects too large to display in their entirety.

Because I split the responsibilities for displaying and managing text between multiple objects, you need to make only a few changes to implement scrolling. First, you need to respond to scrollbar events in the FileView object with two action methods. Second, you need to implement the scrolling behavior in the Viewer.

The first step is fairly simple. The VFrame class already defines two scroll methods—HScrollAction and VScrollAction—that deal with the window's horizontal and vertical scrollbar. All the default methods do is pass the events on to a VScroll object, which associates the scroll bar on screen with a current position.

So, all you have to do to capture scroll events is override the VFrame's methods:

```
Boolean FileView::HScrollAction(VEventRef event)
{
    int pos = horiz_scroll->GetPos();
    VFrame::HScrollAction(event);
    int diff = pos - horiz_scroll->GetPos();
    if (pos)
        viewer.ShiftHorizontal(diff);
    return True;
}

Boolean FileView::VScrollAction(VEventRef event)
{
    int pos = vert_scroll->GetPos();
    VFrame::VScrollAction(event);
    int diff = vert_scroll->GetPos() - pos;
    if (diff)
        viewer.ShiftVertical(diff);
    return True;
}
```

The two functions are almost identical. They first save the current position of the scroll bar, call the VFrame method to set the position of the scroll bar, and calculate the difference between the two positions. If the position changed, they defer to the Viewer so that it actually can scroll the data on the screen.

Implementing scrolling in the Viewer is more difficult. Although Windows provides a simple function to scroll a window:

```
void ScrollWindow(HWND hwnd,
                  int dx,
                  int dy,
                  const RECT FAR *lprcScroll,
                  const RECT FAR *lprcClip)
```

It scrolls only the visible portion of the window. The hard part is figuring out what text to scroll into the window. This work is handled by a new methods in the Viewer:

```
void Viewer::ShiftVertical(int amount)
{
    FileBufferPtr buffer = parent.GetBuffer();
    if (!buffer)
       return;

    int newTop = min(buffer->Size(),
                     max(top_line + amount, 0));
    amount = newTop - top_line;
    int start = top_line = newTop;

    for(int i = 0; i < last_line; i++)
    {
            data[i].line = &(*buffer)[start++];
    }
    int increment = -(amount * char_height);
    ScrollWindow(parent, 0, increment, 0, 0);
}
```

The ShiftVertical method does some sanity checking to make sure you don't try to scroll above the first line or below the last line of the document. Then, it calculates which line needs to be displayed in the window and resets the line pointers in its array. Finally, it calls the Windows ScrollWindow function.

The ScrollWindow function takes care of most of the details of smooth scrolling. Rather than redisplay each line in the window every time the user hits the scroll bar, ScrollWindow allows you to draw only new lines. It shifts the portion of the window that will remain visible, invalidates the other portion, and sends a WM_PAINT message to the window.

I have to admit that scrolling was more difficult than I anticipated. The initial version of the TextBuffer was derived from the VDblList class. However, keeping the current position in the list synchronized with the Viewer caused some problems, so I decided to base the FileBuffer on the VDynArray class, which solved all the problems.

The good news is that the change took only about half an hour to make—with most modifications made to the FileBuffer and minor changes to the

Viewer class. Another benefit of object-oriented techniques: encapsulation. Because representation of the FileBuffer was hidden by public operations that acted on the content of the buffer, changes didn't have big effects elsewhere.

Now that I've examined the most important classes in the FileView program, you're ready to build it. FILEVIEW.H (LISTING 5-5) contains the interface for each of the classes. The application class and WinMain function in VIEWAPP.CPP are displayed in LISTING 5-6.

Listing 5-5
FILEVIEW.H

```
/* -------------------------------------------------------
   fileview.h

        Interface for the FileView class

   Copyright (C) 1992, by Jeff Mackay

   ------------------------------------------------------- */

#ifndef _FILEVIEW_H
#define _FILEVIEW_H

#include <vista.h>
#include <vwindow.h>
#include <vstring.h>
#include <vdynarr.h>
#include <vgrdev.h>


STDCLASS(FileView);
STDCLASS(ViewArray);
STDCLASS(FileBuffer);
STDCLASS(TextLine);


class TextLine : public VString
{

public:
    TextLine(void) : VString() {}
    TextLine(void);
    void DrawOn(VDeviceRef dev, int x_offset, int y_coord, int
                    margin);
    friend istream _FAR &operator >>(istream _FAR &,
                                               TextLineRef);
};

class FileBuffer : public VDblList<TextLinePtr>
{
    public:
```

```cpp
        FileBuffer(void);
        FileBuffer(istream _FAR &strm, charPtr name);
        FileBuffer(void);

        const charPtr GetFileName(void) const;
        void SetFileName(const charPtr name);
        friend istream _FAR &operator >>(istream _FAR &, FileBufferRef);

    private:
        VString file_name;
};


class FileBufferIter : public VDblListIter<TextLinePtr>
{
    public:
        FileBufferIter(FileBuffer _FAR &list)
            : VDblListIter<TextLinePtr>(list) {}
};


struct ViewerLine
{
    TextLinePtr line;
    int         coord;
    ViewerLine(void) : line(0), coord(0) {}
    int operator ==(const ViewerLine _FAR &copy)
        { return copy.line == line; }
};

class Viewer : public VDynArray<ViewerLine>
{
    public:
        Viewer(class FileView _FAR &par);
        void Init(VDeviceRef dev);
        void DrawOn(VDeviceRef dev, RECT _FAR &exposeRect);
        void Resize(RECT _FAR &windowSize);

    private:
        class FileView _FAR &parent;
        int char_width;
        int char_height;
        int x_offset;                   // in characters
        int last_line;
};



class FileView : public VFrame
{
    public:
```

Listing 5-5
Continued.

```
        FileView(VFramePtr par, charPtr title);
        FileView();

        virtual Boolean PaintAction(VEventRef event);
        virtual Boolean CreateAction(VEventRef event);
        virtual Boolean SizeAction(VEventRef event);

        void SetCaption(const charPtr string);
        void SetBuffer(const charPtr name);
        const FileBufferPtr GetBuffer(void) const;

    private:
        FileBufferPtr buffer;
        Viewer        viewer;
};

#endif
```

Listing 5-6
VIEWAPP.CPP

```
/* -------------------------------------------------------------
   viewapp.cpp

   A class to demonstrate the capabilities of the FileView
   object.

   Copyright (C) 1992, by Jeff Mackay
   ----------------------------------------------------------- */
#include <vista.h>
#include <vappl.h>
#include "fileview.h"



class FileViewApp : public VAppl
{
    public:
        FileViewApp(HINSTANCE inst, HINSTANCE prev,
                LPSTR cmdLine, int cmdShow)
          : VAppl("FileView", inst, prev, cmdLine, cmdShow)
        {
        }

        virtual void InitWindow(void)
        {
            main_window = new FileView(NULL, "FileView");
            if (cmd_line.Length() > 0)
```

```
                  ((FileViewPtr) main_window)->SetBuffer(cmd_line);
          }
};

int PASCAL WinMain(HINSTANCE inst, HINSTANCE prev, LPSTR cmdLine, int cmdShow)
{
    FileViewApp app(inst, prev, cmdLine, cmdShow);

    app.Run();
    return app.GetStatus();
}
```

The end result is shown in FIG. 5-2. To run it from Turbo C++, first enter a file name as an argument. Because the program takes a filename on its command line, you also can start it from the File Manager by associating a file extension with it and double-clicking on a file with that extension.

Moving C programs to Vista

Now, I'll give you some hints on moving your C programs to Vista. In chapter 2, I discussed a general strategy for performing the conversion. Here, I'll look at things a little closer.

The majority of operations in most C Windows programs are performed in the program's window procedures. Converting that window procedure into a subclass of VWindow or VFrame is the first step. Many of the case branches in a window procedure will translate almost directly into action methods with a little preparation.

First, examine all of the global variables used in the program with the goal of eliminating them or at least making them members of your application or main window class. Make the functions that manipulate those variables member functions of the object you assign them to.

Next, look at the static and local variables in the window procedure, again with the goal of either eliminating them or making them private or protected members of a window object. By partitioning variables in this way, you'll find that the code becomes easier to understand. Making variables members of a class helps make code more readable, because, to access them outside the class, you have to specifically identify the object they belong to. This makes it much simpler to track down bugs where someone is stomping on variables that they shouldn't be.

After you have rearranged your data, you are ready to translate your case branches into action methods. As you do so, try to eliminate any unnecessary type casting. Earlier Windows programs used type casting extensively to force the compiler to pass the correct type to Windows functions that didn't have prototypes. Because those functions now have prototypes, casting isn't necessary. Either the compiler will convert arguments automatically (if possible) or it will warn you about incompatible data types. The goal is to let the compiler do as much work as possible, instead of trying to fool it into doing something that might not be correct in the first place.

If your windows have menus, you should derive your window class from VFrame, because it provides support for routing WM_COMMAND messages to action methods. If you wish, you can override the CommandAction method and just insert your WM_COMMAND branch into the method. In the next chapter, I'll look at using menus with Vista programs.

While taking this approach might seem like a rather involved process, it definitely is worth the effort. Converting the program will almost definitely make it easier to maintain. The stricter type checking available with the STRICT option in Windows 3.1, and the removal of type casting might even help you find some of those bugs you've written off as unsolvable.

What's next In this chapter, I looked at Vista window objects. I examined the relationship between a Vista window object, its window procedure, events, and action methods. Then, I built FileView to serve as an example of a full-featured window object. In the next chapter, I'll move on to create a program that is more responsive to user commands—and add some interaction with FileView.

6 Getting input with menus & accelerators

The most common form of user input in a Windows program originates from a menu. Menus offer a simple way to provide a hierarchical command interface, without forcing the user to remember a new vocabulary. They are the cornerstone of the consistent interface provided by Windows applications.

This chapter focuses on the use of menus and accelerators to provide a consistent interface in a Vista program. First, I'll examine the Windows menu system and discuss how your program can use menus. Then, I'll look at the Vista objects that deal with menus and build two example programs that uses them. Finally, I'll look at the use of accelerators to provide keyboard shortcuts for menu commands.

Windows menus

One of the most flexible features in the Windows environment is its menu system. It provides a consistent command interface between different programs, while providing a large number of operations to customize the appearance and behavior of individual applications. Windows gives a program access to several types of menus:

- Pull-down menus on a menu bar
- Cascading menus
- Pop-up menus

The different types of menus have a similar appearance and offer both a keyboard and a mouse interface. They share a common set of API functions that create, destroy, and manipulate individual items. A program can load its menu from a resource file, create it dynamically, or use a combination of both techniques to manage the appearance and behavior of a menu.

Menus communicate with a program just like any other Windows component: through messages. When the user selects a command from a menu, the menu sends a WM_COMMAND message to the menu's parent window. The message identifies which command was selected so the program can take the proper action.

Pull-down menus The most common type of menu found in a Windows program is the pull-down menu. Pull-down menus appear as choices on the menu bar displayed above a window's client area. When the user selects one of the items on the menu bar, the menu associated with the item drops down over the window's client area (FIG. 6-1).

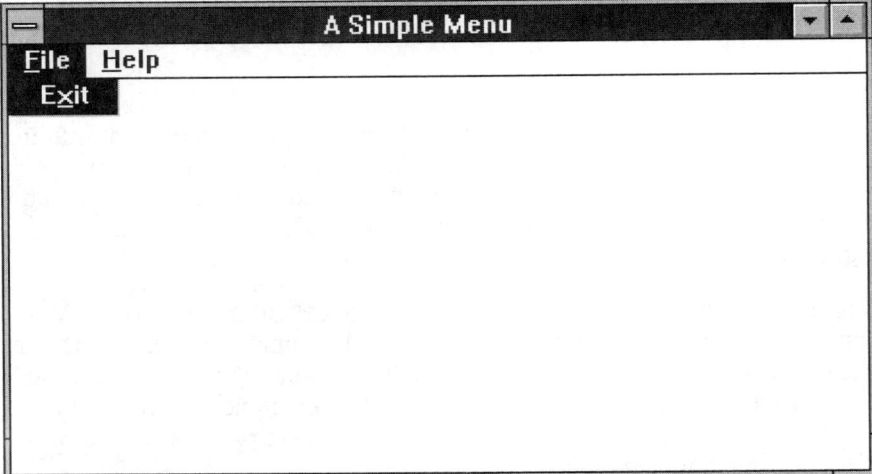

6-1
A sample pull-down menu.

Besides providing a command interface, drop-down menus offer another advantage. By cycling through each of the drop-down menus, a user can browse through the set of commands available for an application. Research on human-computer interaction has shown that people can remember only a few commands a time. It is much easier to navigate through commands than to memorize them.

Drop-down menus are associated with a keyboard mnemonic, which gives the user an alternative to opening a menu with the mouse. The mnemonic is represented by an underlined character. To display a drop-down menu, the user can either use the mouse to select an item on the menu bar or press the Alt key followed by the item's mnemonic. Likewise, items in a pull-down menu, and even child window controls, have their own mnemonic characters represented by an underlined character in the element's label.

Pull-down menus normally are specified in a program's resource script:

```
SimpleMenu MENU
  BEGIN
    POPUP "&File"
      BEGIN
        MENUITEM "E&xit", 101
      END
    POPUP "&Help"
      BEGIN
        MENUITEM "&About...", 201
      END
  END
```

The MENU statement names a specific pull-down menu. While the name is never displayed, the program uses it to identify the menu at runtime. The POPUP statement describes a pull-down menu; the menu bar item for the pull-down displays the POPUP's title. The MENUITEM statement describes an individual menu item, specifying the item's title, identifier, and, if necessary, its initial state. The item's title is displayed to the user, and its identifier is passed to the program when the user selects the item. You can use either a text editor or the Borland Resource Workshop to create menu resource scripts.

Identifiers in a menu need to be unique to allow the program to distinguish one command from another. You can duplicate menu identifiers on separate menus, but it's not a good idea. Most Windows programs offer context-sensitive help, with each menu item having its own help text. Menu identifiers need to be unique among all menus used by the program to allow the help system to present the appropriate help text for an item. For more information on the Windows help system, refer to the Borland C^{++} User's Guide.

Keyboard mnemonics are designated by an ampersand (&) before the mnemonic character. Windows underlines that character when it displays the menu item. Mnemonics should be unique among items on the menu bar and for each pop-up menu. Whenever possible, use the first character as a mnemonic, unless another character makes more sense, like the E&xit command.

Cascading menus

Most items in a pull-down menu correspond directly to commands or options. However, a special type of item—displayed with an arrow to its right (FIG. 6-2)—opens up yet another menu (FIG. 6-3). This type of menu is known

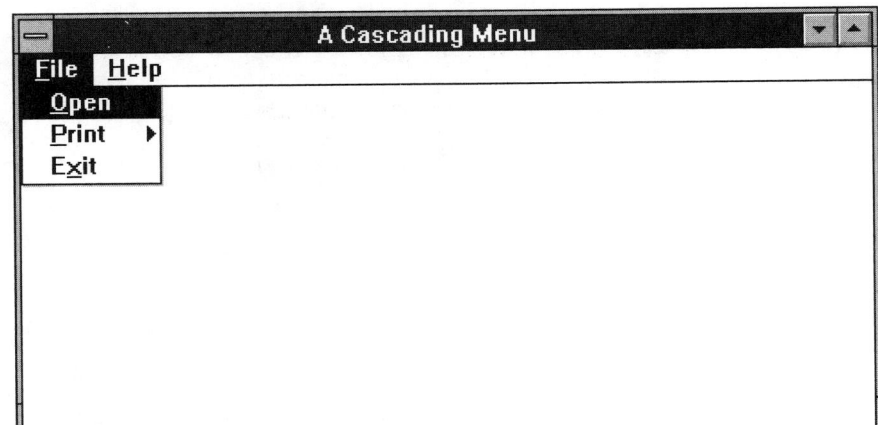

6-2
Another sample menu with a cascading menu item.

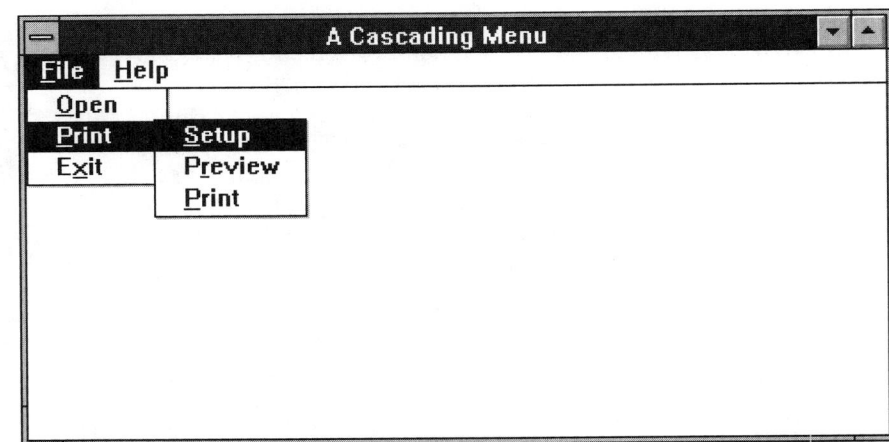

6-3
A cascading menu.

as a cascading menu and can be useful to partition a large number of commands.

While cascading menus can simplify an interface, they also can be distracting. Use them only when they make sense, and try not to cascade at more than one level. Consider alternatives like dialog boxes and tool bars to keep your menus as simple as possible.

Creating a cascading menu in your program's resource script is simple:

```
CascadeMenu MENU
  BEGIN
    POPUP "First"
      BEGIN
        MENUITEM "&1st Item", IDM_FIRST
```

```
            POPUP "&2nd Item"
              BEGIN
                  "&1st Cascade", IDM_SECOND
                  "&2nd Cascade", IDM_THIRD
              END
            MENUITEM "&3rd Item", IDM_FOURTH
        END
END
```

To keep a consistent interface, Windows displays the arrow next to the menu item. It also controls the behavior of the menu, providing both the mouse and keyboard interface.

Pop-up menus

Pop-up menus (FIG. 6-4), a new style of menu first provided with Windows 3.0, allow the program to present a different set of commands at different times. They offer a shortcut to selecting commands and options from pull-down menus. The content of a pop-up menu depends on the task the user is performing when they request the menu. They are especially useful when the user is working with several different objects in a single window.

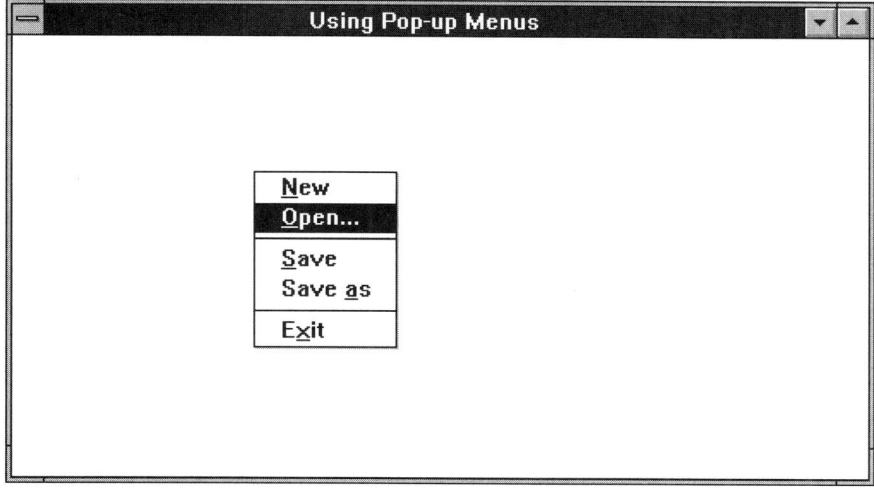

6-4
A dynamic pop-up menu.

For example, a graphics program might offer scaling, shading, and editing operations when the user selects the pop-up menu while editing a bitmap. If they select the pop-up while editing a rectangle, the menu would display options to control sizing, filling, and editing the shape.

Currently, the only standard way to display a pop-up menu is with the mouse, usually when the user clicks the right mouse button on an object. Therefore, the commands on the menu should be available elsewhere. Don't place too many commands on a pop-up menu; that would defeat the purpose of using a pop-up menu in the first place.

Using Vista menu objects

Vista provides a set of menu objects that simplify the Windows menu API. Figure 6-5 shows the class hierarchy for the Vista menu objects.

The VMenu class provides all of the operations necessary to create and manage menus. The VPopupMenu class adds an operation to display a pop-up menu. Also, the VSystemMenu exists to allow a program to modify its system menu.

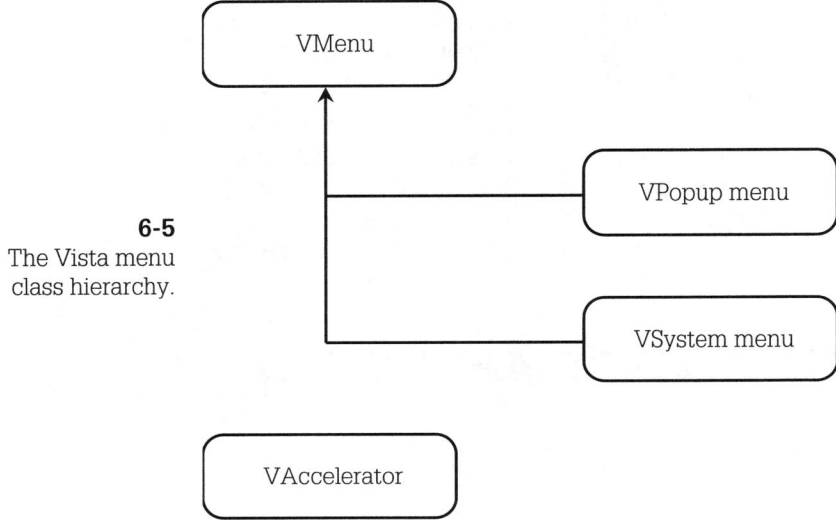

6-5 The Vista menu class hierarchy.

Listing 6-1 contains the code for the SIMPLMNU program, which demonstrates how to load a menu from a resource file and respond to user commands.

Listing 6-1 SIMPLMNU.CPP

```
/* --------------------------------------------------
   simplmnu.cpp

     An example that illustrates using a menu in a Vista
   program

   Copyright (C) 1992, by Jeff Mackay - TAB Books
   -------------------------------------------------- */
#pragma hdrfile "vista.sym"
#include <vista.h>
#pragma hdrstop
#include <vmenu.h>
#include <vmsgbox.h>
#include "simplmnu.h"

class MenuWindow  : public VFrame
```

Getting input with menus & accelerators

```cpp
{
private:

public:

        MenuWindow(void);
    void InitActions(void);
    Boolean ExitCommand(VEventRef event);
    Boolean AboutCommand(VEventRef event);
};

MenuWindow::MenuWindow(void) : VFrame(0, "A Simple Menu")
{
        menu = new VMenu(this, "SimpleMenu");
}

void MenuWindow::InitActions(void)
{
    VFrame::InitActions();
    AddCommand((VAction)&MenuWindow::ExitCommand,  IDM_EXIT);
    AddCommand((VAction)&MenuWindow::AboutCommand, IDM_ABOUT);
}

Boolean MenuWindow::ExitCommand(VEventRef event)
{
    DestroyWindow(*this);
    UNREFERENCED_PARAMETER(event);
    return True;
}

Boolean MenuWindow::AboutCommand(VEventRef event)
{
    VInfoBox aboutBox(this, "A sample About box",
                            "About SimplMenu");
    aboutBox.Execute();
    UNREFERENCED_PARAMETER(event);
    return True;
}



class SimpleMenuApp : public VAppl
{
public:
        SimpleMenuApp(HINSTANCE inst, HINSTANCE prevInst,
                      LPSTR cmdLine, int cmdShow);
        SimpleMenuApp(void);
        void InitWindow(void);
};
```

Using Vista menu objects

Listing 6-1
Continued.

```
SimpleMenuApp::SimpleMenuApp(HINSTANCE inst, HINSTANCE prevInst,
                             LPSTR cmdLine, int
cmdShow) :
             VAppl("simplmnu", inst, prevInst, cmdLine, cmdShow)
{
}


SimpleMenuApp::SimpleMenuApp(void)
{
}

void SimpleMenuApp::InitWindow(void)
{
    main_window = new MenuWindow();
}


int PASCAL WinMain(HINSTANCE hInstance, HINSTANCE hPrevInstance,
                   LPSTR lpszCmdLine, int nCmdShow)
{
    SimpleMenuApp mainApp(hInstance,hPrevInstance,
                lpszCmdLine,nCmdShow);

    return mainApp.Run();
}
```

The resource file used by SIMPLMNU is illustrated in LISTING 6-2. You can use a text editor to create a menu definition in a resource script, but Borland's Resource Workshop provides a good menu editor that simplifies the task.

Listing 6-2
SIMPLMNU.RC

```
/*-------------------------------------------------------
    simplmnu.h

    Resource identifiers for the simplmnu program
-------------------------------------------------------- */

#define IDM_EXIT   101
#define IDM_ABOUT  201
```

SIMPLMNU.H, shown in LISTING 6-3, contains menu identifier definitions used in both the resource script and the source code.

Listing 6-3
SIMPLMNU.H

```
#include "simplmnu.h"

SimpleMenu MENU
BEGIN
        POPUP "&File"
        BEGIN
                MENUITEM "E&xit", IDM_EXIT
        END

        POPUP "&Help"
        BEGIN
                MENUITEM "&About...", IDM_ABOUT
        END

END
```

Adding a menu to a Vista program is simple. First, create a resource file using the Resource Workshop, save the file as a .RC project, then create a new VMenu object in the window's constructor and assign it to the menu data member:

Adding a menu to a window object

```
MenuWindow(void) : VFrame(0, "A Simple Menu")
{
    menu = new VMenu(*this, "SimpleMenu");
}
```

Creating a menu object this way is easy, but it might not be the best method. If you create multiple instances of a window, each window has both a menu object and the Windows data structures representing a menu. Instead, if you plan on creating multiple instances of a window, include a pointer to the menu name in the window class registration structure in the InitWinClass method:

```
void SimpleMenu::InitWinClass(WNDCLASS _FAR &wndclass)
{
    wndclass.lpszMenuName = "SimpleMenu";
}
```

When you use this method, Windows loads the menu resource only once. Each window object creates its own menu object, but they all share the Windows menu data structures.

After the window is created and menu loaded, you need to be able to react to the menu items chosen by the user. This is a two-step process. First, add action items to the window's dispatcher:

Reacting to user commands

```
void MenuWindow::InitActions(void)
{
    VFrame::InitActions();
```

```
    AddCommand((VAction)&MenuWindow::ExitCommand,
               IDM_EXIT);
    AddCommand((VAction)&MenuWindow::AboutCommand,
               IDM_ABOUT);
}
```

This function adds two menu action methods. The first is called when the user selects the Exit command. Actually, the method is activated when the window receives a WM_COMMAND message from a menu item with an identifier of IDM_EXIT. The second is called in response to the About command.

The action methods are similar to those you've seen in previous chapters:

```
Boolean MenuWindow::ExitCommand(VEventRef event)
{
    DestroyWindow(*this);
    return True;
}

Boolean MenuWindow::AboutCommand(VEventRef event)
{
    VInfoBox aboutBox(this, "A sample About box",
                     "About SimplMenu");
    aboutBox.Execute();
    UNREFERENCED_PARAMETER(event);
    return True;
}
```

The first method, ExitCommand, destroys the main window using the DestroyWindow function. When called for an application's main window, DestroyWindow terminates the program.

The second method, AboutCommand, creates a VInfoBox object and executes it. I'll discuss the VInfoBox class in more detail in the next chapter.

Creating dynamic menus with the VMenu class

Although loading a menu from a resource is convenient, Windows programs often change their menu structure as they execute. To accommodate this, the VMenu class and its descendants provide a set of methods that allow you to build and change a menu while a program is executing.

Standard menus consist of three elements: a menu bar, pop-up menus, and menu items. The menu bar, represented by the VMenu class, appears above the window's client area. When the user selects an item on the menu bar, a pop-up menu, represented by the VPopupMenu class, drops down below the selection. Both the VMenu class and the VPopupMenu class contain menu items.

To create a dynamic menu for your window, first create a VMenu object, then create a VPopupMenu object for each of the items on the menu bar. Finally, use the Add method to fill in the commands to appear in the pop-up menus and add the pop-ups to the menu bar.

Listing 6-4 contains DYNMENU.CPP, which demonstrates creating a dynamic menu. Figure 6-4 shows the end result.

Listing 6-4
DYNMENU.CPP

```cpp
/* ------------------------------------------------------------
   dynmenu.cpp

      An example that creates a dynamic menu

   Copyright (C) 1992, by Jeff Mackay
   ------------------------------------------------------------ */
#pragma hdrfile "vista.sym"
#include <vista.h>
#pragma hdrstop

#include <vmenu.h>
#include <vmsgbox.h>


//
// CONSTANTS
//

#define IDM_NEW      101
#define IDM_OPEN     102
#define IDM_SAVE     103
#define IDM_SAVEAS   104
#define IDM_EXIT     105
#define IDM_ABOUT    201


//
// The MenuEntry structure contains information about a single
// menu item.
//
struct MenuEntry
{
    charPtr string;
    int     id;
    int     flags;
} fileEntries[] =
{   { "&New", IDM_NEW },
    { "&Open...", IDM_OPEN },
    { "", -1, VMENU_SEPARATOR },
    { "&Save", IDM_SAVE },
    { "Save &as", IDM_SAVEAS },
    { "", -1, VMENU_SEPARATOR },
```

Listing 6-4
Continued.

```
    { "E&xit", IDM_EXIT }
};

/* -----------------------------------------------------------
MenuWindow:

A class to demonstrate creating dynamic menus
-------------------------------------------------------- */

class MenuWindow : public VFrame
{

private:

public:

        MenuWindow(void);
    void InitActions(void);
    Boolean CreateAction(VEventRef event);
    Boolean NewCommand(VEventRef event);
    Boolean OpenCommand(VEventRef event);
    Boolean ExitCommand(VEventRef event);
    Boolean SaveCommand(VEventRef event);
    Boolean AboutCommand(VEventRef event);
};


MenuWindow::MenuWindow(void) : VFrame(0, "A Simple Menu")
{
}


void MenuWindow::InitActions(void)
{
    VFrame::InitActions();
    AddCommand((VAction)&MenuWindow::NewCommand, IDM_NEW);
    AddCommand((VAction)&MenuWindow::SaveCommand, IDM_SAVE);
    AddCommand((VAction)&MenuWindow::OpenCommand, IDM_OPEN);
    AddCommand((VAction)&MenuWindow::ExitCommand,  IDM_EXIT);
    AddCommand((VAction)&MenuWindow::AboutCommand, IDM_ABOUT);
}


Boolean MenuWindow::CreateAction(VEventRef event)
{
    VFrame::CreateAction(event);
    menu = new VMenu(this);
```

```cpp
    VPopupMenuPtr filePopup = new VPopupMenu();
    for (int i=0; i<dim(fileEntries); i++)
    {
        filePopup->Add(fileEntries[i].string,
                       fileEntries[i].id,
                       fileEntries[i].flags);
    }
    menu->Add("&File", *filePopup);
    VPopupMenuPtr helpPopup = new VPopupMenu();
    helpPopup->Add("&About...", 201);
    menu->Add("&Help", *helpPopup);
    menu->Enable(IDM_SAVE, False);
    menu->Enable(IDM_SAVEAS, False);
    return False;
}


Boolean MenuWindow::NewCommand(VEventRef event)
{
    menu->DeferDrawing();
    menu->Enable(IDM_SAVE);
    menu->Enable(IDM_SAVEAS);
    menu->EnableDrawing();
    menu->Draw();
    UNREFERENCED_PARAMETER(event);
    return True;
}


Boolean MenuWindow::OpenCommand(VEventRef event)
{
    menu->DeferDrawing();
    menu->Enable(IDM_SAVE);
    menu->Enable(IDM_SAVE);
    menu->EnableDrawing();
    menu->Draw();
    UNREFERENCED_PARAMETER(event);
    return True;
}


Boolean MenuWindow::SaveCommand(VEventRef event)
{
    menu->Enable(IDM_SAVE, False);
    UNREFERENCED_PARAMETER(event);
    return True;
}


Boolean MenuWindow::ExitCommand(VEventRef event)
{
```

Listing 6-4
Continued.

```
        DestroyWindow(*this);
        UNREFERENCED_PARAMETER(event);
        return True;
    }


    Boolean MenuWindow::AboutCommand(VEventRef event)
    {
        VInfoBox aboutBox(this, "A sample About box",
                                "About DynMenu");
        aboutBox.Execute();
        UNREFERENCED_PARAMETER(event);
        return True;
    }



    /* -------------------------------------------------------------------

    DynMenuApp:

    The application class

    ------------------------------------------------------------------- */

    class DynMenuApp : public VAppl
    {
    public:
            DynMenuApp(HINSTANCE inst, HINSTANCE prevInst,
                                    LPSTR cmdLine, int cmdShow);
            DynMenuApp(void);
            void InitWindow(void);
    };


    DynMenuApp::DynMenuApp(HINSTANCE inst, HINSTANCE prevInst,
                                    LPSTR cmdLine, int cmdShow) :
    VAppl("simplmnu", inst, prevInst, cmdLine, cmdShow)
    {
    }


    DynMenuApp::DynMenuApp(void)
    {
    }



    void DynMenuApp::InitWindow(void)
    {
        main_window = new MenuWindow();
```

```
}


int PASCAL WinMain(HINSTANCE hInstance, HINSTANCE hPrevInstance,
                                LPSTR lpszCmdLine, int nCmdShow)
{
        DynMenuApp mainApp(hInstance,hPrevInstance,
                                            lpszCmdLine,nCmdShow);

        return mainApp.Run();
}
```

One function in DYNMENU.CPP creates the dynamic menu:

```
struct MenuEntry
{
    charPtr string;
    int id;
    int flags;
} fileEntries[] =
{   { "&New", IDM_NEW },
    { "&Open...", IDM_OPEN },
    { "", -1, VMENU_SEPARATOR },
    { "&Save", IDM_SAVE },
    { "Save &as", IDM_SAVEAS },
    { "", -1, VMENU_SEPARATOR },
    { "E&xit", IDM_EXIT }
};
// ...

Boolean MenuWindow::CreateAction(VEventRef event)
{
    VFrame::CreateAction(event);
    menu = new VMenu(this);
    VPopupMenuPtr filePopup = new VPopupMenu();
    for (int i=0; i<dim(fileEntries); i++)
    {
        filePopup->Add(fileEntries[i].string,
                    fileEntries[i].id,
                    fileEntries[i].flags);
    }
    menu->Add("&File", *filePopup);
    VPopupMenuPtr helpPopup = new VPopupMenu();
    helpPopup->Add("&About...", 201);
    menu->Add("&Help", *helpPopup);
    menu->Enable(IDM_SAVE, False);
    menu->Enable(IDM_SAVEAS, False);
    return False;
}
```

This function first creates an empty menu and an empty pop-up menu. Then, it adds elements from the `fileEntries` array to the pop-up menu. It creates another empty pop-up for the Help menu and adds the About item. Finally, it adds the two pop-ups to the menu bar.

The CreateAction method also disables two of the menu items on the File menu. When the program starts, both of the disabled menu items are dimmed and cannot be selected by the user. When the user selects the New command, its action method enables the menu items:

```
Boolean MenuWindow::NewCommand(VEventRef event)
{
    menu->DeferDrawing();
    menu->Enable(IDM_SAVE);
    menu->Enable(IDM_SAVEAS);
    menu->EnableDrawing();
    menu->Draw();
    return True;
}
```

Notice the calls to DeferDrawing and EnableDrawing. By default, a VMenu object redraws its menu whenever a change is made to the menu's contents. When you need to make several changes at once, this can cause the menu bar to flash as each change is made. The DeferDrawing method temporarily prevents the VMenu object from drawing itself, allowing you to batch menu changes. When you finish with the batch of operations, call the EnableDrawing method to enable redrawing.

The VMenu class provides operations to insert a menu item or pop-up menu before another item (Insert) and operations to remove existing menu items (Remove). It also gives you the ability to check and uncheck menu items, treating them like check boxes to set options rather than perform commands. Appendix B gives more details on these operations.

Creating a floating menu

As I discussed earlier in this chapter, floating pop-up menus can be used as shortcuts to select items normally found on a window's menu bar. In this section, I'll create an example that illustrates using a floating pop-up menu.

Listing 6-5 contains POPMENU.CPP, a program that uses floating pop-up menus in much the same way many Borland programs provide "Menus on Demand." First, the CreateAction method creates a dynamic pop-up menu:

```
Boolean VPopupWindow::CreateAction(VEventRef event)
{
    VFrame::CreateAction(event);
    popup_menu = new VPopupMenu();
    for (int i=0; i<dim(fileEntries); i++)
    {
        popup_menu->Add(fileEntries[i].string,
                        fileEntries[i].id,
```

```cpp
                        fileEntries[i].flags);
    }
    popup_menu->Enable(IDM_SAVE, False);
    popup_menu->Enable(IDM_SAVEAS, False);
    return False;
}
```

Listing 6-5
POPMENU.CPP

```cpp
/* ----------------------------------------------------------
   popmenu.cpp

   An example that uses a floating pop-up menu.

   Copyright (C) 1992, by Jeff Mackay - TAB Books
------------------------------------------------------- */

#pragma hdrfile "vista.sym"
#include <vista.h>
#pragma hdrstop

#include <vmenu.h>

//
// CONSTANTS
//

#define IDM_NEW      101
#define IDM_OPEN     102
#define IDM_SAVE     103
#define IDM_SAVEAS   104
#define IDM_EXIT     105


struct MenuEntry
{
    charPtr string;
    int     id;
    int     flags;
} fileEntries[] =
{   { "&New", IDM_NEW },
    { "&Open...", IDM_OPEN },
    { "", -1, VMENU_SEPARATOR },
    { "&Save", IDM_SAVE },
    { "Save &as", IDM_SAVEAS },
    { "", -1, VMENU_SEPARATOR },
    { "E&xit", IDM_EXIT }
};

/* ----------------------------------------------------------
PopupMenuWindow:
An example window using pop-up menus
-------------------------------------------------------- */
```

Listing 6-5
Continued.

```
*/
class PopupWindow  : public VFrame
{

public:

        PopupWindow(void);
    PopupWindow(void);
    void InitActions(void);
    Boolean CreateAction(VEventRef event);
    Boolean MouseDown(VEventRef event);
    Boolean NewCommand(VEventRef event);
    Boolean OpenCommand(VEventRef event);
    Boolean ExitCommand(VEventRef event);
    Boolean SaveCommand(VEventRef event);

private:
    VPopupMenuPtr popup_menu;

};


PopupWindow::PopupWindow(void) : VFrame(0, "Using Pop-up Menus")
{
}


PopupWindow::PopupWindow(void)
{
    delete popup_menu;
}


void PopupWindow::InitActions(void)
{
    VFrame::InitActions();
    AddAction((VAction)&PopupWindow::MouseDown, WM_RBUTTONDOWN);
    AddCommand((VAction)&PopupWindow::NewCommand, IDM_NEW);
    AddCommand((VAction)&PopupWindow::OpenCommand, IDM_OPEN);
    AddCommand((VAction)&PopupWindow::ExitCommand, IDM_EXIT);
    AddCommand((VAction)&PopupWindow::SaveCommand, IDM_SAVE);
}


Boolean PopupWindow::CreateAction(VEventRef event)
{
    VFrame::CreateAction(event);
    popup_menu = new VPopupMenu();
    for (int i=0; i<dim(fileEntries); i++)
    {
```

```cpp
        popup_menu->Add(fileEntries[i].string,
                        fileEntries[i].id,
                        fileEntries[i].flags);
    }
    popup_menu->Enable(IDM_SAVE, False);
    popup_menu->Enable(IDM_SAVEAS, False);
    UNREFERENCED_PARAMETER(event);
    return False;
}


Boolean PopupWindow::MouseDown(VEventRef event)
{
    int x, y;
    x = LOWORD(event.GetLParam());
    y = HIWORD(event.GetLParam());

    popup_menu->Track(this, x, y);
    return True;
}


Boolean PopupWindow::NewCommand(VEventRef event)
{
    popup_menu->Enable(IDM_SAVE);
    popup_menu->Enable(IDM_SAVEAS);
    UNREFERENCED_PARAMETER(event);
    return True;
}


Boolean PopupWindow::OpenCommand(VEventRef event)
{
    popup_menu->Enable(IDM_SAVE);
    popup_menu->Enable(IDM_SAVEAS);
    UNREFERENCED_PARAMETER(event);
    return True;
}

Boolean PopupWindow::ExitCommand(VEventRef event)
{
    DestroyWindow(*this);
    UNREFERENCED_PARAMETER(event);
    return True;
}

Boolean PopupWindow::SaveCommand(VEventRef event)
{
    popup_menu->Enable(IDM_SAVE, False);
```

Listing 6-5
Continued.

```
        UNREFERENCED_PARAMETER(event);
        return True;
}


/* ----------------------------------------------------------------
PopupMenuApp:

The application class
---------------------------------------------------------------- */
class PopupMenuApp : public VAppl
{
public:
        PopupMenuApp(HINSTANCE inst, HINSTANCE prevInst,
                              LPSTR cmdLine, int cmdShow);
        PopupMenuApp(void);
        void InitWindow(void);
};


PopupMenuApp::PopupMenuApp(HINSTANCE inst, HINSTANCE prevInst,
                                    LPSTR cmdLine, int cmdShow)
        :
        VAppl("simplmnu", inst, prevInst, cmdLine, cmdShow)
{
}


PopupMenuApp::PopupMenuApp(void)
{
}


void PopupMenuApp::InitWindow(void)
{
        main_window = new PopupWindow();
}


int PASCAL WinMain(HINSTANCE hInstance, HINSTANCE hPrevInstance,
                           LPSTR lpszCmdLine, intnCmdShow)
{
        PopupMenuApp mainApp(hInstance,hPrevInstance,
                                        lpszCmdLine,nCmdShow);

        return mainApp.Run();
}
```

108 *Getting input with menus & accelerators*

Notice that the CreateAction method for this program is very similar to the same method in the previous example. Because the VPopupMenu class inherits from the VMenu class, all its operations are available.

After I create the pop-up menu, all I have to do is display it whenever the user clicks the right mouse button on the window's client area. To do this, I'll trap the WM_RBUTTONDOWN event:

```
Boolean VPopupWindow::MouseDown(VEventRef event)
{
    int x, y;
    x = LOWORD(event.GetLParam());
    y = HIWORD(event.GetLParam());
    popup_menu->Track(this, x, y);
    return True;
}
```

Because this pop-up menu isn't attached to a window like a menu bar is, I have to explicitly destroy the menu when I don't need it anymore:

```
PopupWindow::PopupWindow(void)
{
    delete popup_menu;
}
```

A final note about pop-up menus: to keep things simple, in this example I didn't create a menu bar; however, in a real program, you should always provide a menu bar to allow users to select commands without using the mouse. Pop-up menus are convenient, but they shouldn't provide the only command interface for a program.

Using accelerators

Accelerators, like pop-up menus, are shortcuts for selecting menu commands. Unlike a pop-up menu, accelerators are keyboard shortcuts. They allow the user to press a combination of keys instead of selecting a menu item using a mouse or several keyboard mnemonics.

Menus provide a visual representation of the commands available for an application; they make a program suitable for occasional use. Accelerators are for your "power" users; they reduce the number of steps the user must take to access a command.

Listing 6-6 contains ACCELMNU.CPP, which is the SIMPLMNU program modified to use accelerators. Listing 6-7 contains ACCELMNU.RC, which is the SIMPLMNU resource script that also has been modified to include an accelerator table.

Listing 6-6
ACCELMNU.CPP

```
/* -------------------------------------------------------------
   accelmnu.cpp

   An example that illustrates using accelerators in a Vista program

   Copyright (C) 1992, by Jeff Mackay - TAB Books
   ------------------------------------------------------------- */
#pragma hdrfile "vista.sym"
#include <vista.h>
#pragma hdrstop
#include <vmenu.h>
#include <vmsgbox.h>
#include "simplmnu.h"

/* -------------------------------------------------------------
MenuWindow:

The main window class.  Includes support for a menu and
accelerators
   ------------------------------------------------------------- */
class MenuWindow   : public VFrame
{

private:

public:

        MenuWindow(void);
    void InitActions(void);
    Boolean ExitCommand(VEventRef event);
    Boolean AboutCommand(VEventRef event);
};


MenuWindow::MenuWindow(void) : VFrame(0, "A Simple Menu")
{
        menu        = new VMenu(this, "AccelMenu");
        accel_table = new VAccelerator(this, "Accelerators");
}


void MenuWindow::InitActions(void)
{
    VFrame::InitActions();
    AddCommand((VAction)&MenuWindow::ExitCommand,   IDM_EXIT);
    AddCommand((VAction)&MenuWindow::AboutCommand,  IDM_ABOUT);
}


Boolean MenuWindow::ExitCommand(VEventRef event)
{
```

Getting input with menus & accelerators

```
        DestroyWindow(*this);
        UNREFERENCED_PARAMETER(event);
        return True;
}


Boolean MenuWindow::AboutCommand(VEventRef event)
{
    VInfoBox aboutBox(this, "A sample About box", "About
                                    SimplMenu");
    aboutBox.Execute();
    UNREFERENCED_PARAMETER(event);
    return True;
}

/*----------------------------------------------------------------
SimpleMenuApp:

The application class
---------------------------------------------------------------- */

class SimpleMenuApp : public VAppl
{
public:
        SimpleMenuApp(HINSTANCE inst, HINSTANCE prevInst,
                                LPSTR cmdLine, int cmdShow);
        SimpleMenuApp(void);
        void InitWindow(void);
};


SimpleMenuApp::SimpleMenuApp(HINSTANCE inst, HINSTANCE prevInst,
                                        LPSTR cmdLine, int cmdShow) :
            VAppl("simplmnu", inst, prevInst, cmdLine, cmdShow)
{
}


SimpleMenuApp::SimpleMenuApp(void)
{
}


void SimpleMenuApp::InitWindow(void)
{
        main_window = new MenuWindow();
}


int PASCAL WinMain(HINSTANCE hInstance, HINSTANCE hPrevInstance,
                            LPSTR lpszCmdLine, int nCmdShow)
```

Listing 6-6
Continued.

```
        {
                SimpleMenuApp mainApp(hInstance,hPrevInstance,
                                      lpszCmdLine,nCmdShow);

                return mainApp.Run();
        }
```

Listing 6-7
ACCELMNU.RC

```
#include "simplmnu.h"

AccelMenu MENU
BEGIN
        POPUP "&File"
        BEGIN
                MENUITEM "E&xit\tF3", IDM_EXIT
        END

        POPUP "&Help"
        BEGIN
                MENUITEM "&About...\tCtrl+A", IDM_ABOUT
        END

END

Accelerators ACCELERATORS
BEGIN
    VK_F3,   IDM_EXIT,  VIRTKEY
    "^A",    IDM_ABOUT, VIRTKEY
END
```

Adding accelerators to a program takes three steps. The first two involve the resource script. First, modify menu item labels to identify the accelerator used for each item:

```
AccelMenu MENU
BEGIN
  POPUP "&File"
  BEGIN
       MENUITEM "E&xit\tF3", IDM_EXIT
  END
  POPUP "&Help"
  BEGIN
       MENUITEM "&About...\tCtrl+A", IDM_ABOUT
  END
END
```

Accelerators are identified by the key combination used to select the option. It follows the menu item label and is separated by a tab character (\t). Windows right justifies text after the tab character.

The second step is to add an accelerator table to the program:

```
AccelAccelerators ACCELERATORS
BEGIN
    VK_F3, IDM_EXIT, VIRTKEY
    "^A", IDM_ABOUT, VIRTKEY
END
```

Each entry in the accelerator table describes the attributes of a single accelerator. The most common type of accelerator you'll find use function keys or control-letter combinations.

The third step is to load the accelerator table after you load the program's menu:

```
MenuWindow::MenuWindow(void)
    : VFrame(0, "A Menu with Accelerators")
{
    menu = new VMenu(this, "AccelMenu");
    accel_table = new VAccelerator(this, "Accelerators");
}
```

The VWindow class, in cooperation with the VAppl class, handles the actual translation and dispatch of accelerators to your window.

Moving C programs to Vista

In the last chapter, I discussed an approach to take in transforming your C code into C++. If you already have begun the conversion, now's the time to get rid of those huge WM_COMMAND branches. Take each menu item branch and place it into its own member function. If you overrode the CommandAction method as I suggested in the last chapter, be sure to delete that method now or at least chain to the VFrame's method.

When you convert your program, you have two choices when you look at converting the code that manipulates a menu. The easiest approach is to leave the code alone. If you want to assign a menu to a window class, override the InitWinClass method and initialize the `lpzsMenuName` member of the `wndClass` parameter.

A better approach might be to set the window's menu in its constructor by creating a new menu object. Then, use the menu object's member functions to manipulate the menu.

What's next

In this chapter, I've looked at getting input from a user through the use of menus and accelerators. I examined loading menus from a resource file, creating them dynamically, and using floating pop-up menus. I also looked at using accelerators as shortcuts for selecting menu commands. In the next chapter, I'll cover another avenue for obtaining input from users: dialog and message boxes.

7 Dialog & message boxes

Dialog and message boxes provide a consistent and visual means of interacting with the user. Windows application use them extensively to obtain data from and provide information to the user. In this chapter, I'll begin to look at using dialog and message boxes in a Vista program.

Vista provides an extensive hierarchy of classes to manage the many ways in which a program can use dialog boxes (FIG. 7-1). The VDialogBox class, which forms the base of that hierarchy, is derived from the VComposite class.

Vista dialog boxes

The VDialogBox class provides basic support for managing a dialog and its child window controls. While the majority of dialog boxes are loaded from a program's resource file, the dialogs discussed in this chapter are provided by Windows. I'll examine the VDialogBox class further in the next chapter.

Message boxes, which are simple and specialized types of dialog boxes, have been available since the earliest versions of Windows. They consist of a window displaying an icon and a text message, with one or more push buttons to accept user input. Message boxes normally display three types of messages: informational, warning, and error messages. Vista provides classes to represent each type of message box.

Message boxes

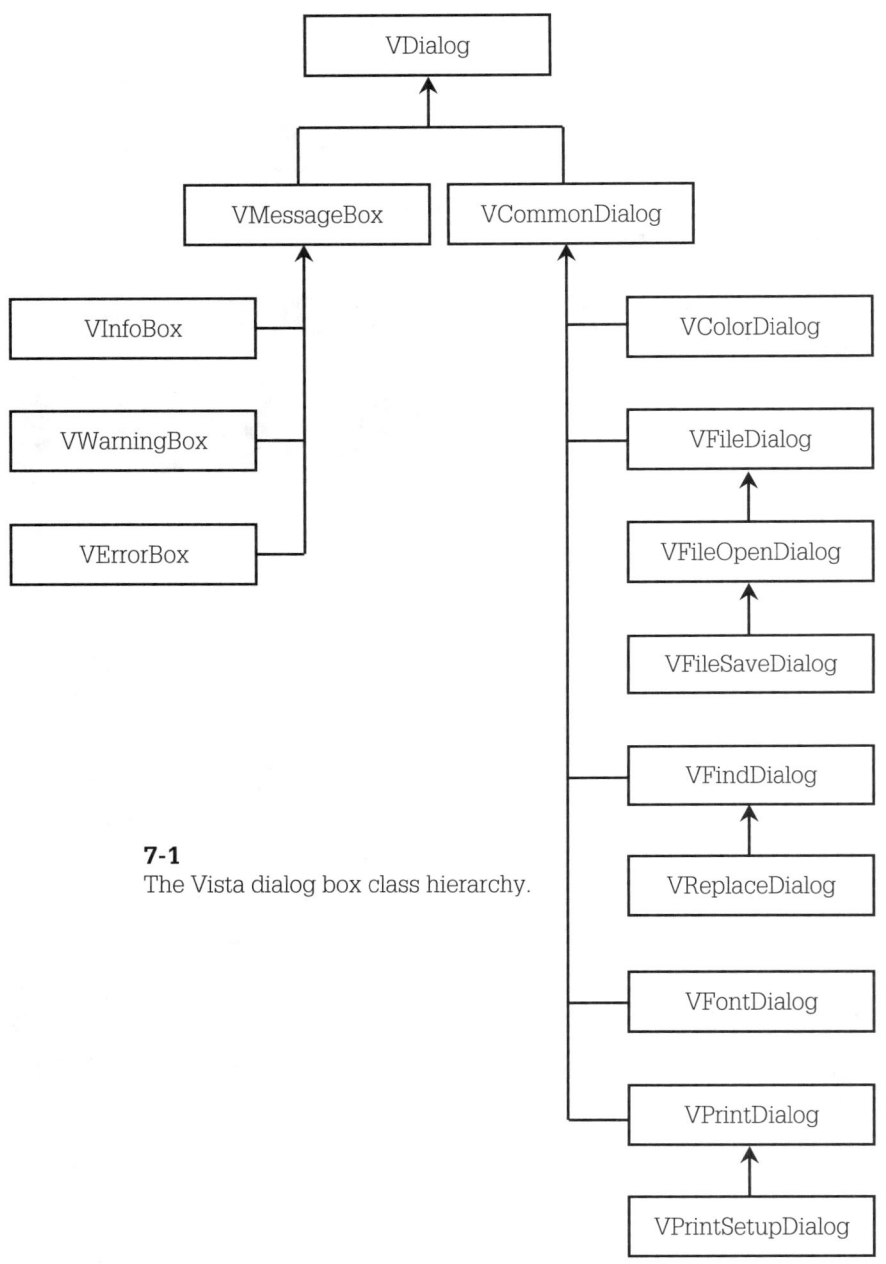

7-1
The Vista dialog box class hierarchy.

As an example of creating message boxes, let's look at the warning box. To create a warning box, just pass it a parent window and the message it should display:

```
VWarningBox warningBox(this, "A warning message");
```

Then, to display the message box, call its Execute member function:

```
int return_code = warningBox.Execute();
```

The resulting warning box is shown in FIG. 7-2. It displays the message you passed with an Ok and a Cancel button. Like the other message boxes, the warning box displays the application's title as its caption.

7-2
A Sample warning box displayed by a VWarningBox dialog object.

Because Windows is a multitasking system, many applications can display messages at the same time. Using the application's title as the title for the message box makes it easier for the user to identify the source of the message. You also can specify a title for the warning box when you create it:

```
VWarningBox warningBox(this, "A warning message",
                      "More warnings");
```

The Execute member function returns the identifier of the button the user selected to dismiss the message box. If the user tries to exit an application without saving a modified record, you can present a warning box giving the user an Ok and Cancel button to select. If the user selects the Cancel button, the Execute function returns IDCANCEL, and the program can refrain from closing the parent window.

While the VInfoBox, VWarningBox, and VErrorBox classes provide enough flexibility for most messages you'll need to display, you can provide further customization by creating VMessageBox objects directly. See appendix B for more information on the VMessageBox class.

Windows common dialogs

Windows 3.1 introduced several dialog boxes to handle the most common user operations. Besides enhancing the consistency of Windows applications, the common dialogs provide a level of sophistication that you probably wouldn't be able to provide in your own applications.

Programs written in C access the common dialogs with function calls and large data structures, with one function handling each type of dialog. To simplify the interface to the common dialogs, Vista provides several classes. TABLE 7-1 lists those classes with their corresponding API functions and data structures.

Table 7-1
Windows common dialog boxes

API function	Structure	Vista class
GetOpenFilename	OPENFILE	VFileOpenDialog
GetSaveFilename		VFileSave Dialog
ChooseColor	CHOOSECOLOR	VColorDialog
ChooseFont	CHOOSEFONT	VFontDialog
PrintDlg	PRINTDLG	VPrintDialog
VPrintSetupDialog		
FindText	FINDREPLACE	VFindDialog
ReplaceText		VReplaceDialog

At the top of the common dialog class hierarchy lies the VCommonDialog class. This class provides operations common to all the common dialogs that allow you to customize the appearance and behavior of the dialogs.

With the SetTemplate function, you can modify the appearance of a common dialog to provide additional child window controls. By providing your own template for the dialog boxes, you can retain some of the behavior of the common dialog but add your own features or change the appearance of a dialog into something more attractive.

You aren't limited to just specifying a custom template for the dialog. Because the Vista custom dialog classes are based on the VWindow class, you can add action methods to filter any event directed to a custom dialog.

In the rest of this section, I'll concentrate on using the custom dialog classes to add features to the FileView program I developed in the last chapter. The first step in adding support for dialogs to FileView is to create its resource and header files (LISTINGS 7-1 and 7-2).

Listing 7-1
FVRCH

```
#include "fvrc.h"

FileView MENU
BEGIN
        POPUP "&File"
        BEGIN
        MENUITEM "&New", IDM_NEW
        MENUITEM "&Open...", IDM_OPEN
        MENUITEM "&Print...", IDM_PRINT
        MENUITEM "Print &setup...", IDM_PRINTSETUP
        MENUITEM SEPARATOR
                MENUITEM "E&xit\tF3", IDM_EXIT
```

```
            END

        POPUP "&Edit"
        BEGIN
            MENUITEM "&Search...", IDM_SEARCH
        END

        POPUP "&Options"
        BEGIN
            MENUITEM "&Font...", IDM_FONT
            MENUITEM SEPARATOR
            MENUITEM "&Background...", IDM_BACKGROUND
            MENUITEM "&Foreground...", IDM_FOREGROUND
        END

            POPUP "&Help"
            BEGIN
                    MENUITEM "&About...\tCtrl+A", IDM_ABOUT
            END
END
```

Listing 7-2
FILEVIEW.CPP, a version of *FileView* using the common dialog classes.

```
/* ------------------------------------------------------
    fvrc.h

    Contains menu identifiers for the FileView program

    Copyright (C) 1992, by Jeff Mackay - TAB Books
   ------------------------------------------------------ */
// File menu
#define IDM_NEW             101
#define IDM_OPEN            102
#define IDM_PRINT           103
#define IDM_PRINTSETUP      104
#define IDM_EXIT            105

// Edit menu
#define IDM_SEARCH          201

// Options menu
#define IDM_FONT            301
#define IDM_BACKGROUND      302
#define IDM_FOREGROUND      303

// Help menu
#define IDM_ABOUT           401
```

The next step is to create "stub" action methods for each of the menu items and add them to the dispatcher:

```
Boolean FileView::OpenCommand(VEventRef event)
{
    UNREFERENCED_PARAMETER(event);
    return True;
}
```

Finally, I can add each of the new action methods to FileView's event dispatcher:

```
void FileView::InitActions(VEventRef event)
{
    AddCommand((VAction)&FileView::OpenCommand,
        IDM_OPEN);
    AddCommand((VAction)&FileView::PrintCommand,
        IDM_PRINT);
    AddCommand((VAction)&FileView::PrintSetupCommand,
        IDM_PRINTSETUP);
    AddCommand((VAction)&FileView::ExitCommand,
        IDM_EXIT);
    AddCommand((VAction)&FileView::SearchCommand,
        IDM_SEARCH);
    AddCommand((VAction)&FileView::FontCommand,
        IDM_FONT);
    AddCommand((VAction)&FileView::ColorCommand,
        IDM_FOREGROUND);
    AddCommand((VAction)&FileView::ColorCommand,
        IDM_BACKGROUND);
}
```

Now, you're ready to fill those stub routines with code that interacts with the common dialogs. First, however, I'll look at an example program, VISTADLG (LISTING 7-3), that just demonstrates the use of the dialogs.

Listing 7-3
VISTADLG.CPP

```
/* -----------------------------------------------------------
   dlgwind.cpp

       An example that illustrates using common dialog boxes.

   Copyright (C) 1992, by Jeff Mackay - TAB Books
   ----------------------------------------------------------- */
#pragma hdrfile "vista.sym"
#include <vista.h>
#pragma hdrstop
#include <vmenu.h>
#include <vmsgbox.h>
#include <vcommon.h>
#include "dlgwind.h"
```

```cpp
/* -------------------------------------------------------
DialogWindow:

The main window class.
------------------------------------------------------- */
class DialogWindow : public VFrame
{
private:
    VPrintDialog      *print_dlg;
    VPrintSetupDialog *setup_dlg;
    VFileOpenDialog   *open_dlg;
    VColorDialog      *back_dlg;
    VColorDialog      *fore_dlg;
    VFontDialog       *font_dlg;
    VFindDialog       *srch_dlg;

public:

    DialogWindow(void);
    void InitActions(void);
    Boolean OpenCommand(VEventRef event);
    Boolean ExitCommand(VEventRef event);
    Boolean AboutCommand(VEventRef event);
    Boolean PrintCommand(VEventRef event);
    Boolean PrintSetupCommand(VEventRef event);
    Boolean BackgroundCommand(VEventRef event);
    Boolean ForegroundCommand(VEventRef event);
    Boolean FontCommand(VEventRef event);
    Boolean SearchCommand(VEventRef event);
    Boolean SearchAction(VEventRef event);
};


DialogWindow::DialogWindow(void)
        : VFrame(0, "Using Dialog Boxes")
{
    menu       = new VMenu(this, "DialogMenu");
    print_dlg  = 0;
    setup_dlg  = 0;
    open_dlg   = 0;
    font_dlg   = 0;
    fore_dlg   = 0;
    back_dlg   = 0;
    srch_dlg   = 0;
}


void DialogWindow::InitActions(void)
{
    VFrame::InitActions();
```

Listing 7-3
Continued.

```
    AddCommand((VAction)&DialogWindow::OpenCommand,
                    IDM_OPEN);
    AddCommand((VAction)&DialogWindow::ExitCommand,
                    IDM_EXIT);
    AddCommand((VAction)&DialogWindow::AboutCommand,
                    IDM_ABOUT);
    AddCommand((VAction)&DialogWindow::PrintCommand,
                    IDM_PRINT);
    AddCommand((VAction)&DialogWindow::PrintSetupCommand,
                    IDM_PRINTERSETUP);
    AddCommand((VAction)&DialogWindow::BackgroundCommand,
                    IDM_BACKGROUND);
    AddCommand((VAction)&DialogWindow::ForegroundCommand,
                    IDM_FOREGROUND);
    AddCommand((VAction)&DialogWindow::FontCommand,
                    IDM_FONT);
    AddCommand((VAction)&DialogWindow::SearchCommand,
                    IDM_SEARCH);
}


Boolean DialogWindow::SearchCommand(VEventRef event)
{
    if (srch_dlg == 0)
    {
        srch_dlg = new VFindDialog(this);
        AddAction((VAction)&DialogWindow::SearchAction,
                VFindDialog::find_replace_message);
    }
    srch_dlg->Execute();
    UNREFERENCED_PARAMETER(event);
    return True;
}


Boolean DialogWindow::SearchAction(VEventRef event)
{
    VFindDialogPtr thisDialog =
            VFindDialog::GetDialogObject(event.GetL
            Param()); if (thisDialog->IsClosing())
    {
        delete thisDialog;
        srch_dlg = 0;
    }
    else
    {
      VInfoBox infoBox(this, thisDialog->GetSearchString());
        infoBox.Execute();
    }
    return True;
```

```
}
Boolean DialogWindow::FontCommand(VEventRef event)
{
    if (font_dlg == 0)
        font_dlg = new VFontDialog(this);

    if (font_dlg->Execute() == IDOK)
    {
        VInfoBox infoBox(this, font_dlg->GetStyle());
        infoBox.Execute();
    }
    UNREFERENCED_PARAMETER(event);
    return True;
}


Boolean DialogWindow::ForegroundCommand(VEventRef event)
{
    if (fore_dlg == 0)
        fore_dlg = new VColorDialog(this);

    if (fore_dlg->Execute() == IDOK)
    {
        VInfoBox infoBox(this, "Selected foreground color");
        infoBox.Execute();
    }
    UNREFERENCED_PARAMETER(event);
    return True;
}


Boolean DialogWindow::BackgroundCommand(VEventRef event)
{
    if (back_dlg == 0)
        back_dlg = new VColorDialog(this);

    if (back_dlg->Execute() == IDOK)
    {
        VInfoBox infoBox(this, "Selected foreground color");
        infoBox.Execute();
    }
    UNREFERENCED_PARAMETER(event);
    return True;
}


Boolean DialogWindow::PrintCommand(VEventRef event)
{
    if (print_dlg == 0)
```

Listing 7-3
Continued.

```
    {
        if (setup_dlg)
            print_dlg = new VPrintDialog(*setup_dlg);
        else
            print_dlg = new VPrintDialog(this);
    }

    if (print_dlg->Execute() == True)
    {
        VInfoBox infoBox(this, "Printing...");
        infoBox.Execute();
    }
    UNREFERENCED_PARAMETER(event);
    return True;
}


Boolean DialogWindow::PrintSetupCommand(VEventRef event)
{
    if (setup_dlg == 0)
        setup_dlg = new VPrintSetupDialog(this);

    if (setup_dlg->Execute() == True)
    {
        VInfoBox infoBox(this, "Printer Setup complete");
        infoBox.Execute();
    }
    UNREFERENCED_PARAMETER(event);
    return True;
}


Boolean DialogWindow::OpenCommand(VEventRef event)
{
    // only create the dialog object the first time
    if (open_dlg == 0)
        open_dlg = new VFileOpenDialog(this,
            "All Files (*.*)|*.*|Text Files(*.txt)|*.txt|");

    // if execute returns True, the user selected a file
    if (open_dlg->Execute() == True)
    {
        VInfoBox info(this, open_dlg->GetFilename());
        info.Execute();
    }
    UNREFERENCED_PARAMETER(event);
    return True;
}
```

```cpp
Boolean DialogWindow::ExitCommand(VEventRef event)
{
    DestroyWindow(*this);
    UNREFERENCED_PARAMETER(event);
    return True;
}


Boolean DialogWindow::AboutCommand(VEventRef event)
{
    VInfoBox aboutBox(this, "A sample About box",
                                    "About MsgWind");
    aboutBox.Execute();
    UNREFERENCED_PARAMETER(event);
    return True;
}

/* -------------------------------------------------------------------
DialogApp:

The application class
------------------------------------------------------------------- */
class DialogApp : public VAppl
{
public:
        DialogApp(HINSTANCE inst, HINSTANCE prevInst,
                                LPSTR cmdLine, int cmdShow);
        DialogApp(void);
        void InitWindow(void);
};

DialogApp::DialogApp(HINSTANCE inst, HINSTANCE prevInst,
                                            LPSTR cmdLine, int cmdShow) :
    VAppl("MsgWind", inst, prevInst, cmdLine, cmdShow)
{
}


DialogApp::DialogApp(void)
{
}


void DialogApp::InitWindow(void)
{
        main_window = new DialogWindow();
}


int PASCAL WinMain(HINSTANCE hInstance, HINSTANCE hPrevInstance,
                                LPSTR lpszCmdLine, int nCmdShow)
```

Listing 7-3
Continued.
```
{
    DialogApp mainApp(hInstance,hPrevInstance,
                                lpszCmdLine,nCmdShow);

    return mainApp.Run();
}
```

Opening files with the VFileOpenDialog class

The VFileOpenDialog class is an interface for the Windows common file dialog (FIG. 7-3). The file open dialog allows the user to choose a file for a program to act on. It gives access to all the drives and directories on a system and, with Windows for Workgroups, full access to network drives.

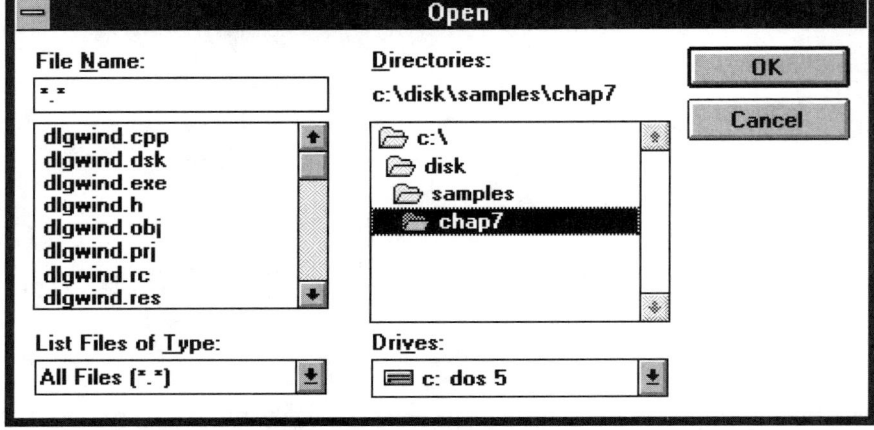

7-3
A file open common dialog box displayed by a VFileOpenDialog object.

Adding the dialog to FileView is a trivial operation. Just create the dialog and execute it:

```
Boolean FileView::OpenCommand(VEventRef event)
{
    if (open_dlg == 0)
        open_dlg = new VFileOpenDialog(this);
    if (open_dlg->Execute() == IDOK)
    {
        HCURSOR old_cursor = SetCursor(wait_cursor);
        SetBuffer(open_dlg->GetFilename(), True);
        SetCursor(old_cursor);
    }
    UNREFERENCED_PARAMETER(event);
    return True;
}
```

This function first checks the `open_dlg` data member to see if the dialog already has been created. If it has not, the function creates it. The dialog is not deleted, so it exists until the user exits the program.

Because the dialog is never deleted, it remembers previous settings every time the user displays it. If the user changes the drive and directory in the dialog box once, it continues to display the files in that location until the user changes them again.

Although it does occupy more memory, this scheme solves a common interface problem. Few things are more aggravating than having to repeatedly give the same instructions to a program. The VFileOpenDialog is an example of allowing the user to control the program rather than the program controlling the user. Instead of forcing the user to open files in the same directory every time, the file open dialog remembers previous settings.

After the OpenCommand function creates the dialog, it displays it with the Execute function. The return value from the Execute function reflects the button the user pressed to dismiss the dialog. If the user dismisses the dialog with the Cancel button, changes to data in the dialog are discarded.

If the user presses the Ok button, the program can load the selected file into FileView. Before loading the file, it changes the cursor into an hourglass to inform the user that the program is active but might not be available for a short period of time.

Managing the printer

The next two items on FileView's File menu manage the program's interaction with the printer. Two methods handle this interaction:

```
Boolean FileView::PrintCommand(VEventRef event)
{
    if (print_dlg == 0)
        print_dlg = new VPrintDialog(this);
    if (setup_dlg != 0)
            *print_dlg = *((VPrintDialogPtr)setup_dlg);
    if (print_dlg->Execute() == IDOK)
    {
       // handle printing operations here
       VInfoBox printBox(this, 'Printing document');
       printBox.Execute();
    }
    UNREFERENCED_PARAMETER(event);
    return True;
}
```

The PrintCommand method creates a VPrintDialog object (FIG. 7-4), which prompts the user for information about a single printing operation.

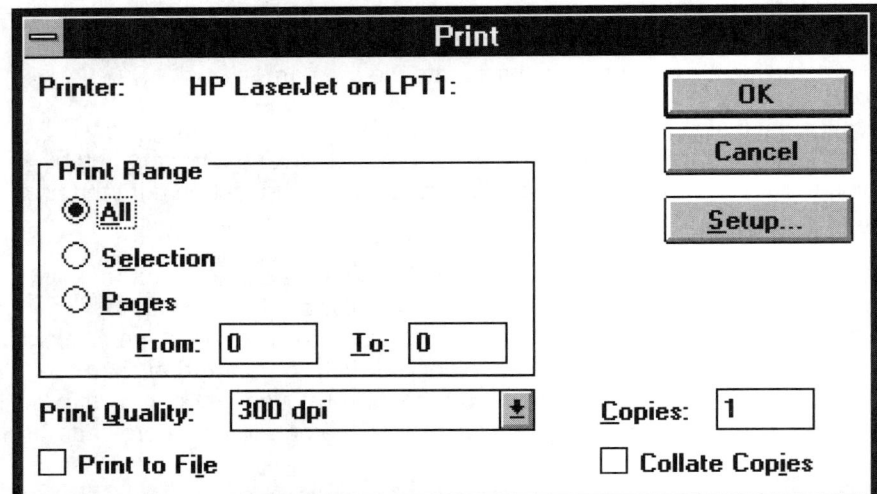

7-4
A print dialog box displayed by a VPrintDialog object.

```
Boolean FileView::PrintSetupCommand(VEventRef event)
{
    if (setup_dlg == 0)
        setup_dlg = new VPrintSetupDialog(this);
    if (print_dlg != 0)
        *setup_dlg = *print_dlg;
    setup_dlg->Execute();
    UNREFERENCED_PARAMETER(event);
    return True;
}
```

The PrintSetupCommand method creates a VPrintSetup object (FIG. 7-5) to allow the user to set printer settings that affect future operations.

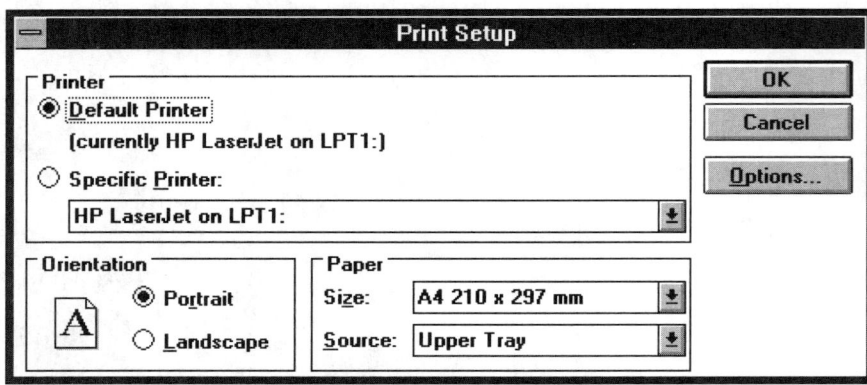

7-5
A print setup dialog box displayed by a VPrintSetupDialog object.

 Dialog & message boxes

The PrintCommand and PrintSetupCommand reference both the `print_dlg` and the `setup_dlg` to keep printer settings synchronized between the two dialogs. For example:

```
*setup_dlg = *print_dlg;
```

The user can access a print setup dialog from the Setup button on the print dialog and, therefore, can change setting on the target printer or switch to a different printer. To accommodate this synchronization, both classes provide an overloaded assignment operator. The VPrintDialog's operator just copies the PRINTDLG structure:

```
VPrintDialogRef VPrintDialog::operator =(VPrintDialogCRef copy)
{
    pd = copy.pd;
    return *this;
}
```

The VPrintSetupDialog's operator calls the VPrintDialog's operator, then sets a flag to tell the PrintDlg function to display only the print setup dialog:

```
VPrintSetupDialogRef::operator =(VPrintDialogCRef copy)
{
    VPrintDialog::operator =(copy);
    pd.Flags |= PD_PRINTSETUP;
    return *this;
}
```

The previous assignment operator is a good example of how C++ treats overloaded operators. The operator can be called in two different ways. First, as an operator:

```
*setup_dlg = *print_dlg;
```

The assignment operator makes the two classes behave just like built-in types; however, behind the scenes, the compiler translates this statement into a function call. The VPrintSetupDialog's assignment operator calls the VPrintDialog function directly:

```
VPrintDialog::operator =(copy);
```

The goal is to reduce the amount of code necessary to complete an operation. Because a VPrintSetupDialog is a specialized form of VPrintDialog, I can reuse its assignment operator without duplicating code.

The remainder of the VPrintDialog and VPrintSetupDialog is very similar to the VFileOpenDialog I covered in the last section. The PrintCommand function isn't complete, I'll finish it in chapter 10. The PrintSetupCommand, as simple as it is, won't need any further modification.

Selecting a font with the VFontDialog class

The FontCommand function creates a VFontDialog object (FIG. 7-6), which allows the user to choose the font used when displaying files. The function is very similar to others that manage a common dialog box object:

```
Boolean DialogWindow::FontCommand(VEventRef event)
{
    if (font_dlg == 0)
        font_dlg = new VFontDialog(this);

    if (font_dlg->Execute() == IDOK)
    {
        VInfoBox infoBox(this, font_dlg->GetStyle());
        infoBox.Execute();
    }
    UNREFERENCED_PARAMETER(event);
    return True;
}
```

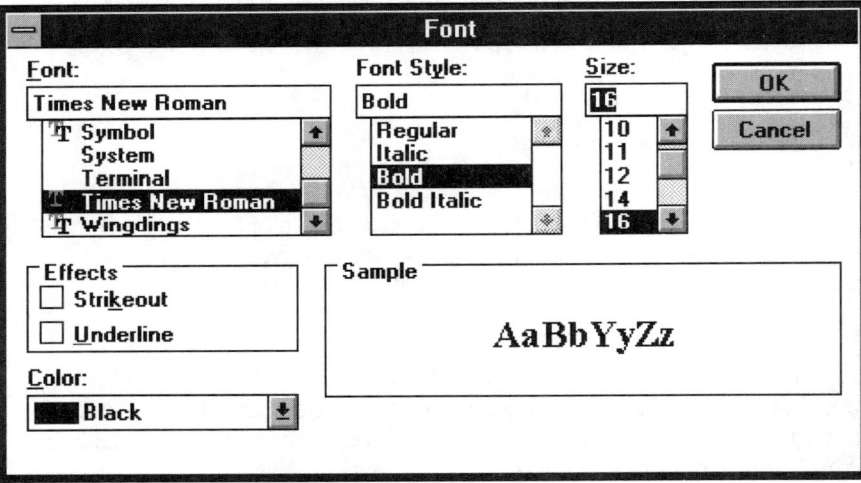

7-6
A Windows common font dialog box displayed by a VFontDialog object.

Setting colors with the VColorDialog class

The ForegroundCommand and BackgroundCommand functions both create a VColorDialog object (FIG. 7-7), which offers an interface to the standard Windows color selection dialog. The color selection dialog probably is the most striking of the new common dialogs (the illustration doesn't do it justice because it's not in color). The code to create the dialog is similar to that used for the other common dialog boxes:

```
Boolean DialogWindow::ForegroundCommand(VEventRef event)
{
    if (fore_dlg == 0)
        fore_dlg = new VColorDialog(this);
```

```
    if (fore_dlg->Execute() == IDOK)
    {
        VInfoBox infoBox(this,
                    "Selected foreground color");
        infoBox.Execute();
    }
    UNREFERENCED_PARAMETER(event);
    return True;
}

Boolean DialogWindow::BackgroundCommand(VEventRef event)
{
    if (back_dlg == 0)
        back_dlg = new VColorDialog(this);

    if (back_dlg->Execute() == IDOK)
    {
        VInfoBox infoBox(this,
                "Selected background color");
        infoBox.Execute();
    }
    UNREFERENCED_PARAMETER(event);
    return True;
}
```

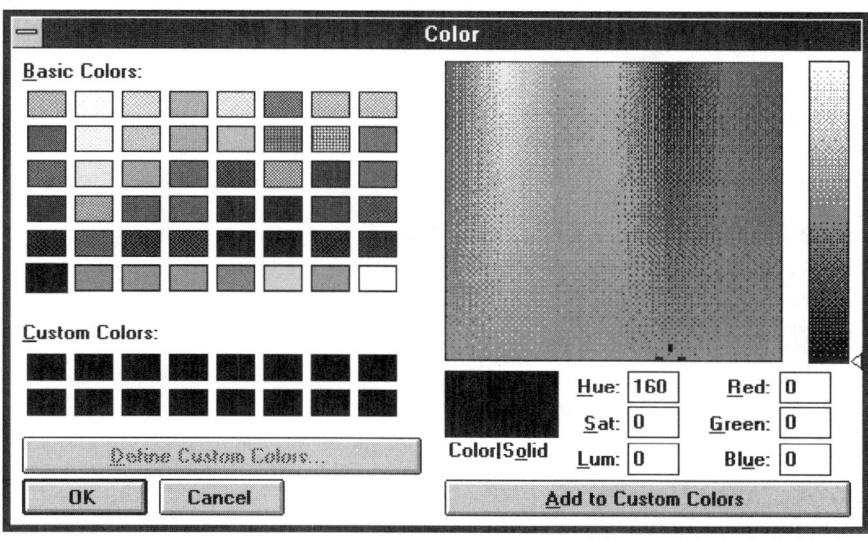

7-7
A Windows common color dialog box displayed by a VColorDialog object.

Search for text with the VFindDialog class

The SearchCommand function displays the last of the Windows common dialogs: the find and replace dialog (FIG. 7-8) represented by the VFindDialog class:

```
Boolean DialogWindow::SearchCommand(VEventRef event)
{
    if (srch_dlg == 0)
    {
        srch_dlg = new VFindDialog(this);
        AddAction((VAction)&DialogWindow::SearchAction,
                  VFindDialog::find_replace_message);
    }
    srch_dlg->Execute();
    UNREFERENCED_PARAMETER(event);
    return True;
}
```

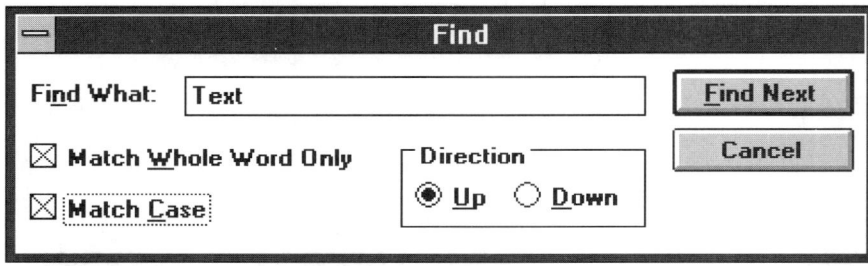

7-8
A find dialog displayed by a VFindDialog object.

While the function is similar in appearance to those managing other common dialogs, there is an important difference. The VFindDialog is a modeless, rather than modal dialog.

A modal dialog, like the font or color choosers, steals the input focus from its parent window when it is displayed. The user must either accept or dismiss the dialog before they can resume in the main application. Because they are simpler to manage, most dialogs are modal.

A modeless dialog offers more flexibility at the cost of more complexity in managing the dialog and the information it collects. The user can continue to work in the main application window while the modeless dialog is displayed.

For example, if the user wishes to search for a string of characters in a text editor, they can display the find dialog to enter the string to search for. When they accept the dialog by pressing the Search button, the editor's cursor is placed on the first occurrence of the target string. To search for the next occurrence, they just press the search button again.

Because the dialog is modeless, the data it collects is not available immediately after the dialog is executed. Instead, a second function is activated when the user presses the Search button:

```
Boolean DialogWindow::SearchAction(VEventRef event)
{
    VFindDialogPtr thisDialog =
      VFindDialog::GetDialogObject(event.GetLParam());
    if (thisDialog->IsClosing())
    {
        delete thisDialog;
        srch_dlg = 0;
    }
    else
    {
        VInfoBox infoBox(this,
           thisDialog->GetSearchString());
        infoBox.Execute();
    }
    return True;
}
```

The SearchAction function is invoked when the user presses either the Search or Cancel buttons on the dialog. The function first checks to see if the user dismissed the dialog. If the user did so, the function deletes the dialog object. If not, it retrieves the search string and displays it in a message box.

The VFindDialog class illustrates another useful feature of the Vista message dispatching scheme: the use of dynamic, or registered, message identifiers. Windows uses three different types of messages:

- System Messages, which start at 0 and run through WM_USER-1, which are global to all applications on the system.
- User Messages, those above WM_USER through 0x7FFF. These are unique to a single application.
- Registered Messages (or string messages), which are unique message identifiers shared between applications.

The VFindDialog retrieves the value of the registered message used by the search dialog using the RegisterMessage API function in its constructor and stores it in a static member variable:

```
VFindDialog::VFindDialog(...)
{
   if (!find_replace_message)
      find_replace_message =
              RegisterWindowMessage(FINDMSGSTRING);
   //...
}
```

Windows common dialogs 133

The FINDMSGSTRING identifier is registered by the common dialog DLL the first time a find dialog is created. The identifier will not change again until the system is restarted. The call to RegisterWindowMessage just returns the registered identifier, it doesn't actually register the message.

After I retrieve the message identifier, the SearchCommand function adds an action method to the object's dispatch array to handle events with the message's identifier:

```
AddAction((VAction)&DialogWindow::SearchAction,
          VFindDialog::find_replace_message);
```

Now, whenever the window receives a registered message from the find dialog, its object can invoke the proper member function.

Registered messages aren't unique to the common dialogs; they can be an excellent way of communicating between your own applications. By using registered messages, you can be sure that the action taken when a message is received is the intended action.

What's next

In this chapter, I looked at standard dialog boxes supplied with Windows. I showed you how each of the dialogs is used in an application, with the standard interface provided by the Vista framework. I also examined the use of registered window messages in communicating with the common dialogs and among applications. In the next chapter, I'll look at using custom dialog boxes to interact with your program's users.

8 Child window control objects

The common dialog boxes covered in the last chapter are great for standardizing common operations, but most programs are much more specialized in their data collection requirements. In this chapter, I'll look at using custom dialog boxes and child window controls to perform more specialized tasks.

Child window controls

As I discussed previously, Windows programs use child window controls to partition a window into distinct areas, each offering its own unique behavior. The push buttons, check boxes, and list boxes you saw on the dialogs in chapter 7 are all examples of child window controls.

A child window control actually is a specialized form of window that has its own window procedure and communicates with its parent window using messages. The parent window reacts to notification of user events from each control. In a C program, this can result in a huge switch statement to handle all the notifications provided by each of its child window controls.

Vista simplifies interaction between a parent window or dialog and its controls. It provides a set of classes (FIG. 8-1) that standardize the interface between the parent and its child objects.

The VControl class, at the top of the hierarchy, provides the operations common to all control objects. It provides a special Create method to allow you to create control objects from the controls specified in a resource script.

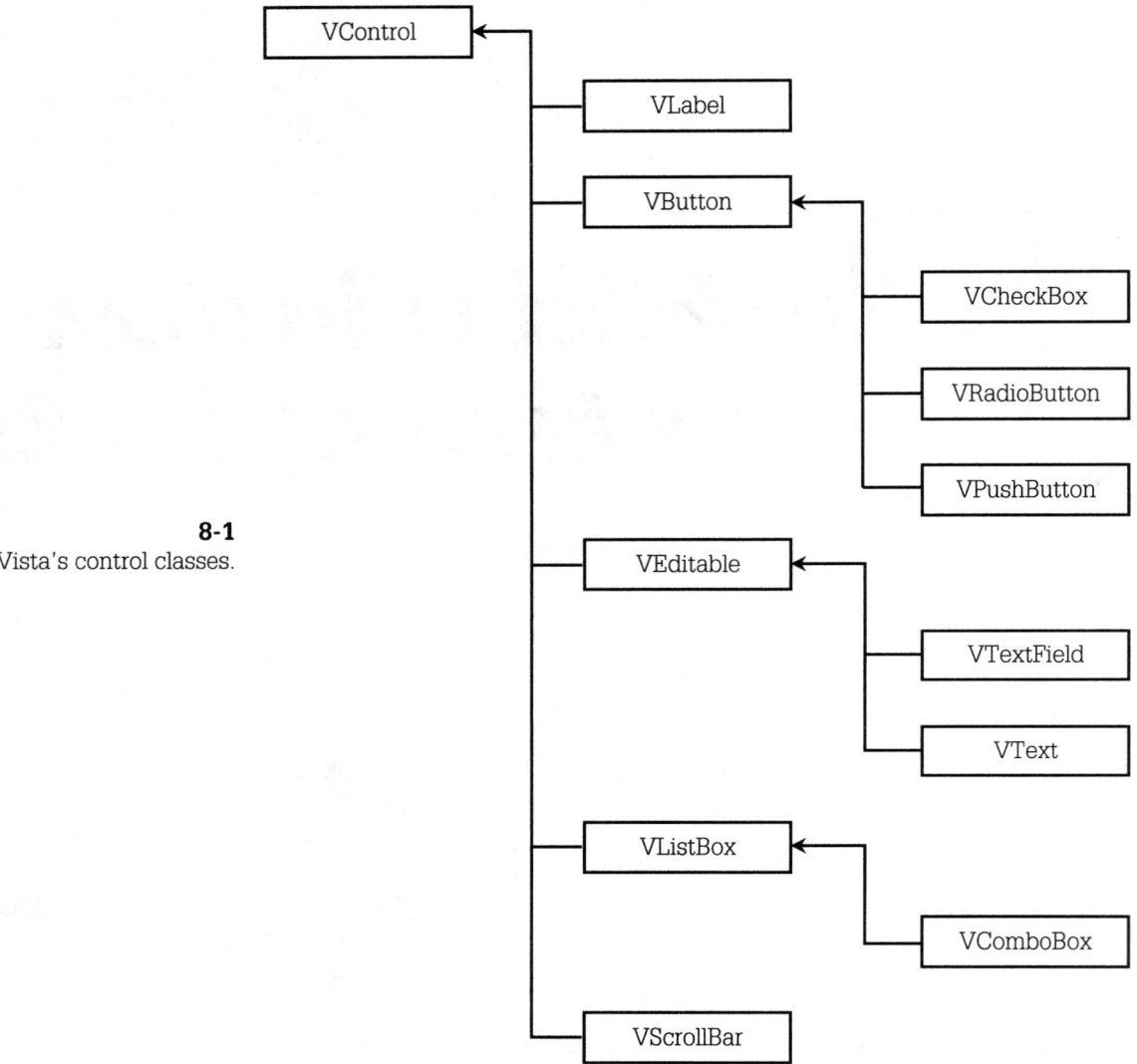

8-1
Vista's control classes.

It also provides empty data transfer and cut, copy, and paste functions that serve as placeholders for subclasses.

The remaining classes in the control hierarchy provide different operations suitable for each type of control. The appendix contains the code and headers for each of the control classes.

Attaching data objects to a dialog box

The Vista library provides a simple mechanism for attaching your program's data structures to the dialog boxes that collect and display the information in those structures. By using the TDataDialog template, you can construct a dialog that serves as a sort of clearing house for another type of object.

For example, suppose you were building an order entry system and needed a dialog to display product information. A simple product object might look like this:

```
struct Product
{
    char product_id[10];
    char description[30];
    char unit[8];
    int on_hand;
    int on_order;
    bcd price;
    Boolean exportable;
    Boolean quantity_discount;
};
```

In a C program, you would set the value of text fields and check box controls in the WM_INITDIALOG case of the product dialog's dialog procedure:

```
Product product;
// ...

BOOL CALLBACK _export ProductDlgProc(HWND hDlg, UINT message,
                                     WPARAM wParam, LPARAM lParam)
{
    switch(message)
    {
        case WM_INITDIALOG:
            // set text of the controls
            SetDlgItemText(hDlg, IDC_PRODUCT_ID,
                        product.product_id);
            // ...
            return TRUE;
        case WM_COMMAND:
            switch (wParam)
            {
                case IDOK:
                    // get text from controls
                    GetDlgItemString(hWnd,
                        IDC_PRODUCT_ID,
                        product.product_id,
                        sizeof(product.product_id));
                    // ...
```

```
                        return TRUE;
            }
    }
    return FALSE;
}
```

When you consider that most Windows program have many such dialogs, you can see why they become so large. The code to transfer every data element to and from every control can become quite unmanageable.

Vista objects provide a much simpler way of doing the same thing. Just build a ProductDialog object to represent the dialog box and attach an instance of the product structure to the dialog in its constructor:

```
class ProductDialog : public TDataDialog<Product>
{
    ProductDialog(VCompositePtr parent,
                Product _FAR *buffer)
        : TDataDialog(parent, buffer)
    {
        new VTextField(this, IDC_PRODUCT_ID,
                sizeof(data_buffer->product_id));
        //...
    }
};
// ...
ProductDialogPtr dialog =
    new TDataDialog(this, "PRODUCT_INFO", &product);
if (dialog->Execute() == IDOK)
  // pass the structure back to a database...
```

The VDataDialog class transfers information from the structure into the controls representing each field before the dialog is displayed. The user then can enter changes to the structure, and, when the dialog is accepted, the VDataDialog class transfers information from the dialog's controls back into the data structure. Instead of writing (and debugging) the code to transfer data yourself, let objects do the transfer on their own.

Each control class implements its own data transfer functions to move information to and from the dialog's attached object. VEditable objects access character arrays, VRadioButton and VCheckBox objects access Boolean variables. VScrollBar, VListBox, and VComboBox objects define their own structures to set and retrieve values from their respective windows. TABLE 8-1 lists the different control classes and their respective transfer buffer types.

Table 8-1
Standard Windows controls and their transfer data types.

Control object	Windows class	Transfer data type
VButton	BUTTON	none
VCheckBox	BUTTON	Boolean
VComboBox	COMBOBOX	VComboData
VEditable VText VTextField	EDIT	char array
VListBox	LISTBOX	VListData
VRadioButton	BUTTON	Boolean
VScrollBar	SCROLLBAR	VScrollData

Control objects handle the transfer of a single data item's value to and from the window associated with the object. Therefore, it is relatively simple to extend the transfer mechanism to perform data conversions. For example, an IntegerEdit control can convert the string in an edit control to and from an integer:

```
void IntegerEdit::ReadBuffer(voidPtr buffer)
{
    char string[32];
    int number = *((int _FAR *)buffer);
    itoa(number, string, 10);
    SetText(string);
}

void IntegerEdit::WriteBuffer(voidPtr buffer)
{
    char string[32];

    int number;
    GetText(string);
    number = atoi(string);
    *((int _FAR *)buffer) = number;
}

int IntegerEdit::GetBufferSize(void)
{
    return sizeof(int);
}
```

The VDataDialog object calls each control's ReadBuffer method to gather their information from the attached object before the dialog is displayed.

Attaching data objects to a dialog box

Likewise, when the dialog is closed successfully, the object calls each control's WriteBuffer method to transfer the information back into the attached object. The end result of using attached objects to transfer data is a significant reduction in code.

Besides drastically reducing the amount of code required to implement a dialog box, object attachment provides other benefits. The VDataDialog class is a template class; the data type of the attached object is passed as a parameter to the template. The compiler won't allow you to pass the wrong data type in a descendant class's constructor. For example, if you try to pass a Customer object to a dialog expecting a Product object, your program won't compile.

Another benefit provided by attached objects is reentrancy. In a multi-threaded environment like Windows NT, global variables in a program will cause problems when you try to split it into multiple threads of execution. If two threads (which can run simultaneously) try to update an object at the same time, the object will very likely become corrupted. Global variables also can cause problems in MDI applications, which I'll discuss in the next chapter.

The ability to run a thread in a program without affecting other threads is called *reentrancy*: a thread can be interrupted and later reenter its execution without any unexpected side-effects. Global variables used by more than one thread will sooner or later run into problems with reentrancy. To get around this problem in C, programs use a window property that points to a handle for the data structure:

```
HANDLE hProduct = LocalAlloc(sizeof(Product), LHND);
Product *product = LocalLock(hProduct);
// fill the structure...

SetProp(hDlg, "DATA", hProduct);
```

Then, when the program needs to access the structure, it retrieves the property and locks the handle to access the structure pointer:

```
HANDLE hProduct = GetProp(hDlg, "DATA");
Product *product = LocalLock(hProduct);
// access the structure ...
```

Using an attached object is a simpler solution. A data object belongs to the parent window instead of residing in some global variable:

```
class OrderWindow : public VFrame
{
    // ...

    protected:
```

```
        Product product;
        // ...

        Boolean ProductCommand(VEventRef event)
        {
            ProductDlg dlg = new ProductDlg(this,
                                                address);
            dlg->Execute();
            return True;
        }
        // ...
};
```

In this example, the OrderWindow object owns the Product data object. Every time the user calls up a ProductDlg, it is displayed with its previous settings. If any other window needs to use a ProductDlg, it defines its own Product object to attach to the dialog.

Vista's object attachment scheme solves some of the reentrancy problems inherent in a multithreaded environment; however, it doesn't address problems dealing with synchronization of displayed information.

For example, suppose your program displays a window or modeless dialog containing a customer order. While viewing this dialog, they decide to update a product record to increase the price of an item on the order. Does the program update the order? How does the order dialog know that the product object was updated? Multi-user applications can complicate this situation even more.

There are a number of solutions to this problem. The simplest probably would be an event broadcasted by the product dialog telling all active windows that its object was updated. Another solution could be smart data objects that have knowledge of dependencies between objects. The details of either solution are beyond the scope of this book, but synchronization is an issue to keep in mind when writing your own programs.

The VDataDialog is an ideal mechanism for separating the objects in your application from the objects used in presentation. It enforces a principle used in GUI application development called *dialog independence*, which separates the form of a program from its function.

The object attachment mechanism reduces your program's dependence on the underlying windowing system, increasing portability. Instead of setting and getting values of controls to set individual data members, attach the data to a dialog. You then can concentrate on the logic unique to your application.

The address book sample application (ADDRESS.CPP) in LISTING 8-1 illustrates attaching a member object to a dialog box. Its resource script (ADDRESS.H) is contained in LISTING 8-2, and the common header file (ADDRC.H) is in LISTING 8-3.

Listing 8-1
ADDRESS.CPP

```
/* --------------------------------------------------------------
   address.cpp

        An address book program that illustrates using custom dialog
        boxes

   Copyright (c) 1992, by Jeff Mackay - TAB Books

   -------------------------------------------------------------- */
#pragma hdrfile "vista.sym"
#include <vista.h>
#pragma hdrstop

#include "addrc.h"
#include <vdlgbox.h>
#include <vallctl.h>


struct Address
{
    char name[31];
    char addr1[31];
    char addr2[31];
    char city[26];
    char state[3];
    char zip_code[10];
    char home_phone[15];
    char work_phone[15];
    char fax_phone[15];
};


STDCLASS(AddressDlg);

class _CLASSTYPE AddressDlg : public VDialogBox
{
    public:
        AddressDlg(VCompositePtr par, Address _FAR *addr);
};


AddressDlg::AddressDlg(VCompositePtr par, Address _FAR *addr)
    : VDialogBox(par, "", "ADDRESS_BOOK")
{
    AttachBuffer(addr, sizeof(*addr));
    new VTextField(this, IDC_NAME,
        sizeof(addr->name));
    new VTextField(this, IDC_ADDR1,
        sizeof(addr->addr1));
```

```cpp
        new VTextField(this, IDC_ADDR2,
            sizeof(addr->addr2));
        new VTextField(this, IDC_CITY,
            sizeof(addr->city));
        new VTextField(this, IDC_STATE,
            sizeof(addr->state));
        new VTextField(this, IDC_ZIPCODE,
            sizeof(addr->zip_code));
        new VTextField(this, IDC_HOMEPHONE,
            sizeof(addr->home_phone));
        new VTextField(this, IDC_WORKPHONE,
            sizeof(addr->work_phone));
        new VTextField(this, IDC_FAXPHONE,
            sizeof(addr->fax_phone));
    }

STDCLASS(LookupDlg);

class _CLASSTYPE LookupDlg : public VDialogBox
{
    public:

        LookupDlg(VCompositePtr par, Address _FAR *addr)
          : VDialogBox(par, "", "ADDRESS_LOOKUP")
        {
            global = this;
            AttachBuffer(addr, sizeof(*addr));
            SetDialogStyle(ModelessDialog);
            new VTextField(this, IDC_LOOKUPNAME,
                                        sizeof(addr->name));
        }

        static LookupDlgPtr GetGlobal(void)
        {
            return global;
        }

        LookupDlg(void)
        {
            global = 0;
        }

    protected:
        virtual void InitActions(void)
        {
            VDialogBox::InitActions();
            AddCommand((VAction)&LookupDlg::SearchCommand, IDC_LOOKUPNAME);
        }

        Boolean SearchCommand(VEventRef event)
        {
```

Listing 8-1
Continued.

```
            memset(data_buffer, '\0', sizeof(Address));

            // perform a search here

            WriteBuffer();

            // display the address
            AddressDlgPtr dlg =
                    new AddressDlg(parent,
                                (Address _FAR *)data_buffer);
            dlg->Execute();
            return True;
        }

    private:
        static LookupDlgPtr global;
};

LookupDlgPtr LookupDlg::global;

STDCLASS(AboutDlg);
class _CLASSTYPE AboutDlg : public VDialogBox
{
    public:
        AboutDlg(VCompositePtr par)
            : VDialogBox(par, "", "ABOUT_ADDRESS") {}
};



STDCLASS(AddrWindow);
class _CLASSTYPE AddrWindow  : public VFrame
{

private:
    struct Address         address;

public:

        AddrWindow(void) : VFrame(NULL, "Address Book")
        {
        memset(&address, '\0', sizeof(address));
        menu = new VMenu(this, "ADDRESS_MENU");
        }

        AddrWindow(void)
        {
        }

    virtual void InitWinClass(WNDCLASSRef wndClass)
        {
```

```cpp
        VFrame::InitWinClass(wndClass);
        wndClass.hIcon = LoadIcon(GetApplication(),
                                                    "ADDRESS_ICON");
    }

    charPtr ClassName(void) const
    {
        return "AddrBook";
    }

    virtual void InitActions(void);
    virtual Boolean NewCommand(VEventRef event);
    virtual Boolean OpenCommand(VEventRef event);
    virtual Boolean SaveCommand(VEventRef event);
    virtual Boolean SaveAsCommand(VEventRef event);
    virtual Boolean NewAddrCommand(VEventRef event);
    virtual Boolean LookupCommand(VEventRef event);
    virtual Boolean AboutCommand(VEventRef event);
};

Boolean AddrWindow::NewCommand(VEventRef event)
{
    UNREFERENCED_PARAMETER(event);
    return True;
}


Boolean AddrWindow::OpenCommand(VEventRef event)
{
    UNREFERENCED_PARAMETER(event);
    return True;
}


Boolean AddrWindow::SaveCommand(VEventRef event)
{
    UNREFERENCED_PARAMETER(event);
    return True;
}


Boolean AddrWindow::SaveAsCommand(VEventRef event)
{
    UNREFERENCED_PARAMETER(event);
    return True;
}


Boolean AddrWindow::NewAddrCommand(VEventRef event)
{
```

Listing 8-1
Continued.

```
        AddressDlgPtr dlg = new AddressDlg(this, &address);
        dlg->Execute();
        UNREFERENCED_PARAMETER(event);
        return True;
    }


    Boolean AddrWindow::LookupCommand(VEventRef event)
    {
        LookupDlgPtr dlg = LookupDlg::GetGlobal();
        if (dlg)
            SetFocus(*dlg);
        else
        {
            dlg = new LookupDlg(this, &address);
            dlg->Execute();
        }
        UNREFERENCED_PARAMETER(event);
        return True;
    }


    Boolean AddrWindow::AboutCommand(VEventRef event)
    {
        AboutDlgPtr dlg = new AboutDlg(this);
        dlg->Execute();
        UNREFERENCED_PARAMETER(event);
        return True;
    }

    void AddrWindow::InitActions(void)
    {
        AddCommand((VAction)&AddrWindow::NewCommand, IDM_NEW);
        AddCommand((VAction)&AddrWindow::OpenCommand, IDM_OPEN);
        AddCommand((VAction)&AddrWindow::SaveCommand, IDM_SAVE);
        AddCommand((VAction)&AddrWindow::SaveAsCommand, IDM_SAVEAS);
        AddCommand((VAction)&AddrWindow::NewAddrCommand, IDM_NEWADDR);
        AddCommand((VAction)&AddrWindow::LookupCommand, IDM_LOOKUP);
        AddCommand((VAction)&AddrWindow::AboutCommand, IDM_ABOUT);
    }


    class AddrBookApp : public VAppl
    {
    public:
            AddrBookApp(const charPtr name, HINSTANCE inst,
                                HINSTANCE prevInst,
                                charPtr cmdLine, int cmdShow) :
                VAppl(name, inst, prevInst, cmdLine, cmdShow) {}

            AddrBookApp(void)
```

```
                {
                        delete main_window;
                }

                void InitWindow(void)
                {
                        main_window = new AddrWindow();
                }

};


int PASCAL WinMain(HINSTANCE hInstance, HINSTANCE hPrevInstance,
                                LPSTR lpszCmdLine, int nCmdShow)
{
        AddrBookApp addrApp("Address Book",hInstance,hPrevInstance,
                                        lpszCmdLine,nCmdShow);

        return addrApp.Run();
}
```

Listing 8-2
ADDRESS.RD

```
#include "addrc.h"

ADDRESS_BOOK DIALOG 21, 19, 287, 140
STYLE DS_MODALFRAME | WS_POPUP | WS_VISIBLE | WS_CAPTION | WS_SYSMENU
CAPTION "Addresses"
FONT 10, "Arial"
BEGIN
        EDITTEXT IDC_NAME,      39, 12, 240, 12,
           ES_LEFT | WS_CHILD | WS_VISIBLE | WS_BORDER |
                WS_TABSTOP
        EDITTEXT IDC_ADDR1,     64, 31, 214, 12,
           ES_LEFT | WS_CHILD | WS_VISIBLE | WS_BORDER |
                WS_TABSTOP
        EDITTEXT IDC_ADDR2,     64, 51, 215, 12,
           ES_LEFT | WS_CHILD | WS_VISIBLE | WS_BORDER |
                WS_TABSTOP
        EDITTEXT IDC_CITY,      28, 72, 99, 12,
           ES_LEFT | ES_AUTOHSCROLL | WS_CHILD | WS_VISIBLE |
                WS_BORDER | WS_TABSTOP
        EDITTEXT IDC_STATE,     157, 72, 24, 12,
           ES_LEFT | WS_CHILD | WS_VISIBLE | WS_BORDER |
                WS_TABSTOP
        EDITTEXT IDC_ZIPCODE,   230, 72, 48, 12,
           ES_LEFT | WS_CHILD | WS_VISIBLE | WS_BORDER |
                WS_TABSTOP
        EDITTEXT IDC_HOMEPHONE, 32, 92, 63, 12,
           ES_LEFT | ES_AUTOHSCROLL | WS_CHILD | WS_VISIBLE |
```

Listing 8-2
Continued.

```
                WS_BORDER | WS_TABSTOP
        EDITTEXT IDC_WORKPHONE, 125, 92, 64,  12,
            ES_LEFT | ES_AUTOHSCROLL | WS_CHILD | WS_VISIBLE |
                WS_BORDER | WS_TABSTOP
        EDITTEXT IDC_FAXPHONE,  219, 92, 56,  12,
            ES_LEFT | ES_AUTOHSCROLL | WS_CHILD | WS_VISIBLE |
                WS_BORDER | WS_TABSTOP
        DEFPUSHBUTTON "&Ok", IDOK, 40, 120, 36, 14,
            WS_CHILD | WS_VISIBLE | WS_TABSTOP
        PUSHBUTTON "&Cancel", IDCANCEL, 129, 120, 36, 14,
            WS_CHILD | WS_VISIBLE | WS_TABSTOP
        PUSHBUTTON "&Help", IDHELP, 218, 120, 36, 14,
            WS_CHILD | WS_VISIBLE | WS_TABSTOP
        LTEXT "Name", -1, 8, 15, 20, 8,
            WS_CHILD | WS_VISIBLE | WS_GROUP
        LTEXT "Address Line 1", -1, 8, 35, 52, 8,
            WS_CHILD | WS_VISIBLE | WS_GROUP
        LTEXT "Address Line 2", -1, 8, 55, 52, 8,
            WS_CHILD | WS_VISIBLE | WS_GROUP
        LTEXT "City", -1, 8, 76, 16, 8,
            WS_CHILD | WS_VISIBLE | WS_GROUP
        LTEXT "State", -1, 136, 76, 20, 8,
            WS_CHILD | WS_VISIBLE | WS_GROUP
        LTEXT "Zip Code", -1, 196, 76, 32, 8,
            WS_CHILD | WS_VISIBLE | WS_GROUP
        LTEXT "Home", -1, 8, 96, 24, 8,
            WS_CHILD | WS_VISIBLE | WS_GROUP
        LTEXT "Work", -1, 100, 96, 20, 8,
            WS_CHILD | WS_VISIBLE | WS_GROUP
        LTEXT "Fax", -1, 200, 96, 16, 8,
            WS_CHILD | WS_VISIBLE | WS_GROUP
END

ADDRESS_MENU MENU
BEGIN
        POPUP "&File"
        BEGIN
                MENUITEM "&New", IDM_NEW
                MENUITEM "&Open...", IDM_OPEN
                MENUITEM "&Save", IDM_SAVE
                MENUITEM "Save &as...", IDM_SAVEAS
                MENUITEM "E&xit", IDM_EXIT
        END

        POPUP "&Addresses"
        BEGIN
                MENUITEM "&New...", IDM_NEWADDR
                MENUITEM "&Lookup...", IDM_LOOKUP
        END

        POPUP "&Help"
```

```
        BEGIN
                MENUITEM "&About", IDM_ABOUT
        END
END

ADDRESS_LOOKUP DIALOG 17, 20, 207, 92
STYLE DS_MODALFRAME | WS_POPUP | WS_CAPTION | WS_SYSMENU
CAPTION "Lookup Address"
FONT 10, "Arial"
BEGIN
        LTEXT "Name", -1, 16, 28, 20, 8,
            WS_CHILD | WS_VISIBLE | WS_GROUP
        EDITTEXT IDC_LOOKUPNAME, 52, 24, 140, 12,
            ES_LEFT | WS_CHILD | WS_VISIBLE | WS_BORDER |
                WS_TABSTOP
        DEFPUSHBUTTON "&Search", IDC_SEARCH, 19, 62, 24, 14,
            WS_CHILD | WS_VISIBLE | WS_TABSTOP
        PUSHBUTTON "&Cancel", IDCANCEL, 91, 63, 32, 14,
            WS_CHILD | WS_VISIBLE | WS_TABSTOP
        PUSHBUTTON "&Help", IDHELP, 167, 64, 24, 14,
            WS_CHILD | WS_VISIBLE | WS_TABSTOP
END


ABOUT_ADDRESS DIALOG 18, 18, 174, 47
STYLE DS_MODALFRAME | WS_POPUP | WS_CAPTION | WS_SYSMENU
CAPTION "About Address Book"
FONT 10, "Arial"
BEGIN
        CONTROL "ADDRESS_ICON", -1, "STATIC",
            SS_ICON | WS_CHILD | WS_VISIBLE | WS_GROUP,
                11, 6, 16, 16
        LTEXT "Address Book", -1, 39, 9, 64, 8,
            WS_CHILD | WS_VISIBLE | WS_GROUP
        LTEXT "Version 1.0", -1, 40, 21, 80, 8,
            WS_CHILD | WS_VISIBLE | WS_GROUP
        LTEXT "Copyright c 1992, Your Name Here",
                -1, 38, 33, 124, 8,
            WS_CHILD | WS_VISIBLE | WS_GROUP
        PUSHBUTTON "&Ok", IDOK, 128, 8, 32, 12,
            WS_CHILD | WS_VISIBLE | WS_TABSTOP
END


ADDRESS_ICON ICON "address.ico"



#define IDC_NAME        1001
#define IDC_ADDR1       1002
#define IDC_ADDR2       1003
```

Listing 8-3
ADDR.C.H

Listing 8-2
Continued.

```
#define IDC_CITY          1004
#define IDC_STATE         1005
#define IDC_ZIPCODE       1006
#define IDC_HOMEPHONE     1007
#define IDC_WORKPHONE     1008
#define IDC_FAXPHONE      1009
#define IDC_LOOKUPNAME    1010
#define IDM_OPEN          102
#define IDM_NEW           101
#define IDM_SAVE          103
#define IDM_SAVEAS        104
#define IDM_EXIT          105
#define IDM_NEWADDR       201
#define IDM_LOOKUP        202
#define IDM_ABOUT         301
#define IDC_SEARCH-       2001
```

Data validation with controls

An important task for any application is validating the data accepted from the user. Objects derived from the VControl class can provide two types of data validation: character-level and field-level.

Character-level validation

Character-level validation is most appropriate for objects derived from the VEditable class. It verifies the validity of each character typed by the user before it reaches the control.

For example, an AlphaTextField object implements an alphabetic character-level validation scheme by intercepting WM_CHAR messages:

```
AddAction((VAction)&AlphaTextField::CharAction,
          WM_CHAR);

Boolean AlphaTextField::CharAction(VEventRef event)
{
    char newKey = event.GetWParam();
    if (iscntrl(newKey) || isalpha(newKey)
                        || isspace(newKey))
        return False;
    else
    {
        MessageBeep(MB_ICONEXCLAMATION);
        return True;
    }
}
```

The WM_CHAR message is sent to a control whenever the user types a character. This function checks the value of the key typed, only allowing alphabetic, space, and control characters to pass through to the control's window procedure. If any other characters are encountered, it beeps to inform the user and returns True to intercept the event.

This same type of validation can be performed to provide numeric validation (signed, unsigned, floating point, etc.) or for validation based on a character mask similar to that used by Borland's dBASE or Paradox products. You could even support regular expressions in a character mask to provide more sophisticated support.

Field-level validation

Although key-level validation can be useful, it often is necessary to provide more sophisticated validation. If an object needs more sophisticated validation, it can be provided at the field level. As part of the object attachment scheme, the VDataDialog cooperates with the objects derived from the VControl class to validate the contents of fields before writing them to an attached object.

The IsValid method is the mechanism Vista uses to perform field-level validation. Before transfer data into an attached object, a dialog object loops through all its child control objects, calling their IsValid method. If any child control object returns False, the dialog won't transfer data into the attached object.

Custom controls

The dialogs I've looked at until now have used only the standard Windows controls. However, many applications need more capabilities than they can find in the standard Windows control set. To address this problem, many vendors are providing their own sets of custom controls that complement or replace those offered by Windows.

There are several ways of using custom controls with Vista objects. First, if the control is based on a standard Windows control, you can use the Vista class representing that base control class directly if you load the controls from a resource script. Second, you can define your own classes to represent the custom control. For example, the following class provides access to the BorBtn class from the Borland Windows Custom Controls library:

```
class _CLASSTYPE VBorBtn : public VButton
{
    public:
        VBorBtn(VCompositePtr parent, int resourceId)
            : VButton(parent, resourceId) {}
    // ....
    virtual const charPtr ClassName(void) const
    {
        return "VBorBtn";
    }
    virtual const charPtr OldClassName(void) const
    {
        return "BORBTN";
    }
    // ...
};
```

The key methods in this class are the ClassName and OldClassName functions. When Vista creates a control object, it uses two different techniques, depending on how the object is being created.

If the control is not created from a resource, Vista registers a new class named by ClassName that "inherits" most of the attributes of the class identified by the name returned by OldClassName. When it registers the class, Vista saves the address of the old window procedure and sets the class window procedure to the VWindow's WindowProc function.

This technique, known as *superclassing*, allows Vista to intercept any messages directed to the control. It translates them into events and reroutes the events to member functions of the object representing the control. If the object doesn't filter an event, the event's message is passed to the control's original window procedure.

The second technique, used when control objects are created from a resource script, is called *subclassing*. Instead of creating a new class, Vista saves the custom control's window procedure and replaces it with VWindow's WindowProc function. The control then will act just as it would had it been superclassed as described earlier.

Both techniques are necessary because Vista gets involved at different points in the window creation process. When you create a control from scratch, Vista can create the new window class. This is more efficient than subclassing every new control— the old window procedure needs to be stored only once.

However, when you create a control object to represent a control created from a dialog resource, Vista doesn't get involved until the control's window has been created. Instead of destroying the original control and recreating it with a Vista class name, Vista just subclasses the original control.

The bottom line is that you need to supply both a ClassName and an OldClassName function. Most custom controls offer additional features through messages. To provide a consistent interface, you also should provide member functions that take care of sending these messages to the control.

Using global window messages

The majority of messages used by controls are local to an application. They usually are identified by a constant that references the value WM_USER. Controls can use messages in the range WM_USER through 0x7FFF for their own private messages. Because the identifiers are constant, you can define action methods for these message just as you would any standard message.

However, some controls use global window message identifiers that are available to all programs but are not constant. Vista's event dispatcher was designed with this capability in mind. To define a member function based on a global message, first register the appropriate message name:

```
void CustomApp::InitApplication(void)
{
    MsgId = RegisterWindowMessage("MessageName");
    VFrame::InitApplication();
}
```

Make sure this function is called before any instance of an object using the message is created. Calling directly from WinMain or the application object's InitApplication method would accomplish this.

Use the name of the variable hold the message identifier when you add the action to handle the message:

```
CustomClass::InitActions(void)
{
    AddAction((VAction)&CustomClass:GlobalMsgAction, MsgId);
}
```

In this example, Vista will call the GlobalMsgAction function whenever a CustomClass object receives a message with the identifier contained in MsgId.

Moving C programs to Vista

In many Windows programs, interacting with dialog boxes and verifying the user responses make up the majority of the program. Converting these programs to Vista can have a significant impact on the size of the program.

The first step is to create a dialog object and, in its constructor, create control objects for all the controls that will collect data from the user. The next step is to get rid of all that code that moves values to and from the controls and replace it with an attached object.

The third step is more complicated: validating data. If the program uses some common routines to perform validation for specific controls, create your own control classes that perform that validation. Another option is to override the WriteBuffer method, validate the content of each control, and chain to the VDialogBox WriteBuffer method.

What's next

In this chapter, I examined child window controls and their use in Vista programs. I also showed you how attached objects can greatly simplify program development by handling many of the details involved in interacting with the user. In the next chapter, I'll look at a different model of user interaction: the Multiple Document Interface.

9 MDI window objects

Many Windows applications deal with more than one type of object at a time or offer multiple views on the same type of object. To standardize the behavior of these multi-object applications, Microsoft introduced the Multiple Document Interface (MDI) standard. In this chapter, I'll look at the Multiple Document Interface and discuss strategies to use in developing your own MDI programs.

The Multiple Document Interface

MDI was introduced to simplify programs that allow the user to manipulate multiple documents. The interface includes three different types of windows: an MDI frame window that serves as the application's main window, MDI child windows to present a view of a document, and an MDI client window that manages an MDI frame's child windows.

Figure 9-1 illustrates an MDI application that you should by now be very familiar with: the Borland C++ IDE. Each time you edit a source file, the IDE places it in its own MDI child window. By taking advantage of the features of the MDI interface, the IDE allows you to tile, cascade, minimize, and maximize child windows.

The best feature of the MDI interface is that all those child window management operations are automatic; you don't need to implement the behavior yourself. The Vista framework simplifies the interface even more so

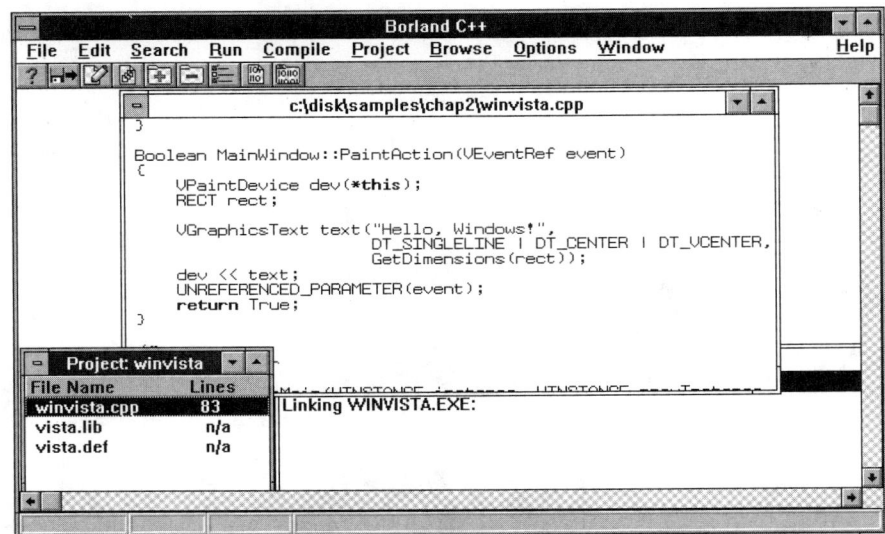

9-1
The Borland C++ IDE uses the MDI interface.

that creating an MDI application is almost as simple as creating any other Windows program.

Vista MDI classes

One of the more complicated aspects of MDI programming is figuring out where to send messages for child window management. Messages can pass from a child to the client, from the client to the parent, from the parent to the client, or from a child directly to the parent. Although many of the operations can be boilerplated from one application to another, it still takes some effort to copy and debug the code.

Vista presents a simplified interface consisting of two classes: VMdiFrame to represent an MDI frame window and VMdiChild to represent the child windows. Operations provided by the client window are encapsulated within the VMdiFrame class. For all practical purposes, the client window no longer exists, although the VMdiClient class is provided in case you need to override the default behavior of the client window.

Managing child windows

Most of the child management functions are provided by the VMdiFrame class, you only need to add a Window menu with predefined items to your frame object. The first example, a minimal MDI program, illustrates the use of the predefined commands. The resource file, MDI.RC, is listed in LISTING 9-1. The code for the program itself, MDI.CPP, is in LISTING 9-2.

Listing 9-1
MDI.RC: resource script for the MDI sample application.

```
#include <vistarc.h>

PARENT_MENU MENU
BEGIN
        POPUP "&File"
        BEGIN
                MENUITEM "&New Window", VID_MDINEWWIN
                MENUITEM "&Close", VID_MDICLOSE
                MENUITEM "E&xit", VID_EXIT
        END

        POPUP "&Window"
        BEGIN
                MENUITEM "&Tile", VID_MDITILE
                MENUITEM "Tile &vertically", VID_MDITILEHORIZ
                MENUITEM "&Cascade", VID_MDICASCADE
                MENUITEM "Arrange &icons", VID_MDIARRANGE
                MENUITEM "Close &all", VID_MDICLOSEALL
        END

END
```

Listing 9-2
MDI.CPP: source code for the MDI sample application.

```
/* --------------------------------------------------------
   mdi.cpp

        A simple MDI application.

   Copyright (C) 1992, by Jeff Mackay - TAB Books
   -------------------------------------------------- */
#pragma hdrfile "vista.sym"
#include <vista.h>
#pragma hdrstop

#include <vmdifrm.h>
#include "mdi.h"

const int WINDOW_MENU_POS = 1;

class MdiWindow  : public VMdiFrame
{

public:
        MdiWindow(void);

protected:
        virtual void InitActions(void);
        virtual Boolean NewChildAction(VEventRef event);

private:
        int child_count;
};
```

Listing 9-2
Continued.

```
MdiWindow::MdiWindow(void)
        : VMdiFrame(NULL, "Sample MDI Window")
{
        child_count = 0;
    SetWindowMenuPos(WINDOW_MENU_POS);
        menu = new VMenu(this, "PARENT_MENU");
}

Boolean MdiWindow::NewChildAction(VEventRef event)
{
        child_count++;
        TCHAR title[10];
        wsprintf(title, "Child %d", child_count);
        VMdiChildPtr child = new VMdiChild(this, title);
        child->Create();
        child->Show();
    UNREFERENCED_PARAMETER(event);
        return True;
}

void MdiWindow::InitActions(void)
{
    VMdiFrame::InitActions();
        AddCommand((VAction) &MdiWindow::NewChildAction,
                                    VID_MDINEWWIN);
}

class MdiApp : public VAppl
{
public:
        MdiApp(charPtr name, HINSTANCE inst, HINSTANCE prevInst,
                        LPSTR cmdLine, int cmdShow) :
            VAppl(name, inst, prevInst, cmdLine, cmdShow) {}

        void InitWindow(void)
        {
                main_window = new MdiWindow();
        }

};


int PASCAL WinMain(HINSTANCE hInstance, HINSTANCE hPrevInstance,
                                    LPSTR lpszCmdLine, int nCmdShow)
{
        MdiApp mdiApp("MDI Sample",hInstance,hPrevInstance,
                                    lpszCmdLine,nCmdShow);

        return mdiApp.Run();
}
```

The NewChildAction function creates a new MDI child window. It keeps a counter of the number of children created, and displays that number as the child's title (FIG. 9-2):

```
Boolean MdiWindow::NewChildAction(VEventRef event)
{
    child_count++;
    TCHAR title[10];
    wsprintf(title, "Child %d", child_count);
    VMdiChildPtr child = new VMdiChild(this, title);
    child->Create();
    child->>Show();
    UNREFERENCED_PARAMETER(event);
    return True;
}
```

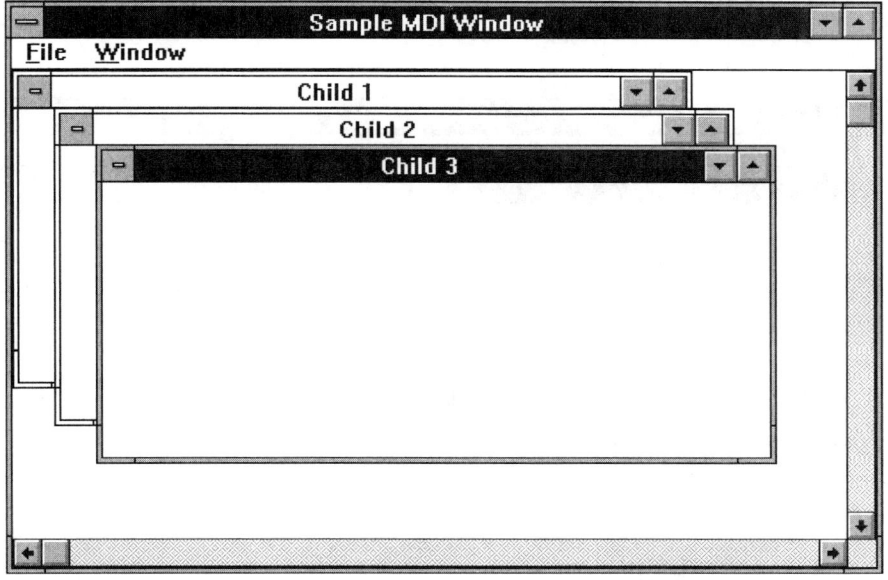

9-2
Output from the MDI sample application.

By convention, all MDI applications include a Window menu that contains options to allow the user to manage the program's child windows (FIG. 9-3). Most of these just arrange child windows and icons. The Tile command tiles the windows so that they fill the entire client are of the MDI frame window, with enough space left over to display the icons for any minimized windows (FIG. 9-4).

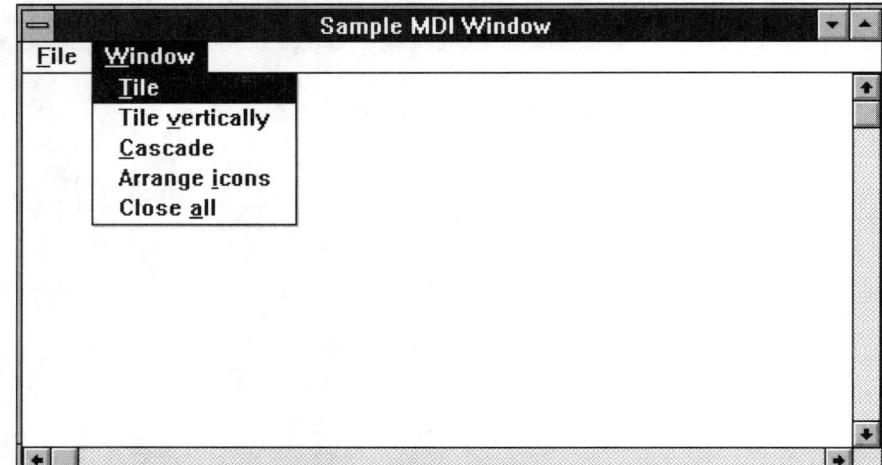

9-3
A sample window menu, common to most MDI applications.

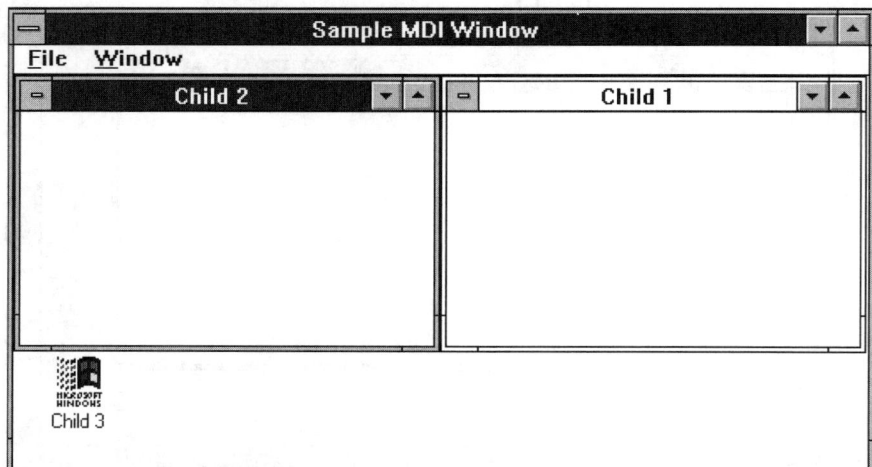

9-4
A tiled MDI window.

The Cascade command arranges the child windows so that they are layered on top of each other, with title bars visible (FIG. 9-5). The arrangement of child windows is handled behind the scenes by the VMdiFrame class:

```
Boolean VMdiFrame::CascadeCommand(VEventRef event)
{
    client->CascadeChildren();
    UNREFERENCED_PARAMETER(event);
    return True;
}
```

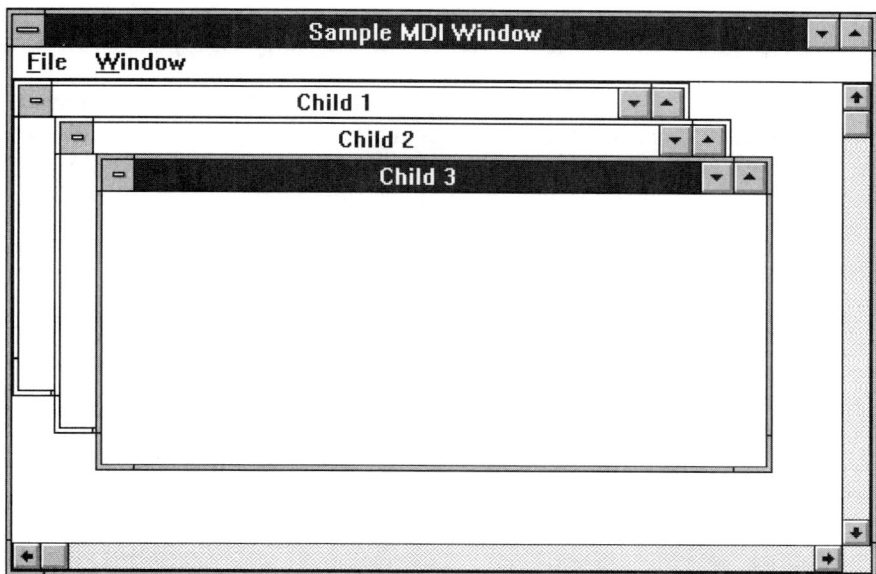

9-5
A cascaded MDI window.

The child management functions are made available to every descendant of the VMdiFrame class through its InitActions member function:

```
void VMdiFrame::InitActions(void)
{
    VFrame::InitActions();
    AddCommand((VAction)&VMdiFrame::CloseCommand,
               VID_MDICLOSE);
    AddCommand((VAction)&VMdiFrame::CloseAllCommand,
               VID_MDICLOSEALL);
    AddCommand((VAction)&VMdiFrame::TileCommand,
               VID_MDITILE);
    AddCommand((VAction)&VMdiFrame::TileCommand,
               VID_MDITILEVERT);
    AddCommand((VAction)&VMdiFrame::CascadeCommand,
               VID_MDICASCADE);
    AddCommand((VAction)&VMdiFrame::ArrangeCommand,
               VID_MDIARRANGE);
}
```

The CloseCommand closes the active MDI child window after calling its QueryClose member function. The CloseAllCommand loops through all MDI child windows and closes each one. The remaining functions: TileCommand, CascadeCommand, and ArrangeCommand all arrange child windows.

Cooperation between the MDI frame and MDI client objects is the key to the simplicity of the Vista MDI interface: the two classes have a special relationship. Although the frame is the most visible entity on the screen, the client object does most of the work. Most of the operations provided by the VMdiFrame class simply forward a request to the client object.

There also is some cooperation between the frame and MDI child windows. The VMdiChild class overrides the Create method supplied by the VWindow class. Instead of directly creating a window using the CreateWindow API function, the VMdiChild's Create method calls its parent's CreateMdiChild method to create a window:

```
void VMdiFrame::CreateMdiChild(VMdiChildPtr child)
{
    VASSERT(child != 0);
    client->CreateChild(child);
}
```

The CreateMdiChild method, in turn, forwards the request to its client object, which fills an MDICREATESTRUCT with information about the child window and sends a WM_MDICREATE message to the client window:

```
void VMdiClient::CreateChild(VMdiChildPtr child)
{
    MDICREATESTRUCT createStruct;
    RECT rect;
    child->GetDimensions(rect);
    createStruct.szClass = child->ClassName();
    createStruct.szTitle = child->GetCaption();
    createStruct.hOwner  = child->appl;
    createStruct.x       = rect.left;
    createStruct.y       = rect.top;
    createStruct.cx      = rect.right;
    createStruct.cy      = rect.bottom;
    createStruct.style   = child->style;
    createStruct.lParam  = 0;

    VWindowPtr oldCreate = _VCreateWindow;
    _VCreateWindow = child;
    SendMessage(*this, WM_MDICREATE, 0,
                (LPARAM)&createStruct);
    _VCreateWindow = oldCreate;
}
```

The VMdiFrame class's DestroyMdiChild is similar. It forwards a request to the client object, which then sends a WM_MDIDESTROY message to the client window:

```
void VMdiClient::DestroyChild(VMdiChildPtr child)
{
 SendMessage(*this, WM_MDIDESTROY,
             (WPARAM)(HWND)*child, 0);
}
```

Swapping menus

The menu interface for MDI programs differs from that of a standard Windows program. Instead of presenting their own menus, MDI child windows borrow the menu bar of their parent window. When a child window is activated, it either adds its own commands to the parent's menu or swaps the parent's menu with its own. The Vista MDI classes provide a convenient way to use the latter approach. Each VMdiChild object can uses its own menu. When the object is activated and receives a WM_MDIACTIVATE event, it uses the SetMenu member function to swap menus with the parent.

The next example program, MDIMENU, consists of an MDI frame window with two different types of MDI child window objects, each with its own menu. The code for the program is in LISTING 9-3, and the resource file is in LISTING 9-4.

Listing 9-3
MDIMENU.CPP

```
/* -------------------------------------------------------
   mdimenu.cpp

        Example of swapping menus in an MDI program.

   Copyright (C) 1992, by Jeff Mackay
   ------------------------------------------------------- */
#pragma hdrfile "vista.sym"
#include <vista.h>
#pragma hdrstop

#include <vgrdev.h>
#include <vmdifrm.h>
#include "mdimenu.h"

STDCLASS(MdiWindow);
STDCLASS(RectWindow);
STDCLASS(HelloWindow);

class _CLASSTYPE HelloChild : public VMdiChild
{
        public:
                HelloChild(VMdiFramePtr par);

        protected:
                Boolean PaintAction(VEventRef event);
};

HelloChild::HelloChild(VMdiFramePtr par)
        : VMdiChild(par, "Hello Window")
{
        win_menu_pos = 2;
    menu = new VMenu(this, "HelloMenu");
}
```

Listing 9-3
Continued.

```
Boolean HelloChild::PaintAction(VEventRef event)
{
        VPaintDevice device(*this);
        TextOut(device, 20, 20, "Hello, World!", 13);
        UNREFERENCED_PARAMETER(event);
        return True;
}


class _CLASSTYPE RectChild : public VMdiChild
{
        public:
                RectChild(VMdiFramePtr par);

        protected:
        Boolean PaintAction(VEventRef event);
};


RectChild::RectChild(VMdiFramePtr par)
        : VMdiChild(par, "Rectangle Window")
{
        win_menu_pos = 2;
    menu = new VMenu(this, "RectMenu");
}


Boolean RectChild::PaintAction(VEventRef event)
{
        RECT rect;
        GetDimensions(rect);

        VPaintDevice device(*this);
        int height = (rect.bottom - rect.top) / 2;
        rect.top = height / 2;
        int width = (rect.right - rect.left) / 2;
        rect.left = width / 2;
        rect.bottom = rect.top + height;
        rect.right = rect.left + width;
        Rectangle(device, rect.left,
                        rect.top, rect.right, rect.bottom);
    UNREFERENCED_PARAMETER(event);
        return True;
}

class _CLASSTYPE MdiWindow  : public VMdiFrame
{
public:
        MdiWindow(void);

protected:
```

```cpp
        virtual void InitActions(void);
        virtual Boolean NewChildAction(VEventRef event);
private:
        int child_count;
};

MdiWindow::MdiWindow(void)
        : VMdiFrame(NULL, "MDI Menus")
{
        child_count = 0;
    SetWindowMenuPos(1);
        menu = new VMenu(this, "ParentMenu");
}


Boolean MdiWindow::NewChildAction(VEventRef event)
{
        child_count++;
        TCHAR title[10];
        wsprintf(title, "Child %d", child_count);
        VMdiChildPtr child;
        if (event.GetWParam() == IDM_NEWHELLOWIN)
                child = new HelloChild(this);
        else
                child = new RectChild(this);
        child->Create();
        child->Show();
    UNREFERENCED_PARAMETER(event);
        return True;
}


void MdiWindow::InitActions(void)
{
    VMdiFrame::InitActions();
        AddCommand((VAction) &MdiWindow::NewChildAction,
                   IDM_NEWHELLOWIN);
        AddCommand((VAction) &MdiWindow::NewChildAction,
                   IDM_NEWRECTWIN);
}


class _CLASSTYPE MdiApp : public VAppl
{
public:
        MdiApp(charPtr name, HINSTANCE inst, HINSTANCE prevInst,
                         LPSTR cmdLine, int cmdShow) :
             VAppl(name, inst, prevInst, cmdLine, cmdShow) {}
```

Listing 9-3
Continued.

```cpp
        void InitWindow(void)
        {
                main_window = new MdiWindow();
        }
};

int PASCAL WinMain(HINSTANCE hInstance, HINSTANCE hPrevInstance,
                                LPSTR lpszCmdLine, int nCmdShow)
{
        MdiApp mdiApp("MDI Sample",hInstance,hPrevInstance,
lpszCmdLine,nCmdShow);

        return mdiApp.Run();
}
```

Listing 9-4
MDIMENU.RC

```
#include "mdimenu.h"
#include <vistarc.h>

ParentMenu MENU
BEGIN
        POPUP "&File"
        BEGIN
                MENUITEM "New &Hello Child", IDM_NEWHELLOWIN
                MENUITEM "New &Rectangle Child", IDM_NEWRECTWIN
                MENUITEM "&Close", VID_MDICLOSE
                MENUITEM "E&xit", VID_EXIT
        END

        POPUP "&Window"
        BEGIN
                MENUITEM "&Tile", VID_MDITILE
                MENUITEM "Tile &vertically", VID_MDITILEHORIZ
                MENUITEM "&Cascade", VID_MDICASCADE
                MENUITEM "Arrange &icons", VID_MDIARRANGE
                MENUITEM "Close &all", VID_MDICLOSEALL
        END
END

HelloMenu MENU
BEGIN
        POPUP "&File"
        BEGIN
                MENUITEM "New &Hello Child", IDM_NEWHELLOWIN
                MENUITEM "New &Rectangle Child", IDM_NEWRECTWIN
                MENUITEM "&Close", VID_MDICLOSE
                MENUITEM "E&xit", VID_EXIT
        END
```

```
        POPUP "&Options"
        BEGIN
                MENUITEM "&Text Size", 101
    END

        POPUP "&Window"
        BEGIN
                MENUITEM "&Tile", VID_MDITILE
    MENUITEM "Tile &vertically", VID_MDITILEHORIZ
                MENUITEM "&Cascade", VID_MDICASCADE
                MENUITEM "Arrange &icons", VID_MDIARRANGE
                MENUITEM "Close &all", VID_MDICLOSEALL
        END
END

RectMenu MENU
BEGIN
        POPUP "&File"
        BEGIN
                MENUITEM "New &Hello Child", IDM_NEWHELLOWIN
    MENUITEM "New &Rectangle Child", IDM_NEWRECTWIN
                MENUITEM "&Close", VID_MDICLOSE
                MENUITEM "E&xit", VID_EXIT
        END

        POPUP "&Options"
        BEGIN
    MENUITEM "&Color...", 101
        END

        POPUP "&Window"
        BEGIN
                MENUITEM "&Tile", VID_MDITILE
    MENUITEM "Tile &vertically", VID_MDITILEHORIZ
                MENUITEM "&Cascade", VID_MDICASCADE
                MENUITEM "Arrange &icons", VID_MDIARRANGE
                MENUITEM "Close &all", VID_MDICLOSEALL
        END
END
```

Getting child windows to swap menus with the parent is simple. Just create a new menu object in the child's constructor and assign the index for the window menu to the window_menu_pos data member. The MDI classes take care of the rest.

To implement the menu sharing, you'll see more cooperation between the VMdiFrame and VMdiChild classes. When the user activates an MDI child window, Windows sends a WM_MDIACTIVATE message to the window. The VMdiChild's MdiActivateAction member function handles the event:

```
Boolean VMdiChild::MdiActivateAction(VEventRef event)
{
```

```
        if (event.GetWParam() == True)
            SetMenu(menu, win_menu_pos);
        else
            // if no other child is being activated, reset
            // the menu.
            if ((HWND)LOWORD(event.GetLParam())==0)
                SetMenu(0, 0);
        return False;
}
```

The parent's SetMenu member function retrieves the child's window pop-up menu and sends a WM_MDISETMENU message to the MDI frame window:

```
VMenuPtr VMdiFrame::SetMenu(VMenuPtr newMenu, int winPos)
{
    if (newMenu == 0)
    {
      newMenu = menu;
      winPos = win_menu_pos;
    }
    VPopupMenu windowMenu(*newMenu, winPos);
    SendMessage(*client, WM_MDISETMENU, 0,
                MAKELONG((HMENU)*newMenu,
                (HMENU)windowMenu));
    DrawMenuBar(*this);
    return newMenu;
}
```

When the MDI frame window receives the message, it swaps its current menu with the child's menu and fills the child's window menu with a list of the existing MDI child windows.

When the child receives a WM_MDIACTIVATE event to notify it that its window is being deactivated, it examines the event's LPARAM member, which contains handles for the window being activated and the window being deactivated. There are two possible scenarios here: either another child will be activated or this is the only active window and no other child will take the active role. If you're dealing with the former case, the child doesn't need to take any action at all because the newly activated child will tell the parent to swap the current menu with its own. If you're dealing with the latter case, the child object passes an invalid menu pointer, which tells the parent to swap back to its own menu.

The VMdiChild class goes a bit further to simplify MDI programs. It not only shares its menu with the parent VMdiFrame object, it also shares the frame's command actions. When a standard window receives a WM_COMMAND event, it tries to dispatch it to an action method, then passes it to the window's DefaultProc member function if the message isn't filtered. The VMDiChild class overrides that behavior to add some consistency to the menu sharing between an MDI child window and its parent. When the window receives a WM_COMMAND message, its CommandAction member function tries to route the event to a member function. If no member function filters the event, it is forwarded to the object's parent:

```
Boolean VMdiChild::CommandAction(VEventRef event)
{
  Boolean filtered = VFrame::CommandAction(event);
  if (!filtered)
  {
      filtered = (*parent)(event);
  }
  return filtered;
}
```

If you examine the menu definitions in FIG. 9-4, you'll notice that the File pop-ups are identical for the parent and both child menus. When the user selects a command in the File menu, the active child receives a WM_COMMAND message. However, because none of its member function filter the event, it passes it on to the parent object. The parent object then handles the event.

The menu-sharing scheme employed by the Vista MDI classes provides several benefits. First, it allows you to treat your child window objects as if they were standard window objects. No special effort is required to share a child's menu with the parent object. Second, the sharing of action methods between parent and child objects reduces dependencies between objects. Your child objects don't need to duplicate the operations implemented by the parent.

Object dependencies

Here's a note on dependencies between objects: the VMenu object originally called its parent Window's SetMenu method when it was created. For standard windows, this worked great—to switch menus on a window, all you needed to do was create a new menu object. However, this introduced a dependency between the menu object and its parent window: you couldn't create a menu object without changing the menu in the parent window. When I moved on to the MDI classes, this "feature" introduced several bugs. Eliminating the call to the SetMenu function got rid of the bug but forced me to go back and fix programs that used this feature. The moral of the story is: reduce dependencies between your objects as much as possible.

Most applications use MDI to provide access to multiple objects within a single program. However, the MDI frame window offers another feature that can be useful in other types of applications: icon management.

An MDI frame object manages its minimized windows by allowing the user to drag icons, providing an "arrange" operation to organize icons, and furnishing scroll bars when the frame contains too many icons to display at one time.

Unconventional MDI windows

This section presents an example that mimics some of the operations of the Windows Program Manager (FIG. 9-6). The main window is an MDI Frame object that manages multiple child windows, each of which also is an MDI Frame object. The child frames manage multiple icon window objects that allow the user to launch applications.

9-6 The Launcher application mimics the Program Manager.

The code for the sample application (the Vista Launcher), MDILNCH.CPP, is contained in LISTING 9-5. The code for the icon window object, ICONWND.CPP, is in LISTING 9-6. Its header file is shown in LISTING 9-7, and the header file for the program is in LISTING 9-8.

Listing 9-5
MDILNCH.RC

```
/* ----------------------------------------------------
   mdilnch.cpp

        Example of using MDI to manage icons.  Also
demonstrates
        use of drag and drop.
   Copyright (C) 1992, by Jeff Mackay - TAB Books
   ---------------------------------------------------- */
#pragma hdrfile "vista.sym"
#include <vista.h>
#pragma hdrstop


#include <shellapi.h>
#include <vmdifrm.h>
#include "lnchicon.h"
```

```cpp
STDCLASS(LaunchWindow);

class _CLASSTYPE LaunchWindow  : public VMdiFrame
{


public:
        LaunchWindow(void);

protected:
        virtual void InitActions(void);
        virtual Boolean DropFileAction(VEventRef event);
    virtual Boolean CreateAction(VEventRef event);
};


LaunchWindow::LaunchWindow(void)
        : VMdiFrame(NULL, "Vista Launcher")
{
}


void LaunchWindow::InitActions(void)
{
    VMdiFrame::InitActions();
        AddAction((VAction) &LaunchWindow::DropFileAction,
                    WM_DROPFILES);
}


Boolean LaunchWindow::CreateAction(VEventRef event)
{
    VMdiFrame::CreateAction(event);
        DragAcceptFiles(*this, True);
        return True;
}


Boolean LaunchWindow::DropFileAction(VEventRef event)
{
        char buffer[128];
     HDROP context = (HDROP)event.GetWParam();
        UINT count = DragQueryFile(context, 0xFFFF, buffer,
                                                    sizeof(buffer));
        for (int i=0; i<count; i++)
        {
                DragQueryFile(context, i, buffer, sizeof(buffer));
                ProgramIconPtr child = new ProgramIcon(this, buffer);
                child->Create();
        child->Show();
        }
```

Listing 9-5
Continued.

```
            DragFinish(context);
            client->ArrangeIcons();
            return True;
    }


    class MdiApp : public VAppl
    {
    public:
            MdiApp(charPtr name, HINSTANCE inst, HINSTANCE prevInst,
                            LPSTR cmdLine, int cmdShow) :
                    VAppl(name, inst, prevInst, cmdLine, cmdShow) {}

            void InitWindow(void)
            {
                    main_window = new LaunchWindow();
            }

    };
```

Listing 9-6
*LNCHICON.
      CP*

```
int PASCAL WinMain(HINSTANCE hInstance, HINSTANCE hPrevInstance,
                            LPSTR lpszCmdLine, int nCmdShow)
{
        MdiApp mdiApp("MDI Sample",hInstance,hPrevInstance,
                                    lpszCmdLine,nCmdShow);

        return mdiApp.Run();
}
/* ---------------------------------------------------------------
   lnchicon.cpp

        Implementation of the ProgramIcon class.

   Copyright (C) 1992, by Jeff Mackay - TAB Books
---------------------------------------------------------------- */

#pragma hdrfile "vista.sym"
#include <vista.h>
#pragma hdrstop

#include <vgrdev.h>
#include <vmsgbox.h>
#include <shellapi.h>
#include <commdlg.h>
#include "lnchicon.h"


ProgramIcon::ProgramIcon(VMdiFramePtr par, charPtr title)
        : VMdiChild(par, 0)
```

```cpp
{
        char name[32];
        program = title;
        GetFileTitle(program, name, sizeof(name));
        for(int i=0;i<sizeof(name)&&name[i]; i++)
                if (name[i] == '.')
                        name[i] = '\0';
        SetCaption(name);
        state = SW_SHOWMINIMIZED;
        style = WS_OVERLAPPED | WS_MINIMIZE | MDIS_ALLCHILDSTYLES;
        icon = ExtractIcon(appl, program, 0);
        if (icon == 0)
        {
        delete_flag = False;
                icon = LoadIcon(appl, IDI_APPLICATION);
        }
        else
        delete_flag = True;
}


ProgramIcon::ProgramIcon(void)
{
        if (delete_flag)
                DestroyIcon(icon);
        icon = 0;
}


void ProgramIcon::InitWinClass(WNDCLASSRef wndClass)
{
        VMdiChild::InitWinClass(wndClass);
        wndClass.style = CS_DBLCLKS;
        wndClass.hIcon = 0;
        wndClass.hCursor = 0;
}


void ProgramIcon::InitActions(void)
{
        VMdiChild::InitActions();
        AddAction((VAction)&ProgramIcon::QueryDragIconAction,
                        WM_QUERYDRAGICON);
        AddAction((VAction)&ProgramIcon::SysCommandAction,
                        WM_SYSCOMMAND);
        AddAction((VAction)&ProgramIcon::DoubleClickAction,
                        WM_NCLBUTTONDBLCLK);
}


Boolean ProgramIcon::PaintAction(VEventRef event)
{
```

Listing 9-6
Continued.

```
            VPaintDevice device(*this);
            DrawIcon(device, 0, 0, icon);
            UNREFERENCED_PARAMETER(event);
            return True;
    }


    Boolean ProgramIcon::QueryDragIconAction(VEventRef event)
    {
            event.SetResponse((LPARAM)MAKELONG(icon, 0));
            return True;
    }


    Boolean ProgramIcon::SysCommandAction(VEventRef event)
    {
            switch(event.GetWParam() & 0xFFF0)
            {
            case SC_SIZE:
            case SC_MINIMIZE:
            case SC_MAXIMIZE:
            case SC_MOUSEMENU:
            case SC_KEYMENU:
            case SC_RESTORE:
                    return True;
            default:
                        return False;
        }
    }
    Boolean ProgramIcon::DoubleClickAction(VEventRef event)
    {
            while (True)
        {
                    int returnCode = WinExec(program, SW_SHOWNORMAL);
                    if (returnCode < 32)
                    {
                            char buffer[128];
                            LoadString(appl, returnCode,
    buffer,
                                            sizeof(buffer));
                            VErrorBox errorBox(this, buffer);
                            returnCode = errorBox.Execute();
                            if (returnCode == IDRETRY)
                                    continue;
                    }
                    break;
            }
            UNREFERENCED_PARAMETER(event);
        return True;
    }
```

Listing 9-7
LNCHICON.H

```
/* ----------------------------------------------------------
   lnchicon.h

        Interface for the ProgramIcon class.

   Copyright (C) 1992, by Jeff Mackay - TAB Books
   ---------------------------------------------------- */
#ifndef _LNCHICON_H
#define _LNCHICON_H

#ifndef _VWINDOW_H
#include <vwindow.h>
#endif

#ifndef _VMDICHLD_H
#include <vmdichld.h>
#endif

STDCLASS(ProgramIcon)

class _CLASSTYPE ProgramIcon : public VMdiChild
{
  public:
        ProgramIcon(VMdiFramePtr par, charPtr title);
        ProgramIcon(void);


  protected:
        virtual void InitWinClass(WNDCLASSRef AWndClass);
        virtual void InitActions(void);
        virtual Boolean PaintAction(VEventRef event);
        virtual Boolean DoubleClickAction(VEventRef event);
        virtual Boolean QueryDragIconAction(VEventRef event);
        virtual Boolean SysCommandAction(VEventRef event);
        VString program;
        HICON   icon;
        Boolean delete_flag;
};

#endif
```

Listing 9-8
String table containing error messages that correspond to error codes returned by WinExec.

```
STRINGTABLE LOADONCALL DISCARDABLE
BEGIN
        0,      "Out of memory or corrupt executable file."
        2,      "File was not found."
        3,      "Path was not found."
        5,      "Sharing or network-protection error."
        8,      "Insufficient memory to start the application."
        10,     "Incorrect Windows version."
```

```
            11,     "Invalid executable file."
            13,     "Application was designed for MS-DOS 4.0."
            14,     "Type of executable file was unknown."
            15,     "Attempt was made to load a real-mode application."
            19,     "File must be decompressed before it can be loaded."
            20,     "Dynamic-link library (DLL) file was invalid."
            21,     "Application requires 32-bit extensions."
END
```

Besides illustrating the versatility of the MDI interface, the Launcher demonstrates another useful Windows feature. When you first run the launcher, it doesn't appear to be an MDI application because it has no menu bar. Instead of using a menu to interact with the user, the program uses the Windows drag-and-drop API to accept files that are dragged on top of it. It then displays the icon for the file and launches the program when the user double clicks on its icon. Let's examine the objects in the launcher program to see how the program works.

Drag-and-drop operations LaunchWindow class in MDILNCH.CPP is derived from VMdiFrame and provides the drag-and-drop interface for the program. Member functions in the class are minimal: two functions provide the entire interface. First, the object's CreateAction function calls the DragAcceptFiles API function to inform Windows that the object's window is interested in files dropped on it:

```
Boolean LaunchWindow::CreateAction(VEventRef event)
{
    VMdiFrame::CreateAction(event);
    DragAcceptFiles(*this, True);
    return True;
}
```

The other function, DropFileAction, is invoked in response to a WM_DROPFILES message. It retrieves information about the files dropped on the window and creates a ProgramIcon object for each file dropped:

```
Boolean LaunchWindow::DropFileAction(VEventRef event)
{
    char buffer[128];
    HDROP context = (HDROP)event.GetWParam();
    UINT count = DragQueryFile(context, 0xFFFF, buffer,
                               sizeof(buffer));
    for (int i=0; i<count; i++)
    {
        DragQueryFile(context, i, buffer, sizeof(buffer));
        ProgramIconPtr child = new ProgramIcon(this,
                                               buffer);
        child->Create();
        child->Show();
    }
}
```

```
    DragFinish(context);
    client->ArrangeIcons();
    return True;
}
```

You first call the DragQueryFile function to get the number of files dropped in the current operation. Then, you retrieve the name of each file dropped and create a new ProgramIcon object to represent the file. Finally, the function calls DragFinish to release memory allocated by the drag-and-drop interface.

The ProgramIcon class simulates an icon used by the program manager to represent a program. While each icon actually is an MDI child window, the ProgramIcon class intercepts some Windows system messages to inhibit the normal behavior of an MDI child window and make it act like an icon.

Simulating a program manager icon

The constructor for the ProgramIcon performs most of the initialization necessary for the object. It saves a copy of the program's file name and sets the caption for the window. Then, it sets its window's state and style attributes and retrieves the icon for the program:

```
ProgramIcon::ProgramIcon(VMdiFramePtr par, charPtr title)
    : VMdiChild(par, 0)
{
    char name[32];
    program = title;
    GetFileTitle(program, name, sizeof(name));
    for(int i=0;i<sizeof(name)&&name[i]; i++)
      if (name[i] == '.')
          name[i] = '\0';
    SetCaption(name);
    state = SW_SHOWMINIMIZED;
    style = WS_OVERLAPPED | WS_MINIMIZE |
            MDIS_ALLCHILDSTYLES;
    icon = ExtractIcon(appl, program, 0);
    if (icon == 0)
    {
        delete_flag = False;
        icon = LoadIcon(appl, IDI_APPLICATION);
    }
    else
        delete_flag = True;
}
```

The ExtractIcon API function, new with Windows 3.1, can be a great convenience. You pass it a program name and an index, and it returns an icon from the program's executable file. This is much easier than trying to read the executable and pull the icon from its resource section. Because both resource and executable formats change with Windows NT, the routine also is much more portable.

To complete initialization, the object's InitWinClass sets some of the members of the window's class structure to allow correct interaction with events:

```
void ProgramIcon::InitWinClass(WNDCLASSRef wndClass)
{
    VMdiChild::InitWinClass(wndClass);
    wndClass.style = CS_DBLCLKS;
    wndClass.hIcon = 0;
    wndClass.hCursor = 0;
}
```

Another method that seems unobtrusive but is very important is the GetClassName function. It returns a string identifying the window class for the ProgramIcon class. If you omit this function, all VMdiChild windows will be displayed with a null cursor—not the desired behavior.

By setting the hIcon and hCursor to 0, the program can draw its own icon and cursor when it is dragged around the window. Setting the CS_DBLCLKS style bit informs Windows that the class wants to receive double-click messages. It is much simpler to allow Windows to determine if two consecutive button clicks are close enough together (in both time and distance) to constitute a double-click, than to maintain state information and do it yourself.

The next notable member function in the ProgramIcon class is its SysCommandAction action method. Called in response to a WM_SYSCOMMAND message, this function disables the system menu and the system accelerators so that the window always stays minimized:

```
Boolean ProgramIcon::SysCommandAction(VEventRef event)
{
    switch(event.GetWParam() & 0xFFF0)
    {
    case SC_SIZE:
    case SC_MINIMIZE:
    case SC_MAXIMIZE:
    case SC_MOUSEMENU:
    case SC_KEYMENU:
    case SC_RESTORE:
            return True;
    default:
        return False;
   }
}
```

Because the window can never be maximized and its icon was set to 0 in the InitWinClass function, the PaintAction method just displays the icon for the window:

```
Boolean ProgramIcon::PaintAction(VEventRef event)
{
    VPaintDevice device(*this);
```

```
    DrawIcon(device, 0, 0, icon);
    UNREFERENCED_PARAMETER(event);
    return True;
}
```

The QueryDragIcon method, called in response to a WM_QUERYDRAGICON message, which is sent because I set the window class's icon to 0 in InitWinClass, responds with the handle to the object's icon. The system creates a black-and-white cursor for the icon and displays it as the icon is dragged.

```
Boolean ProgramIcon::QueryDragIconAction(VEventRef event)
{
    event.SetResponse((LPARAM)MAKELONG(icon, 0));
    return True;
}
```

The previous member functions all work together to simulate the visual behavior of a Program Manager icon. The only remaining member function, DoubleClickAction, called in response to a WM_NCLBUTTONDBLCLK message, implements the functional behavior of the icon. When the user double-clicks on an icon, the icon's program is executed with the WinExec function:

```
Boolean ProgramIcon::DoubleClickAction(VEventRef event)
{
    int returnCode = WinExec(program, SW_SHOWNORMAL);
    if (returnCode < 32)
    {
      char buffer[128];
      LoadString(appl, returnCode, buffer,
              sizeof(buffer));
      VErrorBox errorBox(this, buffer,
                      "Cannot execute program", MB_OK);
      errorBox.Execute();
    }
    UNREFERENCED_PARAMETER(event);
    return True;
}
```

An MDI FileView

Notice the response to errors from the WinExec function. The program's resource script includes a stringtable with messages for each of the possible errors returned from WinExec. The function loads the message corresponding to the error code and displays it in an error box. Windows 3.1 is much more robust in its error-handling than previous versions and reports most errors in a very understandable format. However, it still is better to display readable error messages to the user, than to rely on the system to do it for you.

As a final exercise in MDI applications, I'll convert the FileView program to use an MDI interface (Fig 9-7). Because the single-window version of

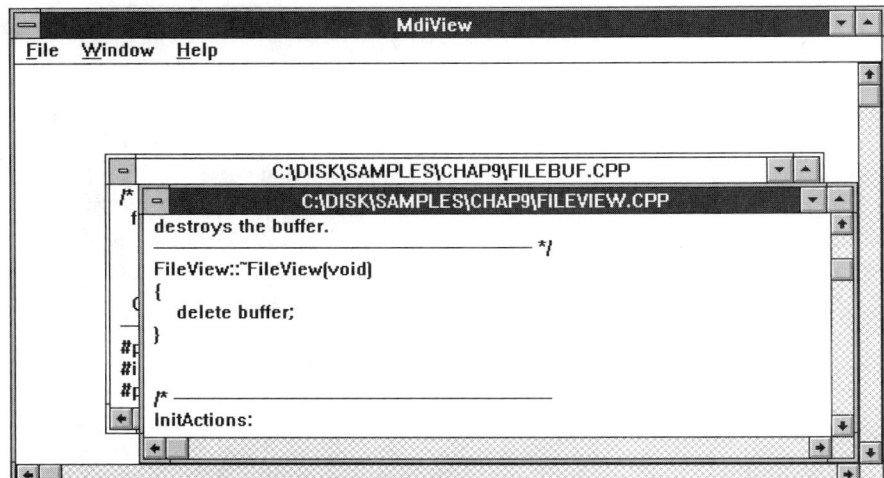

9-7
Output from the new MDIView program.

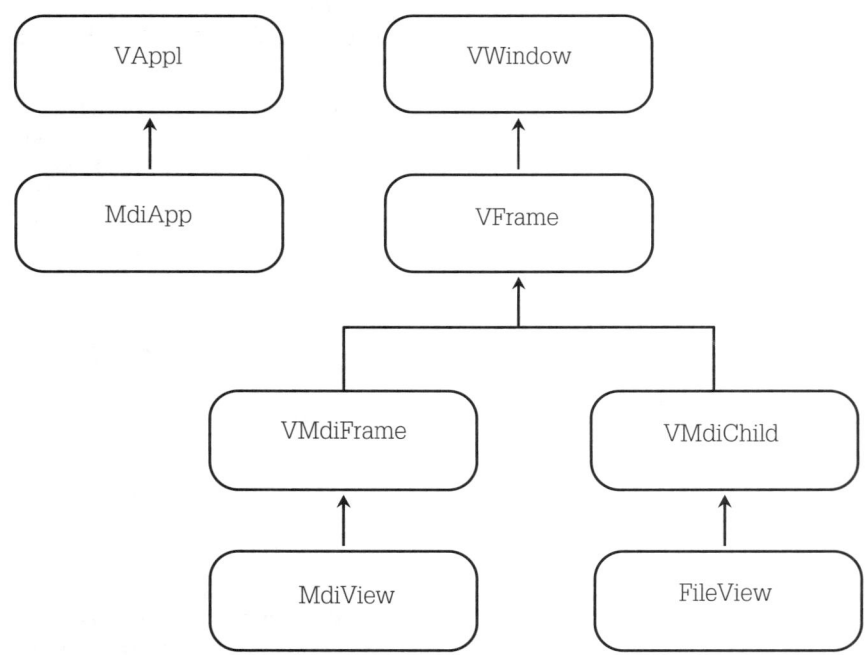

9-8
Class hierarchy for the MDIView program.

FileView was written with reusability in mind, the conversion is trivial. The MdiView program, diagrammed in FIG. 9-8, adds a new application and MDI frame object and makes some minor changes to the FileView object. The new application file, MDIAPP.CPP, is listed in LISTING 9-9, its resource script is in LISTING 9-10, and the updated FILEVIEW.CPP is in LISTING 9-11.

```cpp
/* -----------------------------------------------------------
    mdiview.cpp

            An MDI-style FileView
    Copyright (C) 1992, by Jeff Mackay
----------------------------------------------------------- */
#pragma hdrfile "vista.sym"
#include <vista.h>
#pragma hdrstop
#include <vappl.h>
#include "fvrc.h"
#include "fileview.h"


class MdiView : public VMdiFrame
{
        public:
                MdiView(charPtr initialFile);
                const charPtr ClassName(void) const
                {
                        return "MdiView";
                }


        protected:
        virtual void InitActions(void);
        virtual Boolean CreateAction(VEventRef event);
                virtual Boolean OpenCommand(VEventRef event);
        VFileOpenDialog *open_dlg;
                VString initial_file;
                HCURSOR wait_cursor;
};


MdiView::MdiView(charPtr initialFile)
    : VMdiFrame(0, "MdiView")
{
        initial_file = initialFile;
        menu = new VMenu(this, "MdiViewMenu");
    SetWindowMenuPos(2);
        wait_cursor = LoadCursor(GetApplication(), IDC_WAIT);
        open_dlg = 0;
}


void MdiView::InitActions(void)
{
    VMdiFrame::InitActions();
        AddCommand((VAction)&MdiView::OpenCommand, IDM_OPEN);
```

Listing 9-9
Continued.

```
}

Boolean MdiView::CreateAction(VEventRef event)
{
    VMdiFrame::CreateAction(event);
    if (initial_file.Length() > 0)
        new FileView(this, initial_file);
    return True;
}


Boolean MdiView::OpenCommand(VEventRef event)
{
    if (open_dlg == 0)
        open_dlg = new VFileOpenDialog(this);

    if (open_dlg->Execute() == IDOK)
    {
        HCURSOR old_cursor = SetCursor(wait_cursor);
        FileViewPtr child =
                new FileView(this, open_dlg->GetFilename());
        child->Create();
        child->Show();
        SetCursor(old_cursor);
    }

    UNREFERENCED_PARAMETER(event);
    return True;
}

class MdiViewApp : public VAppl
{
    public:
        MdiViewApp(HINSTANCE inst, HINSTANCE prev,
                LPSTR cmdLine, int cmdShow)
            : VAppl("MdiView", inst, prev, cmdLine, cmdShow)
        {
        }

        virtual void InitWindow(void)
        {
            main_window = new MdiView(cmd_line);
        }
};

int PASCAL WinMain(HINSTANCE inst, HINSTANCE prev,
                              LPSTR cmdLine, int cmdShow)
{
```

Listing 9-10
FILEVIEW.CPP

```
        MdiViewApp app(inst, prev, cmdLine, cmdShow);

        app.Run();
        return app.GetStatus();
}
/* -----------------------------------------------------------
   fileview.cpp

   Implementation of the FileView class.

 Copyright (C) 1992, by Jeff Mackay - TAB Books

------------------------------------------------------------- */
#pragma hdrfile "vista.sym"
#include <vista.h>
#pragma hdrstop

#include <dir.h>
#include <values.h>
#include <fstream.h>
#include <vappl.h>
#include <vmsgbox.h>
#include "fvrc.h"
#include "fileview.h"

FileView::FileView(VMdiFramePtr par, charPtr title)
  : VMdiChild(par, title), viewer(*this), fore_color(RGB(0,0,0)),
    back_color(RGB(255,255,255))
{
        menu = new VMenu(this, "FileView");
        win_menu_pos = 3;
     style |= WS_VSCROLL | WS_HSCROLL;

     buffer    = 0;
     open_dlg  = 0;
     print_dlg = 0;
     setup_dlg = 0;
     find_dlg  = 0;
     color_dlg = 0;
     font_dlg  = 0;
        SetBuffer(title, False);
}


FileView::FileView(void)
{
    delete buffer;
}


void FileView::InitActions(void)
```

Listing 9-10
Continued.

```
{
    VFrame::InitActions();
    AddCommand((VAction)&FileView::PrintCommand, IDM_PRINT);
    AddCommand((VAction)&FileView::PrintSetupCommand,
                    IDM_PRINTSETUP);
    AddCommand((VAction)&FileView::SearchCommand, IDM_SEARCH);
    AddCommand((VAction)&FileView::FontCommand, IDM_FONT);
    AddCommand((VAction)&FileView::ColorCommand, IDM_FOREGROUND);
    AddCommand((VAction)&FileView::ColorCommand, IDM_BACKGROUND);
}


Boolean FileView::PrintCommand(VEventRef event)
{
    if (print_dlg == 0)
        print_dlg = new VPrintDialog(this);

    if (setup_dlg != 0)
        *print_dlg = *((VPrintDialogPtr)setup_dlg);

    if (print_dlg->Execute() == IDOK)
    {
        // handle printing operations here
        VInfoBox printBox(this, "Printing document");
        printBox.Execute();
    }
    UNREFERENCED_PARAMETER(event);
    return True;
}


Boolean FileView::PrintSetupCommand(VEventRef event)
{
    if (setup_dlg == 0)
        setup_dlg = new VPrintSetupDialog(this);

    if (print_dlg != 0)
        *setup_dlg = *print_dlg;

    setup_dlg->Execute();

    UNREFERENCED_PARAMETER(event);
    return True;
}


Boolean FileView::SearchCommand(VEventRef event)
{
    find_dlg = new VFindDialog(this);
    find_dlg->Execute();
    UNREFERENCED_PARAMETER(event);
```

```cpp
    return True;
}


Boolean FileView::SearchAction(VEventRef event)
{
    UNREFERENCED_PARAMETER(event);
    return True;
}


Boolean FileView::FontCommand(VEventRef event)
{
    if (font_dlg == 0)
    {
        font_dlg = new VFontDialog(this);
        font_dlg->SetMinSize(8);
        font_dlg->SetMaxSize(24);
        font_dlg->TrueTypeOnly();
        font_dlg->FixedFontOnly();
    }

    if (font_dlg->Execute() == IDOK)
    {
        // reset the font used to display text
        font = font_dlg->GetFontObject();
    }
    UNREFERENCED_PARAMETER(event);
    return True;
}


Boolean FileView::ColorCommand(VEventRef event)
{
    VColorPtr current;
    if (event.GetId() == IDM_FOREGROUND)
        current = &fore_color;
    else
        current = &back_color;
    if (color_dlg == 0)
    {
        color_dlg = new VColorDialog(this);
    }
    color_dlg->SetColor(*current);
    if (color_dlg->Execute() == IDOK)
    {
        *current = color_dlg->GetNewColor();
    }
    UNREFERENCED_PARAMETER(event);
    return True;
}
```

Listing 9-10
Continued.

```cpp
Boolean FileView::PaintAction(VEventRef event)
{
    if (buffer == 0)
        return False;
    VPaintDevice dev(*this);
    SetTextColor(dev, fore_color);
    SetBkColor(dev, back_color);
    const RECT _FAR &exposeRect = dev.GetExposeRect();
    viewer.DrawOn(dev, exposeRect);
    UNREFERENCED_PARAMETER(event);
    return False;
}


Boolean FileView::CreateAction(VEventRef event)
{
    VFrame::CreateAction(event);
    VDisplayDevice dev(*this);
    viewer.Init(dev);
    return True;
}


Boolean FileView::SizeAction(VEventRef event)
{
    VFrame::SizeAction(event);
    if (buffer == 0)
        return False;
    RECT rect;
    GetDimensions(rect);
    viewer.Resize(rect);
    SetScrollBars(rect);
    return True;
}


Boolean FileView::HScrollAction(VEventRef event)
{
    int oldPos = horiz_scroll->GetPos();
    VFrame::HScrollAction(event);
    int diff = horiz_scroll->GetPos() - oldPos;
    if (diff)
        viewer.ShiftHorizontal(diff);
    return True;
}


Boolean FileView::VScrollAction(VEventRef event)
{
    int oldPos = vert_scroll->GetPos();
    VFrame::VScrollAction(event);
```

```cpp
        int diff = vert_scroll->GetPos() - oldPos;
        if (diff)
            viewer.ShiftVertical(diff);
        return True;
}
void FileView::SetScrollBars(const RECT _FAR &rect)
{
    int pageVSize, pageHSize, charHeight, charWidth,
        maxVRange, maxHRange;

    charWidth   = viewer.CharWidth();
    charHeight  = viewer.CharHeight();
    pageVSize   = ((rect.bottom - rect.top)  / charHeight) - 1;
    pageHSize   = ((rect.right  - rect.left) / charWidth)  - 1;
    maxVRange   = buffer->Size() - (pageVSize+1) ;
    maxHRange   = buffer->MaxLineSize() - (pageHSize+1);
    vert_scroll->SetRange(0, maxVRange, pageVSize, charHeight);
    horiz_scroll->SetRange(0, maxHRange, pageHSize, charWidth);
}


void FileView::SetBuffer(const charPtr name, Boolean reset)
{
    TCHAR fileName[MAXPATH+sizeof(TCHAR)];
    wsprintf(fileName, "%s", name);
    ifstream strm(fileName);
    filebuf *buf = strm.rdbuf();
    // find the size of the file
    streampos fileSize = buf->seekoff(0, ios::end, 0);
    fileSize = max(16, fileSize/60);
    if ((fileSize * sizeof(TextLine)) > MAXINT)
        return;

    buf->seekoff(0, ios::beg, 0);
    delete buffer;
        buffer = new FileBuffer(strm,name,fileSize);

    RECT rect;
    GetDimensions(rect);
    viewer.Resize(rect);
    SetCaption(fileName);
    if (reset)
    {
        SetScrollBars(rect);
        InvalidateRect(*this, &rect, True);
    }
}


const FileBufferPtr FileView::GetBuffer(void) const
```

An MDI FileView

Listing 9-10
Continued.
```
{
    return buffer;
}
```

Listing 9-11
FILEVIEW.CPP
```
/* ------------------------------------------------------------
    fileview.cpp

    Implementation of the FileView class.

    Copyright (C) 1992, by Jeff Mackay - TAB Books

   ------------------------------------------------------------ */
#pragma hdrfile "vista.sym"
#include <vista.h>
#pragma hdrstop

#include <dir.h>
#include <values.h>
#include <fstream.h>
#include <vappl.h>
#include <vmsgbox.h>
#include "fvrc.h"
#include "fileview.h"


FileView::FileView(VMdiFramePtr par, charPtr title)
  : VMdiChild(par, title), viewer(*this), fore_color(RGB(0,0,0)),
    back_color(RGB(255,255,255))
{
    menu = new VMenu(this, "FileView");
    win_menu_pos = 3;
    style |= WS_VSCROLL | WS_HSCROLL;
    buffer    = 0;
    open_dlg  = 0;
    print_dlg = 0;
    setup_dlg = 0;
    find_dlg  = 0;
    color_dlg = 0;
    font_dlg  = 0;
    SetBuffer(title, False);
}



FileView::FileView(void)
{
    delete buffer;
}


void FileView::InitActions(void)
{
```

```cpp
    VFrame::InitActions();
    AddCommand((VAction)&FileView::PrintCommand, IDM_PRINT);
    AddCommand((VAction)&FileView::PrintSetupCommand,
                    IDM_PRINTSETUP);
    AddCommand((VAction)&FileView::SearchCommand, IDM_SEARCH);
    AddCommand((VAction)&FileView::FontCommand, IDM_FONT);
    AddCommand((VAction)&FileView::ColorCommand, IDM_FOREGROUND);
    AddCommand((VAction)&FileView::ColorCommand, IDM_BACKGROUND);
}


Boolean FileView::PrintCommand(VEventRef event)
{
    if (print_dlg == 0)
        print_dlg = new VPrintDialog(this);

    if (setup_dlg != 0)
        *print_dlg = *((VPrintDialogPtr)setup_dlg);

    if (print_dlg->Execute() == IDOK)
    {
        // handle printing operations here
        VInfoBox printBox(this, "Printing document");
        printBox.Execute();
    }
    UNREFERENCED_PARAMETER(event);
    return True;
}

Boolean FileView::PrintSetupCommand(VEventRef event)
{
    if (setup_dlg == 0)
        setup_dlg = new VPrintSetupDialog(this);

    if (print_dlg != 0)
        *setup_dlg = *print_dlg;

    setup_dlg->Execute();

    UNREFERENCED_PARAMETER(event);
    return True;
}


Boolean FileView::SearchCommand(VEventRef event)
{
    find_dlg = new VFindDialog(this);
    find_dlg->Execute();
    UNREFERENCED_PARAMETER(event);
    return True;
}
```

Listing 9-11
Continued.

```cpp
Boolean FileView::SearchAction(VEventRef event)
{
    UNREFERENCED_PARAMETER(event);
    return True;
}


Boolean FileView::FontCommand(VEventRef event)
{
    if (font_dlg == 0)
    {
        font_dlg = new VFontDialog(this);
        font_dlg->SetMinSize(8);
        font_dlg->SetMaxSize(24);
        font_dlg->TrueTypeOnly();
        font_dlg->FixedFontOnly();
    }

    if (font_dlg->Execute() == IDOK)
    {
        // reset the font used to display text
        font = font_dlg->GetFontObject();
    }
    UNREFERENCED_PARAMETER(event);
    return True;
}

Boolean FileView::ColorCommand(VEventRef event)
{
    VColorPtr current;
    if (event.GetId() == IDM_FOREGROUND)
        current = &fore_color;
    else
        current = &back_color;
    if (color_dlg == 0)
    {
        color_dlg = new VColorDialog(this);
    }
    color_dlg->SetColor(*current);
    if (color_dlg->Execute() == IDOK)
    {
        *current = color_dlg->GetNewColor();
    }
    UNREFERENCED_PARAMETER(event);
    return True;
}



Boolean FileView::PaintAction(VEventRef event)
{
```

```cpp
    if (buffer == 0)
        return False;

    VPaintDevice dev(*this);
    SetTextColor(dev, fore_color);
    SetBkColor(dev, back_color);
    const RECT _FAR &exposeRect = dev.GetExposeRect();
    viewer.DrawOn(dev, exposeRect);
    UNREFERENCED_PARAMETER(event);
    return False;
}



Boolean FileView::CreateAction(VEventRef event)
{
    VFrame::CreateAction(event);
    VDisplayDevice dev(*this);
    viewer.Init(dev);
    return True;
}



Boolean FileView::SizeAction(VEventRef event)
{
    VFrame::SizeAction(event);
    if (buffer == 0)
        return False;
    RECT rect;
    GetDimensions(rect);
    viewer.Resize(rect);
    SetScrollBars(rect);
    return True;
}



Boolean FileView::HScrollAction(VEventRef event)
{
    int oldPos = horiz_scroll->GetPos();
    VFrame::HScrollAction(event);
    int diff = horiz_scroll->GetPos() - oldPos;
    if (diff)
        viewer.ShiftHorizontal(diff);
    return True;
}


Boolean FileView::VScrollAction(VEventRef event)
{
    int oldPos = vert_scroll->GetPos();
```

Listing 9-11
Continued.

```cpp
        VFrame::VScrollAction(event);
        int diff = vert_scroll->GetPos() - oldPos;
        if (diff)
            viewer.ShiftVertical(diff);
        return True;
    }



    void FileView::SetScrollBars(const RECT _FAR &rect)
    {
        int pageVSize, pageHSize, charHeight, charWidth,
            maxVRange, maxHRange;

        charWidth   = viewer.CharWidth();
        charHeight  = viewer.CharHeight();
        pageVSize   = ((rect.bottom - rect.top)  / charHeight) - 1;
        pageHSize   = ((rect.right  - rect.left) / charWidth)  - 1;
        maxVRange   = buffer->Size() - (pageVSize+1) ;
        maxHRange   = buffer->MaxLineSize() - (pageHSize+1);
        vert_scroll->SetRange(0, maxVRange, pageVSize, charHeight);
        horiz_scroll->SetRange(0, maxHRange, pageHSize, charWidth);
    }



    void FileView::SetBuffer(const charPtr name, Boolean reset)
    {
        TCHAR fileName[MAXPATH+sizeof(TCHAR)];
        wsprintf(fileName, "%s", name);
        ifstream strm(fileName);
        filebuf *buf = strm.rdbuf();
        // find the size of the file
        streampos fileSize = buf->seekoff(0, ios::end, 0);
        fileSize = max(16, fileSize/60);
        if ((fileSize * sizeof(TextLine)) > MAXINT)
            return;

        buf->seekoff(0, ios::beg, 0);
        delete buffer;
            buffer = new FileBuffer(strm,name,fileSize);

        RECT rect;
        GetDimensions(rect);
        viewer.Resize(rect);
        SetCaption(fileName);
        if (reset)
        {
            SetScrollBars(rect);
```

```
        InvalidateRect(*this, &rect, True);
    }
}


const FileBufferPtr FileView::GetBuffer(void) const
{
    return buffer;
}
```

The resource script includes two separate menus: one for the frame and one for child windows. The OpenCommand method was moved to the new MdiView MDI frame object and changed to create a new FileView instance. Besides some minor changes to the FileView constructor, that's all it took to convert FileView into a full-fledged MDI application.

Why was it so simple to convert FileView into an MDI program? There are two reasons. The first deals with the design of the Vista library. The VMdiChild class is derived from the VFrame class, so adding support for MDI was a simple matter of deriving FileView from VMdiChild rather than VFrame.

The second reason is the original design of the FileView object itself. FileView was self-contained, with no dependency on global variables or its parent object. Therefore, there was no need to remove any dependencies or reorganize the data used by the class. As I discussed earlier, reducing dependencies between objects greatly simplifies the reuse of an object.

Note that, although this example highlights some of the advantages of object-oriented techniques, it is not a good example of reuse. To support MDI operations, I had to change FileView's superclass, deriving it from VMdiChild rather than VFrame. Although the changes were minor, the fact that the class had to be changed at all indicates a deficiency in its original design.

The inheritance scheme implemented by C++ doesn't allow you to change a class's position in the hierarchy. You can't insert a class into some intermediate position in the hierarchy without changing the classes below it. This might appear to be a shortcoming in the base language itself, but it usually indicates a shortcoming in the design of the class hierarchy. The problem might very likely be caused by the framework you're building your application on.

Unfortunately, this problem occurs more often than anyone would like. One of the more difficult tasks in designing a library is determining how objects in the library will be used. Different applications have different—and often conflicting—requirements.

For example, one of the most common "first" objects designed by most C++ programmers is a string class. Because a string probably is the most commonly-used object in C++ programs, many wonder why it hasn't been standardized and provided with the language like the stream library. The problem is in the actual role of the object. Should the class be designed for efficiency in speed or in size? Which operators should be overloaded, and which shouldn't? Should the following statement:

```
String string(10);
```

create a string containing "10," or should it create an empty string with room for 10 characters?

There isn't an easy answer to this dilemma, and you probably will face similar problems in your own programs. With sufficient time and effort, you can solve many of them in a very elegant manner. Sometimes, however, it is easier to either duplicate code or modify base classes to accomplish your goals. Just remember that if you change a base class for a specific project, you might be affecting the behavior of both future and existing programs.

Moving MDI programs from C to Vista

There are three major differences between the MDI classes in the Vista library and the MDI support in most C programs. Topics in previous chapters also apply to your MDI programs, although most MDI programs already are structured in way that makes porting them relatively easy.

First, remember that the VMdiFrame and VMdiChild classes eliminate most of the need for any interaction with the MDI client window. As you convert your code, replace messages passed to the client window with member function calls to the MDI frame object.

Second, because the Vista MDI objects automatically update the parent menu bar with the active child's menu, eliminate unnecessary code that swaps menus between your MDI frame window and MDI child windows. If your program currently updates the menu bar by adding and removing individual elements when a child is activated, you should convert calls to the menu API functions to VMenu member function calls. If you don't assign a menu to a child window object, it won't perform the swap when it is activated.

The third major difference is the most difficult: data management. As I discussed in chapter 8 and earlier in this chapter, C++ programs go to greater lengths to hide implementation details from objects that don't have a need to know.

The best data management strategy for your program depends on whether the program deals with multiple views of one type of object (like the MdiView program) or with a single view of different types of objects (such as an accounting program). In the multiple-view model, the MDI frame object—or an object acting as an agent for the MDI frame—manages the data. With programs based on the single-view model, each MDI child manages its own data, reading it when it in the CreateAction method and saving it in the DestroyAction method.

What's next

In this chapter, I examined the Windows Multiple Document Interface and the MDI classes provided by the Vista library. I looked at the advantages provided by MDI and showed you some unique ways to use the capabilities offered by the MDI objects. In the next chapter, I'll take a brief look at Windows graphics programming by experimenting with the Vista graphics classes.

10 Graphical objects

Windows provides a sophisticated graphics library that works for almost any application. This chapter provides a simple introduction to Windows graphics programming and introduces the graphics classes provided by the Vista library.

I discussed the Windows graphical model briefly in chapter 1 and showed you how it uses some object-oriented approaches to drawing graphics. In this section, I'll go a little more in depth before examining the Vista objects built on top of the Windows graphics interface.

The Windows graphics model

The Windows graphics model is provided by the Graphical Device Interface (GDI), which is a combination of several components. The most visible portion of the GDI is its library of over 200 routines, contained within the GDI.EXE dynamic link library, which is loaded whenever you start Windows. When your program draws a rectangle or circle on the screen, it uses entry points in the GDI library to perform the graphics operations necessary to display the object on the screen.

The GDI doesn't do all the work by itself. It is layered on top of device drivers (FIG. 10-1) that translate the GDI primitives into instructions understood by the device itself. This layering provides device independence. The same GDI function can draw a rectangle on an EGA, VGA, or 24-bit color display or a printer or plotter. With the great number of potential output devices, the GDI

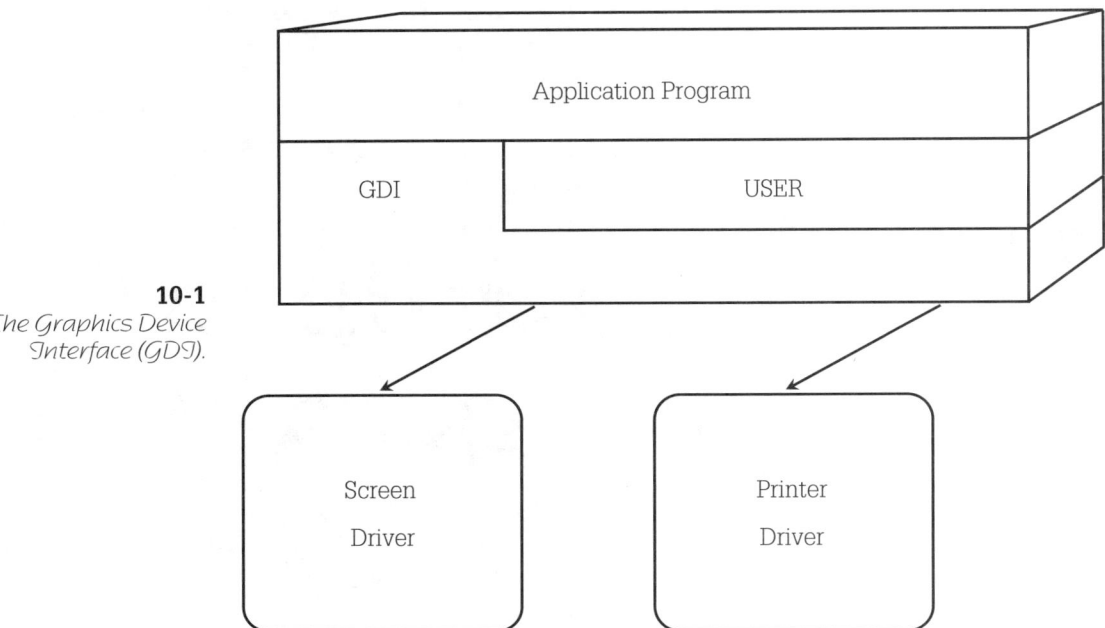

10-1
The Graphics Device Interface (GDI).

takes a great burden off of the programmer. Windows programs don't need to provide the hundreds of drivers found in their DOS counterparts.

Besides device-independence, the layered approach taken by the GDI also offers performance benefits. The sophistication of display devices and laser printers is increasing at least as rapidly as the popularity of graphical user interfaces. If the GDI were to communicate with those devices directly, you would have to wait for updates to the GDI from Microsoft whenever you upgraded your monitor or printer. However, because the GDI uses a device driver approach, hardware vendors can implement their own device drivers optimized to control their own equipment. When you upgrade to a faster monitor or higher-resolution laser printer, the vendor can supply a custom device driver that allows you to take advantage of the new equipment.

The device-independence provided by the GDI is not limited to just its drawing primitives. The resolution of a display device can differ greatly from the resolution of a printer, translating a drawing from device to device can be a complicated task. The GDI simplifies this task by providing a coordinate mapping scheme that allows a program to treat any drawing surface like a piece of graph paper with a flexible grid. For example, to display a bar graph with an X-axis of 1000 units and an Y-axis of 500 units, you just set the mapping mode of a device to be 1000 by 500.

Device contexts Central to all GDI graphics primitives is the device context. The *device context* is a data structure maintained by the GDI that contains information about a device used by the GDI drawing primitives. It maintains information about the current coordinate system, font, color, fill pattern, and other state data that simplify the graphic primitives. Instead of supplying every attribute that affects a drawing command as an argument, you set those attributes in a device context and pass it as an argument.

The device context also serves as permission to draw on a certain area of a device. Because Windows is a multitasking system, programs must cooperate with each other when drawing to the screen. Windows uses the device context to manage this cooperation. When your program needs to draw on a device, it requests a device context, performs its output, and releases the device context.

Windows allows only a limited number of active device contexts at any one time. Misuse of device contexts can lead to serious problems. For example, if your program requests a device context in its PaintAction method but never releases it, before long the GDI will run out of device contexts and the system will hang. The Vista device classes presented in the next section are designed to prevent this problem from occurring.

Drawing tools

With a sophisticated graphics library like the GDI, the amount of information necessary to control graphics output can be overwhelming. While the device context does much to simplify the interface, it can't do it alone. To simplify the interface even further, the GDI provides a set of drawing tools that deal with a specific aspect of graphics output.

The most common tools are the pen, used to draw graphical objects, and the brush, used to fill them with different colors and patterns. Other objects also can be considered drawing tools, including palettes, fonts, colors, and bitmaps. I'll examine the Windows drawing tools closer in the next section.

Graphics primitives

As I mentioned earlier, the GDI consists of more than 200 functions. The majority of these functions, however, manage graphics attributes rather than perform drawing operations. The GDI provides a diverse collection of low-level routines to draw simple graphical objects including points, lines, circles, and rectangles. It also provides a number of high-level functions that draw more complex objects like pie charts and polygons.

Win32 improvements

Like other Windows components, Win32 offers several improvements over the graphics subsystem of Windows 3.*x*. The first difference is the widening of 16-bit parameters into 32 bits. Although most of these changes should be transparent, they might affect existing programs. Of special significance is the fact that coordinates also are widened to 32 bits. There is no longer a 32K limit on coordinate values.

Several new functions were added to the GDI, including functions to manage device-independent color, draw bezier curves, manage graphical object paths, and functions to manipulate and apply transformations to bitmaps. Font support also was improved in several areas.

Perhaps the most significant change in the Win32 GDI is the fact that applications can no longer share GDI objects. Although this shouldn't affect new applications, existing applications that share pens, brushes, or bitmaps must be modified. Because all Win32 programs run in their own protected address space, sharing private tools is no longer appropriate. Bitmaps that must be shared between multiple processes must be created in shared memory and accessed using standard memory API calls.

Vista graphics objects

The Vista graphics objects simplify the Windows graphics interface by encapsulating operations with the data they act on. It also adds a consistent interface suitable for the most common drawing operations. The graphics objects are not meant to replace the GDI; they aren't suitable for applications whose main function in life is to draw graphics. They are meant to hide some of the complexity of the GDI, while allowing you to take an object-oriented approach to displaying simple graphics.

In this section, I'll look at the graphics objects provided by the Vista library and build some reusable objects that you might find useful in your own applications.

Device objects

Vista provides a set of classes used to represent Windows graphics devices (FIG. 10-2). At the base of the hierarchy is the VDevice class, which provides the basic services for all of the device classes. The device classes represent a device context used in normal C programs.

The most commonly used device classes are those that represent a display device: the VDisplayDevice and VPaintDevice classes. The display device classes are used to display graphics on the client area of a window. They take a window object reference as an argument to their constructor.

The device classes can be used immediately after you create them. Unlike the window devices, which require a call to their Create method before they become visible, device objects are fully initialized in their constructors. They also clean up after themselves in their destructor; you don't need to explicitly call a function to release the device context used by a device object.

The VDisplayDevice calls the Windows GetDC API function to retrieve the device context for a window. When the constructor returns, the device object is fully ready for you to display graphics on it. The only real difference between a VDisplayDevice and a VPaintDevice is the VPaintDevice is designed to be used inside the PaintAction method. When the PaintAction method is called (in response to a WM_PAINT message) the device is in a special state where it will display only the areas on a window that need to be

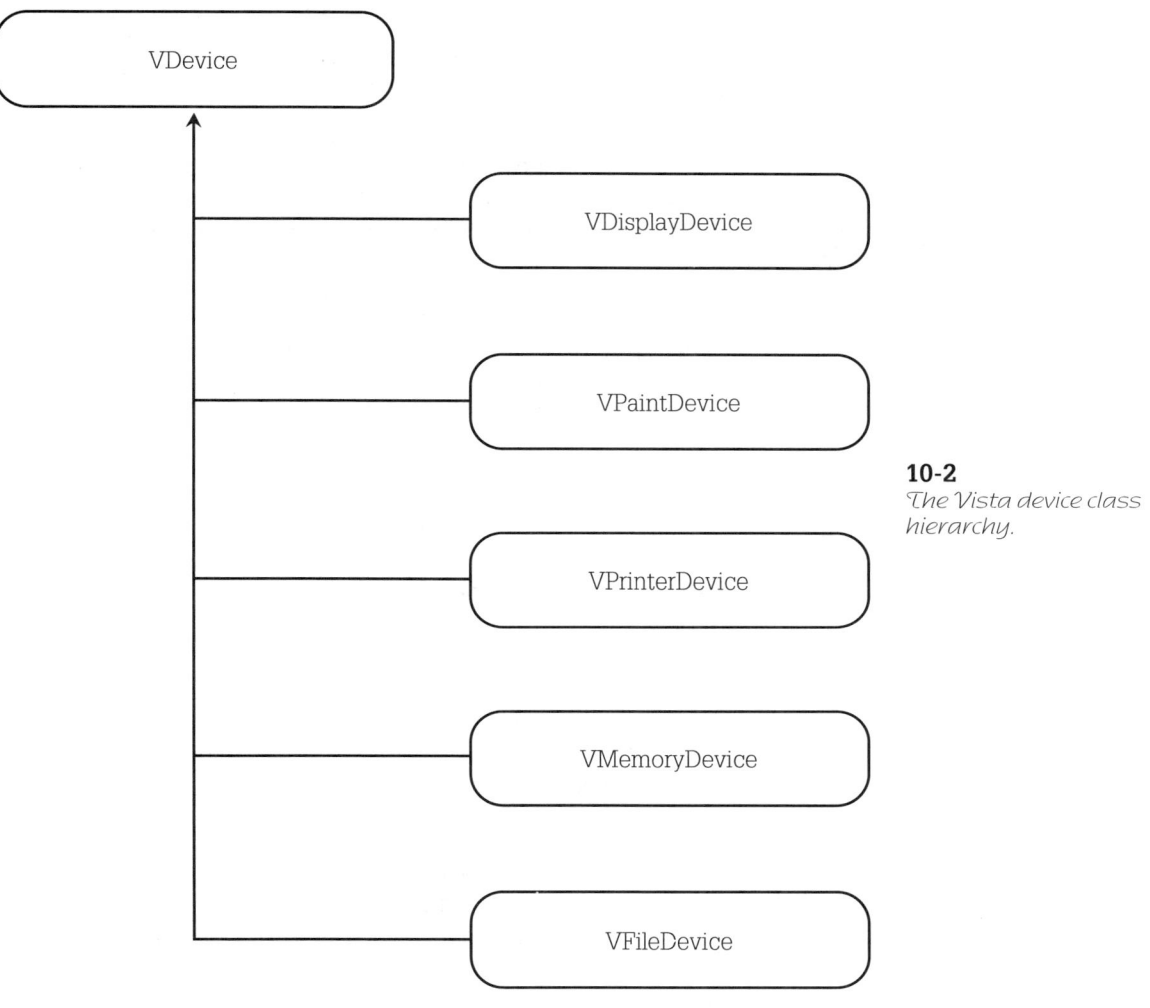

10-2
The Vista device class hierarchy.

updated. It calls the Windows BeginPaint function in its constructor to retrieve the device context for the window.

When the VDisplayDevice is destroyed, it calls the ReleaseDC API function to release its device context back to Windows. Likewise, when the VPaintDevice is destroyed, it calls the EndPaint API function to release its device context.

The other device classes aren't used as often, but they are just as useful. The VMemoryDevice is used for manipulating bitmaps in memory. The VFileDevice represents a metafile and is used to store graphics commands on disk so that they can be "played" on a device at a later time. The VPrinterDevice is used to print graphics on a printer or plotter. All of them work in a way very similar to the display devices. They are ready for drawing on as soon as they are created, and they clean up after themselves when they are destroyed.

The device classes are unlike the window classes in that they are designed to be created either on the stack or on the heap. Creating a window object on the stack normally doesn't give you the results you would want (except for modal dialog and message boxes) because the object's window is destroyed as soon as the function that creates it returns. For the device classes, on the other hand, this is a desirable characteristic. Because the pool of device contexts in the GDI is limited, it normally isn't proper behavior to hold on to one for an extended period of time. If you create one on the stack, device objects enforce proper behavior: when the function that creates them returns, the device context is released back to the GDI.

The device classes are thin wrappers around device contexts, but they don't try to duplicate the entire GDI. Instead, the VDevice class defines a handle operator that returns a handle to the device context represented by the object:

```
inline VDevice::operator HDC(void) const
{
    return handle;
}
```

Just like the VWindow class's handle operator, this function allows you to pass a VDevice object to any function that expects a handle to a device context. Actually, the handle operator is safer because the handle operator is guaranteed to return a valid device context.

The device classes have a special relationship with the graphics tool classes. When you realize a tool onto a device, the tool modifies attributes of the device. The tool object associates itself with the device object by calling the device's Associate member function. When it unrealizes itself, it calls the device object's Dissociate function.

Device objects maintain a list of all active graphics tools that have associated themselves with the device. When the device is destroyed, it loops through the list, dissociates the tool from the device, and calls the tool's Unrealize member function. The next section discusses the graphics tool classes.

Graphics tool objects

As I discussed at the beginning of this chapter, the device context uses graphics tools to assist in setting the device's attributes. Vista provides class that represent those tools and offer a consistent interface to make using them easier. Figure 10-3 illustrates the class hierarchy for the tool objects.

Before looking at the individual tool classes, I'll examine the VGdiTool class. The VGdiTool class is the key to the consistent interface offered by the tool

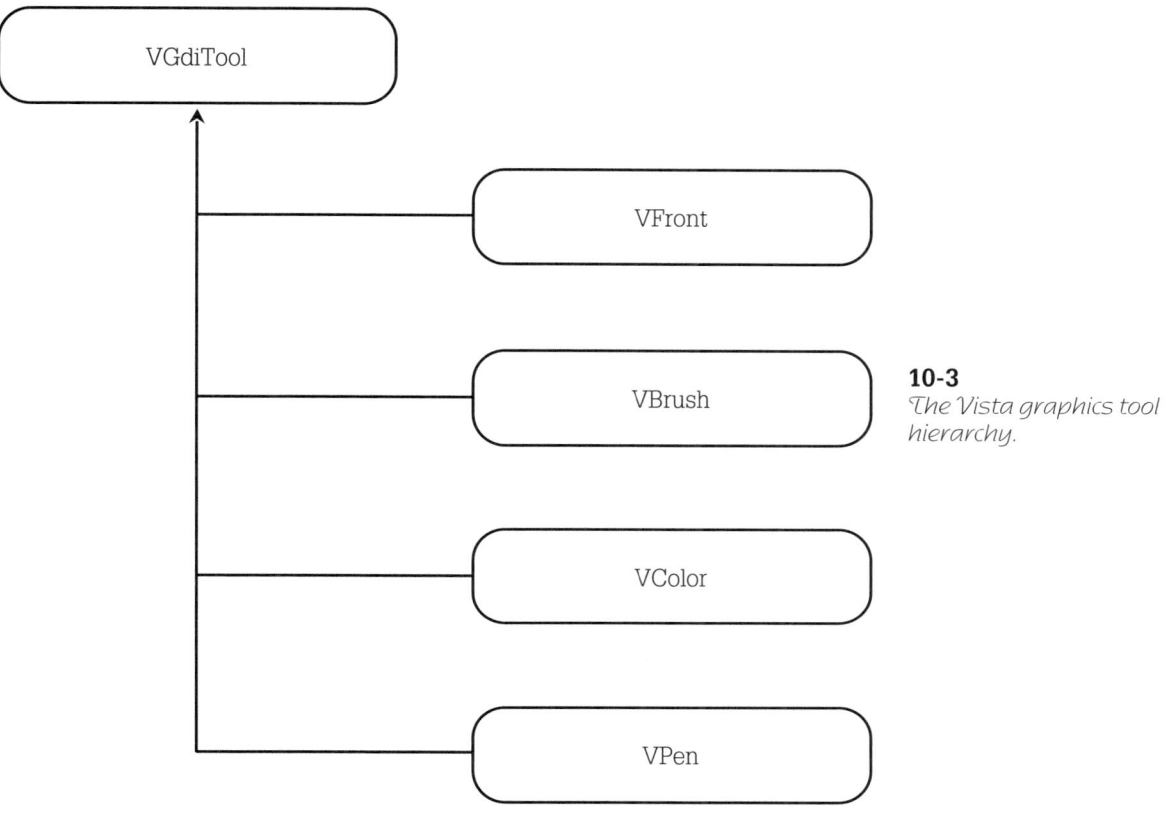

10-3
The Vista graphics tool hierarchy.

classes. It provides member functions that manage the relationship between tools and devices.

The Realize member function associates a tool with a device. It uses the SelectObject API function to retrieve the currently active GDI tool and saves it so that it can be restored when the tool is unrealized. This function is the key to the operation of the graphics tool classes. The Realize method is virtual, but each tool only implements its own unique way of associating itself with a device. Most of the tool classes chain back to this method before performing their own operations.

The Unrealize function is the inverse of the Realize function. It reverses the changes made to the device context state when the tool was realized. The function restores the GDI tool that was active when the object was realized by calling the SelectObject function with the old tool handle.

The VGdiTool class also includes a convenience function that acts like the iostream insertion (<<) operator. This function allows you to streamline your graphics code by realizing a group of tools in one statement:

```
VPaintDevice device(*this);
VColor red(VColor::Red);
VPen pen(VPen::Solid, 3, RGB(0,0,0));
VBrush brush(red);
device << pen << brush;
```

The tool classes themselves are simple and consist mostly of overloaded constructors that allow you to create them in different ways. Refer to the appendix for a complete listing of the vgditool.h header file that contains the class definitions.

High-level graphics objects

In this section, I'll build the Vista high-level graphics objects. With the device and tool classes already provided for you, the graphics objects should be fairly simple to implement. As with any other project, you should step back and look at the design before starting to implement them.

Graphical objects are a classical example of the useful nature of object-oriented programming. Just about every introductory text on C++ programming goes through the exercise of creating a shape hierarchy. I'll do the same, except that I'll concentrate on an efficient implementation for a Windows program rather than a correct object hierarchy.

Because this class hierarchy will represent graphical shapes, I need to determine the characteristics common to all graphical shapes and assign them to an abstract shape class. For the Windows graphics model, almost every shape has both an origin and a size. The key word here is almost: a point doesn't have a size, only an origin. Therefore, I'll add a dimension to classes that need it.

You might have thought of many other attributes that could apply to a shape: line color, fill color, font, etc. However, in the Windows graphic model, these attributes apply to a device not to a shape.

The next step in design is determining the operations that you want to make available for the base class. Because this is an abstract class at the base of a hierarchy, the operations you choose for the base class are available for all of its descendants, so it is important to choose wisely. The first operation should be obvious: drawing. The second might not be: a function to tell whether or not a point is inside the object. The function is used mainly for interacting with the user, so it might not be necessary for programs that only draw graphics. However, remember that you're designing these classes for a framework, so you never know what the classes will be used for.

That should do it for a first try. You're ready to begin specifying your base class, VShape (LISTING 10-1).

```
class _CLASSTYPE VShape
{
 public:
```

```cpp
        VShape(int newX, int newY) : x(newX), y(newY) {}
        VShape(const POINT _FAR &pt) : x(pt.x), y(pt.y) {}
        VShape(void) {}
        virtual void DrawOn(VDeviceRef dev) = 0;
        virtual Boolean HitTest(const POINT _FAR &pt) = 0;
        virtual Boolean HitTest(int x, int y);
        int GetX(void) const { return x }
        int GetY(void) const { return y }
        void SetX(int newX) {x = newX}
        void SetY(int newY) {y = newY}

    protected:
        int x;
        int y;
};
```

```cpp
/* --------------------------------------------------------
vistapr.cpp

        A program to demonstrate printing with Vista

Copyright (C) 1992, by Jeff Mackay

-------------------------------------------------------- */

#pragma hdrfile "vista.sym"
#include <vista.h>
#pragma hdrstop

#include <vgrdev.h>
#include <vcommon.h>
#include <vgrobj.h>


/*
** Application class definition
*/
class PrintAppl : public VAppl
{
    public:
                PrintAppl(HINSTANCE instance, HINSTANCE
                prevInstance,
                    LPSTR cmdLine, int cmdShow);
        virtual void InitWindow(void);
};

/*
** Main window class definition
*/
```

Listing 10-1
PRINTEX.CPP

Listing 10-1
Continued.

```
class PrintWindow : public VFrame
{
    public:
        PrintWindow(void);

        protected:
                void InitActions(void);
            virtual Boolean PrintCommand(VEventRef);
};

PrintAppl::PrintAppl(HINSTANCE instance, HINSTANCE prevInstance,
                        LPSTR cmdLine, int cmdShow)
    : VAppl("Vistapr", instance, prevInstance, cmdLine, cmdShow)
{
}

void PrintAppl::InitWindow(void)
{
   main_window = new PrintWindow();
}

PrintWindow::PrintWindow(void)
    : VFrame(NULL, "Sample Vista Application")
{
    menu = new VMenu(this, "PrintMenu");
}

void PrintWindow::InitActions(void)
{
   VFrame::InitActions();
      AddCommand((VAction)&PrintWindow::PrintCommand, 101);
}

Boolean PrintWindow::PrintCommand(VEventRef event)
{
        VPrintDialog dlg(this);
        dlg.WantDevice();
        if (dlg.Execute() != IDOK)
                return True;

        VPrinterDevice dev(dlg.GetDC());
        dev.PrintTo("Graphics Document");
        dev.NewPage();
    RECT rect;
        VGraphicsText text("Hello, Windows!",

                        DT_SINGLELINE | DT_CENTER | DT_VCENTER,
                GetDimensions(rect));
        dev << text;
```

```
   UNREFERENCED_PARAMETER(event);
   return True;
}

/*
** Main driver
*/
int PASCAL WinMain(HINSTANCE instance, HINSTANCE prevInstance,
                   LPSTR cmdLine, int cmdShow)
{
   PrintAppl appl(instance, prevInstance, cmdLine, cmdShow);

   appl.Run();
   return appl.GetStatus();
   }
```

The class declaration includes several functions that I didn't mention earlier. First, there is an overloaded constructor that takes a reference to a POINT structure as an argument. There also are accessors to retrieve and modifiers to set the value of protected data members. While I could have mentioned them in my design discussion, they are implementation details that don't really add to or subtract from the design of the class.

Now that you've made a first attempt at specifying your base class, try to choose the objects you'll derive from it. If you leaf through the first thousand pages of the Windows reference manuals, you'll come across several functions whose sole purpose is to draw a graphical element. You could take each of those functions and derive an object directly from VShape that uses that routine as its DrawOn method. That would be only a half-hearted attempt at trying to develop a good hierarchy.

Instead, I'll take those functions one at a time and try to come up with a good hierarchy that takes advantage of inheritance and virtual functions.

The first (and simplest) is a pixel, which I'll call a VPoint object. A point is drawn using the SetPixel function, which takes a handle to a device context, an X/Y coordinate, and a COLORREF variable as arguments. You can ignore the handle and the X/Y coordinates because they already are part of the base class. All that's left is the color, so I'll add that as the class's only data member. This new class now looks like this:

```
class _CLASSDEF VPoint : public VShape
{
 public:
    VPoint(int x, int y, COLORREF col)
        : color(col), VPoint(x,y) {}
    VPoint(POINT _FAR &pt, COLORREF col)
        : color(col), VPoint(x,y) {}
    virtual void DrawOn(VDeviceRef dev)
```

```
      { SetPixel(dev, x, y, color); }
   virtual Boolean HitTest(int hitX, int hitY)
      { return (hitX == x && hitY == y); }
   virtual Boolean HitTest(POINT _FAR &pt);
      { return (x == pt.x && y == pt.y); }
public:
   VColor color;
};
```

The next shape I'll implement is the rectangle. The Rectangle function takes a handle to a device context and four integers that specify the top-left and bottom-right corners of the rectangle. I could take the same approach I took with the VPoint object and just include the two other X and Y coordinates and member data in our new object. However, I'm looking for a consistent interface here—with both the GDI and the other classes in the Vista library. So, instead I'll add width and height data members. The class now looks like this:

```
class _CLASSDEF VRectangle : public VShape
{
 public:
    VRectangle(int x, int y, int width, int height);
    VRectangle(POINT first, int width, int height);
    VRectangle(POINT _FAR &first, POINT _FAR &second);
    DrawOn(VDeviceRef dev);
    HitTest(int x, int y);
    HitTest(POINT _FAR &pt);

 private:
    int width;
    int height;
}
```

Notice that I derived VRectangle from VShape and not from VPoint. This was a design decision: a rectangle is not a point. I also had a second, more important reason. The VPoint object needs a color passed to its argument. The rectangle instead uses the current drawing color of the device.

I could continue looking at each class individually, but that would just be redundant. The entire shape class hierarchy is listed in FIG. 10-4. This section should have given you a good idea of the design behind the Vista shape classes. If you need more information, refer to the appendix, which contains the source and header file for the shape classes.

Printing with objects

The final topic I'll cover in this chapter is printing. As I discussed at the beginning of this chapter, the device-independent GDI allows you to print graphics using the same functions you use to display graphics on the screen. Well, almost; there are some differences. The VPrintDevice class hides many of those differences and makes printing much easier.

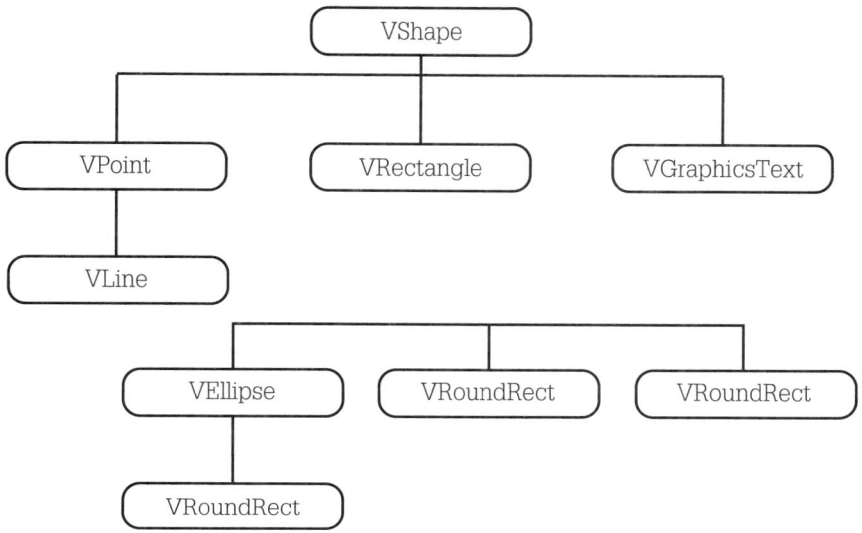

10-4
The Vista graphics object hierarchy.

For a Windows program, everything you print is a graphical document; there is no simple interface for printing text as you would find under DOS. The Windows printing approach makes printing in a business application almost as difficult as printing in a desktop publishing application. On the positive side, however, it is almost as easy to print in a desktop publishing system as it is to print in a business application.

All printing is done through the GDI, with some help from several printer support functions. To start to print, you first must create a device object for the printer. You can do this in one of two ways. The first option is to create it with no parameters and the constructor will read the default printer device's profile settings. The second option is to pass the constructor a handle to a device context received from a VPrintDialog object.

Once you have a printer object, you can initialize a print job by calling the printer object's PrintTo function, passing it the name of the document being printed. This name doesn't need to be a file name and can be up to 31 characters long. The document name will be displayed by the Print Manager while the document is being printed.

The next step is to start a page in the document by calling the printer object's NewPage function. It prepares the printer to begin printing the next page of the document by calling the StartPage API function. If the current page is not the first page of the document, the printer object will call the EndPage API function first. Finally, you can call the GDI functions necessary to display your output. Each time you fill a page of the document, call the NewPage member function. There is no need to inform the printer object when you complete printing. It will complete the document when the device is deleted.

The best way to understand the printing process is to examine the source code in LISTING 10-1. If you need more information on printing, several of the books listed in the bibliography cover Windows printing in detail.

What's next In this chapter, I took a quick look at the graphics support classes provided by the Vista library. I first discussed the Windows graphics model, then looked at the Vista device and graphics tool objects. I looked at the design of the Vista graphics objects and finished up with a short discussion of printing. In the next chapter, I'll look at some more advanced topics: memory management and dynamic link libraries.

11 Memory management & dynamic link libraries

Historically, one of the most difficult tasks in developing a Windows program has been memory management. The standard Windows 3.1 API includes more than 35 memory allocation, deallocation, and management functions. Although many of these function are only for special-purpose use, the average Windows application written in C uses four to eight different memory management functions.

In this chapter, I first will examine the Windows virtual memory scheme to dispel popular myths about Windows memory management that unnecessarily complicate Windows programs. I then will look at some innovative ways to handle the memory requirements of your applications. Finally, I'll look at dynamic link libraries, which can be viewed as a means of reducing the memory requirements of an application.

This chapter goes into more technical material than the rest of the book. This is necessary: Windows memory management is a complicated topic that you need to understand to write industrial-strength Windows applications in C^{++}. I've tried to cover the topics in this chapter in an intelligent manner, presenting you with enough information to understand the most important topics, but without too many extraneous facts. If you need more information on Windows memory management, several of the books listed in the bibliography give much more complete coverage.

The Windows 3.x memory architecture

The earliest versions of Windows were designed to run in a very constrained environment. The average PC at the time was based on an 8086 processor with no more than 640K of memory. It managed to run in this less-than-ideal environment by using a sophisticated memory management scheme.

Since that time, the processing power and memory available to the average machine has increased dramatically. Today, a typical Windows user's computer is based on some variant of the 80386 processor with at least two to four megabytes of memory. To keep pace with the increased sophistication of hardware, the Windows memory management subsystem evolved into a very respectable entity.

Unfortunately, most Windows applications haven't evolved to take advantage of the latest memory management features of the Windows environment. If you have developed previous Windows programs, you undoubtedly have encountered the complexity of Windows memory management. The goal of this section is to convince you that much of the effort you put into memory management in the past may no longer be necessary.

Memory & the Windows operating modes

To provide maximum compatibility with a wide range of hardware, Windows offers three operating modes. Each mode is designed for a specific class of hardware and offers its own advantages and disadvantages.

The earliest versions of Windows ran in "real" mode, which maximized the use of a limited amount of memory. Real mode was based on the segmented architecture of the 8086 processor family: programs were split into multiple segments. Windows as an operating environment provided three mechanisms for minimizing the use of memory in real mode: shared, discardable, and movable memory segments. Each of these mechanisms still is widely used in the more modern operating modes.

Memory segment attributes

Shared memory segments, used mainly for code segments in programs and dynamic link libraries, allow multiple programs to share a single copy of the same code. Users can run multiple instances of the same program without having multiple copies of the program loaded at one time. Dynamic link libraries allow multiple programs to share common functions without maintaining duplicate copies of those functions in memory.

The second mechanism, *discardable segments*, reduced memory requirements for applications even further. Much of the memory required by a program is read-only; the program has no need to change it during the course of its execution. A program's code is a prime target for discardable segments. In the Windows environment, segments containing other common data objects like menu, cursors, and icons also can be discarded. When system memory runs low, Windows can discard these segments, reloading them from disk when necessary.

These first two mechanisms reduce memory requirements a great deal and have little effect on memory management in a program. It's nice to know that they are there, but you don't need to make a conscious effort to use them.

The third mechanism, *movable segments*, has had a profound effect on Windows programming. Movable segments are not fixed in one place in memory; the system can move a segment with the MOVABLE attribute whenever necessary. When memory becomes scarce, the system runs a memory compaction algorithm that rearranges segments to reduce fragmentation and make room for more segments.

Movable segments are a hassle for programmers. Because a program's data can move around in memory, you can't directly store a pointer to the data. That's why handles, which you've seen throughout this book whenever calling a Windows API function, were introduced. A handle essentially is an index into a table of pointers. When Windows moves a data segment, it updates that segment's entry in the pointer table with its new location, but the handle itself doesn't change.

The hassle begins when you need to access the data in a movable segment. You can't use a handle as a pointer, because it doesn't point to your memory, it is only an index into a table. Instead, you need to dereference the handle using an API function. The API function (GlobalLock or LocalLock) returns a pointer to your memory and marks the segment as being fixed in memory. When you finish accessing the memory, you use another API function (GlobalFree or LocalFree) to unlock the segment.

As Windows evolved, its memory management subsystem did also. Support for expanded memory was added, but expanded memory has severe restrictions that prevented Windows from treating it in the same way that it treated conventional memory. Real mode did allow Windows to run on the earlier 8086 processor, as well as the newer 80286, 80836, and 80486 processors. However, as the hardware became smarter, so did Windows memory management, and new operating modes were introduced. As applications got larger and more sophisticated, fewer and fewer were able to run in real mode. As a result, Microsoft removed support for real mode from Windows 3.1.

Removing backward compatibility generally is unacceptable for a system software vendor. In this case, however, the move was necessary and didn't affect a great number of users. A graphical user interface like Windows is processor- and memory-intensive: it takes power to provide the performance necessary to run Windows. The machines targeted by real mode just don't provide the performance or the resources necessary to run Windows applications.

The omission of real mode from Windows 3.1 works to your advantage. It eliminates the need to constantly lock memory before you access it and unlock it when you're through. The newer Windows standard operating mode takes care of these details transparently.

Standard mode

Windows standard mode is supported for 80286 machines and 80386 machines with limited extended memory. It offers several advantages over real mode.

The first advantage is that standard mode switches the processor into protected mode, which provides hardware-based memory protection. Because standard-mode Windows runs the processor in protected mode, one application program normally cannot trash another's data.

If you developed or even ran programs under Windows 3.0, you undoubtedly encountered the all too common "Unrecoverable Application Error" or UAE dialog box. The most common reason for a UAE in Windows 3.0 was violation of the hardware memory protection scheme. In Windows 3.1, the message was changed to "General Protection Fault," but the cause is the same, as is the end result: when a program violates the protection mechanism, it is terminated. The stability of the Windows environment beginning with Windows 3.1 is directly related to its use of protected mode.

Although protected mode operation adds to system stability, it provides another feature that is just as important: access to extended memory. The expanded memory access allowed by real-mode Windows did little to relieve the memory bottleneck caused by the 640K limitation imposed by MS-DOS. The expanded memory specification allowed only a small piece of expanded memory to be mapped into the address space above 640K and below 1Mb. Even if a system had several megabytes of physical expanded memory available, only a little more than 300K could be addressed at any one time.

Extended memory is much more flexible. While the processor runs in protected mode, programs can treat extended memory as an extension to conventional memory. It imposes no restrictions (other than the size of addressing registers) on accessing memory. By running in protected mode, Windows has full access to both conventional memory (the first 640 K) and all available extended memory up to a total of 16Mb.

The third and most important advantage offered by standard-mode Windows is in its memory addressing scheme. If you've programmed an MS-DOS application, you already are familiar with segmented addressing. An individual location in memory is addressed using a segment/offset pair; the segment refers to a block of memory and the offset to a specific location in that block. In simplified terms, a far pointer in your program contains two values: the segment occupies the high word while the low word contains the offset to data being pointed at.

For Windows running in protected mode, the segmented addressing scheme is modified. Instead of pointing to a segment, the high word of a pointer contains a segment selector, which actually is an index into a table. This table, called a *local descriptor table*, serves the same purpose as a table containing handles in real-mode Windows. Windows can move data to eliminate fragmentation and update the descriptor table to keep its segment references valid. The processor automatically dereferences the selector so that pointers always point to the correct location in physical memory.

So, what is the significance of this modified addressing scheme? It eliminates the need for locking and unlocking handles. If you compare FIGS. 11-1 and 11-2, you'll notice very little difference between the two diagrams: the real mode and protected mode addressing schemes provide a slightly different approach to come to the same conclusion. Instead of using API functions to dereference a handle, you can let the processor handle the pointer conversion automatically.

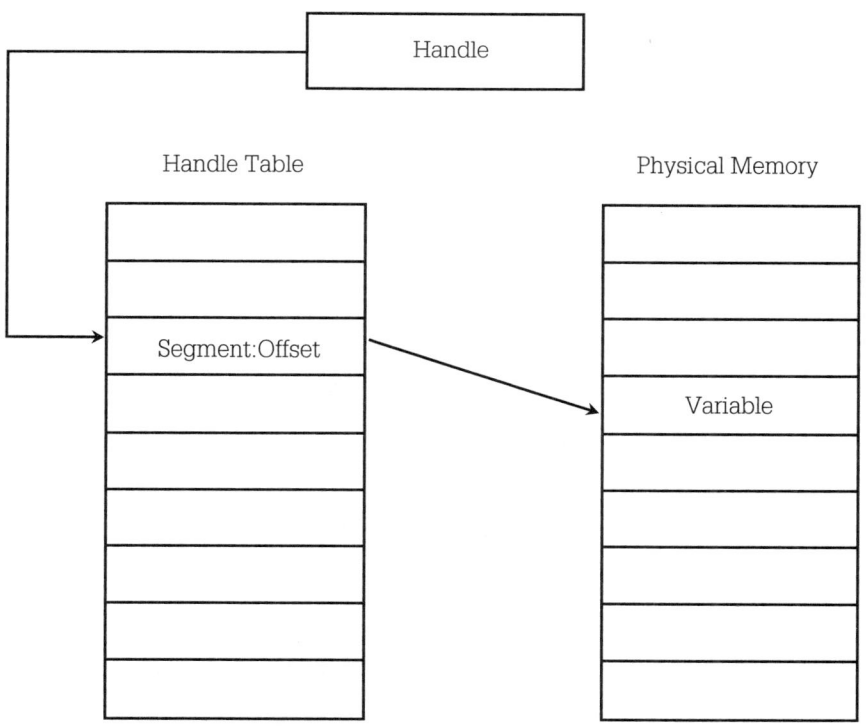

11-1
Windows real mode memory access is based on handles.

The Windows 386-enhanced mode builds on standard mode to add support for up to 64Mb of data and to provide access to true virtual memory. This mode still uses the same addressing scheme provided by standard mode but uses the 80386 processor's paging interrupts to swap pages of memory to and from a disk. What this means to you is that your machine appears to have more memory. Instead of being limited to the actual physical memory

386-enhanced mode

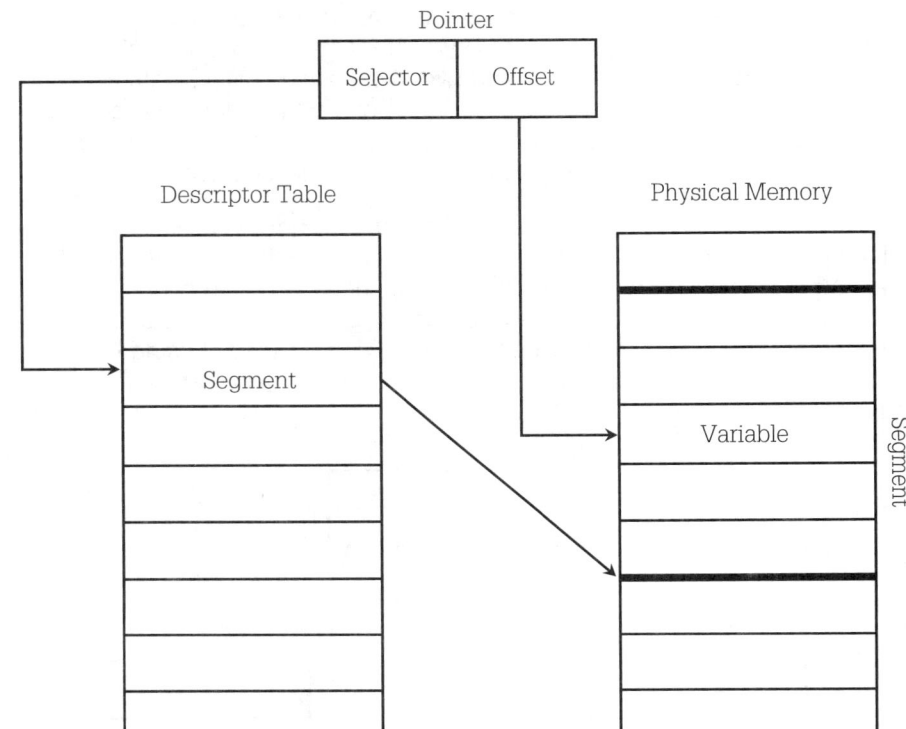

11-2
Under protected mode, the 80286 and 80386 processors use descriptor tables to implement virtual memory.

on the system, Windows running in 386-enhanced mode can address as much as five times more memory than is physically present on a machine.

Windows 386-enhanced mode increases the amount of memory available to the sum of the physical memory present on the system and the size of the systems swap file. It can have a significant effect on the way you do your job because it allows you to run many more programs at the same time and clutter your screen almost as badly as your desk.

Program organization
As I've discussed throughout this chapter, the segment is the major unit of organization in a Windows program. Programs are divided into separate segments, with at least one segment used for code and another for data. In keeping with MS-DOS development terminology, there are four memory models (TABLE 11-1) used for most Windows programs.

The small and medium models only allow a single default data segment. The most common model for Windows programs written in C is the medium model. It allows the program to be divided into multiple code segments with a single default data segment to hold static and global data. In real mode, the segment organization of a program was important: the system could move

216 *Memory management & dynamic link libraries*

Table 11-1
Memory models for Windows programs.

Memory model	Code segments	Data segments
Small	Single	Single
Medium	Multiple	Single
Compact	Single	Multiple
Large	Multiple	Multiple

and discard data only at a segment level. The performance of a program on a machine with limited memory depended on efficient segment organization.

With the protected mode operation of Windows standard and 386-enhanced modes, segment organization becomes less important. The system splits segments into 4K pages; it moves and discards data at the page level. Although a segment initially might occupy consecutive physical pages of memory, in a low-memory situation, the system can split the segment into multiple pages that are moved independently. This effectively fragments the segment, and the program has little control over that fragmentation.

While segmentation takes on a lesser role in protected mode at the system level, it still has an effect on your programs. In the small and medium models, data pointers default to 16-bit near pointers. The compiler assumes that data exists either on the stack or in the default data segment, both of which occupy the same segment. However, all pointers passed to Windows API functions (or other DLL functions) must be far pointers because they have their own default data segments. The compiler converts near pointers to far pointers whenever it can by combining the near pointer with the default data segment's selector. For example:

```
char *menuName = "MyMenu";
LoadMenu(hwnd, menuName);
```

The first statement assigns a string residing the local data segment to the `menuName` variable. The compiler automatically converts the near pointer into a far pointer because the second parameter to LoadMenu is declared as a long pointer in the function's prototype. There is no need to cast the near pointer into a far pointer. The reverse is not true; when the system returns a far pointer, it cannot be converted into a near pointer.

One solution to this problem is to use the compact or large memory model, which default to far pointers for data. However, when you create a program with multiple data segments, Windows will allow you to run only a single instance of the program. In some cases, this is no problem: most users only need to run a single instance of a program at any one time. You can work around the problem by creating a second copy of the program under a different name. Duplicate copies of the program are loaded at runtime, but at least multiple copies can run.

The Windows 3.x memory management API

Windows offers two sets of functions (TABLE 11-2) to manage memory for an application. The first set originally was designed to manage data in your program's local heap. There is little overhead associated with objects allocated from a local heap—only 12 bytes. Memory allocation with the local memory API functions is quick and efficient and are most suitable for a large number of small objects. However, they have one limitation. Because they are designed to operate on a program's default data segment, they will fail when that segment grows too large.

Table 11-2 Windows memory allocation functions.

Local Memory

Function	Description
LocalAlloc	Allocates memory in an application's local heap.
LocalFree	Frees local memory.
LocalLock	Locks a local handle, returning a near pointer.
LocalUnlock	Unlocks a local handle.

Global Memory

Function	Description
GlobalAlloc	Allocates memory from the global heap.
GlobalFree	Frees global memory.
GlobalLock	Locks a global handle, returning a far pointer.
GlobalUnlock	Unlocks a global handle.

The second set of functions manage memory from the global heap. Each newly allocated chunk of memory is placed in its own segment but carries a higher overhead: 24 bytes for each object allocated in the global heap. With this higher overhead, the global memory API functions are more suitable for large objects.

The global memory API functions have their own limitation, brought on by the 64K segment size limitation. A descriptor table can grow only large enough to fill a single segment. Because Windows 3.1 uses a single system-wide descriptor table, only 8192 segments can be allocated at any time. In the next section, I'll discuss the limitations of the Windows memory management API and examine some solutions that overcome those limitations.

The Win32 memory architecture

One of the most significant (and welcome) changes brought on by Windows NT and the Win32S library are in memory management. By definition, a 32-bit environment eliminates the need for near and far pointers required in a segmented operating system like MS-DOS. Therefore, memory management under Win32 can be a much simpler task for most applications.

In keeping with its backward-compatibility theme, Win32 supports the memory allocation functions in Windows 3.x. Most of those functions, however, don't seem appropriate. With the 32-bit memory model implemented by Win32, there is no need for near or far pointers. All pointers are 32 bits in size and consist of a linear number, not a segment:offset or selector:offset pair. So, with Win32, you have a choice. You can continue to use the local and global memory management API or replace them with the standard C++ new and delete operators.

Besides supporting the standard C++ memory management operators and the memory management API provided by Windows 3.1, Win32 adds three additional methods of memory management: heap allocation, virtual memory allocation, and file-mapped shared memory. Each of these new methods is designed for a special purpose but, unfortunately, are beyond the scope of this book.

Memory management with objects

After that long introduction, what else could there possibly be to discuss about memory management? A lot. C++ offers a great deal more flexibility in memory management than a traditional language like C. At first glance, it appears that dynamic memory allocation has been built in to the language because it provides the new and delete operators. This is true to a certain degree, but remember that operators can be overloaded, and that includes the new and delete operators. If the memory management operators don't suit your needs, the language allows you to roll your own.

The default new & delete operators

Before I get into solving the limitations imposed by the Windows API and try to implement our own new and delete, I'm going to review their purpose, then perform some simple tests.

As you've seen in previous chapters, C++ provides operators to handle dynamic memory allocation. The `new` operator takes the place of the standard C `malloc` function (although it often is implemented using `malloc`). The `delete` operator takes the place of the standard C `free` function (although it too often is implemented using this function).

When you deal with objects, you must use the `new` operator to create an object and the `delete` operator to destroy them. Operator `new` not only creates an instance of an object by allocating memory for it, it also initializes the object's virtual tables (if it has any) and invokes constructors for the object and all of its base classes. The `delete` operator not only frees the memory occupied by an object, it also invokes the destructor for the object and all its base classes.

So, let's perform some simple tests on the default new and delete operators. Included with Borland C++ is a useful library called EasyWin, which allows you test the functions you're developing without wrapping a Windows program around them. All you need to do is write a program as if you were developing under DOS—with a main function instead of a WinMain. Then, compile, link, and run the program. It displays any output directed to `cout` in a window.

Listing 11-1 contains the test program, MEMTEST.CPP. The program just loops 10,000 times allocating a buffer of a specified size. Experiment with the program. Compile it first in small model and run it, varying the argument from 10 bytes to 1000 bytes. The results you get should be reasonable. In small model, operator `new` allocates from the local heap, which is limited to 64K in size. Depending on the value you pass as an argument, the amount of memory MEMTEST can allocate will vary from about 4000 bytes to 54,000 bytes.

Listing 11-1
MEMTEST.CPP

```
/* -----------------------------------------------------------
   memtest.cpp

   Tests the Borland C++ implementation of the new and delete operators

   ----------------------------------------------------------- */
#include <stdlib.h>
#include <iostream.h>

int main(int argc, char **argv)
{
        char *var;
        long counter=0;
        long blockSize=atol(argv[1]);

        if (argc < 1)
        {
                cout << "usage: memtest <size>";
                cout << "select Run/Arguments from the IDE and ";
      cout << "enter an allocation size";
                return 1;
        }

    cout << "Allocating memory in " << blockSize ;
    cout << " byte chunks" << endl;
    var = new char[blockSize];

        for(counter=0; counter<10000 && var; counter++)
                var = new char[blockSize];
        cout << "Performed " << counter << " allocations" << endl;
        cout << "Allocated " << counter*blockSize << " bytes ";
        if (counter < 10000) cout << "before failure";
        cout << endl;
        return 0;
}
```

Now, compile it in compact or large model and run it, but be sure to pass it a small value as an argument at first (or you might hang up your system). The results might surprise you—they surprised me. I expected the allocation to fail before it reached the 8000 mark, but it continues on to 10,000. I even changed the loop control to allocate 60,000 times, and it still succeeded.

So, how does the large model operator `new` allow you to allocate so many objects in the global heap? Recall the discussion of the limitation on the size of the descriptor table in the last section. Because operator `new` allocates objects from the global heap in large model programs, it should fail before it allocates 8192 objects. However, the Borland C++ `new` operator uses a technique known as *subsegment allocation* that eliminates the limitations of GlobalLock.

The concept really is very simple. The first time you call operator `new`, it allocates a segment from the global heap using the GlobalAlloc function. Then, it calls an undocumented function, InitHeap, to create a local heap inside the global segment. Finally, it returns a pointer to an area within the segment created using the LocalAlloc and LocalLock functions.

To be honest, I didn't expect the default `new` operator to employ this technique; I wanted to implement it myself as an example. If it isn't broke, I won't try to fix it. However, in the next section, I'll look at ways that I still can improve performance in some situations without reimplementing the global new and delete operators.

The VAllocator class

The `new` operator provided with Borland C++ provides excellent support for general-purpose memory allocation, especially when used in compact- and large-model programs. However, some classes have special memory requirements that can be handled more efficiently. One example of class that could use a specialized allocation scheme is Vista's VString class, because VString objects are used extensively in many Windows programs. Another example of a class needing a specialized allocation strategy is a linked list class like Vista's VList or VDblList template classes.

These classes are prime targets for specialized allocators because a typical program will allocate many of these objects, all of which are the same size. C++ allows customization of the `new` and `delete` operators at a class level to handle situations like this. However, because this is a common optimization technique, it often is better to create an object that performs the allocation. By using an allocator class, you don't need to duplicate the code implementing the optimization in different classes.

Vista's VAllocator class is a general-purpose fixed length allocator designed specifically for small objects that are in high demand in an application. Instead of calling the global operator `new` for each allocation request, the

VAllocator calls the global operator new once, requesting a larger block of memory that it splits into fixed-sized chunks. It creates a free list of those chunks of memory, casting them into links in the list:

```
class _CLASSTYPE VAllocator
{
.
.
.
protected:
    struct link
    {
            link *next;
    };
    link *free_list;
.
.
.
};
void VAllocator::Grow(void)
{
 free_list = (link *)new char[el_size * initial_count];
 VASSERT(free_list != 0);
 for(int i=0; i<initial_count-1; i++)
     free_list[i].next = &free_list[i+1];
 free_list[i].next = 0;
}
```

The New member function removes the first element in the free list and returns it to the calling object for every allocation:

```
void *VAllocator::New(int elSize)
{
  // make sure I aren't being called for an unknown object
  if (elSize > el_size)
      return (void *)new char[elSize];
  if (free_list == 0)
      Grow();
  link *saved = free_list;
  free_list = free_list->next;
  return (void *)saved;
}
```

Notice that if the free list is empty, New calls the Grow member function to add another block of links to the list. The Delete member function performs the inverse, inserting deleted blocks at the front of the list:

```
void VAllocator::Delete(void *el)
{
    link *theLink = (link *)el;
    theLink->next = free_list;
    free_list = theLink;
}
```

The VAllocator class offers two advantages over the default operator new. First, allocations are fast: a system request is needed only when the free list is exhausted. Second, there is virtually no overhead on the small blocks of memory, so allocation is more efficient in terms of space.

Now, let's look at how the new and delete operators are overloaded in the VString class:

```
class _CLASSTYPE VString
{
 public:
  .
  .
  .
    void *operator new(size_t size);
    void operator delete(void *obj);
  .
  .
  .
};
  .
  .
  .

void *VString::operator new(size_t elSize)
{
    return allocator->New(elSize);
}

void VString::operator delete(void *obj)
{
    return allocator->Delete(obj);
}
```

The allocator is defined as a static data member of the VString class and is initialized the first time a VString object is created. The overloaded new and delete operators just pass their requests on to the allocator. Note that when you overload the new and delete operators, they function as static member functions (no implicit this pointer), even if they aren't declared static.

The allocation strategy employed by the VAllocator class improves on the general-purpose allocation techniques implemented by the global new and delete operators. They don't try to replace them; the global operators already hide the details of Windows memory management in a very efficient manner and should be more than sufficient for any application. In the next section, I'll look at a family of classes that hide Windows memory management details in a much different way.

The VHandle class

Many C++ programs need to interact with dynamic link libraries written to be compatible with real mode Windows. The normal interface involves passing global handles back and forth between the program and the functions in the library. When the program needs to access the data structures represented by the handles, it is responsible for locking the handle, accessing the data, and unlocking the handle when it is through. So, even though Vista objects are never represented by handles, you still might end up dealing with the complexities of Windows memory management. Don't panic, there is a better solution.

Vista provides a set of classes designed to hide the implementation details of accessing global and local memory handles. The first class, VHandle, is an abstract class that stores a handle. The other two, VGlobal and VLocal, represent global and local handles.

Using the classes is simple once you get the hang of it. Assume you need to access a database library to access a customer record:

```
struct Customer
{
    char account[8];
    char name[30];
    char address[30];
    char city[30];
    char state[3];
    char zip_code[15];
};
```

When you use the library's GetRecord function to retrieve a Customer record, it returns a global handle that points to an instance of the structure:

```
HGLOBAL custHandle = GetRecord(CUSTOMER);
```

To access the structure, define a VGlobal object to represent the customer record:

```
VGlobal<Customer> customer(custHandle);
```

Now, you can access the VGlobal object as if it were a pointer to a Customer record:

```
strcpy(customer->account, "AB12447");
strcpy(customer->name, "John Dow");
strcpy(customer->street, "123 Main Street");
strcpy(customer->city, "New York");
strcpy(customer->state, "NY");
strcpy(customer->zip_code, "01111");
```

The VGlobal class, in C++ terminology, is called a *handle* or *smart pointer class*. It is an object whose entire purpose in life is to represent another object. The class uses two C++ features: an overloaded pointer dereference operator (->) and templates. Although I've covered both overloaded operators and templates earlier, these classes are unique enough to require more explanation here.

Template classes

The first point of interest is the class definition itself. A *template class* is a mechanism used to apply a concept to any type of object. One common use of templates is in container classes like the BIDS library supplied by Borland C++ or the VList and VArray classes supplied with Vista. Containers probably are the most common data structures in any program. Think about the number of times you've written code to build and traverse a linked list. Now, consider how many times you had to debug that code because you forgot initialize a link or made some other error.

Template classes let you reuse common code on any type of object. Instead of writing and debugging common code every time you need to use it, templates allow you to write and debug it once. The VHandle classes are simple; all they do is lock and unlock a global or local handle. However, you might ask, those operations are trivial, why go to the trouble of creating a template class to provide them? Again, consider the number of times you've forgotten to lock a handle and ended up accessing an uninitialized pointer. Also, how many times you forgot to cast the value returned from GlobalLock into the correct type. The VHandle classes take care of those details for you.

So, how does a template class work? The VHandle class illustrated in LISTING 11-2 is an ideal example. The class is declared with the template specifier, which is a keyword that identifies the class as a template. The class T in brackets identifies the "placeholder" for a type that the template class is representing. The compiler replaces the placeholder with the target class name whenever it encounters the placeholder. For example, for our customer handle:

```
VGlobal<Customer> customer(custHandle);
```

the compiler replaces:
```
virtual T FAR *operator ->(void)
{
    return Lock();
}
```
with:
```
virtual Customer FAR *operator ->(void)
{
    return Lock();
}
```

Listing 11-2
VHANDLE.H

```
/* --------------------------------------------------------
   vhandle.h

         Interface for the VHandle template classes.

   Copyright (C) 1992, by Jeff Mackay

   -------------------------------------------------- */
#ifndef _VHANDLE_H
#define _VHANDLE_H
```

Listing 11-2
Continued

```
#ifndef _VISTA_H
#include <vista.h>
#endif

template <class T> class _CLASSTYPE VHandle
{
    public:
            VHandle(HANDLE hdl, T FAR *obj=0)
                    : handle(hdl){ state = UnLocked; }
            VHandle(void)
            {
            Unlock();
            }

            virtual T FAR *Lock(void) = 0;

            virtual void   Unlock(void) = 0;

            virtual T FAR *operator ->(void)
            {
                    return Lock();
            }

    protected:
        enum HandleState { Locked, Unlocked } state;
    HANDLE handle;
            T FAR *object;
};

template <class T> class _CLASSTYPE VGlobal : public VHandle<T>
{
    public:
            VGlobal(HGLOBAL hdl) :
                    VWindowsHandle<T>(hdl){}

            virtual T FAR *Lock(void)
            {
                    if (state = Locked)
            return object;
                object = (T FAR *)GlobalLock(handle);
                state = Locked;
            return object;
            }

            virtual void Unlock(void)
            {
                    if (state = Unlocked)
            return;
```

```
                    object = 0;
                            GlobalUnlock(handle);
                    }
}
template <class T> class _CLASSTYPE VLocal : public VHandle<T>
{
        public:

                VLocal(HLOCAL hdl) :
                        VWindowsHandle<T>(hdl)

        virtual T FAR *Lock(void)
        {
                return (T FAR *)LocalLock(handle);
        }

        virtual void Unlock(void)
        {
            LocalUnlock(handle);
    }
}
#endif
```

Template classes provide truly polymorphic types. Before templates were introduced, similar features could be attained only by using obscure macros or classes that violated the type-safe nature of C++. With a template class, you gain the full benefits of polymorphism at a class level, without losing major features of the language.

Overloading pointer dereferences

The second point of interest in the VHandle classes is the overloaded pointer dereference operator. By overloading the pointer dereference operator, the VHandle class and its descendants are transformed into smart pointers. You can treat an instance of type VGlobal exactly as you would a pointer to the objects parametrized type.

Let's look at how the operator works. Whenever you dereference a pointer, C++ translates the syntax from:

`customer->zip_code`

to:

`customer.operator->()->zip_code`

which returns a far pointer to a Customer object. The operator itself calls the Lock virtual function to lock the handle and returns a pointer to an instance of the object's parametrized type, which is in this case a Customer structure.

The object's destructor calls the Unlock virtual function to unlock the object represented by its handle.

The Lock and Unlock virtual functions are the keys to the operation of a smart pointer. The two functions are declared as pure virtual functions in the base class and must be implemented by subclasses. The dereference operator is defined in the base class, but the real intelligence is in these two methods.

Because the VGlobal class represents objects allocated on the global heap, it uses the global API functions to lock and unlock its handle. In the VGlobal class, the Lock member function calls GlobalLock function, which translates the object's handle into a far pointer to a Customer record. The Unlock member function calls GlobalUnlock to release the lock on the handle.

Likewise, the VLocal class represents an object allocated on the local heap. Therefore, its Lock member function calls LocalLock, and its Unlock member function calls LocalUnlock.

Extending the VHandle classes

The VHandle classes are a prime target for reuse in the Window NT environment. Windows NT is a multi-threaded operating system: programs can run multiple threads of control simultaneously. One of the most difficult aspects of programming in a multi-threaded environment is the synchronization required to access resources needed by multiple threads. The VHandle class can ease this task a great deal.

The Windows NT API offers a set of routines to manage critical sections, which are used to protect global resources from simultaneous access by multiple threads. If you don't use critical sections or some other exclusion mechanism, your global objects stand the chance of getting corrupted by simultaneous access. For example, assume your program needs a global customer object retrieved from the database library I used in the last example:

```
CRITICAL_SECTION custSection;
HGLOBAL custHandle;
   .
   .
   .
InitializeCriticalSection(&custSection);
   .
   .
   .
custHandle = GetRecord(CUSTOMER);
```

Now, to update the customer record, I'll need to enter a critical section, lock the data handle, update the record, and unlock the data handle. Perform any of those steps out of sequence and you're asking for trouble. So, to make this process simpler, you can derive a class from VGlobal that adds knowledge of critical sections to its Lock and Unlock member functions. Figure 11-3

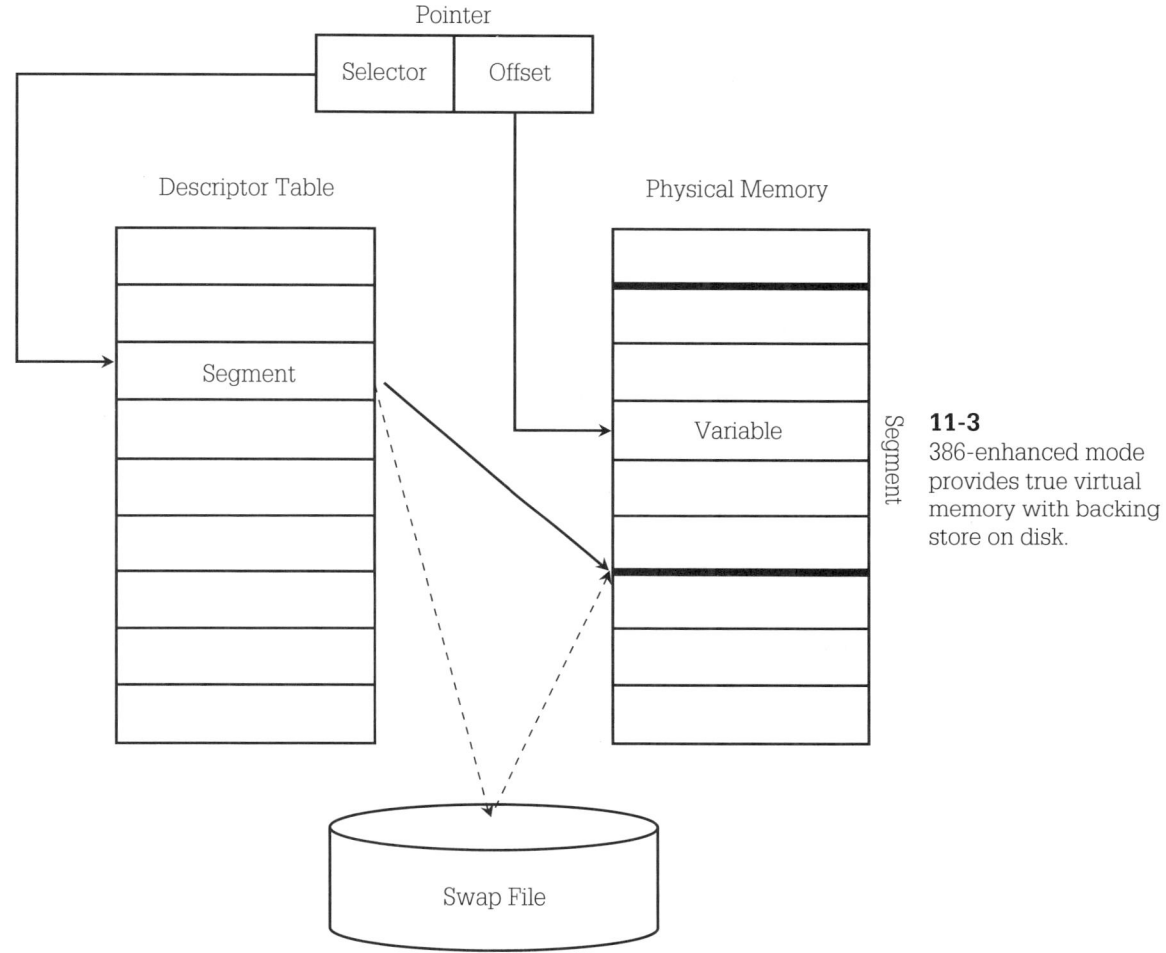

11-3
386-enhanced mode provides true virtual memory with backing store on disk.

contains the class definition for the CriticalGlobal object that implements this. The code for CriticalGlobal is shown in LISTING 11-3.

```
template <class T> CriticalGlobal : public VGlobal<T>
{
        public:
                CriticalGlobal(HANDLE hdl, CRITICAL_SECTION &crit)
                        : VGlobal<T>(hdl), section(crit) {}
            T FAR *Lock(void)
            {
                    EnterCriticalSection(&section);
                    return VGlobal::Lock();
            }

            void Unlock(void)
```

Listing 11-3
An example class to provide support for critical sections on Windows Nt.

Memory management with objects

```
            {
                VGlobal::Unlock();
                LeaveCriticalSection(&section);
            }

    protected:
            CRITICAL_SECTION &section;
};
```

By using the CriticalGlobal class, the code accessing the Customer structure now is almost identical to the last example, but it is safe to use in the multi-threaded Windows NT environment:

```
CriticalGlobal<Customer> customer(custHandle, custSection);
strcpy(customer->name, "John Dow");
strcpy(customer->street, "123 Main Street");
strcpy(customer->city, "New York");
strcpy(customer->state, "NY");
strcpy(customer->zip_code, "01111");
```

Updating a global Invoice record from a Customer record would be very similar:

```
    VCriticalGlobal<Invoice> invoice(invoiceHandle, invoiceSection);
    VCriticalGlobal<Customer> customer(custHandle, custSection);
    strcpy(invoice->account, customer->account);
        .
        .
        .
```

By now, the power of smart pointers and template classes should be obvious. However, a word of caution is in order. Examine the class implementations carefully: the order in which locking and unlocking occurs might not be suitable for your programs. When I first wrote the VHandle classes, the dereference operator looked like this:

```
virtual T FAR *operator ->(void)
{
    T FAR *obj = Lock();
    Unlock();
    return obj;
}
```

The handle was locked immediately after the object pointer was retrieved. This sequence worked when the class was only to handle meant the details of global memory because Windows 3.1 is not preemptive. The memory represented by the handle couldn't be moved until the function accessing the memory returned. When it was extended to encapsulate critical sections, however, I realized this sequence wouldn't work anymore. The handle object would end up leaving the critical section before the object was accessed.

This is an example of the difficulties you'll encounter when implementing template classes. You have to maintain compatibility between the template and its parametrized types, ensure operations directly provided by the class will be appropriate for clients, and anticipate different ways the class can be reused. Template classes can be much more difficult to design than standard classes.

Using dynamic link libraries

Another way of reducing overhead in many applications is through the use of *dynamic link libraries*, or *DLLs*. DLLs provide a way to limit the size of applications so that only the code necessary for the application to run is loaded into memory. DLLs also offer a means to communicate between multiple applications.

A DLL, like a static library, normally is a collection of object modules. Unlike a static library, when you link to a DLL, the code for modules accessed by your program is not copied into the program's executable file. Instead, the linker inserts a reference to the routines residing in the DLL. When the application is loaded and calls functions in the DLL, the system manages loading the DLL and resolving references to functions in the DLL at runtime.

The dynamic loading scheme can have a dramatic effect on the size of an application. Because code residing in DLLs doesn't need to be included in a program's executable file, it reduces the size of the file. The Windows API itself is contained in three DLLs: USER.EXE, GDI.EXE, and the kernel (which actually will be named KRNL386.EXE for 386-enhanced mode or KRNL286.EXE for standard mode). These libraries are over a megabyte in size; without dynamic linking, your programs would be significantly larger.

You can view a DLL as just an extension of your program. When your program calls a function in a DLL, it runs in the context of your program. The function uses your program's stack. Also, unless it intends to do otherwise, any memory allocated by the DLL function belongs to your program. Functions in DLLs do have the option of allocating memory that can be shared between multiple processes. Many programs use DLLs to implement a simple form of interprocess communication.

For a C++ program, dynamic link libraries offer a form of packaging for objects. A DLL can contain the code for a single object, a collection of objects, or even the entire Vista library. In this section, I'll look at the requirements for creating and linking with Vista libraries.

LibMain & WEP

The first component in a library is its LibMain function. As the DLL counterpart for the WinMain function, LibMain is the main driver for a DLL. It usually performs initialization required by objects in the library. However, like WinMain in a Vista program, LibMain has few responsibilities. Normally, the only action it takes is saving the library's instance handle for later use by objects in the library:

```
int FAR PASCAL LibMain(HINSTANCE hInstance,
                       WORD wDataSeg,
                       WORD cbHeapSize, LPSTR lpCmdLine)
{
    VistaDll = hInstance;
    return 1;
}
```

Windows calls the LibMain function when the library is first loaded; that is, when a program that has imported functions from the DLL is loaded or when a program specifically loads the library. Windows calls LibMain only when the DLL is first loaded, not every time a task attaches to the DLL. This limits the usefulness of the LibMain function, but it sometimes can come in handy. The LibMain function is required and must be present in any DLL. In most cases, you can just use the LibMain function in VISTADLL.CPP as a template for your own LibMain.

The first argument to LibMain contains the instance handle for the DLL. Although functions in a DLL (except LibMain) execute in the context of the calling process, the DLL's instance handle can be useful. A DLL can own resources just as a program can, so you can use the DLL's instance handle to access those resources.

The second argument holds the DLLs local data segment identifier (if it has one). By default, a DLL's local data segment is a fixed segment, which means that under real mode it won't be moved. It has been common practice to unlock the data segment; however, under Windows 3.1 this isn't necessary. In protected mode, even fixed data segments can be moved, so there is no reason to unlock the segment.

DLLs normally require a WEP (Windows Exit Procedure) function, which Windows calls when the DLL is unloaded. Like LibMain the WEP function is called only once. An obvious use for the WEP function is to delete objects allocated in LibMain. However, in Windows 3.0, the WEP function couldn't call functions residing in the Windows kernel (including GlobalFree or LocalFree), or it would corrupt data structures maintained in the kernel and occasionally cause a general protection fault. This limited the usefulness of the WEP function so much that most DLLs implement it as an empty function. If not, Borland C++ provides a default WEP function. So, you don't need to create a WEP function if you don't need to use it.

Windows NT dynamic link libraries

Windows NT also implements dynamic link libraries that provide the same features as DLLs under Windows 3.1, but it does so in a much more useful manner. Under NT, the system invokes the LibMain function whenever a process or thread attaches to or detaches from a DLL. Besides allowing a greater level of control, under this architecture, DLLs don't need a WEP function. LibMain takes the place of WEP.

The NT LibMain function takes a different set of arguments than its Windows counterpart:

```
INT LibMain(HINSTANCE hInstance, ULONG reason,
            LPVOID reserved);
```

The first parameter is identical—it contains the DLL's instance handle. The second argument contains an argument that informs why LibMain is being called. The NT LibMain can be called in four circumstances: process attaching, thread attaching, process detaching, and thread detaching. By responding to each of these "events," a DLL can maintain its own context about each client program.

Exporting & importing functions

Before a program can call a function in a DLL, the function must be exported. Exporting a function modifies the entry and exit code to maintain the proper default data segment for the function. Remember that, when your program calls a function in a DLL, it executes within the context of the program. This means that it uses your stack to store local variables and parameters to functions. However, a DLL has its own default data segment; any memory allocated using LocalAlloc (or operator new for DLLs compiled in small and medium memory models) belongs to the DLL.

The entry and exit code for functions in a DLL must be modified to set up registers properly. In the past, this was always done using a module definition file. All exported functions were listed in the module definition file's EXPORTS section. However, Borland C++ eliminates the need for exporting functions using a module definition file. Instead, you can flag a function with the `_export` specifier, which tells the compiler that the function is to be exported.

Exporting functions in a DLL makes them visible outside the DLL. They then can be called from attaching applications or from other DLLs. However, before an application can call an exported function in a DLL, it must inform the linker of the name of the function and the DLL it resides in by importing the function. This usually is accomplished using an import library created by the IMPLIB or IMPLIBW utilities supplied with Borland C++.

Special requirements for objects

Until now, the discussion of Dynamic Link Libraries has been generic: it could apply to C DLL's as well as C++ DLLs. However, there are special requirements for placing classes in a DLL. The Vista library was designed with DLLs in mind, so these requirements don't have too big an effect on the code I already have written.

The first obstacle to overcome when placing classes in a DLL is memory model. Remember that anything allocated using the LocalAlloc API function belongs to the DLL, not to the application calling the DLL. Because operator `new` in the small and medium models returns a near pointer, it uses LocalAlloc. While it is possible to use these models for object DLLs, it isn't an easy task. Therefore, I'll use only large models to build Vista DLLs, compiling with the DLL all functions exported (or -WD) option.

The second obstacle to overcome is exporting member functions. C++ "decorates" function names to enforce type checking. When you call a function, the compiler adds the return type and argument type information to the function name. For example, Borland C++ transforms the name of the constructor for the VAppl class from:

```
VAppl::VAppl(HINSTANCE, HINSTANCE, LPSTR, int);
```

to:

```
O$bctr$qxnzcpx11HINSTANCE__t2t1i
```

Obviously, no one would want to attempt to translate them by hand. One alternative would be to flag every member function with the _export keyword:

```
class VAppl
{
    _export VAppl(HINSTANCE, HINSTANCE, LPSTR, int);
    _export VAppl(void);
    // ...
};
```

This isn't a very good solution either. Glancing at a class definition in a header is one of the most common ways of looking up member functions. The extra identifier obscures the function declaration. Fortunately, Borland C++ allows you to export all the member functions in a class by flagging the class declaration with the _export keyword:

```
class _export VAppl
{
    VAppl(HINSTANCE, HINSTANCE, LPSTR, int);
    ~VAppl(void);
    //...
};
```

This definitely is the best alternative. It takes the least effort and doesn't complicate every function declaration. However, there still is a problem. Classes compiled with the `_export` keyword have all their member functions exported and can be called by other functions in the DLL. However, an application still can't call those functions. Although the functions are exported, the DLL can't share classes with an application unless the application flags the class definitions with the `huge` keyword instead of the `_export` keyword.

You normally will want to share exported classes in a DLL with an application that doesn't export the class. The _CLASSTYPE macro, defined in _defs.h, expands to properly take care of this for us.

The final obstacle to overcome with DLLs applies only to applications linking to a Vista DLL. When a DLL needs to call a function in an application, the entry and exit code for the function must be modified to set the data segment register to the correct value. The traditional solution to this problem is to export the function and use the MakeProcInstance function to create an instance thunk for the function. The instance thunk returned by MakeProcInstance then is called by the DLL function.

If I used this approach, I'd have to determine which functions could be called by classes in a DLL, call MakeProcInstance for each one, and pass the resulting instance thunks to the object. Again, Borland has come up with a better solution. If you compile the application with the smart callbacks option, the MakeProcInstance is unnecessary. The DLL then can call any exported member function in the application.

To sum it all up, there are different requirements for building a Vista DLL and building an application that links to a Vista DLL. To build a Vista DLL:

- Use only the large memory model.
- Compile with the DLL all functions exported model.
- Flag all class declarations in the DLL with the _CLASSTYPE macro.

Note that these requirements apply both to the Vista DLL itself and to any DLL containing Vista objects.

To build an application that links to a Vista DLL:

- Use only the large memory model.
- Compile with the smart callbacks option.
- Add the import libraries for DLLs to the application's project or make file.

For more details on building a Vista DLL, refer to the files on the companion disk.

What's next

I covered a lot of information in this chapter. First, I discussed memory management under Windows, covering the details of the Windows operating modes. I then moved on to discuss memory management for individual classes and examined the Vista VAllocator and VHandle classes. Finally, I discussed the requirements for building and linking with dynamic link libraries. In the next chapter, I'll look at another advanced topic: interprocess communication with the Clipboard, DDE, and OLE.

12 Clipboard, DDE, & OLE objects

One of the major benefits of the Windows environment is the user's ability to share information between multiple applications. This ability enhances productivity and simplifies your programs: they don't need to provide capabilities offered by other programs.

Windows provides several ways to share information between programs. In this chapter, I'll look at three of them: the clipboard, dynamic data exchange (DDE), and object linking and embedding (OLE).

Windows programs don't exist in a vacuum. As with any other multitasking environment, a Window programs can communicate with other programs running on the system. The three most common means of communication—the clipboard, DDE, and OLE—are available on both Windows 3.1 and Win32.

Windows NT provides additional methods of communicating between programs, both local and remote. They include pipes, queues, shared memory, and remote procedure calls similar to those found on most other modern operating systems. While these additional means of communication provide some portability between different environments, they aren't seamlessly integrated with the Windows programming model as the forms we'll discuss in this chapter.

Windows interprocess communication

The clipboard

The first form of communication that I'll look at also is the simplest. The clipboard was introduced with the first version of Windows. It acts as a container that is shared publicly between all applications on the system. The clipboard can hold any type of data: either in a standard format or in a form known only to a single application. Any application can store information in the clipboard, and any application can retrieve that information. The only requirement is that the retrieving application must know what to do with the information.

The clipboard uses a cooperative model of communication similar to that used by the Windows message-passing scheme.(Fig. 12-1) Applications request use of the clipboard by opening it—only a single task can open the clipboard at a time. After the program opens the clipboard, it is free to retrieve or insert data into the clipboard. As soon as it is finished, the application closes the clipboard, making it available to other programs.

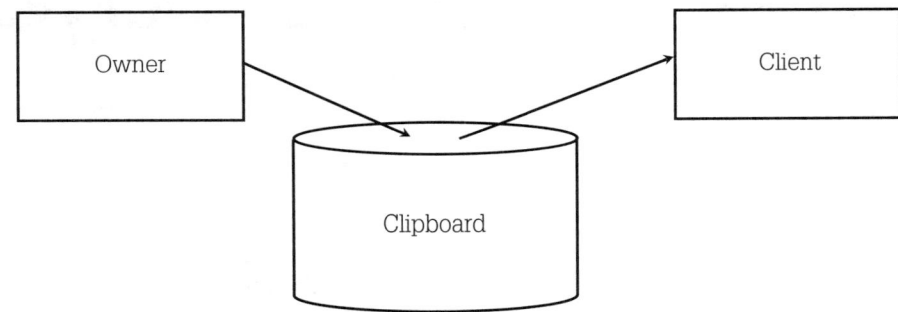

12-1
The relationship between programs and the clipboard.

The VClipboard class

The VClipboard class simplifies clipboard processing. Like most of the graphics classes, the VClipboard initializes itself in its constructor and cleans up after itself in its destructor.

Creating a VClipboard object opens the clipboard, making it ready for data transfer:

```
VClipboard(this, True);
```

Pass it a pointer to a window object as the first parameter. The second parameter is a Boolean flag specifying whether the clipboard should be emptied when it is opened.

When your program creates a clipboard object, the program can either retrieve or set its content. The VClipItem class described here represents the content of the clipboard. Two member functions—GetData and SetData—work with the VClipItem class to deal with the content of the clipboard. Another function, HasFormat returns True if the data on the clipboard is available in the specified format. It can be used to reflect the current state of the clipboard on a program's Edit menu:

```
Boolean EditorWindow::InitMenuPopupAction(VEventRef event)
{
    VClipboard clip(this);
    Boolean pasteEnable;
    pasteEnable = clip.HasFormat(CF_TEXT);
    // ...
    menu->Enable(IDM_PASTE, pasteEnable);
    UNREFERENCED_PARAMETER(event);
    return True;
}
```

The InitMenuPopup action method is called in response to a WM_INITMENUPOPUP event in this section's example program. The event informs the program that a pop-up menu is about to be displayed. This function is used to ensure that menu items only reflect currently available choices. There is no need to allow the user to select the Paste menu choice if the data on the clipboard is in the wrong format. The HasFormat function informs the program of the existence of a specific format.

The format of a data item on the clipboard is important, both to the owning program and the program requesting the item. A word processor can use its own format for representing data and can place its data on the clipboard in that format. However, if another program needs access to the data, it probably won't have knowledge of the word processor's internal format. The clipboard can hold multiple representations of a single data item at the same time. An internal format will be most useful when using the clipboard to transfer data from one place to another within the same application. However, a standard format like CF_TEXT also should be used to allow other programs to access the data.

When the program is through using the clipboard, it should always release it to allow access by other programs. The VClipboard class releases the clipboard in its destructor. Like many of the graphics support classes, the VClipboard class is designed to be created on the stack. It does allow you to explicitly open and close the clipboard, but those operations shouldn't be necessary in most programs: the class handles them internally.

The VClipItem class represents a data item on the clipboard in a specific format. It works in concert with the VClipboard's SetData and GetData functions to ease access to the clipboard. To copy data from the clipboard, a program should create a VClipboard object and a VClipItem object. The VClipboard object opens the clipboard, and the VClipItem holds the data to be placed on the clipboard. Then, the program uses the VClipboard's SetData function to actually place a copy of the data on the clipboard:

The VClipItem class

```
void EditWindow::CopyToClipboard(void)
{
    int start,end;
```

```
        editor->GetSelection(start,end);
        char *buffer=
            new char[editor->GetActualLength(start,end)+1];
        editor->GetTextAt(start, end, buffer);
        VClipboard clip(this, True);
        VClipItem  item(lstrlen(buffer)+1);
        item.SetContent(buffer);
        clip.SetData(item);
        delete buffer;
}
```

The VClipItem creates a global memory object, and its SetContent function copies data from the program into the global memory. It then can be accessed from other applications. Once the data item is placed on the clipboard, the global memory belongs to the clipboard the program never needs to delete it.

An example application: CLIP

Listing 12-1 contains the source for CLIP.CPP, the code implementing a simple text editor. Its header file is in LISTING 12-2. The program creates an Editor object, which is derived from the VText class and supplies a menu for it (see CLIP.RC in LISTING 12-3).

Listing 12-1
EDITOR.CPP

```
/* ------------------------------------------------------------
   editor.cpp

         A simple text editor that demonstrates use of the clipboard.

   Copyright (C) 1992, by Jeff Mackay - TAB Books
   ------------------------------------------------------------ */

#pragma hdrfile "vista.sym"
#include <vista.h>
#pragma hdrstop

#include <vtext.h>
#include <vcommon.h>
#include <vmsgbox.h>
#include <vclip.h>
#include <fstream.h>
#include "editor.h"

STDCLASS(Editor)
class _CLASSTYPE Editor : public VText
{

public:
        Editor(VCompositePtr par, int x, int y, int width, int height);
        void Resize(int newWidth, int newHeight);

};
```

```cpp
Editor::Editor(VCompositePtr par, int x, int y, int width, int
height)
        : VText(par, VString(""), x, y, width, height)
{
        x = y = 0;
        style = style & ES_AUTOHSCROLL;
}
void Editor::Resize(int newWidth, int newHeight)
{
        SetWindowPos(*this, 0, 0, 0, newWidth, newHeight,
                        SWP_NOMOVE | SWP_NOZORDER);
}

STDCLASS(EditWindow);
class _CLASSTYPE EditWindow  : public VFrame
{

public:
        EditWindow(charPtr fileName=0);
        EditWindow(void);
        void InitActions(void);
        void SetText(charPtr name);

protected:
        EditorPtr editor;
    VFileOpenDialogPtr open_dlg;
    VString file_name;
    void CopyToClipboard(void);
        Boolean CreateAction(VEventRef event);
        Boolean SizeAction(VEventRef event);
        Boolean ActivateAction(VEventRef event);
    Boolean InitMenuPopupAction(VEventRef event);
        Boolean NewCommand(VEventRef event);
    Boolean OpenCommand(VEventRef event);
        Boolean CutCommand(VEventRef event);
        Boolean CopyCommand(VEventRef event);
        Boolean PasteCommand(VEventRef event);
        Boolean UndoCommand(VEventRef event);
};


EditWindow::EditWindow(char *fileName)
        : VFrame(NULL, "Vista Editor")
{
        if (fileName && *fileName)
                file_name = fileName;
        menu = new VMenu(this, "EditorMenu");
        open_dlg = 0;
}

EditWindow::EditWindow(void)
{
```

Listing 12-1
Continued.

```cpp
        delete editor;
}

void EditWindow::InitActions(void)
{
        VFrame::InitActions();
AddAction((VAction)&EditWindow::InitMenuPopupAction,
                    WM_INITMENUPOPUP);
AddCommand((VAction)&EditWindow::OpenCommand, IDM_OPEN);
    AddCommand((VAction)&EditWindow::NewCommand, IDM_NEW);
        AddCommand((VAction)&EditWindow::CutCommand, IDM_CUT);
        AddCommand((VAction)&EditWindow::CopyCommand, IDM_COPY);
        AddCommand((VAction)&EditWindow::PasteCommand, IDM_PASTE);
        AddCommand((VAction)&EditWindow::UndoCommand, IDM_UNDO);
}


// create the multi-line edit control
Boolean EditWindow::CreateAction(VEventRef event)
{
        editor = new Editor(this, 0, 0, 0, 0);
        VFrame::CreateAction(event);
        if (file_name.Length() > 0)
        SetText(file_name);
        return False;
}


// resize the edit control to fill the client area
Boolean EditWindow::SizeAction(VEventRef event)
{
        if (event.GetWParam() == SIZE_RESTORED)
    {
                height = HIWORD(event.GetLParam());
                width = LOWORD(event.GetLParam());
                editor->Resize(width, height);
        }
        return VFrame::SizeAction(event);
}


// set focus to the edit control on activation.
Boolean EditWindow::ActivateAction(VEventRef event)
{
    VFrame::ActivateAction(event);
    SetFocus(*editor);
        return True;
}

// open a file...
Boolean EditWindow::OpenCommand(VEventRef event)
{
```

Clipboard, DDE, & OLE objects

```cpp
        if (!open_dlg)
                open_dlg = new VFileOpenDialog(this);
        int result = open_dlg->Execute();
        if (result == IDOK)
        SetText(open_dlg->GetFilename());
        UNREFERENCED_PARAMETER(event);
        return True;
}


// clear the edit control
Boolean EditWindow::NewCommand(VEventRef event)
{
        editor->SetText("");
    UNREFERENCED_PARAMETER(event);
        return True;
}


// read a file into the edit control
void EditWindow::SetText(charPtr fileName)
{
        file_name = fileName;
        ifstream input;
    input.open(fileName, ios::binary);
        if (!input)
        {
                MessageBeep(MB_ICONSTOP);
                return;
        }

    // get the size of the file
        input.seekg(0, ios::end);
        streampos fileSize = input.tellg();
        input.seekg(0, ios::beg);

    // allocate a buffer
    charPtr text = new char[fileSize+1];
        if (text == 0)
        {
                MessageBeep(MB_ICONSTOP);
                return;
        }

        // read the file
        input.read(text, fileSize);
        text[fileSize] = '\0';

        // set the editor's text
        editor->SetText(text);
        delete text;
}
```

Listing 12-1
Continued.

```
// modify the state of edit menu items
Boolean EditWindow::InitMenuPopupAction(VEventRef event)
{
    VClipboard clip(this);
    Boolean pasteEnable, modEnable, undoEnable;

    pasteEnable = clip.HasFormat(CF_TEXT);

    VEditSelection sel = editor->GetSelection(sel);
    modEnable = (Boolean)(sel.start != sel.end);

    undoEnable = editor->CanUndo();

    menu->Enable(IDM_PASTE, pasteEnable);
    menu->Enable(IDM_CUT, modEnable);
    menu->Enable(IDM_COPY, modEnable);
    menu->Enable(IDM_UNDO, undoEnable);
    UNREFERENCED_PARAMETER(event);
    return True;
}


void EditWindow::CopyToClipboard(void)
{
    int start,end;
    editor->GetSelection(start,end);
    char *buffer=
            new char[editor->GetActualLength(start,end)+1];
    editor->GetTextAt(start, end, buffer);
    VClipboard clip(this, True);
    VClipItem  item(lstrlen(buffer)+1);
    item.SetContent(buffer);
    clip.SetData(item);
    delete buffer;
}

// cut text from the edit control
Boolean EditWindow::CutCommand(VEventRef event)
{
    CopyToClipboard();
    editor->ReplaceSelection("");
    UNREFERENCED_PARAMETER(event);
    return True;
}


// copy text from the edit control
Boolean EditWindow::CopyCommand(VEventRef event)
{
    CopyToClipboard();
    UNREFERENCED_PARAMETER(event);
```

```
        return True;
}

// paste text to the edit control
Boolean EditWindow::PasteCommand(VEventRef event)
{
        VClipboard clip(this);
        VClipItem item(clip.GetData());
        editor->ReplaceSelection((charPtr)item.GetContent());
        UNREFERENCED_PARAMETER(event);
    return True;
}


// undo the last editing operation
Boolean EditWindow::UndoCommand(VEventRef event)
{
        // editor->Undo();
        UNREFERENCED_PARAMETER(event);
    return True;
}


STDCLASS(EditApp);
class _CLASSTYPE EditApp : public VAppl
{
public:
        EditApp(charPtr name, HINSTANCE inst, HINSTANCE prevInst,
                    LPSTR cmdLine, int cmdShow)
            : VAppl(name, inst, prevInst, cmdLine, cmdShow) {}

        EditApp(void)
        {
        }

        void InitWindow(void)
        {
                main_window = new EditWindow();
        }

};


int PASCAL WinMain(HINSTANCE hInstance, HINSTANCE hPrevInstance,
                                LPSTR lpszCmdLine, int nCmdShow)
{
        EditApp mainApp("Vista Editor", hInstance, hPrevInstance,
                                    lpszCmdLine, nCmdShow);
        return mainApp.Run();
}
```

Listing 12-2
EDITOR.H

```
#define IDM_OPEN      102
#define IDM_PRINT     103
#define IDM_EXIT      106
#define IDM_SAVE      104
#define IDM_NEW       101
#define IDM_SAVEAS    105
#define IDM_UNDO      201
#define IDM_CUT       202
#define IDM_COPY      203
#define IDM_PASTE     204
```

Listing 12-3
EDITOR.RC

```
#include "editor.h"
#include <vistarc.h>

EditorMenu MENU
BEGIN
    POPUP "&File"
    BEGIN
        MENUITEM "&New", IDM_NEW
        MENUITEM "&Open...", IDM_OPEN
        MENUITEM "&Save", IDM_SAVE
        MENUITEM "Save &as...", IDM_SAVEAS
        MENUITEM SEPARATOR
        MENUITEM "&Print...", IDM_PRINT
        MENUITEM "Print &setup...", 107
        MENUITEM SEPARATOR
        MENUITEM "E&xit\tF3", VID_EXIT
    END

    POPUP "&Edit"
    BEGIN
        MENUITEM "&Undo\tCtrl+Z", IDM_UNDO
        MENUITEM SEPARATOR
        MENUITEM "Cu&t\tCtrl+X", IDM_CUT
        MENUITEM "&Copy\tCtrl+C", IDM_COPY
        MENUITEM "&Paste\tCtrl+V", IDM_PASTE
        MENUITEM SEPARATOR
        MENUITEM "Select &All", 1
    END
END
```

The example in this section illustrates using the clipboard for conventional purposes. However, both DDE and OLE can use the clipboard to ease communication between client and server programs.

Dynamic data exchange

The clipboard provides a simple means of interprocess communication. However, it also imposes many limitations in a multitasking environment that limit its usefulness. The second form of interprocess communication I'll look at, dynamic data exchange (DDE), provides a number of additional advantages.

Like the clipboard, DDE is a method of communicating between cooperating applications. It uses shared memory to pass data objects between applications. Like the clipboard, it can be used for one-time transfers initiated by the user. However, DDE's real power lies in its ability to provide communication on either a one-time or continuing basis, without interaction from the user.

DDE was introduced in Windows version 1.03 and was based entirely on messages. However, there were some drawbacks to the message-based DDE protocol. First, the protocol required a lot of code; it wasn't a simple matter to add DDE capabilities to an application. Second, because of the flexibility of DDE, each application implemented its DDE communication component in a slightly different manner. Integrating with these different communication schemes was a major effort.

After Windows 3.0 was released, Microsoft introduced the DDE management library (DDEML), which offered a simplified interface to the string and data management requirements imposed by DDE. DDEML enforces a consistent protocol implementation, which greatly simplifies integration.

DDEML provides an API built on top of the message-based DDE protocol. It effectively hides the fact that DDE uses Windows messages, but the messages still are used under the covers. When designing the DDE support classes, I considered using the message-based protocol instead of DDEML. This would have simplified my efforts: DDE objects could use the same message dispatch mechanism as window objects. However, DDEML provides a higher level of abstraction: it not only hides the use of messages, it also simplifies use of strings and data objects.

Basing the Vista DDE classes on the DDEML has other benefits. Because it doesn't rely on Vista's message dispatcher, the classes can be used (with minor modifications) in OWL or MFC applications. Another advantage of using DDEML is that the underlying communication protocol doesn't have to use Windows messages. Windows for Workgroups and Windows NT extend DDEML to allow applications to communicate between different nodes of a network. Client programs can communicate with servers residing on other nodes.

In the remainder of this section, I'll examine the Vista DDE classes. (See FIG. 12-2.) Instead of discussing the message-based protocol, I'll concentrate on the Vista classes and their use of DDEML.

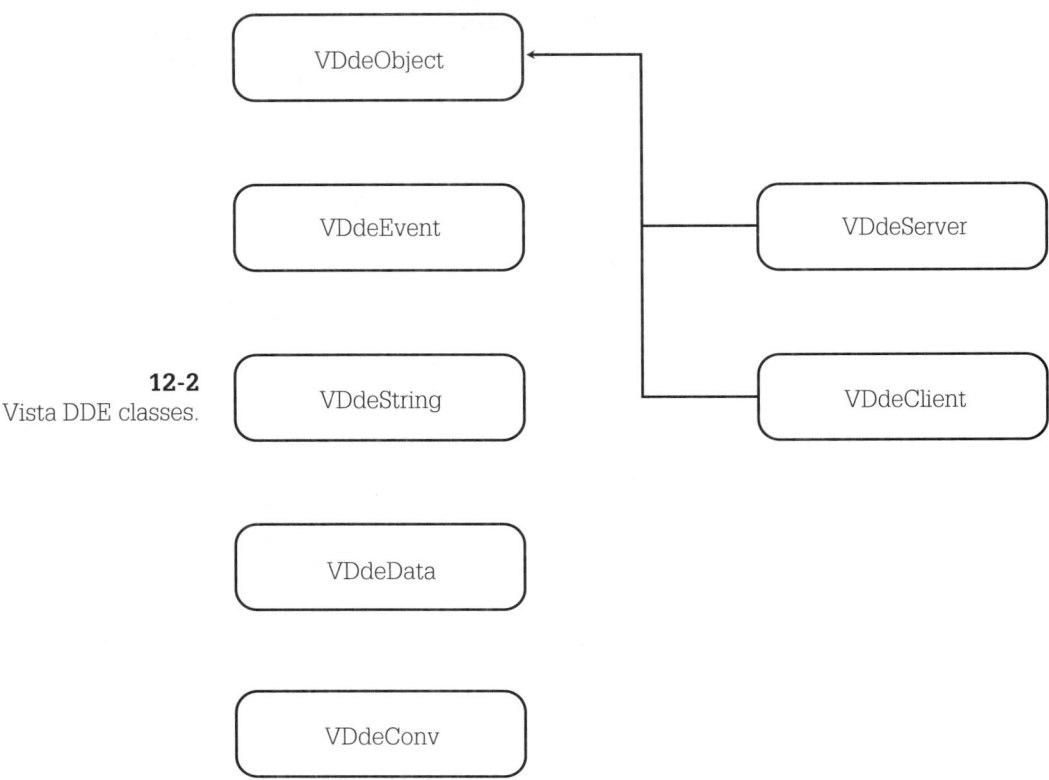

12-2 Vista DDE classes.

DDEML basics   Before looking at the Vista DDE classes, it is important to understand some basic DDEML concepts. In this section, I'll look at four basic concepts: the organization of DDEML applications, the identification scheme used by applications, the components used to identify and pass data between applications, and the channels used to communicate that data. I'll discuss only the basics here; in the next section, I'll dig a little deeper.

A client-server architecture   DDEML applications are based on a client-server architecture. Like the term *object-oriented*, *client-server* has become almost cliche and usually refers to applications distributed among multiple nodes of a network. However, the concept is simple and doesn't require a network: a client application requests data and a server application hands it out. The client and server don't necessarily have to be on separate machines.

The DDEML architecture isolates the application program from typical concerns involved in programming a client-server application. In its original form, DDEML uses Windows messages as its underlying communication channel. However, the NetDDE library provided as a part of Windows for

248 *Clipboard, DDE, & OLE objects*

Workgroups offers the same interface with a network acting as the underlying communication channel.

DDEML applications can act as either a DDE client, a DDE server, or both. The most common examples of DDE applications are word processing and spreadsheet applications that use DDE to provide active links between documents. However, DDE can be just as useful to more specialized applications: it isn't restricted to linking documents. For example, a program needing to access a database can be implemented as a DDE client, with a DDE server dedicated to database access. The same can be said for other types of data access. DDE can be used to access communication ports, network services, or instrumentation, as well as different types of documents.

Identifying DDE data   DDEML servers can use three levels of identification to separate the data objects they provide into a hierarchy (FIG. 12-1). At the top of the hierarchy is one or more service names. Although a server can support more than one service, by convention, each should provide only a single service. Usually, a service name is derived from the name of the application providing the service. The next level is the topic; one service can provide many topics. At the lowest level is the item; each topic can own any number of items.

With this flexible hierarchy, server applications can use an unlimited number of combinations to provide a wide variety of data objects to client applications. For example, a spreadsheet might base a topic name on the name of a spreadsheet file and an item name on a cell address or range of cell addresses. A database server might derive topic names from database names and item names on the tables in that database. To provide a finer level of access, it might use table names as topics, with columns in a table forming the topic's item names.

The problem with DDE's naming scheme is its complexity—both for the server and the client. The server must manage the name space and be able to match a set of names with a data object. Client applications need to know how the server manages those names to gain access to a data item. Unfortunately, there isn't any easy way to simplify the naming scheme without limiting DDE's flexibility. Either the client program or the user needs to know the naming scheme used by server programs to make effective use of the services it provides. Be sure to document your application's naming scheme to allow easier access by client programs.

String management   As I mentioned earlier, the DDEML library simplifies access to data shared between server and client applications. The simplified interface consists of two components: string and data handles.

The first of these components—the string handle—is used in virtually every DDE operation. DDEML string handles identify service, topic, and item names and could potentially eat up a lot of system resources with every application maintaining duplicate names. However, the DDEML uses the system's global atom table to store strings, reducing memory requirements. Instead of keeping their own copies of strings, applications use handles to reference entries in the atom table.

For example, when a server registers a service name, it creates a string handle for the name of the service. DDEML creates a global atom for the string and passes a handle back to the server. When a client application needs to reference the service name and creates a string handle for it, it receives the handle of the string originally created by the server. Each time a string handle is retrieved, DDEML increases a reference count for the string. When the reference count reaches zero, DDEML destroys the string.

Managing DDEML string handles is simple. When you create a string handle and pass it to a DDEML function, the library takes care of deleting the string when it is no longer needed. The only time an application needs to destroy a DDEML string is when DDEML returns an error from a function using the string.

Data objects   Just as string handles represent the names of services, topics, and items; DDEML data handles represent data objects shared between server and client programs. Unlike strings, DDEML data objects are not always owned by the DDEML. When a client sends a data object to a server, DDEML invalidates the data object: the client can't access the object anymore. However, when the server sends a data object to the client, the client must explicitly delete the data object.

Conversations & transactions   When a client application needs to communicate with a server, it opens a conversation between itself and the appropriate server application. You can view a conversation as a connection between the client and server. All communication passes through a conversation, which is always established by a client application.

Under DDEML, conversations are established based on service and topic names. For each unique service/topic combination it needs to access, the client establishes a separate conversation. When multiple servers support the same service, clients can use topic names to determine which server to establish a conversation with. If multiple servers support the same service and topic names, DDEML will choose one server for the client.

After a client and server connect via a conversation, they use transactions to pass data back and forth through that connection. When a client needs a data item from a server, it sends an XTYP_REQUEST transaction. The server responds to the transaction, and the client is notified when it is complete. Clients also can register interest in a specific data item by sending an XTYP_ADVSTART transaction to a server. The server then can send the item to the client whenever it changes.

DDEML transactions can execute in two states: synchronous or asynchronous. A client can send only one synchronous transaction at a time. It is blocked from sending another transaction until the first returns. If the client uses asynchronous transactions instead, it can fire off as many transactions as it needs simultaneously. It will be notified when each transaction completes, or it can cancel transactions that take too long to complete.

As an example of synchronous and asynchronous transactions, consider a client that fills a dialog box with data received from a number of database servers. If it uses synchronous transactions, the client sends a transaction and sets an edit field in the dialog box. It loops through each data item in the dialog box until it is completely filled.

If the client uses asynchronous transactions, it sends all necessary transactions immediately. As it receives a response to each transaction, it fills the corresponding edit control. Because responses are received asynchronously, the third edit control might be filled before the first. However, the client is free to perform other operations while it is waiting for transactions to complete.

The choice between synchronous and asynchronous transactions is yours. Synchronous transactions are simpler, but they affect the responsiveness of applications needing to send many transactions. Asynchronous transactions are a bit more complex, but they offer better performance.

Behind the scenes Conventional DDEML applications use a single function, similar to a window procedure, to respond to DDE events. Like a window procedure, the callback usually contains a large switch statement that branches based on the type of DDE event received.

How are events routed to an application's callback procedure? Remember that the DDEML library is built on top of the message-based DDE protocol. DDEML functions post or send messages to other DDE applications, which receive the messages in a window procedure and call the appropriate callback function. In the Windows environment, messages must be passed to a specific window, so DDEML creates an invisible window on behalf of the application. The window's only purpose is to receive DDE messages. When it receives a DDE message, its window procedure passes the appropriate parameters to the application's callback procedure.

Vista DDE Classes

The Vista library includes several classes designed to simplify the DDE interface. Like the Vista window objects, Vista DLL objects provide a higher level of abstraction while allowing full access to the DDEML API. Vista includes several classes that represent key DDEML concepts; they are illustrated in FIG. 12-3. In this section, I'll look at each class and at some sample applications that implement the DDE protocol using those classes.

12-3
DDE Services, topics, and items.

The VDdeObject class

The VDdeObject class provides operations common to both DDE server and client applications. An instance of the class represents a DDEML instance handle and the object can be passed in place of an instance handle to any DDEML function.

Callback methods The key to any DDEML application is its DDE callback procedure. As I mentioned in the last section, the callback procedure is called to inform the application of DDE events. It is similar in nature to the window procedure, with the most notable similarity being complexity.

The VDdeObject class provides the callback procedure for all Vista DDE applications. It performs much like the VWindow class's window procedure by mapping a single DDE event to a VDdeEvent object and passing it to a specialized member function. By separating transaction support from a single procedure into distinct member functions, DDE support becomes much more manageable.

The callback member function looks and operates much like a window object's action method. It receives a reference to a VDdeEvent object as a parameter and returns a Boolean value specifying whether or not the function filtered the event.

Unlike the VWindow class, the VDdeObject class doesn't need a separate dispatcher object to perform the mapping between events and callback functions. The VDdeObject's callback methods are based on transactions: one callback method handles one type of transaction. Because the number of transactions are limited, the VDdeObject contains a function pointer array as a data member that is used to map transaction identifiers into member functions. The SetCallback and GetCallback member functions access individual elements in the pointer array using a supplied transaction identifier as a direct index into the array.

Like the VWindow class, the VDdeObject class provides a number of default callback methods. A limited number of DDEML transactions can be sent to either client or server applications. These transactions are handled by VDdeObject member functions.

The first, ErrorCallback, is called when DDEML encounters an unrecoverable error, usually resulting from lack of resources. Any object you derive from VDdeObject should implement its own ErrorCallback to release any unneeded resources.

Handling DDEML system errors   The ErrorCallback function is called in response to an XTYP_ERROR transaction. This transaction is sent when the DDEML encounters errors, usually caused by insufficient memory, that prevent it from operating properly. Response to this transaction depends largely on the nature of your application. If your application can release memory when this type of error is encountered, you should override this function in your own class and trigger the release.

A second reason for receiving an XTYP_ERROR event is that the DDEML might have insufficient resources to start a conversation. If you are writing a server application and have blocked transactions, you should unblock them.

Registration callbacks   The RegisterCallback and UnregisterCallback functions are invoked in response to XTYP_REGISTER and XTYP_UNREGISTER transactions. These transactions are triggered whenever a server application registers or unregisters a service. These functions will be invoked for every DDEML application, including the server that registers or unregisters the service name. Although most applications can ignore these functions, you can override them if you need to continually track the service available on your system. If you need to list services only occasionally, use a VDdeConvList object instead.

Disconnect callbacks   The DisconnectCallback member function is invoked in response to a XTYP_DISCONNECT transaction. Either side of a conversation can disconnect from a conversation at any time, so your DDE objects must override this function if your applications depend on conversations being available. Use the DdeReconnect function to attempt to reestablish any disconnected conversations, but don't depend on the function succeeding. If a conversation is disconnected because the application on one side of the conversation has terminated, the function will fail.

The VDdeServer class

Derived from VDdeObject, the VDdeServer adds more callback member functions to those defined by VDdeObject. It also adds some operations and data that automate system topic support. This section covers a lot of information in a very short time, so go grab a cup of coffee.

Connection management callbacks The first callback function I'll look at is the ConnectCallback. The VDdeObject's DDEML callback procedure invokes this function when it receives a XTYP_CONNECT transaction, which is sent whenever a client establishes a conversation with a server application. Until now, most of the default callback member functions performed little or no work at all. They depended on subclasses to specialize and provide additional functionality. However, the ConnectCallback function responds to the XTYP_CONNECT message so that most applications don't need to override this function.

To take advantage of the connection management provided by the VDdeServer class, you must inform your server object of the topics it should support using the AddTopic member function. The server then can verify that the client requesting the connection has passed a valid topic name. The default method allows connections from any client, as long as it requests a supported service and topic name.

If your application needs to limit the number of connections it receives, override this method to verify the connection count, then set the response to the transaction to `False`, call the superclass method to take the default action and increment the counter if it allows the connection. Also, remember to override the DisconnectCallback method to decrement the connection counter when a conversation is terminated. An example of this logic is illustrated in LISTING 12-4.

Listing 12-4
An example of counting connections.

```
const unsigned short MAX_CONNECTIONS = 12;
//...

Boolean MyServer::ConnectCallback(VDdeEventRef event)
{
    if (connect_count >= MAX_CONNECTIONS)
        event.SetResponse(False);
    else
    {
        VDdeServer::ConnectCallback(event);
        if ((Boolean)event.GetResponse() == True)
            connect_count++;
    }
    return True;
}
```

The WildCardCallback function is related to the ConnectCallback function. It is called in response to an XTYP_WILDCONNECT transaction, which is sent when a client requests a list of conversations via a VDdeConvList object. The default action is to create an array of HSZPAIR structures that list the topics supported by the server. If you use the topic management functions of the VDdeServer class, it takes care of this logic for you.

If the server decides to allow a connection from a client application, it responds with a True Boolean value using the VDdeEvent's SetResponse function. The server then receives a XTYP_CONNECT_CONFIRM transaction, which triggers the server's ConfirmCallback member function. If conversations were established with a VDdeConvList object, then this function will be called once for each topic matching the client's selection criteria.

Most applications don't take any action at all when they receive this transaction; however, if your server needs to maintain a list of established conversations, override this method to retrieve the conversation handle from the event. Also, remember to override the DisconnectCallback to remove any disconnected conversations from your list.

I've covered all the callback member functions related to connections between a client and your server. Although they might seem complex at first, you normally don't need to override the default methods. They take the appropriate actions to allow any client to establish one or more conversations with your server application. The next set of methods I'll cover are more complicated: data management callbacks.

Data management callbacks

The real work for a DDE server is in providing data to client applications. The VDdeServer class provides three callback member functions that are invoked to allow the server to format and pass data back to a client application. I'll look at the functions first, then discuss some strategies for using those callbacks in your own server classes.

Request & Advise callbacks   The RequestCallback function is invoked in response to an XTYP_REQUEST transaction, which is sent when a client uses the DdeClientTransaction function to request a data item from the server. The RequestCallback member function is the simplest of the VDdeServer data management callbacks. The server simply determines the topic and item name being requested, formats the data item into a global object, and responds with the global object.

As I discussed earlier, a client can use either synchronous or asynchronous transactions. The transaction model chosen by the client doesn't affect the server. The actions it performs don't change whether the client expects the data immediately or at some time in the future.

If a server is set up to process only a single transaction at a time, it can block incoming transactions when it is busy. The system maintains a queue of blocked transactions that the server can empty at its own pace. There is no need to keep your own queue of waiting transactions.

The default method handles requests for the system topic data items. You should call that method and check the event's response to see if you need to handle the event before going through too much processing. Look at the default method for examples of returning a single data item.

Another callback used to pass data directly back to a client application is the AdviseRequest callback. It is called whenever a server needs to pass a linked data item to a client. It normally takes actions similar to the RequestCallback function. The default AdviseRequest callback just calls the default RequestCallback, so there normally is not any need to override it.

When a client wants to know when a data item changes in value, it sends a XTYP_ADVSTART transaction to the server. The AdvStartCallback member function is called in response to this transaction. The server should use this function to record the topic and item name for the data item. Whenever the data item changes in value, the server calls the server's PostAdvise function, passing the topic and item names. If the client wants to process the data item, the server's AdvRequestCallback will be invoked.

The process of sending updated data for a linked item is called an *advise loop*. The client has several options in how it deals with the data in question. It can create a "hot" link, where the server immediately sends updated data, or it can request a "warm" link, where the server notifies the client that data has changed but the client must request the data from the server. It also can force the server to wait for acknowledgments before it sends notifications or data items. Regardless of the options used by the client, the actions of the server remain the same.

When the client wants to break the link for the data item, it sends a XTYP_ADVSTOP transaction to the server. The AdvStopCallback will be invoked so that the server can remove the topic and item name from its list of active links.

The most common example of a linked data item is when the user links a spreadsheet or graphic to a word processor document. However, data links can be used in other innovative ways. Because a client can have duplicate conversations set up with a single server, it can use links to ensure the data in multiple windows is kept synchronized. Each window object could establish its own link for the items it displays. When the user updates a record in one window, it sends the updated item to the server. The server then notifies any window with that item that its data has changed. The client redraws its window when it receives the new data.

Another novel technique is to use linked items to receive a list of data items from a server. The client requests a link and, each time it receives a data item, adds it to a list. When it receives the final item (denoted by some flag in the item), it terminates the link. This eliminates the need for the server to allocate large buffers for variable length lists of data.

Execute callbacks The most common role for a DDE server is to provide data to client applications. However, it is sometimes useful to allow a server to perform operations for a client instead of or in addition to providing data. The ExecuteCallback member function is invoked when a client sends an XTYP_EXECUTE transaction to the server. The client sends a string that represents the command to be executed by the server. The server defines the command set it supports, and it is responsible for interpreting the command strings passed to it.

Unsolicited callbacks Besides allowing a server to send data items to a client, DDEML provides a means for clients to send unsolicited data to a server. This is an ideal way to allow a server to provide both query and update capabilities. When a client wishes to update a data item, it packages the data into a XTYP_POKE transaction request. The server's PokeCallback accepts the data item from the client and performs whatever actions are necessary to update the item. The PokeCallback member function can work in concert with the advise callbacks to synchronize data displayed in separate windows by a client.

Support objects & operations Besides offering the default callback functions, the VDdeServer class provides a few support functions that ease common actions. The most important of these functions are the Initialize and Cleanup functions, which obtain and release the server's DDEML instance handle. They should be called only once each: Initialize before your programs message loop begins and Cleanup after the message loop ends.

Two other important functions are the Register and Unregister member functions. Register registers the server's service name with DDEML, and Unregister unregisters it (unique names aren't they?). Registering the application's service name with DDEML limits connection requests only to those using the appropriate service name or wildcards.

In the last section, I looked at how servers identify the data items that they can supply to client applications. The VDdeServer uses some small objects that track these identifiers for you, allowing your application to concentrate on providing the data rather than the administrative details involved in responding to system topic requests.

Instances of the VDdeServer object contain a single VDdeService object that represents a service name. It contains a dynamic array of VDdeTopic objects. The VDdeTopic class represents a topic name and contains a dynamic array of VDdeString objects that represent item names.

When an instance of VDdeServer receives a data request for system topic items, it uses these objects to dynamically construct the strings necessary to identify everything it does. The server also maintains a dynamic array of VDdeString objects to hold the names of data formats supported by the specific instance of the server. This array also is used to respond to system topic queries.

An example server: DDESERV   The source code for the example server program, DDESERV.CPP, is contained in LISTING 12-5. Although it is much simpler than a true server application, it does illustrate several of the concepts introduced in this section, including callback functions, global data management, and system topic support. In this next section, I'll look at the other side of the connection: a DDE client application.

Listing 12-5
DDESERV.CPP

```
/* -------------------------------------------------
   ddeserv.cpp

              An example DDE server using the Vista library

   Copyright (C) 1992, by Jeff Mackay
   ------------------------------------------------- */
#pragma hdrfile "vista.sym"
#include <vista.h>
#pragma hdrstop

#include "vddeserv.h"

STDCLASS(TestServer);
class _CLASSTYPE TestServer : public VDdeServer
{
        public:
                TestServer(void)
                {
                        service = VDdeString("Test Service");

                        VDdeTopic topic1(VDdeString("Topic 1"));
                        topic1.AddItem(VDdeString("Item 1"));
                        service.AddTopic(topic1);

                        VDdeTopic topic2(VDdeString("Topic 2"));
                        topic2.AddItem(VDdeString("Item 1"));
                        topic2.AddItem(VDdeString("Item 2"));
                        service.AddTopic(topic2);
                }

        protected:
//              virtual void ConnectCallback(VDdeEventRef);
};

class MainWindow   : public VFrame
{

private:

public:
```

```cpp
            MainWindow(void) : VFrame(NULL,"DDE Server")
            {
            }

            MainWindow(void)
            {
            }


            Boolean CreateAction(VEventRef event)
            {
            VFrame::CreateAction(event);
            return False;
            }
private:
            VDdeString svcName;
};


class ServerApp : public VAppl
{
public:
            ServerApp(charPtr name, HINSTANCE inst, HINSTANCE prevInst,
                            LPSTR cmdLine, int cmdShow) :
                VAppl(name, inst, prevInst, cmdLine, cmdShow) {}

            ServerApp(void)
            {
            }

            void InitConfig(void)
            {
                    server.Initialize();
            }

            void InitWindow(void)
            {
                    main_window = new MainWindow();
            }

            void CleanupConfig(void)
            {
                    server.Cleanup();
        }
private:
            TestServer server;
};
```

```
int PASCAL WinMain(HINSTANCE hInstance, HINSTANCE hPrevInstance,
                   LPSTR lpszCmdLine, int nCmdShow)
{
    _InitEasyWin();
    ServerApp mainApp("DDE Server", hInstance,hPrevInstance,
lpszCmdLine,nCmdShow);
    return mainApp.Run();
}
```

The VDdeClient & Conversation classes

In the last section, I looked at the VDdeServer class and discussed some strategies for implementing your own DDE server applications. In this section, I'll take a quick look at the VDdeClient class and its supporting conversation classes: the VDdeConv and VDdeConvList classes.

Like the VDdeServer class, the VDdeClient class is derived from VDdeObject. It represents a DDEML instance handle and can be used as an argument to any DDEML function. The Initialize and Cleanup functions are similar, and VDdeClient also defines a couple of callback functions. However, the resemblance ends there. Although both client and server applications use DDEML functions, they serve entirely different purposes

For the VDdeServer class, most operations are carried out in response to a callback member function. For the VDdeClient class, the opposite is true: most operations are carried out through normal member functions and an important associated object, the VDdeConv class. The reason for this is that, in the client-server architecture of DDE, the client drives while the server sits back and waits for instructions. The server takes action based on requests from client applications. A client is the active partner in a DDE conversation.

Conversation management The majority of work in a DDE client application involves managing conversations with server applications. The VDdeConv class provides member functions to establish a conversation with a server and to pass requests and data via that conversation. To establish a conversation, use the Connect member function, passing a service and topic name:

```
VDdeString service("Test Service");
VDdeString topic("Topic 1");
VDdeConv conversation;

Boolean result = conversation.Connect(service, topic);
// ...
```

If a server supporting the specified service and topic exists, a conversation will be established and the function will return True. If not, it will return False and the client should take the appropriate action (which usually involves informing the user that the connection couldn't be established).

After a conversation is established, the client can begin to send transactions to the server it is connected to. There are several functions that the client can use to communicate with a server application, with the most common being the Request function.

The Request function asks the server for a data item. Call it with the name of a supported data item and the format you need the data in:

```
VDdeString item("Item 1");
UINT format = RegisterClipboardFormat("Item1Data");
// ...
VDdeHandle<Item1> data = conversation.Request(item, format);

// access the data
charCPtr newName = data->name;

// allow other async transaction requests
conversation.ResetId();
```

By default, the Request function returns a handle to a data item. It uses a synchronous form of transaction that causes the client application to wait until the server returns the data item. However, the VDdeConv class also supports asynchronous transactions, where the client can resume immediately after requesting data—before it receives the data item.

Asynchronous transaction are a bit more complicated than synchronous transactions, but they can provide for smoother communication. For example, if your application displays a dialog with data from multiple servers, it can request all data items at one time and fill the dialog as it receives the data. If the application used synchronous transactions, it would have to wait for one server to return a data item before it could ask for another.

To use asynchronous transactions, specify a timeout value of TIMEOUT_ASYNC in the VDdeConv object's constructor:

```
VDdeConv conversation(TIMEOUT_ASYNC);
```

Any requests that you send with this conversation will be asynchronous transactions. When the server passes a data item back, DDEML will invoke your client object's CompleteCallback member function (which is described later).

Note that only one asynchronous transaction can be active for a conversation at any one time. When you start a transaction, the Request function saves an identifier for the current transaction. If you need to cancel the transaction before the client object receives its data, call the Abandon member function.

The timeout value passed to the VDdeConv constructor is used for all transaction functions. Because DDE deals with communicating between multiple applications, it is important not to let synchronous transactions hang up a client for too long. A server application might become overloaded with too many requests, or it might take too long to process a single request. With synchronous transactions, the client cannot continue until the server finishes processing its request. In a networked DDE connection, this timeout value becomes even more important because networks usually are less reliable than a single system.

The default timeout value of 1000 milliseconds (1 second) should be sufficient for most applications. However, if the server is performing time-intensive tasks or if the server is running on another node of a network, you might need to increase this value.

The Request function is the most commonly used client transaction and is the only one needed for most applications. However, it is limited to other transaction that are available for more specialized tasks. The StartAdvise and StopAdvise functions are used to initiate advise loops on a specific data item. The client object's AdviseDataCallback member function is invoked when the server sends data or notifications on a linked item.

The Execute function instructs a server to execute a command, which is passed as a string. The content of the string must be understood by the server application; there is no standard format for execute command strings.

The Poke function sends unsolicited data to a server. The server must be able to decipher the format and content of the data passed to it. Like execute strings, there is no standard format for data passed to a server with the Poke function.

Transaction complete callbacks Earlier, I looked at the mechanism provided by the VDdeConv class to initiate asynchronous transactions. When a server application responds to an asynchronous transaction, the VDdeClient object's CompleteCallback function is invoked. Override this function if you use asynchronous transactions to access data items.

The VDdeConv class has a static function, GetObject, that converts the conversation handle and transaction identifier in a VDdeEvent received by the CompleteCallback into a VDdeConv pointer:

```
MyClient::CompleteCallback(VDdeEventRef event)
{
    // access the data item
    VDdeHandle<Item1> item(event.hData);
    charCPtr newName = item->name;
    // ...

    // request another item
    VDdeConv conversation = VDdeConv::GetObject(event.conv,
                                                event.data1);
    conversation.ResetId();
    conversation.Request(...);
}
```

Notice the use of the VDdeConv class' ResetId function. Recall that only one asynchronous transaction can be active at any one time for a conversation. The ResetId function informs the VDdeConv object that the transaction is complete and that it can allow another transaction.

Note that only one asynchronous transaction can be active for a conversation at any one time. When you start a transaction, the Request function saves an identifier for the current transaction. If you need to cancel the transaction before the client object receives its data, call the Abandon member function.

Advise data callbacks   A client uses the VDdeConv class' StartAdvise function to begin an advise loop on a specific data item. When the server detects that an item changes, it sends the item (or a notification) to the client. The VDdeClient's AdviseDataCallback function is invoked when it receives the linked item. Override the AdviseDataCallback member function in your own client class if your client application will use advise loops.

The handle for the linked data item is contained in the callback's VDdeEvent parameter. Access it just as you would any other DDE data item. If your application allows multiple active links, you'll need to determine which item the callback was invoked for by comparing the service, topic, and item name strings in the VDdeEvent parameter.

Support classes   In both client and server applications, several classes are used to support common operations. The most common is the VDdeString class. It is used to identify service, topic, and item names and, therefore, is used in almost every operation. While DDEML manages references to DDE strings to minimize the amount of memory needed to refer to those strings, the VDdeString class manages access to DDE string handles. It provides a more natural interface than the DDEML functions.

Two other support classes, the VDdeHandle and VDdeData classes, manage global data passed between client and server applications. Both are template classes that can be used to represent data objects in your application. The VDdeHandle class serves the same role as the VGlobalHandle and VLocalHandle classes discussed in chapter 11. It is derived from the VHandle class to provide simple access to structure members via the pointer dereference operator. Use the VDdeData class for global data objects that originate within your program.

An example client: DDECLNT   The source code for the example DDE client application, DDECLNT.CPP, is contained in LISTING 12-6. The program itself simply connects to the example server application and displays the string received from the server. Again, this program is much simpler than a true DDE client application, but it illustrates the basic concepts without a lot of distractions. In the next section, I'll start looking at a more advanced form of interprocess communication, Object Linking and Embedding.

Listing 12-6
DDECLNT.CPP

```
/* --------------------------------------------------
   ddeclnt.cpp

        An example DDE client using the Vista library

   Copyright (C) 1992, by Jeff Mackay

   -------------------------------------------------- */
#pragma hdrfile "vista.sym"
#include <vista.h>
#pragma hdrstop

#include "vddeclnt.h"
class MainWindow  : public VFrame
{

private:

public:

        MainWindow(void) : VFrame(NULL,"DDE Client")
        {
        }

        MainWindow(void)
        {
        }


        Boolean CreateAction(VEventRef event)
        {
        VFrame::CreateAction(event);
        return False;
        }
private:
        VDdeString svcName;

};


class ClientApp : public VAppl
{
public:
        ClientApp(charPtr name, HINSTANCE inst, HINSTANCE prevInst,
                              LPSTR cmdLine, int cmdShow) :
             VAppl(name, inst, prevInst, cmdLine, cmdShow) {}

        ClientApp(void)
        {
        }
```

Clipboard, DDE, & OLE objects

```
        void InitConfig(void)
        {
                client.Initialize();
    VDdeString service;
                VDdeString topic(SZDDESYS_TOPIC);
                conv_list.Connect(service, topic);
                VDdeConv conv;
                for (conv = conv_list.First();
                                conv.GetHandle() != 0;
                                conv = conv_list.Next())
                {
                        cout << "connected" << endl;
                }
        }

        void InitWindow(void)
        {
                main_window = new MainWindow();
        }

        void CleanupConfig(void)
        {
                conv_list.Disconnect();
                client.Cleanup();
    }
private:
        VDdeClient      client;
    VDdeConvList    conv_list;
};


int PASCAL WinMain(HINSTANCE hInstance, HINSTANCE hPrevInstance,
                                LPSTR lpszCmdLine, int nCmdShow)
{
    _InitEasyWin();
        ClientApp mainApp("DDE Client", hInstance,hPrevInstance,
                                        lpszCmdLine,nCmdShow);

        return mainApp.Run();
}
```

The Vista DDE classes simplify sharing data between a client and server program but leave the presentation of that data to client applications. Object Linking and Embedding or OLE was introduced with Windows 3.0. It offers almost all the features of DDE, while adding an object-oriented flavor to interprocess communication.

Object linking & embedding

Like DDE, OLE is based on a client-server model. Instead of centering around applications, however, OLE is document-centered. An OLE client application presents a document to users and allows them to link or embed objects in that document. OLE server applications manage the linked or embedded objects, which might be of any data type: text, graphics, sound, etc.

The Vista library includes a set of classes (FIG. 12-4) that wrap around standard OLE objects. Besides providing a C^{++} interface to OLE, these classes implement many of the boilerplate functions necessary for all applications. They greatly simplify the task of adding OLE capabilities to your applications.

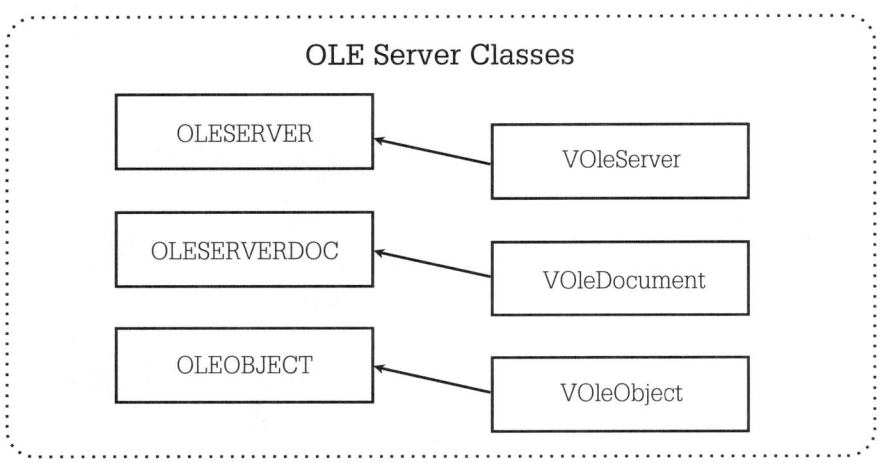

12-4
Vista OLE classes.

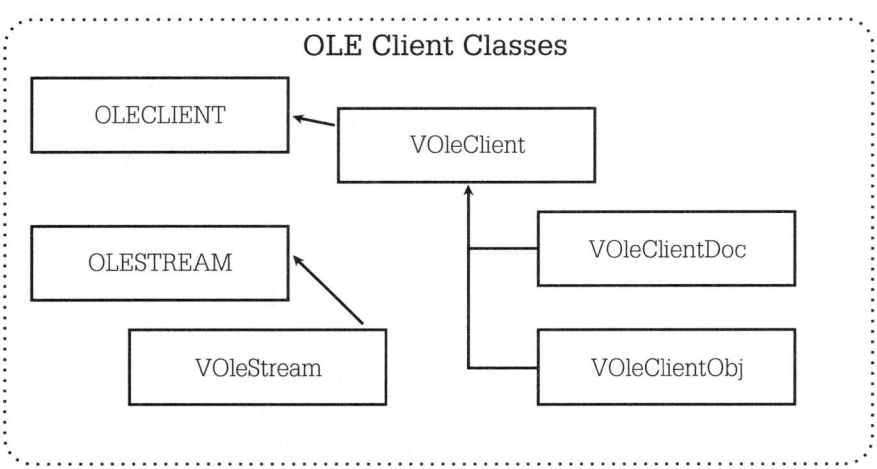

In the next section, I'll discuss some basic OLE concepts before moving on to a discussion of the Vista OLE classes. I won't try to cover the entire subject of OLE in this chapter—only the Vista implementation of the OLE protocol and some ideas for practical application of OLE. Several books listed in the bibliography cover OLE extensively.

Why use OLE?

Graphical user interfaces like Windows brought on a whole new breed of document-based applications. In just a few years, applications moved from simply displaying text to providing a realistic view of a document on screen as it would be seen on paper. User demand for WYSIWYG (what-you-see-is-what-you-get) word processing and desktop publishing applications soared. Spreadsheets and database managers also began to offer many of the features needed to produce presentation-quality graphics.

Through evolution, these new applications have grown unwieldy. Many provide more capabilities in presentation graphics than they do in their own subject areas. Word processors duplicate much of the functionality of spreadsheets, which provide many of the same operations offered by a database management system. All this duplication of effort is self-defeating. When one vendor introduces a new feature, others follow with their own version immediately. Applications have become so loaded down with features that most users need only a fraction of the features offered by their "productivity" programs. They have become so complex that users simply can't learn the operations that should make their jobs simpler.

To address this issue, system software vendors have begun introducing an new model of document-oriented computing. Instead of revolving around applications, a document-oriented system concentrates on documents. A document can consist of many components: text, graphics, images, sound, video, and business or other technical data. Each component in a document is an object; the system manages links between objects, and applications only manage one type of object.

Using this new model simplifies applications. Instead of using a single application to create and manipulate each different type of data, objects in a document manage themselves. The user can create a text document using a word processor, link to a table object from a spreadsheet application, and embed a phone-mail message in the document (FIG. 12-5). The word processor doesn't need to know how to render, manipulate, or store different objects—it concentrates only on what it does best and lets the system manage the rest.

All this is fine for general purpose tools like word processors and spreadsheets, but how does it apply to a developer building business or technical applications? Most of these applications are task-oriented: an accounting application records business transactions, a satellite controller records transmission data. However, more and more modern applications demand use of nontraditional data types: a personnel system needs to display employee pictures along with an address and employment history data, a telemarketing system must store voice mail calls in a to-do list, an accounting system interacts

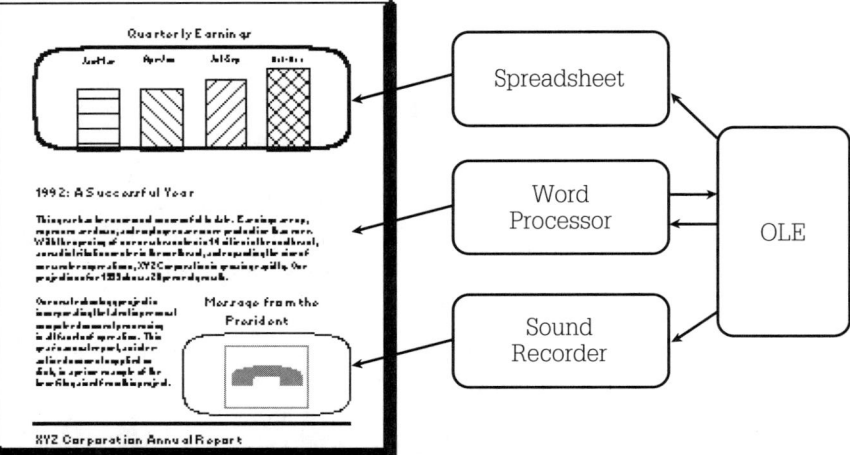

12-5
An OLE document.

with a spreadsheet to calculate financial data. The document-oriented architecture of OLE simplifies the task of adding these features to a system.

Rather than writing the code that displays an image, plays an audio file, or runs a video file, embed an object or link in a traditional database record. Allow the object to display, play, or run itself, and let the spreadsheet work on new ways of calculating returns on investment. Adding new capabilities can be as simple as purchasing a new application that provides those capabilities.

The document-oriented interface offers as many advantages to users as it does to developers. When dealing with a document-oriented interface, users no longer need to concern themselves with the applications used to manipulate data: they concentrate on data objects instead. They don't need to remember where an application is, or even which application to use to modify an object; the system handles that for them.

Unfortunately, the first release of OLE uses a rather complicated interface that uses the clipboard extensively. Using OLE requires a user to know more about an application than they did without using OLE. For example, when a user wants to embed or link to an object, they create the object in a server application and copy it to the clipboard. When the object is pasted into the target document, it becomes an embedded (or linked) object. When they want to modify an embedded object, they double-click on it and OLE activates the object's server application for them (this is at least easier to do than before). The OLE specification covers a large number of user interface rules that must be implemented to fully support OLE.

The second release of OLE provides a much better interface. It supports complex objects (objects that contain other objects), drag-and-drop, and in-place editing. The new release is being tested as I am writing this chapter. It promises many new features, is easier to use, and will definitely make use of OLE much more widespread.

What is OLE?

Object Linking and Embedding enables an application to implement the standard Windows document-oriented interface. It is composed of several API functions and structures that together implement the entire standard.

Like DDE, OLE is built around a client-server architecture. An OLE client is the active partner and calls OLE functions to instruct a server to perform actions on an object. The OLE server, as the passive partner, sits and waits for instructions from a client application. Two separate DLLs (OLECLI.DLL and OLESRV.DLL) contain the client and server API functions. A third OLE entity, the object handler, is not currently supported by the Vista OLE classes.

Figure 12-6 illustrates the communication path used by OLE programs through the OLE client and server DLLs. Notice that the client and server programs don't communicate with each other directly. Instead, all communication is handle by the OLE DLLs. OLE version 1 uses DDE messages entirely for all interprocess communication. With release 2, OLE also can use a more sophisticated form of communication called a remote procedure call (RPC). This new communication scheme allows you to distribute clients and servers across multiple nodes of a network. It also means that it isn't a good idea to rely on the use of DDE messages in your OLE implementation.

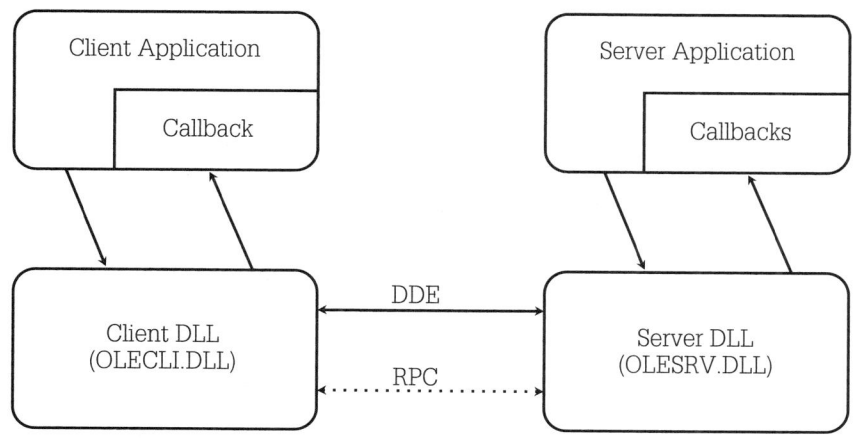

12-6
Communication flow in an OLE program.

The secret behind the OLE API is in its "virtual table" structures that hold a number of pointers to callback functions called by the OLE DLLs. Each OLE object type uses a different virtual table with pointers to the callback functions necessary to implement the behavior of that type of object. An application passes a pointer to an object's virtual table structure when it creates an OLE object, and OLE uses the virtual table to calls the object's functions through the pointers.

Don't confuse OLE's virtual tables with C++ virtual tables. C++ implements virtual functions through hidden tables of function pointers embedded in an object that also are called virtual tables. When you call a virtual function, the compiler takes care of resolving virtual function references through the virtual table. Other than the fact that the OLE virtual table contains function pointers, it has no relationship to a C++ virtual table at all.

When a client or server application needs to use OLE features, it passes a pointer to one of the OLE structures to an API function. Each type of structure contains a single data member: a pointer to the virtual table for that type of structure. Applications normally tack additional data on to the end of these structures to hold the data they need to manage a particular OLE entity.

The behavior of all OLE objects, and the documents that own those objects, is driven entirely by the client and server applications. The OLE DLLs provide only the mechanisms necessary for the client and server applications to work together.

OLE server applications

An OLE server application implements the behavior of an OLE object. Server applications have several responsibilities, all dealing with objects served to a client application. The first is to associate data with an object so that the application can render the object when necessary. The second responsibility is to actually draw a representation of an object, or an object itself into a client device. The third might or might not be necessary for server applications you implement. It allows a client to invoke a command that acts on an embedded or linked object.

Two server characteristics split OLE servers into a couple of distinct groups. The first is whether a single instance of the server can handle one or more than one objects at any one time. A single-instance server usually presents a multiple document interface and can handle multiple objects simultaneously. The single-instance server is more difficult to implement but offers improved performance and, in many cases, a better interface. A multi-instance server can handle only a single object at a time but is easier to implement.

The second characteristic deals with a server's ability to act outside of OLE. Most general-purpose applications such as database managers, spreadsheets, or graphics programs also provide OLE server capabilities. Other applications exist only to serve different objects to client applications. These mini-servers offer fewer features than full servers but are much simpler to implement.

The interface for both client and server applications is similar: a structure containing a pointer to a virtual table is passed to OLE functions. The virtual table contains pointers to functions implementing a certain portion of the application's behavior.

A server application uses three different OLE structures to interact with client applications. The OLESERVER structure contains a pointer to the server's virtual table. Most of the functions in the server's virtual table involve creating and managing documents. The second structure, an OLESERVERDOC structure, contains a pointer to the server's document virtual table. The document virtual table contains pointers to functions that create and manage objects. The final structure, an OLEOBJECT structure, contains a pointer to an object virtual table. The virtual table contains pointers to functions that implement the behavior of a specific type of object.

The server OLE structures form a clean hierarchy: a server can own several documents, each of which can own several objects. The structures themselves can contain anything, the only requirement is that the first data member be a pointer to the structure's virtual table. The Vista library takes advantage of this by deriving all Vista OLE classes directly from the base OLE data types.

OLE client applications

OLE Client applications drive the connection between a document and the servers that implement object behavior. The first responsibility of a client application is to create and register documents, whether they are read from a file or a database or are created from scratch. The second responsibility is to call the OLE API when the user wants to embed an object or insert a link to an object into a document. It also must notify OLE when an object needs to be displayed or edited.

The final requirement is perhaps the most important. A client needs to save enough information about an object so that it can later retrieve, display, and edit or play the object. For linked objects, this usually means saving the path name for the file containing the object along with the object's class name. However, for embedded objects, the client also stores the object itself. Because the client is responsible for storage, an image or audio file can be stored on a remote system or in a database instead of in a local file. The server has full access to the data, although it doesn't know how or where it is stored.

As I mentioned earlier, the first version of OLE has a complicated user interface, and nowhere is this more apparent than in a client application. To implement a full OLE client interface, an application must add several commands to its edit menu, including commands to paste objects, link to objects, insert new objects, and perform actions or "verbs" on selected objects. Most of these options also require interaction with the clipboard. In addition, a client must use OLE to display embedded and linked objects and allow the user to double-click with the mouse on objects to activate their primary verb.

If you are writing your own word processor or spreadsheet application, by all means, include a full-fledged client interface. However, many applications still can take advantage of the benefits offered by OLE without implementing a full client interface. The OLE specification was designed with general-purpose applications in mind. For more specialized applications, a subset of the client interface is more appropriate.

For example, consider the human resources application I mentioned above. The application displays an employee's picture along side address and employment history data. It needs OLE for image processing capabilities, but it only allows one image at a time linked to a database record and it displays it in a specific area of one window or dialog box. The application must allow a user to set the image for a record, possibly using the "insert new object" command or something similar. It should also allow some (probably not all) users to edit or replace the image by double-clicking on it or choosing some menu command that does the same thing. For this application, a full client interface doesn't make sense.

As a second example, consider a financial application that interacts with a spreadsheet. It needs to allow the user to select a set of data, copy it to the clipboard, and manipulate the data in a spreadsheet. It may need to execute macros in the spreadsheet application, and (with OLE 2) it may even use the spreadsheet to create and display data in the first place. This application needs to implement a different (and probably wider) subset of the client interface than the human resources application. But again, a full client interface isn't necessary.

An OLE client application normally uses two structures to interact with OLECLI.DLL. The first, an OLECLIENT structure, contains a single data member: a pointer to the client's virtual table. The client virtual table is simple—it only has a single function pointer. The client callback is called whenever an object it owns is modified in some way.

The second structure is an OLESTREAM structure, which contains a pointer to the stream's virtual table. The streams virtual table contains pointers to functions that read an object from a stream and write it back to a stream. Again, don't confuse an OLE stream with a C^{++} stream. Look at an OLE stream as just a repository for embedded objects. The stream itself could be a file, a database, shared memory, or any means of making an object persist for later access. A C^{++} stream could be used as an OLE stream.

Client applications also use their own representations of documents. For a word processor or spreadsheet, a document is usually a file. For other applications, a database record or some combination of records could serve as a document. The only requirement is that the client be able to determine the identity of embedded and linked objects in the document.

Vista OLE classes

The Vista OLE classes were designed to hide some of the administrative details of building OLE applications. They are thin wrappers around the standard OLE structures and functions. Because of the differences between OLE event handling and standard message handling, member functions in the OLE classes don't provide the same event-response functionality found in other Vista classes.

Figure 12-4 illustrates the OLE classes provided by Vista. Unlike other Vista class hierarchies, the OLE hierarchy is very shallow—only two to three levels deep. Because OLE already is based on objects, choosing the classes was simple; implementing them wasn't.

Other than the difference in event dispatching, which I'll look at later, the Vista OLE classes are similar to other Vista classes. They add a level of consistency and greater simplicity to the OLE API. They make implementing an OLE application much simpler than trying to do it from scratch.

Although the Vista classes are pretty comprehensive, if you implement a full OLE interface, you'll need to resort to using the OLE API for some functions. Some operations can be complex because OLE is an asynchronous communication scheme: when a client communicates with a server, it can continue to work while the server is doing its job.

Event dispatching

Rather than using a message-passing communication scheme, OLE uses the virtual table mechanism to drive the behavior of applications. This mechanism requires a different event dispatching approach.

As I mentioned earlier, the OLE structures contain a single member—a pointer to a virtual table structure. The OLE function depends only on this single data member; however, it must be placed physically as the first longword in the structure. While this might not seem to be a problem, with C++ it is. Recall the earlier discussion of C++ virtual pointers. If a class has any virtual functions, the compiler automatically creates and stores a pointer to the class's virtual table into each instance of the class. Borland C++, by default, places this pointer before any data members. So, if Vista used its own class with virtual functions and a single data member pointing to the OLE virtual table structure, you couldn't pass the structure directly to OLE functions. If you did, OLE would try to use the C++ virtual table as its own—not exactly what you wanted.

However, the OLE structures have no virtual functions and, therefore, no C++ virtual tables or hidden virtual table pointer. Because an OLE structure is used as a base class, passing an instance of a Vista class to OLE works as intended. The compiler translates the pointer to an instance of the Vista class into a pointer to an instance of the OLE structure. OLE receives the data it expects and can use it just as if it were received from a C program.

To hide some of the complexity of OLE event-handling, each of the Vista OLE classes delegates all direct interaction with OLE callbacks to an implementation class. An implementation class includes static member functions for each callback used by its owning interface class. The callback functions are declared as static because they are called directly from the OLE DLLs and receive no hidden `this` pointer. The first argument to each callback function is a pointer to an instance of the OLE structure originally passed by the program to an OLE function. When a static callback function receives the original pointer, it can safely cast it back to a pointer to an instance of a Vista class, producing an interface object. The callback function then forwards the callback to a normal member function for the interface class.

The event dispatching mechanism used by the Vista OLE classes is much harder to describe than it is to understand. If you still are puzzled by how this all works, look at the source code on disk or in the appendix. In the next section, I'll look at an example of OLE event dispatching at work with an OLE mini-server.

Building an OLE server

An OLE server has a simple job: it manages OLE objects. This simple task, however, can require quite a bit of code. The Vista OLE server classes have taken most of the drudgery out of implementing a server application, but you still must implement many details yourself.

Before implementing your own server, consider purchasing one. Most commercial applications today offer an OLE server interface. Most of the "applets" supplied with Windows are themselves OLE server applications. Once you decide that you need a server, plan ahead before creating it. What type of server do you want to create: multi-instance or single-instance? Do you want a full interface or a "mini-server?" The example application takes the easy road on both choices.

The OLESRVR application is a multi-instance server. Each time a client needs to activate or draw an object, OLE creates a new instance of the server. The program offers only a single-document interface (e.g., it deals only with a single main window, instead of being an MDI application). Multi-instance servers are less efficient but easier to implement. Single-instance servers have more information to manage with their multi-document (MDI) interface, but they usually are more efficient.

OLESRVR doesn't include any mechanism for storing and retrieving its own objects and, therefore, is called a "mini-server." To make debugging and demonstration easier, the sample server isn't even a real mini-server. A true mini-server should display an error message if it is invoked outside of OLE. OLESERVER doesn't care: if you start it outside of OLE, it will just sit and wait for an OLE request. I guess you could call it a mini-mini-server. The code for OLESERVER is illustrated in LISTING 12-7; its header in LISTING 12-8; and its resource script in LISTING 12-9.

Listing 12-7
OLESRVR.CPP

```cpp
/* -------------------------------------------------------
    olesrvr.cpp

        A sample OLE server program.

    Copyright (C) 1992, by Jeff Mackay
------------------------------------------------------- */

#pragma hdrfile "vista.sym"
#include <vista.h>
#pragma hdrstop

#include <volesrvr.h>
#include "olesrvr.h"

// object functions:

SampleObject::SampleObject(VOleDocRef par, charCPtr name,
                                          LPOLECLIENT client)
        : VOleObject(par, name, client)
{
        format_count = 3;
        formats = new UINT[format_count];
        formats[0] = VOleServer::native;
        formats[1] = CF_METAFILEPICT;
        formats[3] = 0;
        ServerWindowPtr win =
                (ServerWindowPtr) GetApplication().GetMainWindow();
        win->SetObject(this);
}


void SampleObject::ShowCallback(BOOL setFocus)
{
        if (setFocus)
                SetFocus(*(GetApplication().GetMainWindow()));
        if (string.Length() == 0)
                string = "Hello, World!";
```

Listing 12-7
Continued.

```
}

void SampleObject::Draw(VDeviceRef dev)
{
        SetMapMode(dev, MM_TEXT);
        TextOut(dev, 10, 10, string, string.Length());
}

HGLOBAL SampleObject::GetNative(void)
{
        HGLOBAL handle = GlobalAlloc(GMEM_DDESHARE, string.Length()+1);
        if (handle == 0)
        {
                SetStatus(OLE_ERROR_MEMORY);
                return 0;
        }

        LPSTR buffer = (LPSTR)GlobalLock(handle);
        if (buffer == 0)
        {
                SetStatus(OLE_ERROR_MEMORY);
                return 0;
        }
        lstrcpy(buffer, string);
        GlobalUnlock(handle);
        return handle;
}

SampleObject::SampleObject()
{
    delete formats;
}




// Document functions:
SampleDoc::SampleDoc(VOleServerRef par, charCPtr name)
        : VOleDoc(par,name)
{
}

void SampleDoc::HostNamesCallback(charCPtr client, charCPtr)
{
        char buffer[128];
        wsprintf(buffer, "Vista Object in %s", client);
    GetApplication().GetMainWindow()->SetCaption(buffer);
}

VOleObjectPtr SampleDoc::GetObjectCallback(charCPtr name,
                                LPOLECLIENT client)
{
```

```cpp
        return new SampleObject(*this, name, client);
}

VOleObjectPtr SampleDoc::GetDocCallback(LPOLECLIENT client)
{
        return new SampleObject(*this, 0, client);
}


// Server functions:
Server::Server(charCPtr name)
   : VOleServer(name)
{
}

VOleDocPtr Server::NewDocument(charCPtr docName)
{
        return new SampleDoc(*this, docName);
}



// standard window functions
ServerWindow::ServerWindow(void)
        : VFrame(GetApplication(), 0, "Vista Sample OLE Server")
{
        object=0;
        menu = new VMenu(this, "ServerMenu");
}

ServerWindow::ServerWindow(void)
{
        delete object;
}

void ServerWindow::SetObject(SampleObjectPtr obj)
{
        object = obj;
}

Boolean ServerWindow::UpdateCommand(VEventRef)
{
                VASSERT(object != 0);
                object->NotifyClient(OLE_SAVED);
        return True;
}

Boolean ServerWindow::ExitAction(VEventRef)
{
        SendMessage(*this, WM_CLOSE, 0, 0);
```

Listing 12-7
Continued.

```
        return True;
}

Boolean ServerWindow::PaintAction(VEventRef)
{
        if (!object)
                return False;

        VPaintDevice dev(*this);
        object->Draw(dev);
        return True;
}

void ServerWindow::InitActions(void)
{
        VFrame::InitActions();
        AddCommand((VAction)&ServerWindow::UpdateCommand, 101);
    AddCommand((VAction)&ServerWindow::ExitCommand, 102);
}


class ServerApp : public VAppl
{
public:
        ServerApp(charPtr name, HINSTANCE inst, HINSTANCE prevInst,
                        charPtr cmdLine, int cmdShow) :
                VAppl(name, inst, prevInst, cmdLine, cmdShow)
        {
        }

        ServerApp(void)
        {
        }

        virtual void InitConfig(void)
        {
                server.Register("VistaTest");
        server.SetEmbedded(IsEmbedded());
        }

        virtual void InitWindow(void)
        {
                main_window = new ServerWindow();
        }

        virtual void CleanupConfig(void)
        {
        server.Revoke();
    }

        Boolean IsEmbedded()
        {
```

```
                    if (cmd_line.Length() == 0)
                    return False;

                    LPSTR cmdLine = cmd_line;
                    if (_fstrnicmp(cmdLine+1, "embedding", 9) == 0)
                            return True;
                    else
                    return False;
        }
    Server server;
};


int PASCAL WinMain(HINSTANCE hInstance, HINSTANCE hPrevInstance,
                                LPSTR lpszCmdLine, int nCmdShow)
{
        ServerApp mainApp("Vista OLE Server",hInstance,
                                        hPrevInstance,
                                        lpszCmdLine,nCmdShow);

        return mainApp.Run();
}
```

```
/* ---------------------------------------------------------------
    olesrvr.h

        Interfaces for the classes in the sample OLE server program

    Copyright (C) 1992, by Jeff Mackay - TAB Books

--------------------------------------------------------------- */
#ifndef _OLESRVR_H
#define _OLESRVR_H
STDCLASS(SampleObject);
STDCLASS(SampleDoc);
STDCLASS(Server);
STDCLASS(ServerWindow);

class _CLASSTYPE SampleObject : public VOleObject
{
        public:
                SampleObject(VOleDocRef par, charCPtr name,
                                        LPOLECLIENT client);
                void ShowCallback(BOOL setFocus);
                void Draw(VDeviceRef dev);
                HGLOBAL GetNative(void);
                SampleObject();

        private:
```

Listing 12-8
OLESRVR.H

Listing 12-8
Continued.

```
                    VString string;
        };

        class _CLASSTYPE SampleDoc : public VOleDoc
        {
                public:
                        SampleDoc(VOleServerRef par, charCPtr name);
                        void HostNamesCallback(charCPtr client, charCPtr doc);
                        VOleObjectPtr GetObjectCallback(charCPtr name,
LPOLECLIENT client);
                        VOleObjectPtr GetDocCallback(LPOLECLIENT client);
        };

        class _CLASSTYPE Server : public VOleServer
        {
                public:
                        Server(charCPtr name=0);
                        virtual VOleDocPtr NewDocument(charCPtr docName);
        };

        class ServerWindow  : public VFrame
        {
        public:
                ServerWindow(void);
                ServerWindow(void);
                void SetObject(SampleObjectPtr obj);

        protected:
                Boolean UpdateCommand(VEventRef);
                Boolean ExitAction(VEventRef);
                Boolean PaintAction(VEventRef);
                void InitActions(void);
        private:
                SampleObjectPtr object;
        };


        #endif
```

Listing 12-9
OLESRVR.RC

```
ServerMenu MENU
BEGIN
        POPUP "&File"
        BEGIN
        MENUITEM "&Update", 101
                MENUITEM "E&xit", 102
                END
END
```

Creating a Vista OLE server object The first task in implementing an OLE server application is deriving a class from the VOleServer class. The server class has several callback functions, but the VOleServer class handles most automatically.

The only function you must override is the NewDocument member function. It returns an instance of your derived document class for use in managing objects:

```
VOleDocPtr Server::NewDocument(charCPtr docName)
{
    return new SampleDoc(*this, docName);
}
```

This function returns a new instance of the SampleDoc class. The OLE server DLL will call this function whenever a client creates an object handled by the server.

Creating a Vista OLE server document object A server application's server object is simple but important. It manages the document objects that represent documents in client applications. The server document class, VOleDocument, is just as important: it manages objects within a document. Like the server class, to use a document class, you need to derive your own class from VOleDocument:

```
class MyDocument : public VOleDocument
{
    //...
}
```

The server document class also has several callback functions, but the most important for most applications are the HostNamesCallback, GetObjectCallback, and GetDocCallback.

The HostNamesCallback updates the server window's title bar to reflect a readable name for the object currently being edited. After a client creates a new object, it passes its client and document names for the server to display. The server's document object receives a callback that is passed the strings forwarded by the client. Although this callback function is optional, it is simple enough (and noticeable enough) to implement in every server application.

The GetObjectCallback and GetDocCallback functions are very similar: they both return a new instance of an OLE object. The GetDocCallback is called to return an object that represents an entire client document, while the GetObjectCallback must return a new object that represents the OLE object. A document object is rarely used, but it still is required.

Objects & clipboard formats OLE objects represent themselves in several different ways. The most common representation is called the object's *presentation format* and usually is a metafile picture that contains the GDI instructions necessary to draw an object. Another common format is the bitmap, which is used in place of a metafile format by some applications. Other formats are specific to OLE. At least one is always required: native format. An object's native format is the internal representation of an object. Other OLE-specific formats include OwnerLink, used by the clipboard to identify embedded objects, and ObjectLink, which is used by the clipboard to identify linked objects.

To identify the formats supported by an object, allocate space for and fill the formats data member:

```
SampleObject::SampleObject(VOleDocRef par, charCPtr name,
                                           LPOLECLIENT client)
    : VOleObject(par, name, client)
{
    format_count = 3;
    formats = new UINT[format_count];
    formats[0] = VOleServer::native;
    formats[1] = VOleServer::owner_link;
    formats[2] = CF_METAFILEPICT;
    formats[3] = CF_BITMAP;
    formats[4] = 0;
}
```

The formats supported by an object directly control the operations it will support. If an object includes only the native format, client applications can't display it, embed it, or link to it. If an object includes native, owner_link, and CF_METAFILEPICT formats, a client can display it and embed it but can't link to it. The OLESRVR application is a mini-server; it can't allow links because it doesn't know how to store its own objects.

Managing an OLE object A client object should override several callback functions. The first is the ShowCallback function, which is invoked when the user activates or creates a new object. The function should set focus to and initialize itself:

```
void SampleObject::ShowCallback(BOOL setFocus)
{
    if (setFocus)
            SetFocus(*(GetApplication().GetMainWindow()));
    if (string.Length() == 0)
            string = "Hello, OLE!";
}
```

The Draw member function should draw the object on a device context. Because a device context is received as a parameter to the Draw member function, the object can be drawn on a client application or on the server's window with the same function. The SampleObject's Draw function just prints a greeting:

```
void SampleObject::Draw(VDeviceRef dev)
{
```

```
        SetMapMode(dev, MM_TEXT);
        TextOut(dev, 10, 10, string, string.Length());
}
```

Note the call to SetMapMode. The device passed to the Draw function on behalf of a client application actually is a metafile device that OLE eventually will play to the client's own window or paint device context. OLE always uses the MM_HIMETRIC mapping mode; therefore, if you need to use another mode, you'll have to translate coordinates and dimensions between MM_HIMETRIC and the desired mode.

The final two callback functions that must be implemented by a server application deal with an object's native data format. The GetNative member function packs an object's native data into one block of global memory and returns the handle to the data block. It is called in several different places but is most useful when a client object needs to store an embedded object:

```
HGLOBAL SampleObject::GetNative(void)
{
    HGLOBAL handle = GlobalAlloc(GMEM_DDESHARE, string.Length()+1);
    if (handle == 0)
    {
        SetStatus(OLE_ERROR_MEMORY);
        return 0;
    }
    LPSTR buffer = (LPSTR)GlobalLock(handle);
    if (buffer == 0)
    {
        SetStatus(OLE_ERROR_MEMORY);
        return 0;
    }
    lstrcpy(buffer, string);
    GlobalUnlock(handle);
    return handle;
}
```

The SetNative function is the converse of GetData. It takes a global memory block, pulls the object's native data out, and stores it into member functions. It is invoked when a client reads an object from a stream:

```
void SampleObject::SetNative(HGLOBAL hdl)
{
    charPtr newString = (charPtr)GlobalLock(hdl);
    string = newString;
    GlobalUnlock(hdl);
}
```

Several other callback functions are available but are used only in certain circumstances. Before I go on to discuss client applications, I need to cover an important restriction in server applications. Server callback functions are called in an asynchronous manner and, therefore, are very volatile. Don't call any OLE functions from a callback function, and don't display a message box or other modal dialog that causes the application to enter a secondary message loop. A modal dialog's message loop will discard any DDE messages necessary to communicate with client applications. If you ignore this restriction, you probably will hang up either the client, the server, or the entire system.

If you need to call OLE functions or display a message box in response to a callback function, post a message to the application's window and allow it to take the appropriate action.

Registering an OLE application The system registration database contains information about system entities, including OLE servers and objects. Under Windows 3.1, the registration database is used exclusively for OLE applications. Under Windows NT, the registration database is used extensively for many other purposes. Regardless of which system you are targeting, the registration entries are identical.

I won't get into a full discussion of the registration database here, it is fully covered in the Windows reference manual included with Borland C^{++}. As a brief overview, every server and object type must have an entry in the system registration database so that OLE knows how to activate and where to find server applications for specific objects. There are two ways of registering server applications: through the registration API and via the REGEDIT applet included with Windows 3.1. The OLESRVR application uses the OLESRVR.REG file to register its information:

```
REGEDIT
ENTRIES FOR VistaTest SERVER
HKEY_CLASSES_ROOT\.vst = VistaTest
HKEY_CLASSES_ROOT\VistaTest = VistaTest Object
HKEY_CLASSES_ROOT\VistaTest\protocol\StdFileEditing\verb\0 = EDIT
HKEY_CLASSES_ROOT\VistaTest\protocol\StdFileEditing\server = olesrvr.exe
```

Before you can run the OLESERVER sample application, you'll need to merge this file with the registration database using REGEDIT. For more information, see the online help for REGEDIT.

One final requirement for using the OLESERVER application. All OLE server applications, including OLESERVER, must reside in a directory included in the path, in the Windows directory, or in the Windows system directory. Move the OLESRVR.EXE file before trying to create objects.

Building an OLE client I mentioned earlier that implementing a full OLE client interface can be a daunting task. In this section, I'll implement a subset of the OLE client interface to present an example of using OLE. Although it covers only a portion of the interface, you can use the concepts introduced in this section to add OLE client functionality to your own applications.

The code for the sample OLE client program, OLECLNT, is illustrated in LISTING 12-10. Its header file is in LISTING 12-11, and its resource script is in LISTING 12-12.

Listing 12-10
OLECLNT.CPP

```cpp
/* --------------------------------------------------------
   oleclnt.cpp

        Sample OLE client application

   Copyright (C) 1992, by Jeff Mackay - TAB Books
   -------------------------------------------------- */
#pragma hdrfile "vista.sym"
#include <vista.h>
#pragma hdrstop

#include <voleclnt.h>
#include "oleclnt.h"

STDCLASS(ClientDoc);
STDCLASS(ClientObj);
STDCLASS(ClientWindow);
STDCLASS(ClientApp);

class _CLASSTYPE ClientObj : public VOleClientObj
{
        public:
                ClientObj(VOleClientDocPtr doc=0, VWindowPtr win=0,
                        LPOLEOBJECT obj=0)
                        : VOleClientObj(doc, win, obj)
                {
                }

        protected:
                virtual void SavedCallback(LPOLEOBJECT)
                {
                VASSERT(owner);
                        owner->Invalidate();
                }

                virtual void ChangedCallback(LPOLEOBJECT)
                {
                        VASSERT(owner);
            owner->Invalidate();
        }
};

class _CLASSTYPE ClientDoc : public VOleClientDoc
{
```

Listing 12-10
Continued.

```
                public:
                    ClientDoc(charPtr name, VWindowPtr win)
                        : VOleClientDoc(name, win)
                    {
                    }

                protected:
                    virtual VOleClientObjPtr NewObject(void)
                    {
                    // may create a window associated with the object
                        return new ClientObj(this, owner);
                    }

                    virtual void SavedCallback(LPOLEOBJECT)
                    {
            VASSERT(owner);
                owner->Invalidate();
                    }

                    virtual void ChangedCallback(LPOLEOBJECT)
                    {
                        VASSERT(owner);
                        owner->Invalidate();
                    }
        };
        class _CLASSTYPE ClientWindow  : public VFrame
        {

        public:

                ClientWindow(void) : VFrame(NULL, "Vista OLE Client -
        test.doc")
                {
                        menu = new VMenu(this, "ClientMenu");
                        doc = new ClientDoc("test.doc", this);
                        doc->Register("VistaClient", "test.doc");
                }

                ClientWindow(void)
                {
                        delete doc;
                }


        protected:
                Boolean InitMenuAction(VEventRef)
                {
                        LPOLEOBJECT obj = doc->First();
                        Boolean hasObject = (Boolean)(obj != 0);
        menu->DeferDrawing();
                        menu->Enable(IDM_CUT, hasObject);
        menu->Enable(IDM_COPY, hasObject);
```

```cpp
                menu->Enable(IDM_ACTIVATE, hasObject);

                if (!undoObj)
                        menu->Enable(IDM_UNDO, hasObject);
                menu->Enable(IDM_PASTE, doc->CanPaste());
                menu->EnableDrawing();
                return True;
        }

        virtual Boolean PaintAction(VEventRef)
        {
                VPaintDevice dev(*this);
ClientObj currentObj(doc, this, doc->First());
if (currentObj)
                currentObj.Draw(&dev);
return True;
}

        void CopyObject()
        {
                ClientObj currentObj(doc, this, doc->First());
if (currentObj)
                        undoObj = currentObj;
        }

        void DeleteObject(void)
        {
                ClientObj currentObj(doc, this, doc->First());
                if (currentObj)
                {
                        undoObj = currentObj;
                        currentObj.Delete();
            Invalidate();
}
}

Boolean ExitCommand(VEventRef)
{
PostMessage(*this, WM_CLOSE, 0, 0);
        return True;
}

Boolean UndoCommand(VEventRef)
{
// ?
return True;
}

Boolean CutCommand(VEventRef event)
{
        CopyCommand(event);
        DeleteObject();
```

Object linking & embedding

Listing 12-10
Continued.

```
        Invalidate();
            return True;
    }

    Boolean CopyCommand(VEventRef)
    {
            ClientObj currentObj(doc, this, doc->First());
            if (currentObj)
                    currentObj.CopyToClipboard();
            return True;
    }

    Boolean PasteCommand(VEventRef)
    {
            DeleteObject();
            doc->FromClip();
Invalidate();
            return True;
    }

    Boolean InsertCommand(VEventRef)
    {
            DeleteObject();
            VOleClientObjPtr obj = doc->Create("PBRUSH");
            obj->SetHostNames("VistaClient");
            return True;
    }

    Boolean ActivateCommand(VEventRef)
    {
            ClientObj object(doc, this, doc->First());
            if (object)
                    object.Activate();
            return True;
            }

    void InitActions(void)
    {
            VFrame::InitActions();
            AddAction((VAction)&ClientWindow::InitMenuAction,
                            WM_INITMENUPOPUP);
            AddCommand((VAction)&ClientWindow::ExitCommand,
                            IDM_EXIT);
            AddCommand((VAction)&ClientWindow::UndoCommand,
                            IDM_UNDO);
              AddCommand((VAction)&ClientWindow::CutCommand,
                            IDM_CUT);
            AddCommand((VAction)&ClientWindow::CopyCommand,
                            IDM_COPY);
            AddCommand((VAction)&ClientWindow::PasteCommand,
```

288 *Clipboard, DDE, & OLE objects*

```
                                        IDM_PASTE);
                AddCommand((VAction)&ClientWindow::InsertCommand,
                                        DM_INSERT);
                AddCommand((VAction)&ClientWindow::ActivateCommand,
                                IDM_ACTIVATE);
        }

        ClientDocPtr doc;
        ClientObj    undoObj;
};


class _CLASSTYPE ClientApp : public VAppl
{

public:
        ClientApp(charPtr name, HINSTANCE inst, HINSTANCE prevInst,
                        charPtr cmdLine, int cmdShow) :
                VAppl(name, inst, prevInst, cmdLine, cmdShow)
        {
        }

        ClientApp(void)
        {
        }

        virtual void InitConfig(void)
        {
        }

        virtual void InitWindow(void)
        {
                main_window = new ClientWindow();
        }

        virtual void CleanupConfig(void)
        {
        }
};


int PASCAL WinMain(HINSTANCE hInstance, HINSTANCE hPrevInstance,
                                LPSTR lpszCmdLine, int nCmdShow)
{
        ClientApp mainApp("Vista OLE Client",hInstance,
                                        hPrevInstance,
                                        lpszCmdLine,nCmdShow);

        return mainApp.Run();
}
```

Listing 12-11
OLECLNT.H

```
/* -----------------------------------------------------------------
    oleclnt.cpp

            Sample OLE client application

    Copyright (C) 1992, by Jeff Mackay - TAB Books
   ------------------------------------------------------------- */

#define IDM_EXIT 101
#define IDM_UNDO 201
#define IDM_CUT  202
#define IDM_COPY 203
#define IDM_PASTE 204
#define IDM_INSERT 205
#define IDM_ACTIVATE 206
```

Listing 12-12
OLECLNT.RC

```
ClientMenu MENU
BEGIN
        POPUP "&File"
        BEGIN
                MENUITEM "E&xit", IDM_EXIT
        END
        POPUP "&Edit"
        BEGIN
                MENUITEM "&Undo", IDM_UNDO
                MENUITEM "Cu&t", IDM_CUT
                MENUITEM "&Copy", IDM_COPY
                MENUITEM "&Paste", IDM_PASTE
        END
        POPUP "&Object"
        BEGIN
                MENUITEM "&New Paintbrush Object", IDM_INSERT
        MENUITEM "&Activate", IDM_ACTIVATE
        END
END
```

Using a Vista OLE container document   The major difference between the OLE interface and a more traditional Windows interface is the fact that an OLE application is based on documents. To the client application, however, an OLE document doesn't actually have to be a document. Instead, view the document as a container for OLE objects. It provides the functions necessary for creating and managing objects.

The first step in creating an OLE client application is to create an OLE container document class. The container document normally corresponds to a window—either the application's top-level window, an MDI child window, or a dialog box. To create a container object, derive a class from the VOleClientDoc class:

```
class ClientDoc : public VOleClientDoc
{
public:
    ClientDoc(charPtr name, VWindowPtr owner)
        : VOleClientDoc(name, owner) { //... }
// ...
};
```

The constructor for the document class should accept a name and an owning window as arguments. The name is used to identify the document to OLE and normally consists of a file name or other unique key. The owning window is used to either display child objects or to act as a parent for the child windows displaying child objects. An ideal place to create a container document object is in the constructor for the owning window. To ease references to the document object, keep a pointer to it as a data member of the window.

After you create a document object and display its window, you can start to create child objects. Normally, the window's menu contains choices that allow the user to create objects or load documents containing objects. There basically are four sources for OLE objects: the clipboard, an external file, an internal data source or stream, or the object's server. The VOleClientDoc class contains several functions allowing you to create embedded objects or links to external objects from each of these sources.

For example, the ClientWindow's InsertCommand function, uses the Create member function to activate the Window Paintbrush application to create a new Paintbrush document from scratch:

```
VOleClientObjPtr obj = doc->Create("PBRUSH");
```

In this example, the Create function creates an object of a specific class: PBRUSH, which is the class name for all Windows Paintbrush objects. Object class names are stored in the system's registration database. When you invoke the Create function, OLE activates the object's server, allowing the user to create a new object. When the user is through creating the new object, they select the server's Update command to display the object on the client's window. Note that the object is not available to the client application until the user finishes editing it.

Likewise, the Paste member function creates an object from the clipboard:

```
doc->FromClip();
```

Notice that the FromClip member function doesn't require you to pass a class name. When an object is copied to the clipboard, its class name already is known to the OLE DLLs. There is no need to pass it explicitly. If your application expects a certain type of object (e.g., a spreadsheet, graph, or image), you might need to perform additional validation before allowing the user to paste an object into your container document.

In your derived container document class, you need to override only a single function: NewObject. Each of the object creation functions calls this virtual function to associate a server object with a client object. The function should return a new instance of your derived client object class.

Using a Vista OLE client object   A client object forms the visible (or audible) portion of an OLE connection. Basic management of client objects with the Vista library is surprisingly simple when you consider the amount of work that would have been involved had you tried to implement objects in your application.

While an OLE container document normally corresponds to a top-level window, an OLE client object can be associated with either a portion of the window or a separate child window. In a generic application like a spreadsheet or word processor, object management can be quite complicated because you need to track the size and position of each object, as well as the object's own data. However, in a specialized application, you can assign an object to its own window and allow the Vista VOleClientObj class take care of the details.Creating Client Objects

Use the container document's object creation functions to create an OLE object. The VOleClientObj class doesn't represent an OLE object directly; it is used only as a proxy to simplify operations on the object. The container document's member functions associate a VOleClientObj object with an OLE object using the VOleClientDoc's NewObject function.

Managing client objects   Because the VOleClient object is only a proxy for an object, it doesn't consume very many resources. In the OLECLNT application, the object created by the NewObject command is used only to react to client callback functions. When the program needs to perform other operations directly on an object, it creates another proxy object for it. For example:

```
void ClientWindow::CopyObject()
{
    ClientObj currentObj(doc, this, doc->First());
    if (currentObj)
            undoObj = currentObj;
}
```

The CopyObject command clones an OLE object to allow support for an Undo command. It first creates a proxy for the currently displayed object and uses the VOleClientObj's assignment operator to create the proxy object and assign it to the undoObj data member. It uses the document's First member function to retrieve a handle to the first object in the document and passes it to the proxy's constructor. The VOleClientDoc class is a true container; it contains functions to traverse the object contained within a document.

Although the creation of a proxy client object is cheap, you might need to keep track of the original proxy objects created by your document class's NewObject function. There are several ways to do this, including maintaining an array or list of child objects in the document or attaching the object to a window and keeping a pointer to the object as a data member in the window class.

A client object has several callback member functions, but the most important are the SavedCallback and ChangedCallback:

```
virtual void SavedCallback(LPOLEOBJECT)
{
    VASSERT(owner);
    owner->Invalidate();
}
virtual void ChangedCallback(LPOLEOBJECT)
{
    VASSERT(owner);
    owner->Invalidate();
}
```

The SavedCallback is called when the user updates an object in its server application. The ChangedCallback is invoked when the user makes some sort of change to a linked object. Both callbacks should ensure the object is redrawn. In the sample client application, the ClientObj class just invalidates the contents of the owner window, which causes the PaintAction member function to be invoked. It calls the OLE client DLL to draw the object. Like server callbacks, client callbacks cannot call OLE functions or display modal dialogs or message boxes. Instead, post messages to the owning window and allow it to take the appropriate action.

Drawing an object   The VOleClientObj class provides a number of functions for managing a client object, but none is more important than the Draw member function. Instead of drawing an object by itself, a client application relies on objects to draw themselves. The Draw function forwards a request to the client DLL, which passes it to the OLE server DLL, which finally passes the request on to the server application to do the actual drawing.

The ClientWindow's PaintAction member function handles the drawing of the document's child object:

```
virtual Boolean ClientWindow::PaintAction(VEventRef)
{
    VPaintDevice dev(*this);
      ClientObj currentObj(doc, this, doc->First());
    if (currentObj)
```

```
        currentObj.Draw(&dev);
    return True;
}
```

The function passes a VPaintDevice pointer to the Draw function. The OLE DLLs pass the drawing request, along the device context, to the server application for processing.

Activating or editing an object   If your program needs to allow the user to edit embedded or linked objects, call the selected object's Activate member function:

```
Boolean ClientWindow::ActivateCommand(VEventRef)
{
    ClientObj object(doc, this, doc->First());
    if (object)
        object.Activate();
    return True;
}
```

OLE objects can have any number of verbs associated with them, although most implement only a primary and possibly one secondary verb. The primary verb usually is Edit and is selected by default by the Activate member function. If you need to allow the user to access other verbs, obtain them from the system registration database and display them on the application's Edit menu when the object is selected.

Using a Vista OLE stream object   When you need to save an embedded object, derive a class from the VOleStream class to do the work of reading and writing the object to persistent storage. The location or type of storage doesn't matter: it could be in a local file, a remote file, or a database.

The VOleStream class has two callback functions: the GetCallback, which physically reads data from a stream, and the PutCallback, which writes data to a stream:

```
virtual DWORD VOleStream::GetCallback(voidPtr buf, DWORD
bufSize);
virtual DWORD VOleStream::PutCallback(voidCPtr buf, DWORD
bufSize);
```

These functions are invoked by the VOleClientObj's Save and Load member functions. When you call these functions, pass a pointer to an instance of the appropriate stream object. The OLE client DLL will take care of invoking the stream callback functions.

Debugging OLE applications   One of the most difficult aspects of developing an OLE application is debugging. Microsoft recognized this and developed several tools to assist in debugging OLE applications. The tools consist of an OLESPY monitor application similar to Borland's WINSIGHT program, CLTEST to test server applications, and SRTEST to test client applications.

If you plan to develop production OLE applications, these tools are absolutely necessary. You can obtain them on CompuServe in the Microsoft Developers Forum or from the Microsoft Developer Network Compact Disk.

Wrapping up

This chapter covered a lot of material on interprocess communication using the Vista library. I started with the clipboard, moved on to the Dynamic Data Exchange Management Library, and finished by discussing Object Linking and Embedding. By building on the features covered in this chapter, you can add the newest Windows technology to your own programs.

Appendix

This appendix contains the source code and header files for all the classes in the Vista library.

Listing A-1
VALLOC.H

```
/* -----------------------------------------------------
   valloc.h

        Interface for the VAllocator class.

   Copyright (C) 1992, by Jeff Mackay

   ----------------------------------------------------- */

#ifndef _VALLOC_H
#define _VALLOC_H

#ifndef _VISTA_H
#pragma hdrfile "vista.sym"
#include <vista.h>
#pragma hdrstop
#endif

STDCLASS(VAllocator);

class _CLASSTYPE VAllocator
{
```

The Vista library

Listing A-1
Continued.

```
        public:
                VAllocator(int elSize, int initCount=100);
                void *New(int elSize);
                void Delete(void *el);

        protected:
                virtual void Grow(void);
                struct link
                {
                        link *next;
                };
                int el_size;
                int initial_count;
                link *free_list;
};

#endif   // _VALLOC_H
```

Listing A-2
VALLOC.CPP

```
/*-------------------------------------------------------------
   valloc.cpp

   Implementation of the VAllocator class.

   Copyright (C) 1992, by Jeff Mackay

-------------------------------------------------------- */
#pragma hdrfile "vista.sym"
#include <vista.h>
#pragma hdrstop

#include <valloc.h>

VAllocator::VAllocator(int elSize, int initCount)
{
        el_size = max((size_t)elSize, sizeof(link));
        initial_count = initCount;
        free_list = 0;
        Grow();
}

void *VAllocator::New(int elSize)
{
        // make sure we aren't being called for an unknown object
        if (elSize > el_size)
                return (void *)new char[elSize];

        if (free_list == 0)
                Grow();
        link *saved = free_list;
```

```
        free_list = free_list->next;
        return (void *)saved;
}

void VAllocator::Delete(void *el)
{
        link *theLink = (link *)el;
        theLink->next = free_list;
        free_list = theLink;
}

void VAllocator::Grow(void)
{
        free_list = (link *)new char[el_size * initial_count];
        VASSERT(free_list != 0);
        for(int i=0; i<initial_count-1; i++)
                free_list[i].next = &free_list[i+1];
        free_list[i].next = 0;
}
```

```
/* --------------------------------------------------------
   VAppl.h

        VAppl class interface definition.

   Copyright (c) 1992, by Jeff Mackay

   -------------------------------------------------------- */

#ifndef _WINAPP_H
#define _WINAPP_H

#ifndef _VISTA_H
#include "Vista.h"
#endif

#ifndef _VSTRING_H
#include "VString.h"
#endif

#ifndef _VWINDOW_H
#include "VWindow.h"
#endif

const VApplRef GetApplication(void);

_REFTYPE(MSG);

STDCLASS(VAppl);
```

Listing A-3
VAPPL.H

Listing A-3
Continued.

```
class _CLASSTYPE VAppl
{
            public:
                VAppl(const charPtr name, HINSTANCE hInstance,
                        HINSTANCE hPrev, charPtr cmd, int doShow);
                VAppl();

            operator    HINSTANCE(void) const;

                virtual void InitApplication(void);
                virtual void InitConfig(void);
                virtual void InitWindow(void);
                virtual void CleanupConfig(void);
                virtual void CleanupApplication(void);
                VStatus       Run(void);
                VStatus       EventLoop(void);
                Boolean       ConvertKeyMessage(MSGRef msg);
                void          SetActiveWindow(VWindowPtr window);
                void          SetMainWindow(VWindowPtr window);
                void           SetStatus(VStatus value);
                void          SetAccelerators(VAcceleratorPtr accels);
                void           Error(charPtr message=0);

                int            GetWinState(void) const;
                charPtr     GetAppDir(void) const;
                VStatus       GetStatus(void) const;
                charPtr     GetAppName(void) const;
                VWindowPtr   GetMainWindow(void) const;
                VWindowPtr   GetActiveWindow(void) const;
                VAcceleratorPtr GetAccelerators(void) const;
                friend VApplRef GetApplication(void);

            protected:

                VString         app_name;
                HINSTANCE       instance;
                HINSTANCE       prev_instance;
                VString         cmd_line;
                int             win_state;
                VStatus         error_status;
                VWindowPtr      main_window;
                VWindowPtr      active_window;
                VAcceleratorPtr accel_table;
                static VApplPtr appl;
};

inline void VAppl::SetStatus(VStatus value)
{
       error_status = value;
}
```

```cpp
inline void VAppl::SetActiveWindow(VWindowPtr window)
{
    active_window = window;
}

inline void VAppl::SetMainWindow(VWindowPtr window)
{
    main_window = window;
}

inline void VAppl::SetAccelerators(VAcceleratorPtr accel)
{
    accel_table = accel;
}

inline VStatus VAppl::GetStatus(void) const
{
        return error_status;
}

inline int VAppl::GetWinState(void) const
{
        return win_state;
}

inline charPtr VAppl::GetAppName(void) const
{
        return app_name;
}

inline VAcceleratorPtr VAppl::GetAccelerators(void) const
{
    return accel_table;
}

inline VAppl::operator HINSTANCE(void) const
{
        return instance;
}

inline const VApplRef GetApplication(void)
{
        return *VAppl::appl;
}

inline const VWindowPtr VAppl::GetMainWindow(void) const
{
        return main_window;
}

inline const VWindowPtr VAppl::GetActiveWindow(void) const
```

Listing A-3
Continued.
```
        return active_window;
}
#endif // _VAPPL_H
```

Listing A-4
VAPPLH.CPP
```
/* -----------------------------------------------------------
    VAppl.cpp

                    Implementation of the VAppl class.

    Copyright (c) Jeff Mackay, 1992

----------------------------------------------------------- */
#pragma hdrfile "vista.sym"
#include <vista.h>
#pragma hdrstop
#include <vappl.h>
#include <dir.h>

VApplPtr VAppl::appl;

VAppl::VAppl(const charPtr name, HINSTANCE hInstance,
                    HINSTANCE hPrev,
                  charPtr cmd,    int doShow)
{
        if (!appl)
                appl = (VApplPtr) this;
        app _name = name;
        instance = hInstance;
        prev _instance = hPrev;
        cmd _line = cmd;
        win _state = doShow;
        error _status = V _SUCCESS;
        active _window = 0;
        main _window = 0;
        accel _table = 0;
}

VAppl::VAppl(void)
{
}

const charPtr VAppl::GetAppDir(void) const
{
        static TCHAR nameBuf[MAXPATH+sizeof(TCHAR)];

        GetModuleFileName(*this, nameBuf, sizeof(nameBuf)-1);
        for (int i=lstrlen(nameBuf)-sizeof(TCHAR); i; i--)
        {
```

```
                    if (nameBuf[i-sizeof(TCHAR)] == TEXT('\\'))
                            nameBuf[i] = TEXT('\0');
            }
            return nameBuf;
}


void VAppl::InitApplication(void)
{
        if (GetStatus() != V_SUCCESS)
                return;

        InitWindow();
        if (GetStatus() != V_SUCCESS)
                return;

        if (GetMainWindow())
        {
                main_window->Create();
                if (GetStatus() != V_SUCCESS)
                        return;

                main_window->Show();
                if (GetStatus() != V_SUCCESS)
                        return;

                main_window->Update();
        }
        else
        {
                SetStatus(V_APPNOWND);
        }
}

void VAppl::InitWindow(void)
{
}


void VAppl::InitConfig()
{
}

void VAppl::CleanupApplication(void)
{
   CleanupConfig();
}

void VAppl::CleanupConfig(void)
{
        SetStatus(V_SUCCESS);
}
```

Listing A-4
Continued.

```
Boolean VAppl::ConvertKeyMessage(MSGRef msg)
{
    Boolean retVal = False;

    if (active _window)
    {
        retVal = (Boolean) IsDialogMessage(*active _window, &msg);
        if (retVal == 0 && accel _table != 0)
            retVal = (Boolean) TranslateAccelerator(*active _window,
                                                   *accel _table, &msg);
    }
    return retVal;
}

VStatus VAppl::EventLoop(void)
{
    MSG msg;

    if (GetStatus())
        Error();

    while (GetMessage(&msg, 0, 0, 0))
    {
        if (!ConvertKeyMessage(msg))
        {
            TranslateMessage(&msg);
            DispatchMessage(&msg);
            if (GetStatus())
                Error();
        }
    }
    return (VStatus) msg.wParam;
}

VStatus VAppl::Run(void)
{
    InitConfig();
    if (GetStatus() != V _SUCCESS)
        return GetStatus();

    InitApplication();
    if (GetStatus() != V _SUCCESS)
        return GetStatus();

    VStatus retVal = EventLoop();

    CleanupApplication();

    return retVal;
}
```

```cpp
void VAppl::Error(charPtr message)
{
        int flag;
        HWND wnd;
        VString msg2 = message;
        char buffer[128];

        if (msg2 == NullString)
                msg2 = "Vista Error: %d.  Continue?";

        //
        // if there is no main window, message box has to be
        // task modal so that it uses the desktop as its parent.
        //
        if (!GetMainWindow())
        {
                wnd = 0;
                flag = MB _TASKMODAL;
        }
        else
        {
                wnd = *GetMainWindow();
                flag = MB _APPLMODAL;
        }

        wsprintf(buffer, msg2, GetStatus());
        flag |= (MB _ICONEXCLAMATION | MB _OKCANCEL);
        int answer = MessageBox(wnd, buffer, 0, flag);

        //
        // if answer is 0, there wasn't enough memory to
        // create the message box.  Windows guarantees a
        // message box will be created if flags are passed
        // as follows.
        //
        if (answer == 0)
        {
                flag = MB _ICONHAND | MB _SYSTEMMODAL;
                answer = MessageBox(wnd, buffer, 0, flag);
        }

        if (answer == IDCANCEL)
        {
                PostQuitMessage(GetStatus());
        }
        else
        {
                SetStatus(V _SUCCESS);
        }
}
```

Listing A-5
VARRAY.H

```c
/* -----------------------------------------------------------
    VArray.h

       Interface for the VArray template class.

    Copyright (C) 1992, by Jeff Mackay
   ----------------------------------------------------------- */
#ifndef _VARRAY_H
#define _VARRAY_H

#include <vista.h>
#include <stdlib.h>
#include <limits.h>

class VContainer
{
    public:
        virtual void Clear() = 0;
        virtual int Size() = 0;
};

template <class T> class VArray : public VContainer
{
    public:
        VArray(int sz, T defaultVal);
        VArray(const VArray _FAR &);
        VArray _FAR &operator=(const VArray _FAR &);
        VArray();
        T _FAR &operator[](int ndx);
        virtual int Insert(T _FAR &obj, int ndx);
        virtual int Append(T _FAR &obj);
        virtual void Clear(void);
        virtual int Size(void)
        {
            return arr_size;
        }
        virtual int Find(T _FAR &obj);

    protected:
        T    *data;
        T default_value;
        int arr_size;
                int top;
};

template <class T> VArray<T>::VArray(int sz, T defVal)
{
    top = 0;
        arr_size = sz;
    default_value = defVal;
    data = new T[arr_size];
```

```cpp
    VASSERT(data != 0);
    for (int i=0; i<arr_size; i++)
        data[i] = default_value;
}

template <class T>
        VArray<T>::VArray(const VArray<T> _FAR& copy)
{
    delete data;
        arr_size = copy.arr_size;
    data = new T [arr_size];
        VASSERT(data != 0);

    for (int i=0; i<arr_size; i++)
        data[i] = copy.data[i];
        top = copy.top;
}

template <class T> VArray<T> _FAR &
        VArray<T>::operator =(const VArray<T> _FAR &copy)
{
    delete data;
    arr_size = copy.arr_size;
    data = new T [arr_size];
    for (size_t i=0; i<arr_size; i++)
        data[i] = copy.data[i];
    top = copy.top;
    return *this;
}

template <class T> VArray<T>::VArray()
{
    delete [] data;
}

template <class T> inline T _FAR &VArray<T>::operator[](int n)
{
        VASSERT(n < arr_size);
        return data[n];
}

template <class T> int VArray<T>::Append(T _FAR &obj)
{
        VASSERT(top < arr_size);
        data[top++] = obj;
    return top;
}

template <class T> int VArray<T>::Insert(T _FAR &obj, int ndx)
{
        VASSERT(ndx < arr_size);
```

Listing A-5
Continued.

```
            if (top < ndx)
                    top = ndx+1;
            data[ndx] = obj;
            return ndx;
    }

    template <class T> int VArray<T>::Find(T _FAR &obj)
    {
            for(int i=0; i<arr_size; i++)
            {
                    if (data[i] == obj)
                            return i;
        }
            return INT_MAX;
    }


    template <class T> void VArray<T>::Clear(void)
    {
        for(int i=0; i<arr_size; i++)
        {
            data[i] = default_value;
        }
    }

    #endif
```

Listing A-6
VBITMAP.H

```
/* ---------------------------------------------------------
    VBitmap.h

    Interface for the VBitmap class

    Copyright (C) 1992, by Jeff Mackay - TAB BOOKS

----------------------------------------------------------- */
#ifndef _VBITMAP_H
#define _VBITMAP_H

#ifndef _VISTA_H
#include <Vista.h>
#endif

#ifndef _VAPPL_H
#include <VAppl.h>
#endif

class VBitmap
{
    public:
```

```
            VBitmap(charPtr name);
            VBitmap(int id);
            VBitmap(VCoord width, VCoord height, const voidPtr bits);
            VBitmap();
            operator HBITMAP(void) const;

    private:
        HBITMAP handle;

};

// load a bitmap from a resource based on a resource string
inline VBitmap::VBitmap(charPtr name)
{
    handle = LoadBitmap(GetApplication(), name);
}

// load a bitmap from a resource based on a resource identifier
inline VBitmap::VBitmap(int id)
{
    handle = LoadBitmap(GetApplication(), MAKEINTRESOURCE(id));
}

// create a black-and-white bitmap from an array of bits
inline VBitmap::VBitmap(VCoord width, VCoord height, const voidPtr bits)
{
    handle = CreateBitmap(width, height, 1, 1, bits);
}

inline VBitmap::VBitmap()
{
    DeleteObject(handle);
}

inline VBitmap::operator HBITMAP(void) const
{
    return handle;
}

#endif
```

Listing A-7
VBUTTON.H

```
/* ---------------------------------------------------------------
    VButton.h

            Interface for the VButton class

        Copyright (C) 1992, by Jeff Mackay

------------------------------------------------------------ */
```

Listing A-7
Continued.

```c
#ifndef _VBUTTON_H
#define _VBUTTON_H

#ifndef _VCONTROL_H
#include <vcontrol.h>
#endif

#define VC_PUSHBUTTON            BS_PUSHBUTTON
#define VC_DEFPUSHBUTTON         BS_DEFPUSHBUTTON

class _CLASSTYPE VButton : public VControl
{
    public:
                int button_style;
                VButton(VCompositePtr parent, charPtr title,
                        int x, int y, int width, int height,
                    int styleFlag=VC_PUSHBUTTON);
        VButton(VCompositePtr parent, int resourceId);
                virtual const charPtr ClassName(void) const;
                virtual const charPtr OldClassName(void) const;
        virtual void InitActions(void);
                virtual Boolean ClickedAction(VEventRef event);
                virtual Boolean DoubleClickedAction(VEventRef event);
                virtual void Cut(void) {}
                virtual void Copy(void) {}
                virtual void Paste(void) {}
                virtual void Clear(void) {}
                void SetStyle(int style);
                void Push(void);
                void Release(void);
};

#endif
```

Listing A-8
VBUTTON.CPP

```cpp
/* ----------------------------------------------------------------
            VButton.cpp

                Implementation of the VButton class

Copyright (C) 1992, by Jeff Mackay

---------------------------------------------------------------- */
#pragma hdrfile "vista.sym"
#include <vista.h>
#pragma hdrstop
#include <vbutton.h>

VButton::VButton(VCompositePtr parent, charPtr title,
                    int x, int y, int width, int height,
                    int styleFlag)
```

```cpp
        : VControl(parent, title, x, y, width, height)
{
    button_style = styleFlag;
    style |= button_style;
}

VButton::VButton(VCompositePtr parent, int resourceId)
    : VControl(parent, resourceId)
{
}

const charPtr VButton::ClassName(void) const
{
        return "VButton";
}

const charPtr VButton::OldClassName(void) const
{
        return "button";
}

void VButton::SetStyle(int style)
{
        button_style = style;
        if (handle)
        {
                VEvent event(*this, BM_SETSTYLE, style, 1);
                event.Send();
        }
}

void VButton::Push()
{
        if (!handle)
                return;

        VEvent event(*this, BM_SETSTATE, 1);
        event.Send();
}

void VButton::Release()
{
        if (!handle)
                return;

        VEvent event(*this, BM_SETSTATE, 1);
        event.Send();
}

void VButton::InitActions(void)
{
```

Listing A-8
Continued.

```
        VControl::InitActions();
    AddAction((VAction) &VButton::ClickedAction, WM_COMMAND,
                            resource_id, BN_CLICKED);
    AddAction((VAction) &VButton::DoubleClickedAction,
WM_COMMAND, resource_id, BN_DOUBLECLICKED);
}

Boolean VButton::ClickedAction(VEventRef event)
{
    UNREFERENCED_PARAMETER(event);
        return False;
}


Boolean VButton::DoubleClickedAction(VEventRef event)
{
    UNREFERENCED_PARAMETER(event);
        return False;
}
```

Listing A-9
VCHECK.H

```
/* ---------------------------------------------------------------
    vcheck.h

    Interface for the VCheckBox class.

    Copyright (C) 1992, by Jeff Mackay
--------------------------------------------------------------- */
#ifndef _VCHECK_H
#define _VCHECK_H

#ifndef _VBUTTON_H
#include <vbutton.h>
#endif

// values for the button style
#define VC_CHECKBOX      BS_CHECKBOX
#define VC_AUTOCHECKBOX  BS_CHECKBOX
#define VC_3STATE        BS_3STATE
#define VC_AUTO3STATE    BS_AUTO3STATE
#define VC_LEFTTEXT      BS_LEFTTEXT

// values for the button state - VCB_GRAYED only valid for 3-state controls
#define VC_UNCHECKED        0
#define VC_CHECKED          1
#define VC_GRAYED           2

STDCLASS(VCheckBox);
class _CLASSTYPE VCheckBox : public VButton
{
```

```cpp
public:
    VCheckBox(VCompositePtr parent, charPtr title,
              int x, int y, int width, int height,
              int style=VC_UNCHECKED, int checked=VC_UNCHECKED);
    VCheckBox(VCompositePtr parent, int resourceId,
              int check=VC_UNCHECKED);
    virtual void SetCheck(int value=VC_CHECKED);
    virtual int  GetCheck(void);

protected:
    virtual Boolean CreateAction(VEventRef event);
    virtual Boolean ClickedAction(VEventRef event);
    virtual void GetValue(voidPtr buffer);
    virtual void SetValue(voidPtr buffer);
    virtual int  GetValueLength(void);

    int initial_state;
};


inline VCheckBox::VCheckBox(VCompositePtr parent, charPtr title,
                     int x, int y, int width, int height,
                     int style, int checked)
  : VButton(parent, title, x, y, width, height, style)
{
    initial_state = checked;
}

inline VCheckBox::VCheckBox(VCompositePtr parent, int resourceId,
                            int checked)
  : VButton(parent, resourceId)
{
    initial_state = checked;
}


inline Boolean VCheckBox::CreateAction(VEventRef event)
{
    SetCheck(initial_state);
    VButton::CreateAction(event);
    int ctlStyle = GetWindowLong(*this, GWL_STYLE);
    button_style = (ctlStyle & VC_LEFTTEXT);
    return True;
}

inline Boolean VCheckBox::ClickedAction(VEventRef event)
{
    VButton::ClickedAction(event);
    if (button_style == VC_CHECKBOX)
        SetCheck(!GetCheck());
    return True;
}
```

Listing A-9
Continued.

```
inline void VCheckBox::SetValue(voidPtr buffer)
{
    SetCheck(*((int _FAR *)buffer));
}


inline void VCheckBox::GetValue(voidPtr buffer)
{
    *((int _FAR *)buffer) = GetCheck();
}


int VCheckBox::GetValueLength(void)
{
    return sizeof(int);
}


inline void VCheckBox::SetCheck(int value)
{
    SendMessage(*this, BM_SETCHECK, value, 0);
}


inline int VCheckBox::GetCheck(void)
{
    return SendMessage(*this, BM_GETCHECK, 0, 0);
}


#endif
```

Listing A-10
VCOMCLR.H

```
/* -----------------------------------------------------------
    vcomclr.h

    Interface for the common color dialog

    Copyright (C) 1992, by Jeff Mackay
----------------------------------------------------------- */
#ifndef _VCOMCLR_H
#define _VCOMCLR_H

#ifndef _VCOMMON_H
#include <vcommon.h>
#endif

#ifndef _VGDITOOL_H
#include <vgditool.h>
#endif
```

```cpp
STDCLASS(VColorDialog);

class _CLASSTYPE VColorDialog : public VCommonDialog
{
    public:
        VColorDialog(VFramePtr parent);
        int Execute(void);
        VColorRef operator [](int index);
        VColorRef GetNewColor(void);
        void SetColor(VColorRef color);

    private:
        Boolean     modified;
        CHOOSECOLOR cc;
        VColor      colors[16];
        VColor      current;
        COLORREF    custom_colors[16];
};

#endif
```

```cpp
/*--------------------------------------------------------------
   vcomclr.cpp

      Implementation of the common color selection dialog box

   Copyright (C) 1992, by Jeff Mackay
---------------------------------------------------------------- */

#pragma hdrfile "vista.sym"
#include <vista.h>
#pragma hdrstop
#include <vcomclr.h>


VColorDialog::VColorDialog(VFramePtr par)
        : VCommonDialog(par)
{
    memset(&cc, '\0', sizeof(cc));
    cc.lStructSize = sizeof(cc);
    cc.hwndOwner = *par;
    cc.lpCustColors = custom_colors;
    cc.lCustData = (LPARAM) this;
    cc.Flags = CC_RGBINIT;
    for (int i=0; i<dim(custom_colors); i++)
        colors[i] = custom_colors[i] = RGB(0,0,0);
    modified = False;
}
```

Listing A-11
VCOMCLR.CPP

Listing A-11
Continued.

```
VColorRef VColorDialog::operator[](int index)
{
    modified = True;
    return colors[index];
}

void VColorDialog::SetColor(VColorRef color)
{
    current = color;
}

VColorRef VColorDialog::GetNewColor(void)
{
    return current;
}

int VColorDialog::Execute(void)
{
    int i;
    cc.rgbResult = current;
    if (modified)
    {
        for (i=0; i<dim(colors); i++)
            custom_colors[i] = colors[i];
        modified = False;
    }

    int retVal = ChooseColor(&cc);

    current = cc.rgbResult;
    for (i=0; i<dim(colors); i++)
        colors[i] = custom_colors[i];
    return retVal;
}
```

Listing A-12
VCOMFILE.H

```
/* -----------------------------------------------------------
    vcomfile.h

    Interface for the VFileDialog Class

    Copyright (C) 1992, by Jeff Mackay
   ----------------------------------------------------------- */
#ifndef _VCOMFILE_H
#define _VCOMFILE_H

#ifndef _VCOMMON_H
#include <vcommon.h>
#endif
```

```cpp
#define MAX_PATH 128
#define MAX_FILE 16

STDCLASS(VFileDialog);
STDCLASS(VFileOpenDialog);
STDCLASS(VFileSaveDialog);

class VFileDialog : public VCommonDialog
{
    public:
        VFileDialog(VFramePtr par, const charPtr filterStr=0);
        VFileDialog(VFileDialogRef copy);
        VFileDialog(void);
        VFileDialogRef operator =(VFileDialogRef copy);

        const charPtr GetFilename(void) const;
        const charPtr GetFileTitle(void) const;

        int Execute(void);
        void SetRemember(Boolean value) { do_remember = value; }
        void SetFilter(const charPtr filterStr);
        void SetInitialDir(const charPtr dir);
        void SetDefaultExt(const charPtr ext);
        void ShowHelpButton(void)
        {
            of.Flags |= OFN_SHOWHELP;
        }

    protected:
        virtual void Initialize(void);
        virtual void Remember(void);
        virtual int ExecFunction(void)=0;
        Boolean do_remember;
        Boolean executed;
        VString file_name;
        VString file_title;
        VString initial_dir;
        VString filter;
        VString custom_filter;
        VString def_ext;
        OPENFILENAME of;
};

class VFileOpenDialog : public VFileDialog
{
    public:
        VFileOpenDialog(VFramePtr parent,
                        const charPtr string=0);
        void AllowReadOnly(void);
        void PreventReadOnly(void);
```

Listing A-12
Continued.

```cpp
            void ShowReadOnlyOption(void);
                    void HideReadOnlyOption(void);
            void SetInitialReadOnlyOption(void);
            void FileMustExist(void);

    protected:
        virtual int ExecFunction(void);
};

class _CLASSTYPE VFileSaveDialog : public VFileDialog
{
    public:
        VFileSaveDialog(VFramePtr parent,
                        const charPtr string=0);

    protected:
        virtual int ExecFunction(void);
};

#endif
```

Listing A-13
VCOMFILE.CPP

```cpp
/*--------------------------------------------------------------
    vcomfile.cpp

    Implementation of the common file dialog box classes.

    Copyright (C) 1992, by Jeff Mackay
--------------------------------------------------------------- */

#pragma hdrfile "vista.sym"
#include <vista.h>
#pragma hdrstop
#include <vcomfile.h>


VFileDialog::VFileDialog(VFramePtr par, const charPtr filterStr) :
  VCommonDialog(par),
  file_name(MAX_PATH), file_title(MAX_FILE),
  initial_dir(MAX_PATH), filter(MAX_PATH),
  custom_filter(MAX_PATH), def_ext(4)
{
    do_remember = True;
    Initialize();
    if (filterStr)
        SetFilter(filterStr);
    else
        SetFilter("All Files (*.*)|*.*|");
    of.hwndOwner = *par;
}
```

```cpp
VFileDialog::VFileDialog(VFileDialogRef copy) :
  VCommonDialog(VFramePtr(copy.parent)),
  file_name(MAX_PATH), file_title(MAX_FILE),
  initial_dir(MAX_PATH), filter(MAX_PATH),
  custom_filter(MAX_PATH), def_ext(4)
{
    of.hwndOwner = copy.of.hwndOwner;
    do_remember = True;
    file_name = copy.file_name;
    file_title = copy.file_title;
    initial_dir = copy.initial_dir;
    filter = copy.filter;
    custom_filter = copy.custom_filter;
    def_ext = copy.def_ext;
    Initialize();
}

void VFileDialog::Initialize()
{
    executed = False;
    memset(&of, 0, sizeof(of));
    of.lStructSize = sizeof(of);
    of.lpstrFile = file_name.Buffer();
    of.nMaxFile  = file_name.Allocated();
    of.lpstrFilter = filter.Buffer();
    of.lpstrCustomFilter = custom_filter.Buffer();
    of.nMaxCustFilter = custom_filter.Allocated();
    of.nFilterIndex = 1;
    of.lpstrFileTitle = file_title.Buffer();
    of.nMaxFileTitle = file_title.Allocated();
    of.lpstrInitialDir = initial_dir.Buffer();
    of.lpstrDefExt = def_ext.Buffer();
}

VFileDialogRef VFileDialog::operator =(VFileDialogRef copy)
{
    if (&copy != this)
    {
        do_remember = True;
        file_name = copy.file_name;
        file_title = copy.file_title;
        initial_dir = copy.initial_dir;
        filter = copy.filter;
        custom_filter = copy.custom_filter;
        def_ext = copy.def_ext;
        Initialize();
    }
    return *this;
}

VFileDialog::VFileDialog(void)
{
```

Listing A-13
Continued.

```
}

int VFileDialog::Execute(void)
{
    if (executed)
        Remember();

    VString old_dir(MAX_PATH);   old_dir   = initial_dir;
    VString old_name(MAX_PATH);  old_name  = file_name;
    VString old_title(MAX_FILE); old_title = file_title;

    int result = ExecFunction();
    if (result == IDCANCEL)
    {
        executed    = False;
        initial_dir = old_dir;
        file_name   = old_name;
        file_title  = old_title;
    }
    else
    {
        executed = True;
        initial_dir.ResetLength();
        file_name.ResetLength();
        file_title.ResetLength();
    }
    return result;
}

void VFileDialog::Remember(void)
{
    initial_dir = file_name;
    file_name   = GetFileTitle();
    file_title[0] = TEXT('\0');
}


const charPtr VFileDialog::GetFilename(void) const
{
    return (const charPtr) file_name;
}

const charPtr VFileDialog::GetFileTitle(void) const
{
    return (const charPtr) file_title;
}

void VFileDialog::SetFilter(const charPtr filterStr)
{
    filter = filterStr;
    int len = filter.Length();
```

```cpp
        TCHAR delim = filter[len-1];
        for (int i=0; i<len; i++)
        {
            if (filter[i] == delim)
                filter[i] = TEXT('\0');
        }
}

VFileOpenDialog::VFileOpenDialog(VFramePtr parent, const charPtr string)
    : VFileDialog(parent, string)
{
    AllowReadOnly();
    HideReadOnlyOption();
    FileMustExist();
}

void VFileOpenDialog::AllowReadOnly(void)
{
    of.Flags = (of.Flags & OFN_NOREADONLYRETURN);
}

void VFileOpenDialog::PreventReadOnly(void)
{
    of.Flags |= OFN_NOREADONLYRETURN;
}

void VFileOpenDialog::ShowReadOnlyOption(void)
{
    of.Flags = (of.Flags & OFN_HIDEREADONLY);
}

void VFileOpenDialog::HideReadOnlyOption(void)
{
    of.Flags |= OFN_HIDEREADONLY;
}

void VFileOpenDialog::SetInitialReadOnlyOption(void)
{
    of.Flags |= OFN_READONLY;
}

void VFileOpenDialog::FileMustExist(void)
{
    of.Flags |= OFN_CREATEPROMPT;
}

int VFileOpenDialog::ExecFunction(void)
{
    return GetOpenFileName(&of);
}
```

Listing A-13 *Continued.*

```
VFileSaveDialog::VFileSaveDialog(VFramePtr parent, const charPtr string)
    : VFileDialog(parent, string)
{
}

int VFileSaveDialog::ExecFunction(void)
{
    return GetSaveFileName(&of);
}
```

Listing A-14 *VCOMFIND.H*

```
/*----------------------------------------------------------------
    vcomfind.h

    Interface for the common search and replace dialogs

    Copyright (C) 1992, by Jeff Mackay
---------------------------------------------------------------- */
#ifndef _VCOMFIND_H
#define _VCOMFIND_H

#ifndef _VCOMMON_H
#include <vcommon.h>
#endif

STDCLASS(VFindDialog);
STDCLASS(VReplaceDialog);

class _CLASSTYPE VFindDialog : public VCommonDialog
{
    public:
        VFindDialog(VFramePtr parent, int string_size=128);
        int Execute(void);
        charPtr GetSearchString(void) const;
        Boolean IsClosing(void) const;
        Boolean FindNext(void) const;
        Boolean FindDown(void) const;
        Boolean FindUp(void) const;
        Boolean MatchCase(void) const;
        Boolean WholeWord(void) const;
        static UINT find_replace_message;
        static VFindDialogPtr GetDialogObject(LPARAM lParam);

    protected:
        FINDREPLACE fr;
        VString     search_string;
};


class _CLASSTYPE VReplaceDialog : public VFindDialog
{
```

```cpp
    public:
        VReplaceDialog(VFramePtr parent, UINT stringSize=128);
        int Execute(void);
        const charPtr GetReplaceString(void) const;
        Boolean Replace(void) const;
        Boolean ReplaceAll(void) const;

    protected:
        VString replace_string;

};

#endif
```

Listing A-15
VCOMFIND.CPP

```cpp
/*------------------------------------------------------------
    vcomfind.cpp

    Implementation of the common find and replace dialogs

    Copyright (C) 1992, by Jeff Mackay
------------------------------------------------------------ */

#pragma hdrfile "vista.sym"
#include <vista.h>
#pragma hdrstop

#include <vcomfind.h>

UINT VFindDialog::find_replace_message;

VFindDialog::VFindDialog(VFramePtr parent, int stringSize)
    : VCommonDialog(parent), search_string(stringSize)
{
    if (!find_replace_message)
        find_replace_message =
            RegisterWindowMessage(FINDMSGSTRING);

    memset(&fr, '\0', sizeof(fr));
    fr.lStructSize = sizeof(fr);
    if (parent)
        fr.hwndOwner = *parent;
    fr.lpstrFindWhat = search_string.Buffer();
    fr.wFindWhatLen  = search_string.Allocated();
    fr.lCustData     = (LPARAM)this;
}


const charPtr VFindDialog::GetSearchString(void) const
{
```

Listing A-15
Continued.

```cpp
    return search_string;
}

int VFindDialog::Execute(void)
{
    HWND dlg = FindText(&fr);
    return (dlg != 0);
}

VFindDialogPtr VFindDialog::GetDialogObject(LPARAM lParam)
{
    FINDREPLACE FAR *lpfr = (FINDREPLACE FAR *)lParam;
    return (VFindDialogPtr)lpfr->lCustData;
}

Boolean VFindDialog::IsClosing(void) const
{
    return (Boolean)(fr.Flags & FR_DIALOGTERM);
}

Boolean VFindDialog::FindNext(void) const
{
    return (Boolean)(fr.Flags & FR_FINDNEXT);
}

Boolean VFindDialog::FindUp(void) const
{
    return (Boolean)(!FindDown());
}

Boolean VFindDialog::FindDown(void) const
{
    return (Boolean)(fr.Flags & FR_DOWN);
}

Boolean VFindDialog::MatchCase(void) const
{
    return (Boolean)(fr.Flags & FR_MATCHCASE);
}

Boolean VFindDialog::WholeWord(void) const
{
    return (Boolean)(fr.Flags & FR_WHOLEWORD);
}

VReplaceDialog::VReplaceDialog(VFramePtr parent, UINT stringSize)
    : VFindDialog(parent, stringSize), replace_string(stringSize)
{
    fr.lpstrReplaceWith = replace_string.Buffer();
    fr.wReplaceWithLen  = replace_string.Allocated();

}
```

```
int VReplaceDialog::Execute(void)
{
    HWND dlg = ReplaceText(&fr);
    return (dlg != 0);
}

const charPtr VReplaceDialog::GetReplaceString(void) const
{
    return replace_string;
}

Boolean VReplaceDialog::Replace(void) const
{
    return (Boolean)(fr.Flags & FR_REPLACE);
}

Boolean VReplaceDialog::ReplaceAll(void) const
{
    return (Boolean)(fr.Flags & FR_REPLACEALL);
}
```

Listing A-16
VCOMFONT.H

```
/*---------------------------------------------------------
    vcomfont.h

    Interface for the common font selection dialog

    Copyright (C) 1992, by Jeff Mackay
---------------------------------------------------------- */
#ifndef _VCOMFONT_H
#define _VCOMFONT_H


#ifndef _VCOMMON_H
#include <vcommon.h>
#endif

#ifndef _VGDITOOL_H
#include <vgditool.h>
#endif

STDCLASS(VFontDialog);

class _CLASSTYPE VFontDialog : public VCommonDialog
{
    public:
        VFontDialog(VFramePtr frame);
        int Execute(void);
        void SetMinSize(int pointSize);
        void SetMaxSize(int pointSize);
```

Listing A-16
Continued.

```cpp
        void TrueTypeOnly(void);
        void FixedFontOnly(void);

        const charPtr GetStyle(void) const;
        int GetPointSize(void) const;
        const LOGFONT _FAR &GetLogFont(void) const;
        VFontRef GetFontObject(void);

    private:
        CHOOSEFONT cf;
        VString    font_name;
        VFont      font_object;
        LOGFONT    lf;
};

inline void VFontDialog::TrueTypeOnly(void)
{
    cf.Flags |= CF_TTONLY;
}

inline void VFontDialog::FixedFontOnly(void)
{
    cf.Flags |= CF_FIXEDPITCHONLY;
}
#endif
```

Listing A-17
VCOMFONT.CPP

```cpp
/*-----------------------------------------------------------
    vcomfont.cpp

    Implementation of the common font selection dialog

    Copyright (C) 1992, by Jeff Mackay
-------------------------------------------------------- */

#pragma hdrfile "vista.sym"
#include <vista.h>
#pragma hdrstop
#include <vcomfont.h>

VFontDialog::VFontDialog(VFramePtr frame)
    : VCommonDialog(frame), font_name(LF_FACESIZE)
{
    memset(&cf, '\0', sizeof(cf));
    memset(&lf, '\0', sizeof(lf));
    cf.lStructSize = sizeof(cf);
    cf.Flags = CF_FORCEFONTEXIST | CF_SCREENFONTS | CF_EFFECTS;
    cf.nFontType = SCREEN_FONTTYPE;
    cf.lpszStyle = font_name.Buffer();
    cf.lpLogFont = &lf;
}
```

```
int VFontDialog::Execute(void)
{
    if (cf.nSizeMin > 0 ||  cf.nSizeMax > 0)
        flags |= CF_LIMITSIZE;
    return ChooseFont(&cf);
}

void VFontDialog::SetMinSize(int pointSize)
{
    cf.nSizeMin = pointSize;
}

void VFontDialog::SetMaxSize(int pointSize)
{
    cf.nSizeMax = pointSize;
}

int VFontDialog::GetPointSize(void) const
{
    return cf.iPointSize;
}

const LOGFONT _FAR &VFontDialog::GetLogFont(void) const
{
    return lf;
}

VFontRef VFontDialog::GetFontObject(void)
{
    font_object = lf;
    return font_object;
}

const charPtr VFontDialog::GetStyle(void) const
{
    return (const charPtr) lf.lfFaceName;
}


/* ----------------------------------------------------------
   vcommon.h

        Interface for the VCommonDialog class.  Also includes
     headers for the other common dialog classes.

   Copyright (C) 1992, by Jeff Mackay
   ---------------------------------------------------------- */
#ifndef _VCOMMON_H
#define _VCOMMON_H
```

Listing A-18
VCOMMON.H

Listing A-18
Continued.

```cpp
#include <commdlg.h>        // windows include file

#ifndef _VDLGBOX_H
#include <vdlgbox.h>
#endif

STDCLASS(VCommonDialog);

class _CLASSTYPE VCommonDialog : public VDialogBox
{
        public:
                VCommonDialog(VFramePtr parent)
                   : VDialogBox(parent) {}
                virtual void   Create(void) {}
                virtual int    Execute(void) {return IDCANCEL;}
                virtual Boolean Destroy(Boolean flg) { return True;}
};

#ifndef _VCOMCLR_H
#include <vcomclr.h>
#endif

#ifndef _VCOMFILE_H
#include <vcomfile.h>
#endif

#ifndef _VCOMFIND_H
#include <vcomfind.h>
#endif

#ifndef _VCOMFONT_H
#include <vcomfont.h>
#endif

#ifndef _VCOMPRNT_H
#include <vcomprnt.h>
#endif

#endif
```

Listing A-19
VCOMPOST.CPP

```cpp
/*---------------------------------------------------------------
    VCompost.cpp

        Implementation of the VComposite class.

    Copyright (C) 1992, by Jeff Mackay
---------------------------------------------------------------- */
#pragma hdrfile "vista.sym"
#include <vista.h>
```

```c++
#pragma hdrstop
#include <vwindow.h>
#include <vappl.h>


VComposite::VComposite(void)
{
    VWindowPtr child;

    while((child = children.First()) != 0)
        delete child;
}


void VComposite::InitActions(void)
{
        VWindow::InitActions();
        AddAction((VAction)&VComposite::CloseAction, WM_CLOSE);
        AddAction((VAction)&VComposite::CommandAction, WM_COMMAND);
}


void VComposite::Create(void)
{
        VWindow::Create();
}


void VComposite::AddCommand(VAction action, short cmdId,
                            short ntfyId)
{
    AddAction(action, WM_COMMAND, cmdId, ntfyId);
}


void VComposite::AddChild(VWindowPtr child)
{
        children.Append(child);
}


void VComposite::RemoveChild(VWindowPtr child)
{
        children.Remove(child);
}


void VComposite::CreateChildren(void)
{
        ChildIterator iter(children);
        VWindowPtr _FAR *current;
```

Listing A-19
Continued.

```cpp
        while ((current = iter()) != 0)
        {
                (*current)->Create();
        }
}

Boolean VComposite::IsValid(void)
{
    ChildIterator iter(children);
    VWindowPtr _FAR *child;
    while ((child = iter()) != 0)
    {
        if ((*child)->IsValid() == False)
            return False;
    }
    return True;
}


Boolean VComposite::QueryClose(void)
{
    ChildIterator iter(children);
    VWindowPtr _FAR *child;
    while ((child = iter()) != 0)
    {
        if ((*child)->QueryClose() == False)
            return False;
    }
    return True;
}

Boolean VComposite::CommandAction(VEventRef event)
{
        Boolean filtered = False;

        // Controls set the low word to the control's window handle.
        HWND hwnd = (HWND)LOWORD(event.GetLParam());
        VWindowPtr control = GetWinPointer(hwnd);
    if (control != 0)
        filtered = (*control)(event);
    else
        filtered = False;
        return filtered;
}


Boolean VComposite::CloseAction(VEventRef event)
{
        UNREFERENCED_PARAMETER(event);
        Destroy(True);
        delete this;
```

```
        return True;
}

Boolean VComposite::CreateAction(VEventRef event)
{
    UNREFERENCED_PARAMETER(event);
    VWindow::CreateAction(event);
    CreateChildren();
    return True;
}
```

Listing A-20
VCOMPRNT.H

```
/*---------------------------------------------------------------
   vcomprnt.h

   Interface for the common print and print setup dialogs

   Copyright (C) 1992, by Jeff Mackay
----------------------------------------------------------- */

#ifndef _VCOMPRNT_H
#define _VCOMPRNT_H

#ifndef _VCOMMON_H
#include <vcommon.h>
#endif

STDCLASS(VPrintDialog);
STDCLASS(VPrintSetupDialog);

class _CLASSTYPE VPrintDialog : public VCommonDialog
{
    public:
        VPrintDialog(VFramePtr parent);
        VPrintDialog(const VPrintDialogRef copy);
        VPrintDialog(void);
        VPrintDialogRef operator =(const VPrintDialogRef copy);
        // modifiers
        int  Execute(void);
        void SetMaxPage(int max);
        void SetMinPage(int min);
        void SetDevice(charPtr name, charPtr driver,
                       charPtr port);
        void WantDevice(void);
        void DisablePages(void);
        void DisableSelection(void);

        // accessors
        int GetFromPage(void) const;
```

Listing A-20
Continued.

```cpp
        int GetToPage(void) const;
            int GetCopies(void) const;
            HDC GetDC(void) const { return pd.hDC; }

    protected:
        PRINTDLG pd;
};


class _CLASSTYPE VPrintSetupDialog : public VPrintDialog
{
    public:
        VPrintSetupDialog(VFramePtr window) :
            VPrintDialog(window)
        {
            pd.Flags |= PD_PRINTSETUP;
        }
        VPrintSetupDialogRef operator =(
                            VPrintSetupDialogRef const copy)
        {
            VPrintDialog::operator =(copy);
            pd.Flags |= PD_PRINTSETUP;
            return *this;
        }
        VPrintSetupDialogRef operator =(
                            VPrintDialogRef const copy)
        {
            VPrintDialog::operator =(copy);
            pd.Flags |= PD_PRINTSETUP;
            return *this;
        }
};

#endif
```

Listing A-21
VCOMPRNT.CPP

```cpp
/*------------------------------------------------------------
    vcomprnt.cpp

        Implementation of the common print and print setup dialogs

    Copyright (C) 1992, by Jeff Mackay
------------------------------------------------------------ */

#pragma hdrfile "vista.sym"
#include <vista.h>
#pragma hdrstop
#include <vcomprnt.h>

VPrintDialog::VPrintDialog(VFramePtr parent)
```

```cpp
        : VCommonDialog(parent)
{
    memset(&pd, '\0', sizeof(pd));
    pd.lStructSize = sizeof(pd);
    if (parent != 0)
        pd.hwndOwner   = *parent;
}

VPrintDialog::VPrintDialog(const VPrintDialogRef copy)
        : VCommonDialog(VFramePtr(copy.parent))
{
    pd = copy.pd;
}

VPrintDialog::VPrintDialog(void)
{
}

VPrintDialogRef VPrintDialog::operator =(
                                        const VPrintDialogRef copy)
{
    pd = copy.pd;
    return *this;
}

int VPrintDialog::Execute(void)
{
    return PrintDlg(&pd);
}

void VPrintDialog::SetMaxPage(int max)
{
    pd.nMaxPage = max;
}

void VPrintDialog::SetMinPage(int min)
{
    pd.nMinPage = min;
}

int VPrintDialog::GetFromPage(void) const
{
    return pd.nFromPage;
}

int VPrintDialog::GetToPage(void) const
{
    return pd.nToPage;
}

int VPrintDialog::GetCopies(void) const
{
```

Listing A-21
Continued.

```cpp
    return pd.nCopies;
}

void VPrintDialog::SetDevice(charPtr name, charPtr driver,
                             charPtr port)
{
    VString devString = name;
    devString += "|";
    devString += driver;
    devString += "|";
    devString += port;
    devString += "|";
}

void VPrintDialog::WantDevice(void)
{
    pd.Flags |= PD_RETURNDC;
}

void VPrintDialog::DisablePages(void)
{
    pd.Flags |= PD_NOPAGENUMS;
}

void VPrintDialog::DisableSelection(void)
{
    pd.Flags |= PD_NOSELECTION;
}
```

Listing A-22
VCONTROL.H

```cpp
/* ------------------------------------------------------
   vcontrl.h

       VControl class interface definition.

   Copyright (c) Jeff Mackay, 1992

   ------------------------------------------------------ */

#ifndef _VCONTROL_H
#define _VCONTROL_H

#ifndef _VWINDOW_H
#include <vwindow.h>
#endif

STDCLASS(VControl);
class _CLASSTYPE VControl : public VWindow
{
```

```cpp
public:

    // constructors
        VControl(VCompositePtr parent, charPtr title,
                        int x, int y, int width, int height,
            int style= 0);
        VControl(VCompositePtr parent, int resourceId);

    // destructor
        virtual VControl(void);

    // accessors
        virtual const charPtr OldClassName(void) const;
        virtual const charPtr ClassName(void) const;
    virtual void    GetValue(voidPtr bufer);
    virtual int     GetValueLength(void);

    // modifiers
    virtual void Create(void);
        virtual void InitWinClass(WNDCLASSRef wndclass);
        virtual void Cut();
        virtual void Copy();
        virtual void Paste();
        virtual void Clear();
        virtual void SetValue(voidPtr buffer);

protected:
    static LRESULT CALLBACK _export
            ControlProc(HWND hwnd, UINT message,
                                    WPARAM wParam, LPARAM lParam);
    Boolean CommandAction(VEventRef event);
    static  WNDENUMPROC   init_child_proc;
    static  BOOL CALLBACK _export
                        InitChildProc(HWND child, LPARAM target_id);
        virtual LRESULT DefaultProc(VEventRef event);
    int     resource_id;
    Boolean resource_item;
};

inline void VControl::Cut(void)
{
}

inline void VControl::Copy(void)
{
}

inline void VControl::Paste(void)
{
}
```

Listing A-22
Continued.

```cpp
inline void VControl::Clear(void)
{
}

inline LRESULT VControl::DefaultProc(VEventRef event)
{
    return CallWindowProc(old_proc, *this, event.GetId(),
                          event.GetWParam(), event.GetLParam());
}

#endif
```

Listing A-23
VCONTROL.CPP

```cpp
/* ----------------------------------------------------------
** VContrl.cpp
**
**      VControl class implementation.
**
** Copyright (c) Jeff Mackay, 1992
**
** ----------------------------------------------------------
*/
#pragma hdrfile "vista.sym"
#include <vista.h>
#pragma hdrstop
#include <vcontrol.h>
#include <vappl.h>

WNDENUMPROC VControl::init_child_proc;

VControl::VControl(VCompositePtr par, charPtr title,
                                    int X, int Y, int W, int H, int
styleFlags) :
        VWindow(par, title)
{
    ex_style = WS_EX_NOPARENTNOTIFY;
    style    = WS_VISIBLE | WS_CHILD;
    x = X;
    y = Y;
    width = W;
    height = H;
    resource_id = VDEF_CTL_ID;
    resource_item = False;
    if (styleFlags)
        style = styleFlags;
}

VControl::VControl(VCompositePtr par, int resourceId) :
    VWindow(par, 0)
{
    wnd_proc =
```

```cpp
                    (WNDPROC)MakeProcInstance(
                                            (FARPROC)&VControl::ControlProc,
                                            GetApplication());
    if (init_child_proc == 0)
    {
       init_child_proc = (WNDENUMPROC)
            MakeProcInstance((FARPROC)VControl::InitChildProc, appl);
    }
    resource_id = resourceId;
    resource_item = True;
}

VControl::VControl(void)
{
}

// this is only called for controls not created from a resource
// script.  Effectively subclasses the control
void VControl::InitWinClass(WNDCLASSRef wndClass)
{
        if (!GetClassInfo(0, OldClassName(), &wndClass))
        {
        VWindow::InitWinClass(wndClass);
            appl.SetStatus(V_NOOLDCLASS);
            return;
        }
        old_proc              = wndClass.lpfnWndProc;
        wndClass.lpfnWndProc  = wnd_proc;
        wndClass.lpszClassName = (LPSTR) ClassName();
        wndClass.lpszMenuName  = 0;
        wndClass.hInstance     = appl;
}


const charPtr VControl::ClassName(void) const
{
        return "VControl";
}

const charPtr VControl::OldClassName(void) const
{
        return "CONTROL";
}

void VControl::GetValue(voidPtr buffer)
{
    UNREFERENCED_PARAMETER(buffer);
}

int VControl::GetValueLength(void)
{
```

Listing A-23
Continued.

```
        return 0;
}

void VControl::SetValue(voidPtr buffer)
{
    UNREFERENCED_PARAMETER(buffer);
}

void VControl::Create(void)
{
    if (registered == False)
    {
            Register();
    }
    if (resource_item == False)
    {
            VWindow::Create();
    }
    else
    {
        VWindowPtr oldCreate = _VCreateWindow;
        _VCreateWindow = this;
        EnumChildWindows(*parent, init_child_proc,
                    (LPARAM)(VControl FAR *)this);
        _VCreateWindow = oldCreate;
        if (handle == 0)
        {
                appl.SetStatus(V_WININVCHILD);
                return;
        }
        style = GetWindowLong(*this, GWL_STYLE);
        ex_style = GetWindowLong(*this, GWL_WNDPROC);
        old_proc = (WNDPROC)SetWindowLong(*this, GWL_WNDPROC,
(LONG)wnd_proc);
        VEvent event(*this, WM_CREATE);
        (*this)(event);
    }
}

// child window enum proc used to find the window handle for a
// control with an id (couldn't get GetDlgItem() to work from
// the WM_INITDIALOG message
BOOL CALLBACK _export VControl::InitChildProc(HWND hWnd, LPARAM param)
{
    VControl FAR *control = (VControl FAR *)param;
    UINT ctlId = GetWindowWord(hWnd, GWW_ID);
    if (ctlId == control->resource_id)
    {
            control->handle = hWnd;
            control->SetWinPointer();
```

```
                    return FALSE;
        }
    else
        {
                    return TRUE;
        }
}

Boolean VControl::CommandAction(VEventRef event)
{
    UNREFERENCED_PARAMETER(event);
    return False;
}


LRESULT CALLBACK _export
VControl::ControlProc(HWND hWnd, UINT id,
                                    WPARAM wParam, LPARAM lParam)
{
        VControlPtr control = (VControlPtr)GetWinPointer(hWnd);
    if (control == 0)
        return 0;

        VEvent  event(*control, id, wParam, lParam);
        Boolean filtered = (*control)(event);
        if (!filtered)
        return CallWindowProc(control->old_proc, *control,
                            event.GetId(), event.GetWParam(),
                                    event.GetLParam());
        else
            return event.GetResponse();
}
```

Listing A-24
VDATADLG.H

```
/* ----------------------------------------------------------------
   vdatadlg.h

    Interface for the VDataDialog template class.

   Copyright (C) 1992, by Jeff Mackay
   ---------------------------------------------------------------- */

#ifndef _VDATADLG_H
#define _VDATADLG_H

#ifndef _VDLGBOX_H
#include <vdlgbox.h>
#endif

template <class T> _CLASSTYPE VDataDialog : public VDialogBox
```

Listing A-24
Continued.

```
{
public:
    VDataDialog(VCompositePtr parent, charPtr template,
                T _FAR *buffer);
    {
        Attach(buffer);
    }

    void Attach(T _FAR *buffer)
    {
        AttachBuffer((void _FAR *)buffer);
    }

    T _FAR *Detach(T _FAR *buffer)
    {
        return DetachBuffer(void);
    }

    T _FAR *GetBuffer(void)
    {
        return (T _FAR *)data_buffer;
    }
};

#endif
```

Listing A-25
VDBLLIST.H

```
/* -------------------------------------------------------
    vdbllist.h

        Implementation of the VDblList template class

    Copyright (C) 1992, by Jeff Mackay - TAB BOOKS

   -------------------------------------------------------- */

#ifndef _VDBLLIST_H
#define _VDBLLIST_H

#ifndef _VISTA_H
#include <vista.h>
#endif

STDCLASS(VDblNode);
class _CLASSTYPE VDblNode
{
public:
    VDblNode *next;
    VDblNode *prev;
    VDblNode(void) : next(0), prev(0) {}
```

```cpp
};
STDCLASS(VDblListBase);
class _CLASSTYPE VDblListBase
{
    public:
                VDblListBase(void) : head(0) {}
        ~VDblListBase(void) { Clear(); }

        // Accessors
        VDblNodePtr First(void)
        {
            return head;
        }

        VDblNodePtr Last(void)
        {
            return (head) ? head->prev : 0;
        }

        VDblNodePtr Next(VDblNodePtr prev)
        {
            return (prev->next == head) ? prev->next : 0;
        }

        VDblNodePtr Prev(VDblNodePtr next)
        {
            return (next->prev == head) ? next->prev : 0;
        }


        // Modifiers
        virtual void Clear(void);
        virtual void Delete(VDblNodePtr el)
        {
            el = Remove(el);
            delete el;
        }
        virtual void Delete(void)
        {
            VDblNodePtr node = Remove(head);
            delete node;
        }

        void Insert(VDblNodePtr el);
            void Append(VDblNodePtr el);
            VDblNode _FAR *Remove(VDblNodePtr el);
        VDblNode _FAR *Remove(void) { return Remove(head); }
            friend class VDblListBaseIter;

    protected:
        VDblNodePtr head;
```

Appendix 341

Listing A-25
Continued.

```cpp
};
class VDblListBaseIter
{
    public:

        VDblNode _FAR *Next(void)
        {
            if (list->head == 0 || curr == 0)
                return 0;

            VDblNode _FAR *node = curr;
            curr = curr->next;
            if (curr == list->head)
                curr = 0;
            return node;
        }

        VDblNode _FAR *Prev(void)
        {
            if (list->head == 0 || curr == 0)
                return 0;

            VDblNode _FAR *node = curr;
            if (curr == list->head->prev)
                curr = 0;
            return node;
        }

    enum IterDirection
    {
        Forward,
        Reverse
    };

        VDblListBaseIter(const VDblListBase _FAR &l,
                            IterDirection dir=Forward)
        {
            list = &l;
    SetDirection(dir);
            Rewind();
        }

        VDblListBaseIter _FAR &operator =(
                    const VDblListBaseIter _FAR &copy)
    {
        list = copy.list;
        curr = copy.curr;
        SetDirection(Forward);
        return *this;
    }

    void SetDirection(IterDirection dir)
```

```cpp
    {
        direction = dir;
        if (direction == Forward)
            traverse = &VDblListBaseIter::Next;
        else
            traverse = &VDblListBaseIter::Prev;
    }

        VDblNode _FAR *operator()()
        {
            VDblNode _FAR *node = (this->*traverse)();
            return node;
        }

        VDblNode _FAR *Start(void)
        {
            curr = list->head;
            return curr;
        }

        VDblNode _FAR *End(void)
        {
            curr = list->head ? list->head->prev : 0;
            return curr;
        }

    VDblNode _FAR *SetCurrent(VDblNode _FAR *node)
    {
        VASSERT(node);
        curr = node;
        return curr;
    }

        VDblNode _FAR *Rewind(void)
        {
            if (direction == Forward)
                return Start();
            else
                return End();
        }

    VDblNode _FAR *Current(void) const
    {
        return curr;
    }

protected:
        const VDblListBase _FAR *list;
    IterDirection direction;
    VDblNode      _FAR *curr;
    VDblNode _FAR * (_FAR VDblListBaseIter::*traverse)(void);
```

Listing A-25
Continued.

```cpp
};
template <class T> struct VDblLink : public VDblNode
{
        T data;
        VDblLink(const T _FAR &val) : data(val) {}
};

template <class T> class VDblList : public VDblListBase
{
        public:
        VDblList(T defVal)
            : VDblListBase()
        {
            default_value = defVal;
        }

            void Insert(const T _FAR &el)
            {
                    VDblListBase::Insert(new VDblLink<T>(el));
            }

            void Append(const T _FAR &el)
            {
                    VDblListBase::Append(new VDblLink<T>(el));
            }

            T Remove(void)
            {
        if (head == 0)
            return default_value;

        if (current == head)
            current = 0;

        T data = ((VDblLink<T> _FAR *)head)->data;
        VDblListBase::Delete();
                    return data;
            }

            T Remove(const T _FAR &el);

        T Current(void)
        {
            return (current) ? current->data : default_value;
        }

        T First(void)
        {
            current = (VDblLink<T> _FAR *)VDblListBase::First();
            return Current();
        }
```

```cpp
        T Next(T _FAR &el)
        {
            if (current && current->data == el)
                current = (VDblLink<T> _FAR *)
                            VDblListBase::Next(current);
            else
                current = Find(el);
            return Current();
        }

        T Prev(T _FAR &el)
        {
            if (current && current->data == el)
                current = (VDblLink<T> _FAR *)
                            VDblListBase::Prev(current);
            else
                current = Find(el);
            return Current();
        }

        T Last(void)
        {
            current = (VDblLink<T> _FAR *)VDblListBase::Last();
            return Current();
        }

        T Contains(T _FAR &el)
        {
            current = Find(el);
            return Current();
        }

    protected:
            VDblLink<T> _FAR *Find(const T _FAR &el);
        VDblLink<T> _FAR *current;
        T default_value;

};

template <class T>
T VDblList<T>::Remove(const T _FAR &el)
{
    VDblLink<T> _FAR *link = current;
    if (link == 0 || link->data != el)
    {
        link = Find(el);
        if (link == 0)
            return default_value;
    }
    if (link == current)
```

Listing A-25
Continued.

```
        current = 0;
    VDblListBase::Remove(link);
        return el;
}


template <class T>
VDblLink<T> _FAR *VDblList<T>::Find(const T _FAR &el)
{
        VDblListBaseIter iter=*this;
        VDblLink<T> _FAR *node;
        while((node = (VDblLink<T> _FAR *)iter()) != 0)
        {
                if (node->data == el)
                        return node;
        }
        return 0;
}

template <class T>
class VDblListIter : public VDblListBaseIter
{
            public:
            VDblListIter(const VDblList<T> &l)
                    : VDblListBaseIter(l) {}
            T _FAR *operator()()
            {
                    VDblLink<T> _FAR *link;
                    link = (VDblLink<T> _FAR *)
                            VDblListBaseIter::operator()();
                    if (link)
                            return &link->data;
                    else
                            return 0;
            }

            T _FAR *Start(void)
            {
        VDblLink<T> _FAR *link = (VDblLink<T> _FAR *)
                        VDblListBaseIter::Start();
        if (link)
            return &link->data;
        else
            return 0;
            }

            T _FAR *End(void)
            {
        VDblLink<T> _FAR *link = (VDblLink<T> _FAR *)
                            VDblListBaseIter::End();
        if (link)
```

```cpp
                    return &link->data;
                else
                    return 0;
                }

            T _FAR *Current(void) const
            {
                VDblLink<T> _FAR *link = (VDblLink<T> _FAR *)
                                    VDblListBaseIter::Current();
                if (link)
                    return &link->data;
                else
                    return 0;

            }
};

#endif
```

```cpp
/*---------------------------------------------------------
    vdbllist.cpp

        Implementation of the VDblListBase class

    Copyright (C) 1992, by Jeff Mackay - TAB BOOKS
--------------------------------------------------------- */
#pragma hdrfile "vista.sym"
#include <vista.h>
#pragma hdrstop
#include <vdbllist.h>

void VDblListBase::Insert(VDblNode _FAR *el)
{
        if (!head)
        {
                el->prev = el->next = el;
        }
        else
        {
                el->prev = head->prev;
                el->next = head;
                el->prev->next = el->next->prev = el;
        }
        head = el;
}


VDblNode _FAR *VDblListBase::Remove(VDblNode _FAR *el)
{
    VASSERT(el != 0);
        if (el->next == el->prev)              // only element
        {
```

Listing A-26
VDBLLIST.CPP

Listing A-26
Continued.

```
                        head = 0;
        }
        else
        {
                el->next->prev = el->prev;
                el->prev->next = el->next;
                if (el == head)
        {
                        head = el->next;
        }
        }
        return el;
}

void VDblListBase::Append(VDblNode _FAR *el)
{
        if (head == 0)
        {
                head = el;
                head->prev = head->next = el;
        }
        else
        {
                el->prev = head->prev;
                el->next = head;
                el->prev->next = el->next->prev = el;
        }
}

void VDblListBase::Clear(void)
{
    if (head == 0)
        return;

    VDblNode _FAR *child;
    VDblNode _FAR *nextChild;
    child = head->next;
    while (child && child != head)
    {
        nextChild = child->next;
        delete child;
        child = nextChild;
    }
    delete head;
}

/* -----------------------------------------------------------
   VDisptch.h            Implementation of the VDispatcher class.

   Copyright (C) 1992, by Jeff Mackay
   ----------------------------------------------------------- */
```

Listing A-27
VDISPTCH.H

```cpp
#if !defined(_VDISPTCH_H)
#define _VDISPTCH_H

#include <vista.h>
#include <vdbllist.h>
#include <limits.h>

STDCLASS(VDispatcher);
STDCLASS(VEvent);
STDCLASS(VActionItem);
STDCLASS(VWindow);

const short VDEF_CTL_ID    = -10;
const short VDEF_NOTIFY_ID = -10;

typedef Boolean (_FAR VWindow::*VAction)(VEventRef);


class VActionItem
{
public:
        VAction action;
        UINT    message_id;
        short   ctl_id;
    short   notify_id;

        VActionItem(VAction act = 0, UINT msg = 0,
            short ctl=VDEF_CTL_ID,
                short notify=VDEF_NOTIFY_ID) :
            action(act), message_id(msg),
            ctl_id(ctl), notify_id(notify)
        {
        }
};

class _CLASSTYPE VDispatcher
{

public:

    VDispatcher(void) : actions(0) {}
        VDispatcher(void);
        void AddAction(VAction action, UINT id,
                                short ctl=VDEF_CTL_ID,
                                shortntfy=VDEF_CTL_ID);
        void RemoveAction(VAction action);
        void RemoveAction(UINT id, short ctl=VDEF_CTL_ID,
                                short ntfy=VDEF_NOTIFY_ID);
        VAction operator [](const VEventRef) const;
        VAction operator [](int) const;

private:
```

Listing A-27
Continued.

```
            VDblList<VActionItemPtr> actions;
                VActionItemPtr Find(VAction action) const;
                VActionItemPtr Find(UINT id, short ctl = VDEF_CTL_ID,
                                short ntfy = VDEF_CTL_ID) const;
        };

        #endif
```

Listing A-28
VDISPTCH.CPP

```
/* -----------------------------------------------------------------
    VDisptch.cpp

                    Interface for the VDispatcher class

    Copyright (C) 1992, by Jeff Mackay

----------------------------------------------------------------- */
#pragma hdrfile "vista.sym"
#include <vista.h>
#pragma hdrstop
#pragma hdrstop
#include <vdisptch.h>
#include <vevent.h>

const int INVALID_VACTION = (-1);

/* -----------------------------------------------------------------
destructor:

Deletes the action array.
----------------------------------------------------------------- */
VDispatcher::VDispatcher(void)
{
    VDblListIter<VActionItemPtr> iter(actions);
    VActionItemPtr _FAR *itemPtr;
    while((itemPtr = iter()) != 0)
    {
        delete *itemPtr;
    }
}



/* -----------------------------------------------------------------
AddAction:

Adds an action item to the action array.
----------------------------------------------------------------- */
void VDispatcher::AddAction(VAction action, UINT id, short ctlId,
                                            short notifyId)
{
        VActionItemPtr item =
```

```cpp
                    new VActionItem(action, id, ctlId, notifyId);
    actions.Append(item);
}

/* ------------------------------------------------------------
RemoveAction:

Removes an action item
------------------------------------------------------------ */
void VDispatcher::RemoveAction(VAction action)
{
        VActionItemPtr item = Find(action);
    if (item == 0)
        return;

    actions.Remove(item);
}

void VDispatcher::RemoveAction(UINT id, short ctl, short ntfy)
{
    VActionItemPtr item = Find(id, ctl, ntfy);
    if (item == 0)
        return;

    actions.Remove(item);
}

/* ------------------------------------------------------------
operator [](event):

Indexes the action list with an event object.  For most messages, it
uses only the event id as an index; however, for WM_COMMAND messages
it can use a combination of the event id, the control id, and the
notification code as the index.
------------------------------------------------------------ */
const VAction VDispatcher::operator [](const VEventRef event) const
{
        VActionItemPtr item;

        if (event.GetId() == WM_COMMAND)
                item = Find(event.GetId(), event.GetWParam(),
                        HIWORD(event.GetLParam()));
        else
                item = Find(event.GetId());

    if (item == 0)
        return 0;
    else
        return item->action;
}
```

Appendix 351

Listing A-28
Continued.

```cpp
/* ----------------------------------------------------------
operator [](int)

Index operator used when only an event id is available
---------------------------------------------------------- */
const VAction VDispatcher::operator [](int id) const
{
    VActionItemPtr item = Find(id);
    if (item == 0)
        return 0;
    else
        return item->action;
}
/* ----------------------------------------------------------
---------------------------------------------------------- */
VActionItem *VDispatcher::Find(VAction act) const
{
    VDblListIter<VActionItemPtr> iter(actions);
    VActionItemPtr _FAR *itemPtr;

    while ((itemPtr = iter()) != 0)
    {
        if ((*itemPtr)->action == act)
            return *itemPtr;
    }
    return 0;
}

#define _VCONTROL_MATCH        (8)
#define _VNOTIFY_MATCH         (4)
#define _VCONTROL_WILDCARD     (2)
#define _VNOTIFY_WILDCARD      (1)
#define _VFULL_MATCH           (_VCONTROL_MATCH + _VNOTIFY_MATCH)

VActionItem *VDispatcher::Find(UINT id, short ctl, short ntfy)
const
{
    VActionItemPtr _FAR *itemPtr;
    VDblListIter<VActionItemPtr> iter(actions);

        if (id != WM_COMMAND)
    {
        while((itemPtr = iter()) != 0)
        {
            if ((*itemPtr)->message_id == id)
            {
                return(*itemPtr);
            }
        }
    }
        else
        {
```

```cpp
        VActionItemPtr  bestMatch = 0;
        BYTE            bestScore = 0;

            // perform a best-match search through the action list
            // control id match takes priority over a notify id match
        while ((itemPtr = iter()) != 0)
        {
            if ((*itemPtr)->message_id != id)
                continue;

            BYTE score = 0;

            // check the control id
            if ((*itemPtr)->ctl_id == ctl)
                score += _VCONTROL-MATCH;
            else
                if ((*itemPtr)->ctl_id != VDEF_CTL_ID)
                    continue;
                else
                    score += _VCONTROL_WILD CARD;
            // check the notification code
            if ((*itemPtr)->notify_id == ntfy)
                score += -VNOTIFY_MATCH;
            else
                if ((*itemPtr)->notify_id != VDEF_NOTIFY_ID)
                    continue;
                else
                    score += _VNOTIFY_WILDCARD;

            if (score > bestScore)
            {
                bestMatch = *itemPtr;
                bestScore = score;
                if (bestScore == _VFULL_MATCH)
                    break;
            }
        }
        return bestMatch;
        }
    return 0;
}


/* ---------------------------------------------------------------
        VDlgBox.h

                Interface for the VDialogBox class

        Copyright (C) 1992, by Jeff Mackay
---------------------------------------------------------------*/
#ifndef _VDLGBOX_H
```

Listing A-29
VDLGBOX.H

Listing A-29
Continued.

```cpp
#define _VDLGBOX_H

#ifndef _VISTA_H
#include <vista.h>
#endif

STDCLASS(VDialogBox);

class _CLASSTYPE VDialogBox : public VComposite
{
    public:
        enum DialogStyle
        {
            ModalDialog,
            ModelessDialog
        } dialog_style;

        VDialogBox(VCompositePtr parent, charPtr title=0,
                    charPtr templateName=0);

        VDialogBox(VCompositePtr parent, charPtr title,
                        int resourceId);

        VDialogBox();
        virtual Boolean operator ()(VEventRef event);
        void SetDialogStyle(DialogStyle style);
    int SendChildEvent(int childId, VEventRef event);
        virtual const charPtr ClassName(void) const;
    virtual int Execute(void);
    virtual void ReadBuffer(void);
    virtual void WriteBuffer(void);
    void SetDeleteFlag(Boolean value);
    Boolean GetDeleteFlag(void);
    virtual Boolean QueryClose(void);
    virtual Boolean Destroy(Boolean query);

    protected:
    Boolean delete_flag;
        voidPtr data_buffer;
    int     buffer_size;
        VString template_name;
        int resource_id;
    int result;
    static DLGPROC dlg_proc;

    void AttachBuffer(voidPtr buffer, int bufSize);
    voidPtr DetachBuffer(void);
        virtual Boolean CreateAction(VEventRef event);
    virtual Boolean NCDestroyAction(VEventRef event);
    virtual Boolean CloseAction(VEventRef event);
```

```cpp
        virtual Boolean OkCommand(VEventRef event);
        virtual Boolean CancelCommand(VEventRef event);

            virtual void    InitActions(void);
            virtual void Create(void);
        virtual LRESULT DefaultProc(VEventRef event);
            static BOOL FAR PASCAL _export DialogFunc(HWNDhwnd,
                UINT message, WPARAM wParam, LPARAM lParam);
};

inline void VDialogBox::AttachBuffer(voidPtr buffer,
int

bufSize)

{
    data_buffer = buffer;
    buffer_size = bufSize;
}

inline voidPtr VDialogBox::DetachBuffer(void)
{
    voidPtr retVal = data_buffer;
    data_buffer = 0;
    buffer_size = 0;
    return retVal;
}

inline void VDialogBox::SetDeleteFlag(Boolean value)
{
    delete_flag = value;
}

inline Boolean VDialogBox::GetDeleteFlag(void)
{
    return delete_flag;
}


inline LRESULT VDialogBox::DefaultProc(VEventRef event)
{
     return DefDlgProc(*this, event.GetId(),
                event.GetWParam(), event.GetLParam());
}

inline int VDialogBox::SendChildEvent(int childId,

VEventRef event)
{
    return SendDlgItemMessage(*this, childId, event.GetId(),
                event.GetWParam(), event.GetLParam());
```

Listing A-29
Continued.

```cpp
}
#endif
```

Listing A-30
VDLGBOX.CPP

```cpp
/*-----------------------------------------------------------------
                VDlgBox.cpp

                    Implementation of the Dialog Box class

                Copyright (C) 1992, by Jeff Mackay

------------------------------------------------------------------*/
#pragma hdrfile "vista.sym"
#include <vista.h>
#pragma hdrstop

#include <vdlgbox.h>
#include <vcontrol.h>
#include <vappl.h>
#include <stdio.h>
#include <vmsgbox.h>

static VDialogBoxPtr createDialog;
DLGPROC VDialogBox::dlg_proc = 0;

// constructor for dialog box with template name as a string
VDialogBox::VDialogBox(VCompositePtr parent, charPtr title,
                    charPtr templateName) :
        VComposite(parent, title), template_name(templateName)
{
    if (!dlg_proc)
        dlg_proc  = (DLGPROC) MakeProcInstance(
                        (FARPROC)&VDialogBox::DialogFunc, appl);
        resource_id   = 0;
    data_buffer   = 0;
    buffer_size   = 0;
        dialog_style  = ModalDialog;
    translate_tabs = True;
    delete_flag   = True;
}

// constructor with template name as an int
VDialogBox::VDialogBox(VCompositePtr parent, charPtr title,
                                            int resourceId) :
        VComposite(parent, title), template_name(NULL)
{
    if (!dlg_proc)
        dlg_proc  = (DLGPROC) MakeProcInstance(
                        (FARPROC)&VDialogBox::DialogFunc,
appl);
```

```cpp
        resource_id    = resourceId;
        dialog_style   = ModalDialog;
    translate_tabs = True;
    data_buffer    = 0;
    buffer_size    = 0;
    delete_flag    = True;
}

VDialogBox::VDialogBox()
{
    if (dialog_style == ModalDialog)
        parent = 0;
}

const charPtr VDialogBox::ClassName(void) const
{
    if (dialog_style == ModalDialog)
        return (charPtr) 32770L;   // from Windows
    else
        return "VDialogBox";
}

void VDialogBox::SetDialogStyle(DialogStyle style)
{
        if (handle)
                return;
        dialog_style = style;
}

void VDialogBox::Create(void)
{
    if (!registered)
    {
            Register();
            if (appl.GetStatus() != V_SUCCESS)
                    return;
    }

        VDialogBoxPtr oldCreate = createDialog;
        createDialog = this;
        LPSTR templateName;
        if (template_name == NullString)
                templateName = (LPSTR) MAKELONG(resource_id, 0);
        else
                templateName = template_name;
        if (dialog_style == ModalDialog)
        {
                result = DialogBoxParam(appl, templateName, *parent,
                                        dlg_proc, (DWORD) this);
        }
        else
        {
```

Listing A-30
Continued.

```
                    handle = CreateDialogParam(appl, templateName, *parent,
                                        dlg_proc, (DWORD) this);
                    result = (handle) ? True : False;
            if (parent)
                parent->AddChild(this);
            }
            createDialog = oldCreate;
            if (!result)
            {
                    appl.SetStatus(V_WINCANTCRE);
                    return;
            }

        if (dialog_style != ModalDialog)
        {
            state = SW_SHOWNORMAL;
                Show();
        }
    }

    int VDialogBox::Execute()
    {
        Create();
        return result;
    }

    BOOL FAR PASCAL _export
    VDialogBox::DialogFunc(HWND hWnd, UINT message,
                        WPARAM wParam, LPARAM lParam)
    {
        VDialogBoxPtr dialog = (VDialogBoxPtr) GetWinPointer(hWnd);
            if (!dialog)
        {
            if (message == WM_INITDIALOG)
                {
                    dialog = (VDialogBoxPtr) lParam;
                    dialog->handle = hWnd;
                    dialog->>SetWinPointer();
            }
            else
            {
                return FALSE;
            }
        }
        VEvent  event(*dialog, message, wParam, lParam);
        Boolean filtered = (*dialog)(event);
    return (filtered) ? event.GetResponse() : False;
    }

    Boolean VDialogBox::operator ()(VEventRef event)
    {
```

```cpp
        VAction action = dispatcher[event];
    return (action) ? (this->*action)(event) : False;
}


Boolean VDialogBox::CreateAction(VEventRef event)
{
    VComposite::CreateAction(event);
    ReadBuffer();
    event.SetResponse(True);
        return True;
}

void    VDialogBox::InitActions(void)
{
    VComposite::InitActions();
    AddAction((VAction)&VDialogBox::CreateAction, WM_INITDIALOG);
    AddCommand((VAction)&VDialogBox::OkCommand, IDOK);
    AddCommand((VAction)&VDialogBox::CancelCommand, IDCANCEL);
}
Boolean VDialogBox::NCDestroyAction(VEventRef event)
{
    VComposite::NCDestroyAction(event);
    if (delete_flag == True)
        delete VDialogBoxPtr(this);
    return False;   // make sure this event is passed on
}

Boolean VDialogBox::CloseAction(VEventRef event)
{
    Destroy(False);
    UNREFERENCED_PARAMETER(event);
    return True;
}

Boolean VDialogBox::QueryClose(void)
{
    return IsValid();
}

Boolean VDialogBox::Destroy(Boolean query)
{
    if (dialog_style == ModalDialog)
    {
        if (query == True)
        {
            if (QueryClose() == True)
            {
              EndDialog(*this, IDOK);
              return True;
            }
```

Listing A-30
Continued.

```
            else
            {
               return False;
            }
         }
         else
         {
            EndDialog(*this, IDCANCEL);
            return True;
         }
      }
      else
         return VComposite::Destroy(query);
}


Boolean VDialogBox::OkCommand(VEventRef event)
{
    WriteBuffer();
    Destroy(True);
    UNREFERENCED_PARAMETER(event);
    return True;
}

Boolean VDialogBox::CancelCommand(VEventRef event)
{
    Destroy(False);
    UNREFERENCED_PARAMETER(event);
    return True;
}



void VDialogBox::ReadBuffer(void)
{
    if (data_buffer == 0)
        return;

    ChildIterator iter(children);
    VControlPtr _FAR *child;
    charPtr buff = charPtr(data_buffer);
    while ((child = (VControlPtr _FAR *)iter()) != 0)
    {
        VASSERT(buff + (*child)->GetValueLength() <=
                charPtr(data_buffer) <+ buffer_size);
        (*child)->SetValue(voidPtr(buff));
        buff += (*child)->GetValueLength();
    }

}
```

```
void VDialogBox::WriteBuffer(void)
{
    if (!data_buffer)
        return;

    ChildIterator iter(children);
    VControlPtr _FAR *child;
    charPtr buff = charPtr(data_buffer);
    while ((child = (VControlPtr _FAR *)iter()) != 0)
    {
        VASSERT(buff + (*child)->GetValueLength() <=
                charPtr(data_buffer) + buffer_size);
        (*child)->GetValue(voidPtr(buff));
        buff += (*child)->GetValueLength();
    }
}
```

Listing A-31
VDYNARR.H

```
/* ------------------------------------------------------------------
   VDynArray.h

        Interface for the VDynArray template classes derived from
    the BIDS array templates.

    Copyright (C) 1992, by Jeff Mackay - TAB BOOKS
   ------------------------------------------------------------  */
#ifndef _VDYNARR_H
#define _VDYNARR_H

#ifndef _VARRAY_H
#include <varray.h>
#endif

#ifndef __ARRAYS_H
#include <arrays.h>
#endif

template <class T>
class VDynArray : public BI_ArrayAsVector<T>
{
        public:
                VDynArray(int upper=16, int delta=0)
                : BI_ArrayAsVector<T>(upper, 0, delta) {}
                void Add(T t) { add(t); }
                void AddAt(T t, int loc) { addAt(t, loc); }
                sizeType Count(void) const { return arraySize(); }
                sizeType Members(void) const { return getItemsInContainer(); }
};
```

Listing A-31
Continued.
```
template <class T>
class VDynArrayIterator : public BI_ArrayAsVectorIterator<T>
{
        public:
                VArrayIterator(const VArray<T> _FAR &a)
                : BI_ArrayAsVectorIterator<T>(a) {}
};

#endif
```

Listing A-32
VEDIT.H
```
/* -------------------------------------------------------------
   VEditable.h

                 VEditable abstract class interface.

   Copyright (c) 1992, by Jeff Mackay

   ------------------------------------------------------------- */

#ifndef _VEDIT_H
#define _VEDIT_H

#ifndef _VCONTROL_H
#include <vcontrol.h>
#endif

STDCLASS(VEditable);

struct VEditSelection
{
    int start;
    int end;
};
_REFTYPE(VEditSelection);


class _CLASSTYPE VEditable : public VControl
{
public:
        VEditable(VCompositePtr parent, VStringRef text, int x,
                        int y, int width, int height, int maxSize=(-1));
        VEditable(VCompositePtr parent, int resourceId,
                            int maxSize=(-1));
        VEditable() {}

        virtual const charPtr ClassName(void) const;
        virtual const charPtr OldClassName(void) const;
        virtual Boolean CanUndo(void);
        virtual VEditSelectionRef GetSelection(VEditSelectionRef sel);
```

```cpp
        virtual void GetSelection(int _FAR &start, int _FAR &end);
        virtual void SetSelection(VEditSelectionRef sel);
    virtual void SetSelection(int start, int end);
        virtual void ReplaceSelection(charPtr string);
        virtual charPtr GetText(charPtr buffer);
        virtual int    GetTextLength(void);
        virtual Boolean IsValid(void);
        virtual void InitActions(void);
        virtual Boolean CreateAction(VEventRef event);
        virtual Boolean ChangeAction(VEventRef event);
        virtual Boolean OverflowAction(VEventRef event);
        virtual Boolean LoseFocusAction(VEventRef event);
        virtual Boolean SetFocusAction(VEventRef event);

        virtual void Cut(void);
        virtual void Copy(void);
        virtual void Paste(void);
        virtual void Clear(void);
    virtual void Undo(void);
        virtual Boolean Modified(void);
        virtual void SetSize(UINT size);
        virtual void SetReadOnly(Boolean flag);
        virtual void GetValue(voidPtr value);
        virtual void SetValue(voidPtr value);
        virtual int  GetValueLength(void);
        virtual void SetText(charPtr buffer);

protected:
    int max_size;
};

inline VEditable::VEditable(VCompositePtr parent,
                                              VStringRef text, int x, int y,
            int width, int height, int maxSize)
    : VControl(parent, text, x,y,width,height)
{
    max_size = maxSize;
}

inline VEditable::VEditable(VCompositePtr parent,
                                               int resourceId, int maxSize)
    : VControl(parent, resourceId)
{
    max_size = maxSize;
}


inline Boolean VEditable::CreateAction(VEventRef event)
{
```

Listing A-32
Continued.

```cpp
    if (max_size >= (-1))
        SetSize(max_size);
    UNREFERENCED_PARAMETER(event);
    return False;
}

inline Boolean VEditable::ChangeAction(VEventRef event)
{
    UNREFERENCED_PARAMETER(event);
    return False;
}

inline Boolean VEditable::OverflowAction(VEventRef event)
{
    UNREFERENCED_PARAMETER(event);
    return False;
}

inline Boolean VEditable::LoseFocusAction(VEventRef event)
{
    UNREFERENCED_PARAMETER(event);
    return False;
}

inline Boolean VEditable::SetFocusAction(VEventRef event)
{
    UNREFERENCED_PARAMETER(event);
    return False;
}

inline Boolean VEditable::IsValid(void)
{
    return True;
}
#endif
```

Listing A-33
VEDIT.CPP

```cpp
/* --------------------------------------------------------
    vedit.cpp

                VEdit class implementation.
    Copyright (c) 1992, by Jeff Mackay

----------------------------------------------------------- */
#pragma hdrfile "vista.sym"
#include <vista.h>
#pragma hdrstop

#include <vedit.h>

const charPtr VEditable::ClassName(void) const
```

```cpp
{
        return "VEditable";
}

const charPtr VEditable::OldClassName(void) const
{
        return "edit";
}

void VEditable::InitActions(void)
{
    AddAction((VAction)&VEditable::CreateAction, WM_CREATE);
        AddAction((VAction)&VEditable::ChangeAction, WM_COMMAND,
            resource_id, EN_UPDATE);
    AddAction((VAction)&VEditable::OverflowAction, WM_COMMAND,
            resource_id, EN_MAXTEXT);
    AddAction((VAction)&VEditable::SetFocusAction, WM_COMMAND,
            resource_id, EN_SETFOCUS);
    AddAction((VAction)&VEditable::LoseFocusAction, WM_COMMAND,
            resource_id, EN_UPDATE);
}

void VEditable::Cut(void)
{
    SendMessage(*this, WM_CUT, 0, 0);
}

void VEditable::Copy(void)
{
    SendMessage(*this, WM_COPY, 0, 0);
}

void VEditable::Paste(void)
{
    SendMessage(*this, WM_PASTE, 0, 0);
}

void VEditable::Clear(void)
{
    SendMessage(*this, WM_CLEAR, 0, 0);
}

void VEditable::Undo(void)
{
        SendMessage(*this, WM_UNDO, 0, 0);
}

void VEditable::GetValue(voidPtr buffer)
{
    GetText((charPtr) buffer);
```

Listing A-33
Continued.

```cpp
}
int  VEditable::GetValueLength(void)
{
    return GetTextLength();
}

void VEditable::SetValue(voidPtr value)
{
    if (max_size > -1)
        ((charPtr)value)[max_size-1] = '\0';
    SetText((charPtr)value);
}

void VEditable::SetText(charPtr buffer)
{
    SetWindowText(*this, buffer);
}

charPtr VEditable::GetText(charPtr buffer)
{
    int len = GetWindowText(*this, buffer,
GetTextLength());
    UNREFERENCED_PARAMETER(len);
    return buffer;
}

int VEditable::GetTextLength(void)
{
    int text_length;
    if (max_size > 0)
        text_length = max_size;
    else
        text_length = GetWindowTextLength(*this);
    return text_length;
}

Boolean VEditable::CanUndo(void)
{
    return (Boolean) SendMessage(*this, EM_CANUNDO, 0, 0);
}

Boolean VEditable::Modified(void)
{
    return (Boolean) SendMessage(*this, EM_GETMODIFY, 0,
0);
}

VEditSelectionRef
VEditable::GetSelection(VEditSelectionRef sel)
{
        GetSelection(sel.start, sel.end);
```

```
                return sel;
}

void VEditable::GetSelection(int _FAR &start, int _FAR &end)
{
        DWORD result;

        result = (DWORD) SendMessage(*this, EM_GETSEL, 0, 0);
        start = LOWORD(result);
    end   = HIWORD(result);
}

void VEditable::SetSelection(VEditSelection _FAR &sel)
{
        SetSelection(sel.start, sel.end);
}

void VEditable::SetSelection(int start, int end)
{
        SendMessage(*this, EM_SETSEL, 1, MAKELONG(start, end));
}

void VEditable::SetSize(UINT newSize)
{
    max_size = newSize;
    SendMessage(*this, EM_LIMITTEXT, max_size, 0);
}

void VEditable::ReplaceSelection(charPtr string)
{
        SendMessage(*this, EM_REPLACESEL, 0,
                    (LPARAM)(LPCSTR)string);
}

void VEditable::SetReadOnly(Boolean flag)
{
    SendMessage(*this, EM_SETREADONLY, (WPARAM)flag, 0);
}


/* --------------------------------------------------------
    VEvent.h

        Event class interface definition.

    Copyright (C) 1992, by Jeff Mackay

   -------------------------------------------------------- */
```

Listing A-34
VEVENT.H

Listing A-33
Continued.

```c
#ifndef _VEVENT_H
#define _VEVENT_H

#ifndef _VISTA_H
#include <vista.h>
#endif

STDCLASS(VEvent);

typedef UINT    VEventId;
typedef LRESULT VResponse;

class _CLASSTYPE VEvent
{

public:

        // constructors
        VEvent(VWindowRef wnd, UINT id=0, WPARAM wParam=0,
                        LPARAM lParam=0);
    VEvent(const VEventRef);

        // destructor
        virtual VEvent(void);

        // operators
        VEventRef operator =(const VEventRef evt);
    operator UINT(void) const;

        LRESULT Send(void);
        int     Post(void);

        void    GetPosition(int *x, int *y) const;
        void    GetPosition(POINT *point) const;
        int     GetTime(void) const;
        WPARAM  GetWParam(void) const;
        LPARAM  GetLParam(void) const;
        HWND    GetHandle(void) const;
        VEventId GetId(void) const;
        VResponse GetResponse(void) const;
    VWindowRef GetWindow(void) const;
        void    SetResponse(VResponse val);
        int     SetQueue(int number) const;
protected:

        WPARAM      wparam;
        LPARAM      lparam;
        HWND        hwnd;
    VEventId    message;
        VResponse   response;
    VWindowPtr  window;
```

```cpp
};

// virtual destructor (does nothing)
inline VEvent::VEvent(void)
{
}

// Get the position for an event - overloaded
inline void VEvent::GetPosition(int *x, int *y) const
{
        DWORD value = GetMessagePos();
    POINT point = MAKEPOINT(value);
        *x = point.x;
        *y = point.y;
}

// Get the mouse position for an event - overloaded
inline void VEvent::GetPosition(POINT *pt) const
{
        DWORD value = GetMessagePos();
        *pt = MAKEPOINT(value);
}

// Send an event to a window

inline LRESULT VEvent::Send(void)
{
        return SendMessage(hwnd, message, wparam, lparam);
}

// Post an event for a window

inline int VEvent::Post(void)
{
        return PostMessage(hwnd, message, wparam, lparam);
}

// Get a message's word param

inline WPARAM VEvent::GetWParam(void) const
{
        return wparam;
}
// Get a message's long param

inline LPARAM VEvent::GetLParam(void) const
{
        return lparam;
}

// get the return value
```

Listing A-34
Continued.

```
inline VResponse VEvent::GetResponse(void) const
{
        return response;
}

// set the return value
inline void VEvent::SetResponse(VResponse val)
{
        response = val;
}

// get the message identifier
inline VEventId VEvent::GetId(void) const
{
        return message;
}

// get the target window handle
inline HWND VEvent::GetHandle(void) const
{
        return hwnd;
}

// get the target window object
// don't need to check the window for 0, it was
// initialized with a reference
inline VWindowRef VEvent::GetWindow(void) const
{
        return *window;
}
#endif
```

Listing A-35
VEVENT.CPP

```
/*-----------------------------------------------------------
    vevent.cpp

    Implementation of the VEvent class.

    Copyright (C) 1992, by Jeff Mackay

------------------------------------------------------------ */
#pragma hdrfile "vista.sym"
#include <vista.h>
#pragma hdrstop

VEvent::VEvent(VWindowRef wnd, UINT id, WPARAM wParam, LPARAM lParam)
{
    window      = &wnd;
```

```cpp
        hwnd        = wnd;
        message     = id;
        wparam      = wParam;
        lparam      = lParam;
        response    = 0;
}

VEvent::VEvent(const VEventRef evt)
{
        window      = evt.window;
        hwnd        = evt.hwnd;
        message     = evt.message;
        wparam      = evt.wparam;
        lparam      = evt.lparam;
        response    = evt.response;
}

VEventRef VEvent::operator =(const VEventRef evt)
{
        window      = evt.window;
        hwnd        = evt.hwnd;
        message     = evt.message;
        wparam      = evt.wparam;
        lparam      = evt.lparam;
        response    = evt.response;
        return(*this);
}
```

Listing A-36
VFRAME.CPP

```cpp
/*----------------------------------------------------------------
    vframe.cpp

         Implementation of the VFrame class

    Copyright (C) 1992, by Jeff Mackay

----------------------------------------------------------------- */
#pragma hdrfile "vista.sym"
#include <vista.h>
#pragma hdrstop

VFrame::VFrame(VApplRef appl, VCompositePtr par, charPtr caption)
: VComposite(appl, par, caption)
{
        menu_name = 0;
        menu = 0;
        vert_scroll = 0;
        horiz_scroll = 0;

        width = height = CW_USEDEFAULT;
```

Listing A-36
Continued.

```
              x       = y       = CW_USEDEFAULT;
        state = appl.GetWinState();
}

VFrame::VFrame(VCompositePtr par, charPtr caption) :
        VComposite(par, caption)
{
        menu_name = 0;
        menu = 0;
        vert_scroll = 0;
        horiz_scroll = 0;

        width = height = CW_USEDEFAULT;
        x       = y       = CW_USEDEFAULT;
        state = appl.GetWinState();
}

VFrame::VFrame(void)
{
        delete menu;
        delete vert_scroll;
        delete horiz_scroll;
}

const VMenuPtr VFrame::GetMenu(void) const
{
        return menu;
}


VMenuPtr VFrame::SetMenu(VMenuPtr newMenu, int winPos)
{
        UNREFERENCED_PARAMETER(winPos);
        VMenuPtr oldMenu = menu;
    if (oldMenu != 0)
        oldMenu->SetParent(0);

        menu = newMenu;
        if (handle)
        {
                ::SetMenu(*this, *menu);
        }
        return oldMenu;
}
void VFrame::Create(void)
{
        if (!menu)
                menu_or_child = child_id;
        else
                menu_or_child = (UINT)(HMENU) *menu;
```

```cpp
        VComposite::Create();
}

void VFrame::InitActions()
{
    VComposite::InitActions();
        AddAction((VAction)&VFrame::DestroyAction,       WM_DESTROY);
    AddAction((VAction)&VFrame::QueryEndSessionAction,
                            WM_QUERYENDSESSION);
        if (style & WS_VSCROLL)
            AddAction((VAction)&VFrame::VScrollAction, WM_VSCROLL);
        if (style & WS_HSCROLL)
            AddAction((VAction)&VFrame::HScrollAction, WM_HSCROLL);
    AddCommand((VAction)&VFrame::ExitCommand,        VID_EXIT);
}

Boolean VFrame::CommandAction(VEventRef event)
{
        Boolean filtered = False;
        UINT result = LOWORD(event.GetLParam());

    // menus set the loword of lparam to 0, accelerators to 1
        if (result == 0 || result == 1)
        {
            filtered = (*this)(event.GetWParam(), event);
        }
        else
        {
            filtered = VComposite::CommandAction(event);
        }
    return filtered;

}


Boolean VFrame::DestroyAction(VEventRef event)
{
        UNREFERENCED_PARAMETER(event);
    // frames can be secondary windows
        if (this == appl.GetMainWindow())
        {
            PostQuitMessage(0);
            return True;
        }
        return False;
}


Boolean VFrame::HScrollAction(VEventRef event)
{
        return (*horiz_scroll)(event);
```

Listing A-36
Continued.

```
}

Boolean VFrame::VScrollAction(VEventRef event)
{
        return (*vert_scroll)(event);
}


Boolean VFrame::CreateAction(VEventRef event)
{
    VComposite::CreateAction(event);
        if (style & WS_VSCROLL)
                vert_scroll = new VScroll(*this, Vertical);
        if (style & WS_HSCROLL)
                horiz_scroll = new VScroll(*this, Horizontal);
        return False;
}


Boolean VFrame::QueryEndSessionAction(VEventRef event)
{
    Boolean canQuit = QueryClose();
    if (canQuit == True)
        event.SetResponse(1);
    return True;
}


Boolean VFrame::ExitCommand(VEventRef event)
{
    Destroy(True);
    UNREFERENCED_PARAMETER(event);
    return True;
}
```

Listing A-37
VGDITOOL.H

```
/* ----------------------------------------------------------------
    VGdiTool.h

        Interface for the GDI tool classes

    Copyright (C) 1992, by Jeff Mackay
----------------------------------------------------------------*/

#ifndef _VGDITOOL_H
#define _VGDITOOL_H
```

```
#ifndef _VISTA_H
#include <vista.h>
#endif

#include <string.h>

STDCLASS(VGdiTool);
STDCLASS(VDevice);
STDCLASS(VFont);
STDCLASS(VBrush);
STDCLASS(VColor);
STDCLASS(VPen);
STDCLASS(VPalette);

class _CLASSTYPE VGdiTool
{
public:

        VGdiTool(int stock_type);
        VGdiTool(void);
        VGdiTool(void);
        operator HGDIOBJ(void);
        virtual void Realize(VDeviceRef dev);
        virtual void Unrealize(void);
        virtual void Detach(void);
        friend VDeviceRef operator <<(VDeviceRef dev, VGdiTool tool);

protected:
        HGDIOBJ handle;
        int     stock_type;
        Boolean stock_object;

private:
        void Initialize(void)
        {
            handle          = 0;
            stock_object    = False;
            device          = 0;
         realized          = False;
        }

        VGdiTool(VGdiToolRef) {}                              // restrict
   VGdiToolRef operator =(VGdiToolRef) {return *this;}        // restrict
   HGDIOBJ old_handle;
        Boolean realized;
        VDevicePtr device;
};
class _CLASSTYPE VBitmap : public VGdiTool
{
 public:
```

Listing A-37
Continued.

```cpp
                VBitmap(void) : VGdiTool()
                {
                }

        private:
                VBitmap(int stock_type) : VGdiTool(stock_type) {} // restrict
        };

        class _CLASSTYPE VBrush : public VGdiTool
        {
                public:
                        typedef enum
                        {
                                BDiagonal   = HS_BDIAGONAL,
                                Cross       = HS_CROSS,
                                DiagCross   = HS_DIAGCROSS,
                                FDiagonal   = HS_FDIAGONAL,
                                Horizontal  = HS_HORIZONTAL,
                                Vertical    = HS_VERTICAL,
                        } HatchType;

                        VBrush(int stock_type) : VGdiTool(stock_type)
                        {
                        }

                        VBrush(VBrushCRef copy)
                        {
                        handle = copy.handle;
                        }

                        VBrushRef operator =(VBrushCRef copy)
                        {
                                if (handle != copy.handle)
                                {
                                        Detach();
                                        handle = copy.handle;
                                        stock_type = copy.stock_type;
                        stock_object = copy.stock_object;
                                }
                        return *this;
                        }

                        VBrush(HBRUSH copy)
                        {
                        handle = copy;
                        }

                        VBrushRef operator =(HBRUSH copy)
                        {
                        Detach();
                                handle = copy;
```

```cpp
            return *this;
        }

        VBrush(HBITMAP bitmap)
        {
    Detach();
            handle = bitmap;
        }

        VBrushRef operator =(HBITMAP bitmap)
        {
    Detach();
            handle = (HGDIOBJ)CreatePatternBrush(bitmap);
            return *this;
        }

        VBrush(HatchType hatch, COLORREF color)
        {
            handle = (HGDIOBJ)CreateHatchBrush(hatch, color);
        }

        VBrush(COLORREF color)
        {
            handle = (HGDIOBJ)CreateSolidBrush(color);
    }

        VBrushRef operator =(COLORREF color)
        {
        Detach();
            handle = (HGDIOBJ)CreateSolidBrush(color);
        return *this;
    }

        VBrush(void)
        {
        }

        virtual void Realize(VDeviceRef dev)
        {
        VGdiTool::Realize(dev);
        }

    operator HBRUSH(void) { return (HBRUSH) handle; }
};
class _CLASSTYPE VColor
{
    private:
    COLORREF color;

    public:
        typedef enum
```

Listing A-37
Continued.

```cpp
        {
            ActiveBorder = COLOR_ACTIVEBORDER + 1,
            ActiveCaption = COLOR_ACTIVECAPTION + 1,
            AppWorkspace = COLOR_APPWORKSPACE + 1,
            Background = COLOR_BACKGROUND + 1,
            BtnFace = COLOR_BTNFACE + 1,
            BtnHighlight = COLOR_BTNHIGHLIGHT +1,
            BtnText = COLOR_BTNTEXT + 1,
            CaptionText = COLOR_CAPTIONTEXT + 1,
            GrayText = COLOR_GRAYTEXT + 1,
            HighLight = COLOR_HIGHLIGHT + 1,
            InactiveBorder = COLOR_INACTIVEBORDER + 1,
            InactiveCaption = COLOR_INACTIVECAPTION + 1,
            InactiveCaptionText = COLOR_INACTIVECAPTIONTEXT + 1,
            Menu = COLOR_MENU + 1,
            Scrollbar = COLOR_SCROLLBAR + 1,
            Window = COLOR_WINDOW + 1,
            WindowFrame = COLOR_WINDOWFRAME + 1,
            WindowText = COLOR_WINDOWTEXT + 1,
        } SysColor;

        typedef enum
        {
            Black,
            White,
            Red,
            Green,
            Blue,
            Cyan,
            Magenta,
    Yellow,
} StdColor;
        VColor(int r=0, int g=0, int b=0);
        VColor(COLORREF col);
        VColor(SysColor syscol);
VColor(StdColor col);
        virtual void Realize(void);
        virtual void Unrealize(void);
        operator COLORREF(void);
VColorRef operator =(COLORREF col);
        VColor(VColorCRef col);

};
inline UINT PixelsToPoints(HDC hdc, UINT pix)
{
        return pix * (1/GetDeviceCaps(hdc, LOGPIXELSY)) * 12;
}

inline UINT PointsToPixels(HDC hdc, UINT points)
{
```

```cpp
            return points * GetDeviceCaps(hdc, LOGPIXELSY) / 12;
}

class _CLASSTYPE VFont : public VGdiTool
{
        public:
                VFont(charPtr name, UINT pixHeight,
                        Boolean useItalic=False,
                        Boolean useBold=False,
                        Boolean useUnder=False,
                        int charSet=ANSI_CHARSET)
                {
                lf = new LOGFONT;
                memset(lf, 0, sizeof(*lf));
                        _fstrcpy(lf->lfFaceName, name);
            lf->lfItalic = useItalic;
            lf->lfUnderline = useUnder;
            if (useBold)
                                lf->lfWeight = FW_BOLD;
                    lf->lfCharSet = charSet;
                delete lf;
                }

                VFont(LOGFONT _FAR &logFont)
                {
                        lf = new LOGFONT;
                        *lf = logFont;
                        handle = (HGDIOBJ)CreateFontIndirect(lf);
                delete lf;
                lf = 0;
                }

        VFont(void)
        {
            lf = 0;
            handle = 0;
        }

        VFontRef operator =(LOGFONT _FAR &copy)
        {
            lf = new LOGFONT;
            *lf = copy;
            handle = (HGDIOBJ)CreateFontIndirect(lf);
            delete lf;
            lf = 0;
            return *this;
        }

                VFont(int stock_type) : VGdiTool(stock_type)
```

Listing A-37
Continued.

```cpp
                {
                    lf = 0;
                }

                virtual void Realize(VDeviceRef dev)
                {
                    VGdiTool::Realize(dev);
                }

            operator HFONT(void) { return (HFONT) handle; }
            private:
                LOGFONT *lf;
};

class _CLASSTYPE VPen : public VGdiTool
{
        public:
            typedef enum
            {
                        Solid = PS_SOLID,
                        Dash  = PS_DASH,
                        Dot   = PS_DOT,
                        DashDot = PS_DASHDOT,
                        DashDotDot = PS_DASHDOTDOT,
                        Null = PS_NULL,
                        InsideFrame = PS_INSIDEFRAME,
            } PenStyle;

                VPen(void) : VGdiTool()
                {
                handle = CreatePen(Solid, 0,
VColor(VColor::Black));
                }

            VPen(int stock_type) : VGdiTool(stock_type)
            {
            }

            VPen(PenStyle style, int width, COLORREF color)
            {
                handle = (HGDIOBJ) CreatePen(style, width, color);
            }

                VPen(VPenCRef copy)
                {
                        if (handle != copy.handle)
                handle = copy.handle;
                }

                VPenRef operator =(VPenCRef copy)
```

```cpp
            {
                if (handle != copy.handle)
                {
        Detach();
                    handle = copy.handle;
                    stock_type = copy.stock_type;
                }
        return *this;
    }

            VPen(HPEN copy)
            {
            handle = copy;
    }

            VPenRef operator =(HPEN copy)
            {
                    Detach();
                    handle = copy;
        return *this;
            }

            operator HPEN(void) { return (HPEN) handle; }
};
class _CLASSTYPE VPalette : public VGdiTool
{
        public:

            VPalette(void)
            {
            }

            VPalette(VPaletteRef copy)
            {
            *this = copy;
            }

            VPaletteRef operator =(VPaletteRef copy)
            {
                    if (handle != copy.handle)
                    {
                            Detach();
                            handle = copy.handle;
                    }
        return *this;
            }

            VPalette(const LOGPALETTE FAR &palette)
            {
            handle = (HGDIOBJ) CreatePalette(&palette);
```

Listing A-37
Continued.

```cpp
            }
            VPaletteRef operator =(const LOGPALETTE FAR &palette)
            {
                Detach();
                    handle = (HGDIOBJ) CreatePalette(&palette);
            return *this;
        }

            operator HPALETTE(void) { return (HPALETTE) handle; }
        private:
            VPalette(int stock_type){} // restrict
};

// VColor inline functions
inline VColor::VColor(int r, int g, int b)
{
        color = RGB(r,g,b);
}

inline VColor::VColor(COLORREF col)
{
        color = col;
}


inline VColor::VColor(SysColor syscol)
{
        color = GetSysColor(syscol);
}


inline void VColor::Realize(void)
{
}

inline void VColor::Unrealize(void)
{
}

inline VColor::operator COLORREF(void)
{
        return color;
}
inline VColorRef VColor::operator =(COLORREF col)
{
    color = col;
    return *this;
}
```

```cpp
inline VColor::VColor(VColorCRef col)
{
    color = col.color;
}


#endif
```

```cpp
/*
-----------------------------------------------------------
    vgditool.cpp

        Implementation of the VGdiTool class

    Copyright (C) 1992, by Jeff Mackay
-----------------------------------------------------   */
#pragma hdrfile "vista.sym"
#include <vista.h>
#pragma hdrstop

#include <vgditool.h>
#include <vgrdev.h>


VGdiTool::VGdiTool(int stock_type)
{
        Initialize();
                handle = GetStockObject(stock_type);
}

VGdiTool::VGdiTool(void)
{
        Initialize();
}

VGdiTool::VGdiTool(void)
{
        if (device)
        {
                Unrealize();
                device = 0;
        }
        Detach();
}

VGdiTool::operator HGDIOBJ(void)
{
```

Listing A-38
VGDITOOL.CPP

Listing A-38
Continued.

```cpp
        return handle;
}

void VGdiTool::Realize(VDeviceRef dev)
{
        device = &dev;
        device->Associate(*this);
        old_handle = SelectObject(*device, handle);
        realized = True;
}

void VGdiTool::Unrealize(void)
{
        if (!realized)
                return;

        SelectObject(*device, old_handle);
    device   = 0;
        realized = False;
}

void VGdiTool::Detach(void)
{
        if (handle && !stock_object)
            DeleteObject((HGDIOBJ)handle);
    handle = 0;
}

VDeviceRef operator <<(VDeviceRef dev, VGdiTool tool)
{
        tool.Realize(dev);
    return dev;
}

static COLORREF colors[] =
{
        RGB(0,0,0),
        RGB(255,255,255),
        RGB(255,0,0),
        RGB(0,255,0),
        RGB(0,0,255),
        RGB(0,128,128),
        RGB(128,0,128),
    RGB(128,128,0),
};
VColor::VColor(StdColor col)
{
        color = colors[(int)col];
}
```

Listing A-39
VGRDEV.H

```c
/* --------------------------------------------------------
   vgrdev.h

     Interface for the graphics device classes.

   Copyright (C) 1992, by Jeff Mackay

   -------------------------------------------------------- */

#ifndef _GRDEV_H
#define _GRDEV_H

#include <Vista.h>
#include <VString.h>
#include <VWindow.h>
#include <VGdiTool.h>
#include <VDblList.h>

STDCLASS(VDevice);
STDCLASS(VDisplayDevice);
STDCLASS(VPaintDevice);
STDCLASS(VFileDevice);
STDCLASS(VMemoryDevice);
STDCLASS(VPrinterDevice);

class _CLASSTYPE VDevice
{
        public:
        // constructor
                VDevice(VWindowPtr win=NULL);

        // destructor
                virtual VDevice();

        // operators
                operator HDC(void) const;

        // accessors
                VWindowPtr GetParent(void) const;

        // modifiers
                void SetParent(VWindowPtr win);
        virtual void Save(void);
                virtual void Restore(void);
                void DoDis(void);
                void Associate(VGdiToolRef tool);
                void Dissociate(VGdiToolRef tool);

    protected:
        HDC handle;
```

Listing A-39
Continued.

```cpp
            VWindowPtr parent;
            typedef VDblList<VGdiToolPtr> ToolStack;
            typedef VDblListIter<VGdiToolPtr> ToolIterator;
            ToolStack  tools;

    private:
};
inline VDevice::VDevice(VWindowPtr win) :
        parent(win), handle(0), tools(0)
{
}


inline VDevice::operator HDC(void) const
{
    return handle;
}

inline VWindowPtr VDevice::GetParent(void) const
{
    return parent;
}

inline void VDevice::Save(void)
{
    SaveDC(handle);
}

inline void VDevice::Restore(void)
{
    RestoreDC(handle, -1);
}

class _CLASSTYPE VDisplayDevice : public VDevice
{
    public:
        VDisplayDevice(VWindowRef win);
        VDisplayDevice();

    protected:

    private:
};
inline VDisplayDevice::VDisplayDevice(VWindowRef win)
        : VDevice(&win)
{
    handle = GetDC(*parent);
}

inline VDisplayDevice::VDisplayDevice()
```

```cpp
{
    ReleaseDC(*parent, *this);
    handle = NULL;
}

class _CLASSTYPE VPaintDevice : public VDevice
{
    public:
        VPaintDevice(VWindowRef win);
        VPaintDevice();
        const RECT _FAR &GetExposeRect(void) const;

    protected:

    private:
        PAINTSTRUCT ps;
};

inline VPaintDevice::VPaintDevice(VWindowRef win)
        : VDevice(&win)
{
    handle = BeginPaint(*parent, &ps);
}

inline VPaintDevice::VPaintDevice()
{
    EndPaint(*parent, &ps);
}

inline const RECT _FAR &
VPaintDevice::GetExposeRect(void) const
{
    return ps.rcPaint;
}

class _CLASSTYPE VPrinterDevice : public VDevice
{
    public:
                VPrinterDevice(charPtr driverName=0,
                                        charPtr deviceName=0,
                                        charPtr portName=0);
        VPrinterDevice(HDC printDlgDc);
        VPrinterDevice();
                void PrintTo(charPtr doc, charPtr file=0);
                void NewPage(void);
        protected:
        Boolean SetDefaultDevice();

    private:
        Boolean started;
        Boolean page_printed;
        Boolean need_end;
```

Listing A-39
Continued.

```cpp
            VString driver_name;
            VString device_name;
            VString port_name;
};

inline VPrinterDevice::VPrinterDevice(HDC printDlgDC)
      : VDevice(NULL)
{
      need_end = False;
   started = False;
      handle = printDlgDC;
}


class _CLASSTYPE VFileDevice : public VDevice
{
      public:
            VFileDevice(charPtr fileName=0, charPtr mode="w");
            VFileDevice(void);
            void PlayOn(VDeviceRef dev);
            HMETAFILE Close(void);

      private:
            VString file_name;

};

inline VFileDevice::VFileDevice(charPtr fileName,
                                                  charPtr mode
{
      file_name = fileName;
      if (!mode ||  mode[0] == TEXT('w'))
            handle = (HDC)CreateMetaFile(file_name);
      else
            handle = (HDC)GetMetaFile(file_name);
}

inline VFileDevice::VFileDevice(void)
{
      if (handle != 0)
            DeleteMetaFile((HMETAFILE)handle);
}

// client is responsible for deleting the returned handle
inline HMETAFILE VFileDevice::Close(void)
{
      HMETAFILE hMeta = CloseMetaFile(handle);
      handle = 0;
      return hMeta;
}

inline void VFileDevice::PlayOn(VDeviceRef dev)
```

```cpp
{
    PlayMetaFile(dev, (HMETAFILE)handle);
}

class _CLASSTYPE VMemoryDevice : public VDevice
{
    public:
        VMemoryDevice(VDeviceRef dev);
        VMemoryDevice();

    protected:

    private:
        HDC target_dc;
};

inline VMemoryDevice::VMemoryDevice(VDeviceRef dev) :
    VDevice(NULL), target_dc(dev)
{
    handle = CreateCompatibleDC(target_dc);
}

inline VMemoryDevice::VMemoryDevice()
{
    DeleteDC(handle);
}

#endif
```

Listing A-40
VGRDEV.CPP

```cpp
/*----------------------------------------------------------
    vgrdev.cpp

    Implementation of the graphics device classes.

    Copyright (C) 1992, by Jeff Mackay

---------------------------------------------------------- */
#pragma hdrfile "vista.sym"
#include <vista.h>
#pragma hdrstop
#include <vgrdev.h>
#include <vgditool.h>


VDevice::VDevice()
{
    ToolIterator iter(tools);
    VGdiToolPtr _FAR *tool;
```

Listing A-40
Continued.

```cpp
                    while((tool = iter()) != 0)
        {
            Dissociate(*(*tool));
        }
}

void VDevice::Associate(VGdiToolRef tool)
{
        tools.Append(&tool);
}

void VDevice::Dissociate(VGdiToolRef tool)
{
        tool.Unrealize();
    tools.Remove();
}


VPrinterDevice::VPrinterDevice(charPtr driverName,
                                        charPtr deviceName, charPtr portName)
        : VDevice(NULL), driver_name(driverName),
        device_name(deviceName), port_name(portName)
{
    Boolean success;
        if (driverName == 0)
    {
        success = SetDefaultDevice();
        if (!success)
                        return;
        }
        handle = CreateDC(driver_name, device_name,
                                                port_name, NULL);
    need_end = False;
        started = False;
}

Boolean VPrinterDevice::SetDefaultDevice(void)
{
    char prof_line[128];
    int  length;

        length = GetProfileString("windows", "device",
                                                        "",prof_line, sizeof(prof_line));
    if (!length)
       return False;

        device_name = strtok(prof_line, ",");
    driver_name = strtok(prof_line, NULL);
    port_name   = strtok(prof_line, NULL);
```

```
        return True;
}

void VPrinterDevice::PrintTo(charPtr doc, charPtr file)
{
        DOCINFO info;

        info.cbSize = sizeof(info);
        info.lpszDocName = doc;
    info.lpszOutput  = file;
    StartDoc(*this, &info);
        started = True;
}

void VPrinterDevice::NewPage(void)
{
    VASSERT(started == True);
        if (need_end)
        EndPage(*this);
        StartPage(*this);
        need_end = True;
}

VPrinterDevice::VPrinterDevice(void)
{
        if (need_end)
                EndPage(*this);
        if (started)
        EndDoc(*this);
}
```

```
/*----------------------------------------------------------
   VGrObj.h

      Interface for the Vista graphical objects

   Copyright (C) 1992, by Jeff Mackay - TAB BOOKS

---------------------------------------------------------- */

#ifndef _VGROBJ_H
#define _VGROBJ_H
#ifndef _VISTA_H
#include <Vista.h>
#endif

#ifndef _VGRDEV_H
#include <VGrDev.h>
```

Listing A-41
VGROBJ.H

Listing A-41
Continued.

```cpp
#endif

STDCLASS(VGraphicsObject);
STDCLASS(VGraphicsText);
STDTYPE(RECT);

class VShape
{
    public:
        VShape();
        virtual VShape();
            friend VDeviceRef operator <<(VDeviceRef, VShape);

    protected:
        virtual void DrawOn(VDeviceRef dev) = 0;

    private:
};

VShape::VShape()
{
}

VShape::VShape()
{
}

VDeviceRef operator <<(VDeviceRef dev,
                                                   VShape obj)
{
    obj.DrawOn(dev);
    return dev;
}

class VGraphicsText : public VShape
{
    public:
                VGraphicsText(charPtr string, int flagVar,
                                        RECTPtr box=NULL);

    protected:
        virtual void DrawOn(VDeviceRef dev);

    private:
        VString string;
        UINT    flags;
        RECT    bounding_box;
};

void VGraphicsText::VGraphicsText(charPtr str,
                                                                    int flagVar, RECTPtr box)
```

```
        : VShape(), string(str), flags(flagVar)
{

    if (box)
    {
        bounding_box = *box;
    }
    else
    {
        bounding_box.left = bounding_box.right  =
        bounding_box.top  = bounding_box.bottom = 0;
    }
}

void VGraphicsText::DrawOn(VDeviceRef dev)
{
    DrawText(dev, string, -1, &bounding_box, flags);
}
#endif
```

```
/*----------------------------------------------------------
    vgrobj.cpp

        Implementation of the graphics objects

    Copyright (C) 1992, by Jeff Mackay

---------------------------------------------------------- */

#include <vgrobj.h>
#include <vgrdev.h>
#include <vgditool.h>
```

Listing A-42
VGROBJ.CPP

```
/* ---------------------------------------------------------
    vhandle.h

          Interface for the VHandle template classes.

    Copyright (C) 1992, by Jeff Mackay

--------------------------------------------------------- */
#ifndef _VHANDLE_H
#define _VHANDLE_H

#ifndef _VISTA_H
#include <vista.h>
```

Listing A-43
VHANDLE.H

Listing A-43
Continued.

```cpp
#endif

template <class T, class H> class _CLASSTYPE VHandle
{
    public:
        enum HandleState { Locked, Unlocked } state;
        VHandle(H hdl, T FAR *obj=0)
                : handle(hdl){ /* state = UnLocked; */}

        virtual VHandle(void)
        {
        // subclass *must* call Unlock from their destructors
        }

        T FAR *Lock(void)
        {
                if (state == Locked)
        return object;
                object = DoLock();
                state = Locked;
        return object;
        }

        virtual T FAR *DoLock(void) = 0;

        void   Unlock(void)
        {
                if (state == Unlocked)
        return;
                object = 0;
                DoUnlock();
        }

        virtual void DoUnlock(void) = 0;

        virtual T FAR *operator ->(void)
        {
                return Lock();
        }

    protected:
        H handle;
        T FAR *object;
};


template <class T> class _CLASSTYPE VGlobal : public VHandle<T,
HGLOBAL>
{
    public:
```

```cpp
                VGlobal(HGLOBAL hdl) :
                        VHandle<T, HGLOBAL>(hdl){}

                VGlobal(void)
                {
                        Unlock();
                }

                virtual T FAR *DoLock(void)
                {
                        return (T FAR *)GlobalLock(handle);
                }

                virtual void DoUnlock(void)
                {
                        GlobalUnlock(handle);
                }
}
template <class T> class _CLASSTYPE VLocal : public VHandle<T,
HLOCAL>
{
        public:

                VLocal(HLOCAL hdl)
                        : VHandle<T, HLOCAL>(hdl) {}

                VLocal(void)
                {
                        Unlock();
                }

                virtual T FAR *DoLock(void)
                {
                        return (T FAR *)LocalLock(handle);
                }

                virtual void DoUnlock(void)
                {
                        LocalUnlock(handle);
                }
}

#endif
```

/*--
   VIcon.h

Listing A-44
VICON.H

Listing A-44
Continued.

Interface for the VIcon class
Copyright (C) 1992, by Jeff Mackay - TAB BOOKS

```
--------------------------------------------------------- */
#ifndef _VICON_H
#define _VICON_H

#ifndef _VISTA_H
#include <vista.h>
#endif

class VIcon
{
    public:
    enum IconType
    {
        Application = IDI_APPLICATION,
        Asterisk = IDI_ASTERISK,
        Exclamation = IDI_EXCLAMATION,
        Hand = IDI_HAND,
        Question = IDI_QUESTION
    };
    VIcon(IconType type=Application);
        VIcon(charPtr name);
        VIcon(int id);
        VIcon();
        HICON Handle(void) const;

    private:
        HICON handle;
        Boolean do_destroy;
};

// load a predefined icon
inline VIcon::VIcon(IconType type)
{
    do_destroy = False;
        handle = LoadIcon(GetApplication(),
MAKEINTRESOURCE(type));
}

// load an icon from the resource file
inline VIcon::VIcon(charPtr name)
{
    do_destroy = True;
    handle = LoadIcon(GetApplication(), name);
}
// use an integer for the resource name
inline VIcon::VIcon(int id)
{
    do_destroy = True;
```

```
                handle = LoadIcon(GetApplication(),
                                            MAKEINTRESOURCE(id));
}

inline VIcon::VIcon()
{
    if (do_destroy)
        DestroyIcon(handle);
}


#endif




/* -----------------------------------------------------------
 Vista.h

            Common Vista definitions — for all classes

  Copyright (c) Jeff Mackay, 1992

------------------------------------------------------------*/

#ifndef _VISTA_H
#define _VISTA_H

#ifndef _WINDOWS_H
#define _WINDOWS_H
#define NOSOUND
#define NOCOMM
#define NOPROFILER
#define STRICT
#include <windows.h>
#endif

#ifndef __DLL__
#include <strstream.h>
#endif

#ifndef UNREFERENCED_PARAMETER
#define UNREFERENCED_PARAMETER(name) ((void) name)
#endif

#ifndef _VSTATUS_H
#include <vstatus.h>
#endif
#ifndef __ARRAYS_H
#include <arrays.h>
#endif
```

Listing A-45
VISTA.H

Listing A-45
Continued.

```c
#ifndef __LISTIMP_H
#include <listimp.h>
#endif

#ifndef __DEFS_H
#include <_defs.h>
#endif

#ifndef _VISTARC_H
#include <vistarc.h>
#endif


// macros to standardize type names
// (and hide the Windows details)
#define _PTRTYPE(name) typedef name _FAR *name##Ptr;
#define _CPTRTYPE(name) typedef const name _FAR *name##CPtr;
#define _REFTYPE(name) typedef name _FAR &name##Ref;
#define _CREFTYPE(name) typedef const name _FAR &name##CRef;

// STDCLASS is used for all classes
#define STDCLASS(name) class _CLASSTYPE name; \
        _PTRTYPE(name) \
    _CPTRTYPE(name) \
        _REFTYPE(name) \
    _CREFTYPE(name)


// STDTYPE is used for typedefs and built-in data types
#define STDTYPE(name) _PTRTYPE(name) \
                     _CPTRTYPE(name) \
                     _REFTYPE(name) \
                     _CREFTYPE(name)

#ifndef WIN32
typedef char TCHAR;
#define CHAR(x) 'x'
#define TEXT(n) n
#endif

typedef TCHAR FAR *charPtr;    // all strings treated as FAR
typedef const TCHAR FAR *charCPtr;
typedef void FAR *voidPtr;     // generic buffers too
typedef const void FAR *voidCPtr;
typedef int VCoord;
typedef int VDimension;
typedef enum { False, True } Boolean;
#define dim(arr) (sizeof(arr)/sizeof(arr[0]))
#ifndef __STDTEMPL_H
template <class T> inline T min(T t1, T t2)
{
        return t1<t2 ? t1 : t2;
```

```cpp
}

template <class T> inline T max(T t1, T t2)
{
        return t1<t2 ? t2 : t1;
}
#endif

// forward declarations
STDCLASS(VWindow);
STDCLASS(VAppl);

// include the most commonly used header files

#ifndef _VSTRING_H
#include <vstring.h>
#endif

#ifndef _VEVENT_H
#include <vevent.h>
#endif

#ifndef _VWINDOW_H
#include <vwindow.h>
#endif

#ifndef _VAPPL_H
#include <vappl.h>
#endif

#endif // _VISTA_H
```

Listing A-46
VISTARC.H

```c
/* -------------------------------------------------------
   vistarc.h

        Common definitions used by resource scripts

   Copyright (C) 1992, by Jeff Mackay
   ------------------------------------------------------- */

//
// Counter for MDI children
//
#define VID_MDICHILD 0x0601
//
// common id values for resources and child windows
//
#define VID_EXIT                        0x0701
```

Listing A-46
Continued.

```
#define VID_CUT                 0x0702
#define VID_COPY                0x0703
#define VID_PASTE               0x0704
#define VID_CLEAR               0x0705
#define VID_UNDO        0x0706
//
// MDI Command IDs
//
#define VID_MDIARRANGE   0x0710
#define VID_MDITILE             0x0711
#define VID_MDITILEHORIZ 0x0711
#define VID_MDITILEVERT  0x0712
#define VID_MDICASCADE   0x0713
#define VID_MDICLOSE     0x0714
#define VID_MDICLOSEALL  0x0715
#define VID_MDINEWWIN    0x0716
#define VID_LAST                0x0717
```

Listing A-47
VLABEL.H

```
/* -------------------------------------------------------
    vlabel.h

                VLabel control class interface.

    Copyright (c) 1992, by Jeff Mackay

   ------------------------------------------------------- */

#ifndef _VLABEL_H
#define _VLABEL_H

#ifndef _VCONTROL_H
#include "vcontrol.h"
#endif

STDCLASS(VLabel);

class _CLASSTYPE VLabel : public VControl
{
protected:
        enum LabelStyle
        {
                        LeftText   = SS_LEFT,
                        RightText  = SS_RIGHT,
                        CenterText = SS_CENTER
        } label_style;
public:

        VLabel(VCompositePtr parent, charPtr text,
```

```
                              int x, int y, int width, int height)
                    : VControl(parent, text, x,y,width,height)
{}
    VLabel(VCompositePtr parent, int resourceId)
        : VControl(parent, resourceId) {}
        void SetJustify(const LabelStyle just);
        LabelStyle GetJustify(void)  { return label_style; }
        virtual const charPtr ClassName(void) const;
        virtual const charPtr OldClassName(void) const;
        virtual void Cut(void) {}
        virtual void Copy(void) {}
        virtual void Paste(void) {}
        virtual void Clear(void) {}
        VLabel() {}
};

#endif
```

Listing A-48
VLABEL.CPP

```
/* --------------------------------------------------------
   VLabel.cpp

             VLabel class implementation.

   Copyright (c) 1992, by Jeff Mackay

   -------------------------------------------------------- */
#pragma hdrfile "vista.sym"
#include <vista.h>
#pragma hdrstop
#include <vlabel.h>

const charPtr VLabel::ClassName(void) const
{
        return "VLabel";
}

const charPtr VLabel::OldClassName(void) const
{
        return "static";
}

//
// Set the justification for a label.  If this is
// called after the window for the label has been
// created, it forces a PAINT event.
//
void VLabel::SetJustify(const LabelStyle just)
{
```

Listing A-48
Continued.

```
        label_style = just;
        style |= label_style;
        if (handle)
        {
                UpdateWindow(handle);
        }
}
```

Listing A-49
VLIST.H

```c
/* ------------------------------------------------------
    VList.h

        Interface for the VList (linked list) template class

   Copyright (C) 1992, by Jeff Mackay

   ------------------------------------------------------ */
#ifndef _VLIST_H
#define _VLIST_H

#ifndef _VISTA_H
#include <vista.h>
#endif

struct VNode
{
        VNode _FAR *next;
    VNode(VNode _FAR *ptr=0) {next = ptr;}
};

class VListBase
{
        public:
        VListBase(void) : last(0), list_size(0) {}
        VListBase(void) { delete last; }
                void Insert(VNode *arg);
                void Append(VNode *arg);
                VNode _FAR *Remove(void);
        size_t GetSize(void) const { return list_size; }
                friend class VListBaseIter;

        private:
        size_t list_size;
                VNode _FAR *last;
};
// Insert a node at the head of the list
void VListBase::Insert(VNode _FAR *arg)
{
```

```cpp
                if (last)
                        arg->next = last;
                else
                        last = arg;
                last->next = arg;              // head of the list
}

// add a node at the end of the list
void VListBase::Append(VNode _FAR *arg)
{
        if (last)
        {
                arg->next = last->next;
                last = last->next = arg;
        }
        else
                last = arg->next = arg;
}

// Remove (and return) the head of the list
VNode _FAR *VListBase::Remove(void)
{
        VASSERT(last != 0);
        VNode _FAR *theNode = last->next;
        if (theNode == last)
                last = 0;
        else
                last->next = theNode->next;
    return theNode;
}

class VListBaseIter
{
        public:
                VListBaseIter(VListBase _FAR &l);
                VNode _FAR *operator()();
                void Rewind(void);
        private:
                VListBase _FAR *list;
        VNode     _FAR *curr;
};

inline VListBaseIter::VListBaseIter(VListBase _FAR &l)
{
        list = &l;
        Rewind();
}

VNode _FAR *VListBaseIter::operator ()()
{
```

Listing A-49
Continued.

```cpp
            VNode _FAR *node = curr ? (curr=curr->next) : 0;
            if (node == list->last)
                    curr = 0;
     return node;
}

inline void VListBaseIter::Rewind(void)
{
     curr = list->last;
}


template <class T> struct VLink : public VNode
{
     T data;
     VLink(const T _FAR &arg) : data(arg) {}
};

template <class T> class VList : public VListBase
{
     public:
//       friendclass VListInter<T>;
            void Insert(const T _FAR &el)
                    { VListBase::Insert(new VLink<T>(el)); }
            void Append(const T _FAR &el)
                    { VListBase::Append(new VLink<T>(el)); }
     T Remove(void);
};

template <class T> T VList<T>::Remove(void)
{
     VLink<T> _FAR *lnk =
             (VLink<T> _FAR *) VListBase::Remove();
     T data = lnk->data;
     delete lnk;
     return data;
}


template <class T> class VListIter : public VListBaseIter
{
     public:
            VListIter(VList<T>& l) : VListBaseIter(l)
                     {}
            T _FAR *operator()();
};

template <class T> inline T _FAR VListIter<T>::operator()()
{
     VLink<T> _FAR *link;
     link = (VLink<T> _FAR *) VListBaseIter::operator()();
     return link ? link->data : 0;
```

```
}
#endif



/* -------------------------------------------------------          Listing A-50
        VLstBox.h                                                   VLSTBOX.H

                Implementation of the VListBox class.

        Copyright (C) 1992, by Jeff Mackay

----------------------------------------------------------- */
#ifndef _VLSTBOX_H
#define _VLSTBOX_H

#ifndef _VCONTROL_H
#include <vcontrol.h>
#endif

#ifndef _VDYNARR_H
#include <vdynarr.h>
#endif

STDCLASS(VListBox);

STDCLASS(VListEntry);
struct VListEntry
{
    charPtr string;
    voidPtr context;
    int     index;
};

class VListArray : public VDynArray<VListEntry>
{
    VListArray(int count=36)
        : VDynArray<VListEntry>(count) {}
};

STDCLASS(VListData);
struct VListData
{
    int                 sel_count;
    int                 *selection;
        int                 item_count;
    VListArray          items;
};
```

Listing A-50
Continued.

```cpp
class VListBox : public VControl
{
    public :

        VListBox(VCompositePtr parent, charPtr title,
                    int x, int y, int width, int height,
                    int ctlStyle)
            : VControl(parent, title, x, y,
                                width, height, ctlStyle)
        {
    style |= WS_BORDER | LBS_NOTIFY |
            LBS_WANTKEYBOARDINPUT;
        }

        VListBox(VCompositePtr parent, int resource_id) :
                VControl(parent, resource_id)
    {
    }
        virtual const charPtr ClassName(void) const;
        virtual const charPtr OldClassName(void) const;

        virtual void Add(charPtr string, voidPtr context=0);
    virtual void Add(VListEntryRef entry);
    virtual void Add(VListArray _FAR &array);

        virtual void Insert(charPtr string,
                voidPtr context=0, int index = -1);
    virtual void Insert(VListEntryRef entry);

        virtual void Delete(charPtr string, int index = -1);
    virtual void Delete(VListEntryRef entry);

        virtual int  Find(charPtr string,
                voidPtr _FAR *context=0, int index = -1);
    virtual int  Find(VListEntryRef entry);

        virtual void GetEntry(charPtr _FAR *string,
                voidPtr _FAR *context, int index);
    virtual void GetEntry(VListEntryRef entry);
    virtual int  GetContents(VListArray _FAR &array);

        virtual void GetContext(int index,
                voidPtr _FAR *context);
    virtual void GetContext(VListEntryRef entry);
    virtual void SetContext(int index, voidPtr context);

        virtual int  GetSelection(int _FAR * _FAR *selection);
    virtual int  Count(void);

    protected:
    virtual Boolean ClickedAction(VEventRef event);
```

```
        virtual Boolean DoubleClickedAction(VEventRef event);
        virtual void SetValue(voidPtr val);
        virtual void GetValue(voidPtr val);
        virtual int  GetValueLength(void);
};

inline int VListBox::GetValueLength(void)
{
    return sizeof(VListDataPtr);
}

#endif
```

Listing A-51
VLSTBOX.CPP

```
/* ---------------------------------------------------------------
        VLstBox.cpp

                Implementation of the VListBox class.

        Copyright (C) 1992, by Jeff Mackay

--------------------------------------------------------------- */
#pragma hdrfile "vista.sym"
#include <vista.h>
#pragma hdrstop
#include <VLstBox.h>
#include <VString.h>

const charPtr VListBox::ClassName(void) const
{
        return "VListBox";
}

const charPtr VListBox::OldClassName(void) const
{
        return "listbox";
}

void VListBox::Add(charPtr string, voidPtr context)
{
    int index = SendMessage(*this, LB_ADDSTRING, 0, (LPARAM)(LPSTR)string);
    SetContext(index, context);
}

void VListBox::Add(VListEntryRef item)
{
    Add(item.string, item.context);
}

void VListBox::Add(VListArray _FAR &array)
```

Listing A-51
Continued.

```cpp
{
    SetRedraw(False);
    for(int i=0; i<array.arraySize(); i++)
    {
        if(array[i].string)
            Add(array[i]);
    }
    SetRedraw(True);
}


void VListBox::Insert(charPtr string, voidPtr context, int index)
{
    SendMessage(*this, LB_INSERTSTRING, index,
                        (LPARAM)(LPSTR)string);
    SetContext(index, context);
}

void VListBox::Insert(VListEntryRef item)
{
    Insert(item.string, item.context, item.index);
}


void VListBox::Delete(charPtr string, int index)
{
    if (index == -1)
        index = Find(string);
    SendMessage(*this, LB_DELETESTRING, index, 0);
}

void VListBox::Delete(VListEntryRef item)
{
    Delete(item.string, item.index);
}

int VListBox::Find(charPtr string,
                        voidPtr _FAR *context, int index)
{
    int pos = (int)SendMessage(*this, LB_FINDSTRING, index,
                        (LPARAM)(LPSTR)string);
    GetContext(pos, context);
    return pos;
}

void VListBox::GetEntry(charPtr _FAR *string,
                                voidPtr _FAR *context, int index)
{
    if (string == 0)
        return;
```

```cpp
    int strLen = SendMessage(*this, LB_GETTEXTLEN, index, 0) + 1;
    *string = new char[strLen];
    SendMessage(*this, LB_GETTEXT, index,
                            (LPARAM)(char FAR *)string);
    GetContext(index,context);
}

void VListBox::GetEntry(VListEntryRef item)
{
    GetEntry(&item.string, &item.context, item.index);
}

int VListBox::GetContents(VListArray _FAR &array)
{
    int count = Count();
    for (int i=0; i<count; i++)
    {
        GetEntry(array[i]);
    }
    return count;
}

void VListBox::GetContext(int index, voidPtr _FAR *context)
{
    if (context != 0)
        SendMessage(*this, LB_GETITEMDATA, index,
                            (LPARAM)*context);
}

void VListBox::SetContext(int index, voidPtr context)
{
    SendMessage(*this, LB_SETITEMDATA, index, (LPARAM)context);
}

int VListBox::GetSelection(int _FAR * _FAR *selection)
{
    int selCount = SendMessage(*this, LB_GETSELCOUNT, 0, 0);
    if (selCount == LB_ERR)
        {
        *selection = new int[1];
            (*selection)[0] = SendMessage(*this, LB_GETCURSEL, 0, 0);
    }
    else
    {
        *selection = new int[selCount];
        SendMessage(*this, LB_GETSELITEMS, selCount,
                    (LPARAM)(int FAR *)*selection);
    }
    return selCount;
}

int VListBox::Count(void)
```

Listing A-51
Continued.
```
    {
        return SendMessage(*this, LB_GETCOUNT, 0, 0);
    }

    void VListBox::SetValue(voidPtr newVal)
    {
        VListData _FAR *data =
                    (VListData _FAR *) *((VListData _FAR * _FAR *)newVal);
        if (data)
            Add(data->items);
    }

    void VListBox::GetValue(voidPtr value)
    {
        VListData _FAR *data =
                    (VListData FAR *)*((VListData _FAR * _FAR *)value);
        if (data)
        {
            data->item_count = GetContents(data->items);
            data->sel_count  = GetSelection(&data->selection);
        }
    }
```

Listing A-52
VMAIN.CPP
```
/*-----------------------------------------------------------
    vmain.c

        Contains LibMain for the Vista dll.

    Copyright (C) 1992, by Jeff Mackay

------------------------------------------------------------ */
#include <windows.h>

HINSTANCE _VistaDll;

int FAR PASCAL LibMain(HINSTANCE hInstance, WORD wDataSeg,
                                WORD cbHeapSize, LPSTR lpCmdLine)
{
    _VistaDll = hInstance;
    return 1;
}
```

Listing A-53
VMDICHLD.H
```
/* ---------------------------------------------------------
    VMdiChld.h

        Interface for the VMdiChld class.
```

```cpp
        Copyright (C) 1992, by Jeff Mackay

---------------------------------------------------------- */

#ifndef _VMDICHLD_H
#define _VMDICHLD_H

#ifndef _VWINDOW_H
#include <vwindow.h>
#endif

STDCLASS(VMdiFrame);
STDCLASS(VMdiChild);

class _CLASSTYPE VMdiChild : public VFrame
{
        public:
                VMdiChild(VMdiFramePtr parent, charPtr caption);
                VMdiChild(void);
                virtual const charPtr ClassName(void) const;
                virtual void Create(void);
        virtual VMenuPtr SetMenu(VMenuPtr menu, int winPos=0);
                virtual void SetWindowMenuPos(int pos);
                virtual int GetWindowMenuPos();
                friend class VMdiClient;
                friend class VMdiFrame;

        protected:
                virtual void InitWinClass(WNDCLASSRef wndClass);
                virtual void InitActions(void);
                virtual Boolean Destroy(Boolean query);
                virtual Boolean MdiActivateAction(VEventRef event);
                virtual Boolean CommandAction(VEventRef event);
                virtual LRESULT DefaultProc(VEventRef event);
                int win_menu_pos;
};

inline LRESULT VMdiChild::DefaultProc(VEventRef event)
{
        return DefMDIChildProc(*this, event.GetId(),
                                                event.GetWParam(),
                                                event.GetLParam());
}

inline void VMdiChild::SetWindowMenuPos(int pos)
{
        win_menu_pos = pos;
}
```

Listing A-53
Continued.

```cpp
inline int VMdiChild::GetWindowMenuPos(void)
{
        return win_menu_pos;
}

#endif
```

Listing A-54
VMDICHILD.CPP

```cpp
/* -----------------------------------------------------
    vmdichld.cpp

        Implementation of the VMdiChild class.

    Copyright (C) 1992, by Jeff Mackay

   ----------------------------------------------------- */
#pragma hdrfile "vista.sym"
#include <vista.h>
#pragma hdrstop
#include <vmdichld.h>
#include <vmdiFrm.h>
#include <vappl.h>

VMdiChild::VMdiChild(VMdiFramePtr parent, charPtr caption)
        : VFrame((VFramePtr)parent, caption)
{
        win_menu_pos = 0;
        width = CW_USEDEFAULT;
        height = CW_USEDEFAULT;
}

VMdiChild::VMdiChild(void)
{
}

const charPtr VMdiChild::ClassName(void) const
{
        return "VMdiChild";
}

void VMdiChild::Create(void)
{
    if (!registered)
    {
            Register();
            if (appl.GetStatus() != V_SUCCESS)
                return;
    }
        ((VMdiFramePtr) parent)->CreateMdiChild(this);
```

```cpp
}

void VMdiChild::InitWinClass(WNDCLASSRef wndclass)
{
        VFrame::InitWinClass(wndclass);
}

void VMdiChild::InitActions(void)
{
        VFrame::InitActions();
        AddAction((VAction) &VMdiChild::MdiActivateAction,
                        WM_MDIACTIVATE);
}

VMenuPtr VMdiChild::SetMenu(VMenuPtr newMenu, int winPos)
{
        VMenuPtr oldMenu = menu;
        win_menu_pos = winPos;
    menu = newMenu;
        VMdiFramePtr(parent)->SetMenu(menu, win_menu_pos);
        return oldMenu;
}

Boolean VMdiChild::MdiActivateAction(VEventRef event)
{
        if (menu == 0)
                return False;

        if (event.GetWParam() == True)
                SetMenu(menu, win_menu_pos);
        else
                // if no other child is being activated, reset
        // the menu.
                if ((HWND)LOWORD(event.GetLParam())==0)
                        SetMenu(0, 0);
        return False;
}

Boolean VMdiChild::Destroy(Boolean query)
{
        if (query == True && QueryClose() == False)
                return False;
        else
    {
                (VMdiFramePtr(parent))->DestroyMdiChild(this);
                return True;
        }
}

Boolean VMdiChild::CommandAction(VEventRef event)
{
```

Listing A-54
Continued

```
        Boolean filtered = VFrame::CommandAction(event);
        if (!filtered)
        {
                filtered = (*parent)(event);
        }
        return filtered;
}
```

Listing A-55
VMDICLI.H

```
/* ----------------------------------------------------------------
    VMdiCli.h

        Interface for the VMdiClient class.

    Copyright (C) 1992, by Jeff Mackay

   ---------------------------------------------------------------- */

#ifndef _VMDICLI_H
#define _VMDICLI_H

#ifndef _VWINDOW_H
#include <vwindow.h>
#endif

#ifndef _VMDIFRM_H
#include <VMdiFrm.h>
#endif

#ifndef _VMDICHLD_H
#include <VMdiChld.h>
#endif

STDCLASS(VMdiClient);

class _CLASSTYPE VMdiClient : public VComposite
{
        public:

                VMdiClient(VMdiFramePtr par);
                VMdiClient()
                {
                }
                const charPtr ClassName(void) const;
                const charPtr OldClassName(void) const;
                virtual void InitWinClass(WNDCLASSRef wndClass);
                virtual VMdiChildPtr GetActive(void);
                virtual void CreateChild(VMdiChildPtr child);
        virtual void ActivateChild(VMdiChildPtr child);
                virtual void DestroyChild(VMdiChildPtr child);
```

```
            virtual void TileChildren(UINT flag);
            virtual void CascadeChildren(void);
            virtual void ArrangeIcons(void);

        protected:

        virtual LRESULT DefaultProc(VEventRef event);

        private:

            CLIENTCREATESTRUCT createStruct;

};

inline LRESULT VMdiClient::DefaultProc(VEventRef event)
{
   return CallWindowProc(old_proc, *this, event.GetId(),
                                          event.GetWParam(),
                                          event.GetLParam());

}
#endif
```

```
/* -----------------------------------------------------------
   VMdiFrm.h

        Interface for the VMdiFrame class.

   Copyright (C) 1992, by Jeff Mackay

   ---------------------------------------------------------- */

#ifndef _VMDIFRM_H
#define _VMDIFRM_H

#ifndef _VWINDOW_H
#include <vwindow.h>
#endif

#ifndef _VMDICLI_H
#include <vmdicli.h>
#endif

STDCLASS(VMdiClient);
STDCLASS(VMdiFrame);
STDCLASS(VMdiChild);

class _CLASSTYPE VMdiFrame : public VFrame
```

Listing A-56
VMDIFRM.H

Listing A-56
Continued.

```cpp
        {
        public:
                VMdiFrame(VCompositePtr par, charPtr caption);
                VMdiFrame();
                virtual VMdiChildPtr GetActiveChild(void);
                const charPtr ClassName(void) const;
                virtual void InitWinClass(WNDCLASSRef wndClass);
                virtual void InitActions(void);
                virtual void CreateMdiChild(VMdiChildPtr child);
                virtual void DestroyMdiChild(VMdiChildPtr child);
                virtual VMenuPtr SetMenu(VMenuPtr newMenu,
                                                            int winPos);
                void SetWindowMenuPos(int pos);
                int GetWindowMenuPos(void);
                virtual Boolean CreateAction(VEventRef event);
                virtual Boolean CascadeCommand(VEventRef event);
                virtual Boolean TileCommand(VEventRef event);
                virtual Boolean ArrangeCommand(VEventRef event);
                virtual Boolean CloseAllCommand(VEventRef event);
                virtual Boolean CloseCommand(VEventRef event);

        protected:
                VMdiClientPtr client;
                virtual void InitCommandActions(void);
                virtual LRESULT DefaultProc(VEventRef event);
                virtual void AddChild(VWindowPtr child);

        private:
                int win_menu_pos;

        };

        inline void VMdiFrame::SetWindowMenuPos(int pos)
        {
                    win_menu_pos = pos;
        }

        inline int VMdiFrame::GetWindowMenuPos(void)
        {
                    return win_menu_pos;
        }
        #endif
```

Listing A-57
VMDIFRM.CPP

```cpp
/* --------------------------------------------------------
   vmdifrm.cpp

   Implementation of the VMdiFrame class.
```

```c
   Copyright (C) 1992, by Jeff Mackay

----------------------------------------------------------- */
#pragma hdrfile "vista.sym"
#include <vista.h>
#pragma hdrstop

#include <vmdifrm.h>
#include <vmdicli.h>
#include <vmdichld.h>
#include <vappl.h>

VMdiFrame::VMdiFrame(VCompositePtr par, charPtr caption)
        : VFrame(par, caption)
{
    client = 0;
        win_menu_pos = 0;
        width = height = CW_USEDEFAULT;
        style = WS_OVERLAPPEDWINDOW | WS_CLIPCHILDREN;
}

VMdiFrame::VMdiFrame(void)
{
        delete client;
}

LRESULT VMdiFrame::DefaultProc(VEventRef event)
{
    HWND clientWnd;
    if (client)
            clientWnd = *client;
    else
            clientWnd = 0;
        return DefFrameProc(*this, clientWnd, event.GetId(),
                            event.GetWParam(), event.GetLParam());
}

//
// CreateMdiChild fills an MDICREATESTRUCT with parameters from
// a child window's attr structure, and sends a WM_MDICREATE
// event to the client window.  The client will create the
// window.
//
void VMdiFrame::CreateMdiChild(VMdiChildPtr child)
{
        VASSERT(child != 0);
        client->CreateChild(child);
}

void VMdiFrame::DestroyMdiChild(VMdiChildPtr child)
```

Listing A-57
Continued.

```cpp
{
        VASSERT(child != 0);
        client->DestroyChild(child);
}

void VMdiFrame::AddChild(VWindowPtr child)
{
        // the client window is not a true child
        if (strcmp(child->ClassName(), "VMdiClient")==0)
                return;
    VFrame::AddChild(child);
}

//
// standard ClassName method
//
const charPtr VMdiFrame::ClassName(void) const
{
        return "VMdiFrame";
}

//
// The frame's InitWinClass method overrides the background
// color.  This isn't absolutely necessary, but it makes the
// window look better at startup
//
void VMdiFrame::InitWinClass(WNDCLASSRef wndClass)
{
        VWindow::InitWinClass(wndClass);
        wndClass.hbrBackground = (HBRUSH) COLOR_APPWORKSPACE + 1;
        wndClass.style = 0;
}

void VMdiFrame::InitActions(void)
{
        VFrame::InitActions();
        AddCommand((VAction)&VMdiFrame::CloseCommand,    VID_MDICLOSE);
    AddCommand((VAction)&VMdiFrame::CloseAllCommand, VID_MDICLOSEALL);
        AddCommand((VAction)&VMdiFrame::TileCommand,     VID_MDITILE);
    AddCommand((VAction)&VMdiFrame::TileCommand,     VID_MDITILEVERT);
        AddCommand((VAction)&VMdiFrame::CascadeCommand,  VID_MDICASCADE);
        AddCommand((VAction)&VMdiFrame::ArrangeCommand,  VID_MDIARRANGE);
}

void VMdiFrame::InitCommandActions(void)
{
}
Boolean VMdiFrame::CreateAction(VEventRef event)
{
    VFrame::CreateAction(event);
```

```cpp
        client = new VMdiClient(this);
    VASSERT(client != 0);
        client->Create();
        return True;
}

VMenuPtr VMdiFrame::SetMenu(VMenuPtr newMenu, int winPos)
{
        if (newMenu == 0)
    {
                newMenu = menu;
                winPos = win_menu_pos;
        }
        VPopupMenu windowMenu(*newMenu, winPos);
        SendMessage(*client, WM_MDISETMENU, 0,
                                MAKELONG((HMENU)*newMenu,
(HMENU)windowMenu));
    DrawMenuBar(*this);
        return newMenu;
}

Boolean VMdiFrame::CloseCommand(VEventRef event)
{
        VMdiChildPtr child = GetActiveChild();
        if (child)
        {
        child->Destroy(True);
    }
    UNREFERENCED_PARAMETER(event);
        return True;
}

Boolean VMdiFrame::CloseAllCommand(VEventRef event)
{
        VMdiChildPtr child = GetActiveChild();
        while (child)
        {
                child->Destroy(True);
        child = client->GetActive();
    }
        UNREFERENCED_PARAMETER(event);
        return False;
}


Boolean VMdiFrame::TileCommand(VEventRef event)
{
        client->TileChildren(event.GetId());
        return True;
}
```

Listing A-57
Continued.

```
Boolean VMdiFrame::CascadeCommand(VEventRef event)
{
    client->CascadeChildren();
    UNREFERENCED_PARAMETER(event);
        return True;
}

Boolean VMdiFrame::ArrangeCommand(VEventRef event)
{
    client->ArrangeIcons();
        UNREFERENCED_PARAMETER(event);
        return True;
}

VMdiChildPtr VMdiFrame::GetActiveChild(void)
{
        return client->GetActive();
}
```

Listing A-58
VMENU.H

```
/* ------------------------------------------------------------
    VMenu.h

        VMenu class interface

    Copyright (C) 1992, by Jeff Mackay

------------------------------------------------------------ */

#ifndef _VMENU_H
#define _VMENU_H

#ifndef _VISTA_H
#include <vista.h>
#endif

STDCLASS(VEvent);
STDCLASS(VFrame);
STDCLASS(VMenu);
STDCLASS(VPopupMenu);
STDCLASS(VSystemMenu);
STDCLASS(VAccelerator);

#define VMENU_SEPARATOR   MF_SEPARATOR
#define VMENU_BREAK       MF_MENUBREAK
#define VMENU_BYPOSITION  MF_BYPOSITION
#define VMENU_BYCOMMAND   MF_BYCOMMAND
#define VMENU_OWNERDRAW   MF_OWNERDRAW
```

```cpp
class _CLASSTYPE VMenu
{
    public:

    // constructors
        VMenu(VFramePtr window, const charPtr menuName);
        VMenu(VFramePtr window=0, int id=0);
    VMenu(void);

        // destructor
        VMenu(void);

    // operators
        operator HMENU(void) const;

        // modifiers
    void Create(const charPtr string);
    void Create(int id);

        void Add(const charPtr item, UINT id, UINT flags=0);
        void Add(const charPtr string, VMenuRef   item,
                                    UINT flags=0);
        void Insert(UINT pos, const charPtr item, UINT id,
                                    UINT flags=0);
        void Insert(UINT pos, const charPtr string,
                                VPopupMenuRef menu,
            UINT flags=0);
    void Remove(UINT id);
    void Remove(VPopupMenuRef menu);

        void Check(UINT id, Boolean state=True,
                            UINT flags=VMENU_BYCOMMAND);
        Boolean IsChecked(UINT id,
                                UINT flags=VMENU_BYCOMMAND);
        void ToggleCheck(UINT id,
                                UINT flags=VMENU_BYCOMMAND);

        void Enable(UINT id,
                                    Boolean state=True,
                            UINT flags=VMENU_BYCOMMAND);
        Boolean IsEnabled(UINT id,
                                UINT flags=VMENU_BYCOMMAND);
        void ToggleEnable(UINT id,
                                UINT flags=VMENU_BYCOMMAND);

        void Draw();
        void DeferDrawing(void);
        void EnableDrawing(void);
    void SetParent(VFramePtr win);
```

Listing A-58
Continued.

```cpp
    protected:
        VMenu(Boolean isPopup);
            VString     menu_name;
            VFramePtr   parent;
            HMENU       handle;
            UINT                        position_state;
            Boolean     do_draw;
        Boolean    is_popup;
};

class _CLASSTYPE VPopupMenu : public VMenu
{
    public:
        VPopupMenu(VMenuRef menuBar, UINT id);
        VPopupMenu(void);
        VPopupMenu(void);
        void Track(VFramePtr win, int x, int y,
                UINT flags=TPM_LEFTALIGN | TPM_RIGHTBUTTON);
        void SetDelete(Boolean state) { do_destroy = state; }
        void SetPosition(UINT pos) { position = pos; }
        UINT  GetPosition(void) const { return position; }
    protected:
        Boolean do_destroy;
        UINT    position;
};

class VSystemMenu : public VMenu
{
    public:
        VSystemMenu(VFramePtr win);
        VSystemMenu(void);
};

class _CLASSTYPE VAccelerator
{
        private:

                HACCEL handle;
                VString name;
                VFramePtr parent;

        public:
                VAccelerator(VFramePtr window, charPtr string=0);
                VAccelerator(VFramePtr window, UINT id);
        operator HACCEL(void) const;
};

inline VAccelerator::operator HACCEL(void) const
{
    return handle;
```

```
}

#endif    // _VMENU_H


/* ----------------------------------------------------------
   VMenu.cpp

                 Implementation of the VMenu class

   Copyright (C) 1992, Jeff Mackay

   ---------------------------------------------------------- */
#pragma hdrfile "vista.sym"
#include <vista.h>
#pragma hdrstop

#include <vappl.h>
#include <vwindow.h>
#include <vstring.h>

VMenu::VMenu(VFramePtr window, const charPtr string) :
        parent(window)
{
        do_draw         = True;
    handle          = 0;
    is_popup        = False;
    Create(string);
}

VMenu::VMenu(VFramePtr window, int id) :
        parent(window)
{
        do_draw         = True;
    handle          = 0;
    is_popup        = False;
    Create(id);
}

VMenu::VMenu(Boolean isPopup)
{
    is_popup = isPopup;
    do_draw  = True;
    handle   = 0;
    parent   = 0;
}
// menus are always destroyed.  The destructor sets the parent's // menu to NULL
to prevent Windows from destroying the menu when
// the window is destroyed.  A parent's menu object *MUST* be
// destroyed before the WM_NCDESTROY completes.
```

Listing A-59
VMENU.CPP

Listing A-59
Continued.

```cpp
VMenu::VMenu(void)
{
    if (parent)
        parent->SetMenu(0);
    DestroyMenu(handle);
    handle = 0;
}

void VMenu::Create(int id)
{
        Create((charPtr)MAKEINTRESOURCE(id));
}

void VMenu::Create(const charPtr name)
{
    VASSERT(handle == 0);
    handle = LoadMenu(GetApplication(), name);
    if (handle == 0)
            handle = ::CreateMenu();
}

VMenu::operator HMENU(void) const
{
        return handle;
}

void VMenu::Add(const charPtr item, UINT id, UINT flags)
{
        AppendMenu(handle, MF_ENABLED | MF_STRING | flags, id, item);
        Draw();
}

void VMenu::Add(const charPtr string, VMenuRef item, UINT flags)
{
    AppendMenu(handle, MF_POPUP | flags, (UINT) item.handle,
                            string);
    item.SetParent(parent);
    Draw();
}

void VMenu::Remove(UINT id)
{
    RemoveMenu(handle, id, MF_BYPOSITION);
        Draw();
}

void VMenu::Remove(VPopupMenuRef menu)
{
    RemoveMenu(handle, menu.GetPosition(), MF_BYPOSITION);
    menu.SetParent(0);
    menu.SetDelete(True);
}
```

```cpp
void VMenu::Insert(UINT pos, const charPtr item, UINT id,
                                    UINT flags)
{
        InsertMenu(handle, pos+1, flags, id, item);
        Draw();
}

void VMenu::Insert(UINT pos, const charPtr string,
                                    VPopupMenuRef item, UINT flags)
{
    InsertMenu(handle, pos+1, flags, (UINT) item.handle, string);
    item.SetPosition(pos);
    item.SetParent(parent);
    Draw();
}


void VMenu::Check(UINT id, Boolean state, UINT flags)
{
        flags |= (state==True) ? MF_CHECKED : MF_UNCHECKED;
        CheckMenuItem(handle, id, flags);
        Draw();
}

Boolean VMenu::IsChecked(UINT id, UINT flags)
{
    UINT state = GetMenuState(handle, id, flags);
    return ((state & MF_CHECKED) == 1 ? True : False);
}

void VMenu::ToggleCheck(UINT id, UINT flags)
{
    Check(id, IsChecked(id, flags) ? False : True, flags);
}

void VMenu::Enable(UINT id, Boolean state, UINT flags)
{
    flags |= (state==True) ? MF_ENABLED : MF_GRAYED;
    EnableMenuItem(handle, id, flags);
    Draw();
}


Boolean VMenu::IsEnabled(UINT id, UINT flags)
{
    UINT state = GetMenuState(handle, id, flags);
    return ((state & MF_ENABLED) == 1 ? True : False);
}
```

Listing A-59
Continued.

```cpp
void VMenu::ToggleEnable(UINT id, UINT flags)
{
    Enable(id, IsEnabled(id, flags) ? False : True, flags);
}

void VMenu::Draw()
{
    if (parent && do_draw)
        DrawMenuBar(*parent);
}

void VMenu::DeferDrawing(void)
{
    do_draw = False;
}

void VMenu::EnableDrawing(void)
{
    do_draw = True;
    Draw();
}

void VMenu::SetParent(VFramePtr frame)
{
    parent = frame;
}

VPopupMenu::VPopupMenu(VMenuRef menuBar, UINT pos) : VMenu(True)
{
    handle = GetSubMenu(menuBar, pos);
    do_destroy = False;
    position = pos;
}

VPopupMenu::VPopupMenu(void) : VMenu(True)
{
    do_destroy = True;
    position = -1;
    handle = CreatePopupMenu();
}

VPopupMenu::VPopupMenu(void)
{
    if (do_destroy == False)
        handle = 0;
}

void VPopupMenu::Track(VFramePtr win, int x, int y, UINT flags)
{
    if (win == 0)
        return;
```

```
        POINT pt;
        pt.x = x;
        pt.y = y;
        ClientToScreen(*win, &pt);
        TrackPopupMenu(handle, flags, pt.x, pt.y, 0, *win, 0);
}


void VSystemMenu::VSystemMenu(VFramePtr window) : VMenu(True)
{
    parent = window;
    handle = GetSystemMenu(*parent, True);
}

void VSystemMenu::VSystemMenu(void)
{
    GetSystemMenu(*parent, False);
    parent = 0;
    handle = 0;
}

VAccelerator::VAccelerator(VFramePtr window, charPtr string) :
        parent(window), name(string)
{
        if (!name)
                name = parent->GetCaption();
        handle = LoadAccelerators(GetApplication(), name);
}

VAccelerator::VAccelerator(VFramePtr window, UINT id) :
        parent(window)
{
        handle = LoadAccelerators(GetApplication(),
MAKEINTRESOURCE(id));
}




/* ----------------------------------------------------------
   VMsgBox.h

   Interface for several message box classes.

   Copyright (C) 1992, by Jeff Mackay

---------------------------------------------------------- */
#ifndef _VMSGBOX_H
#define _VMSGBOX_H

#ifndef _VISTA_H
```

Listing A-60
VMSGBOX.H

Listing A-60
Continued.

```cpp
#include <Vista.h>
#endif

#define VMSG_STRING_MAX 256

class _CLASSTYPE VMessageBox
{
    public:
                VMessageBox(const VWindowPtr parentWin=0,
                                const charPtr msgStr=0,
                      int msgStyle=0, const charPtr titleStr=0);
        void SetMessage(const charPtr msg, ...);
        Execute();

    private:
        const VWindowPtr parent;
        VString title;
        VString message;
        int     style;
};

class _CLASSTYPE VInfoBox : public VMessageBox
{
    public:
                VInfoBox(const VWindowPtr parent=0,
                                const charPtr message=0,
                    const charPtr title=0);
};

inline VInfoBox::VInfoBox(const VWindowPtr parent,
                                        const charPtr message,
                    const charPtr title)
    : VMessageBox(parent, message,
                    MB_ICONINFORMATION | MB_OK, title)
{
}

class _CLASSTYPE VErrorBox : public VMessageBox
{
    public:
                VErrorBox(const VWindowPtr parent=0,
                                const charPtr msgStr=0,
                    const charPtr titleStr=0);
};

inline VErrorBox::VErrorBox(const VWindowPtr parent,
                                        const charPtr msgStr,
                        const charPtr titleStr)
        : VMessageBox(parent, msgStr,
                        MB_ICONSTOP | MB_ABORTRETRYIGNORE,
                titleStr)
```

```
{
}

class _CLASSTYPE VWarningBox : public VMessageBox
{
    public:
                VWarningBox(const VWindowPtr parent=0,
                                    const charPtr msgStr=0,
                    const charPtr titleStr=0);
};

inline VWarningBox::VWarningBox(const VWindowPtr parent,
                                            const charPtr msgStr,
                                const charPtr titleStr)
        : VMessageBox(parent, msgStr,
                        MB_ICONEXCLAMATION | MB_OKCANCEL, titleStr)
{
}

#endif
```

```
/*-----------------------------------------------------------------
    VMsgBox.cpp

    Implementation of the  message box classes.

    Copyright (C) 1992, by Jeff Mackay

-------------------------------------------------------------- */

#pragma hdrfile "vista.sym"
#include <vista.h>
#pragma hdrstop

#include <stdarg.h>
#include <vmsgbox.h>
#include <vappl.h>
#include <vwindow.h>

VMessageBox::VMessageBox(const VWindowPtr parentWin, const
                                            charPtr msgStr,
                        int msgStyle, const charPtr titleStr)
        : parent(parentWin), title(titleStr),
            message(msgStr), style(msgStyle)
{
    if (style == 0)
        style = MB_ICONINFORMATION | MB_OK;
```

Listing A-61
VMSGBOX.cpp

Listing A-61
Continued.

```
        if (parent == 0)
            style |= MB_TASKMODAL;

        if (titleStr == 0)
            title = GetApplication().GetAppName();
    }

    int VMessageBox::Execute(void)
    {
        HWND parentWin;

        if (parent != 0)
            parentWin = *parent;
        else
            parentWin = NULL;

        return MessageBox(parentWin, message, title, style);
    }

    void VMessageBox::SetMessage(const charPtr format, ...)
    {
        TCHAR buffer[VMSG_STRING_MAX];
        va_list argPtr;

        va_start(argPtr, format);
        wvsprintf(buffer, format, argPtr);
        va_end(argPtr);
        message = buffer;
    }
```

Listing A-62
VRADBTN.H

```
/* -------------------------------------------------------
            VRadBtn.h

                    Implementation of the VRadioButton class

            Copyright (C) 1992, by Jeff Mackay

   ------------------------------------------------------- */

#ifndef _VRADBTN_H
#define _VRADBTN_H

#ifndef _VCHECK_H
#include <vcheck.h>
#endif
#define VC_RADIOBUTTON          BS_RADIOBUTTON
#define VC_AUTORADIOBUTTON      BS_AUTORADIOBUTTON
```

```
STDCLASS(VRadioButton);

class _CLASSTYPE VRadioButton : public VCheckBox
{
    public:
        VRadioButton(VCompositePtr parent, VStringRef title,
                     int x, int y, int width, int height,
                     int radStyle=VC_AUTORADIOBUTTON,
                     int checked=VC_UNCHECKED)
        : VCheckBox(parent, title, x, y, width, height)
        {
            button_style = radStyle;
            style = radStyle;
        }

        VRadioButton(VCompositePtr parent, int resourceId,
                     int checked) :
                VCheckBox(parent, resourceId, checked)
        {
        }
};

#endif
```

Listing A-63
VSCROLL.H

```
/* ---------------------------------------------------------------
   VScroll.h

     Interface for the VScroll class.  The VScroll implements
     an automatic scrollbar (not a scrollbar control).

     Copyright (C) 1992, by Jeff Mackay

   --------------------------------------------------------- */

#ifndef _VSCROLL_H
#define _VSCROLL_H

#ifndef _VISTA_H
#include <Vista.h>
#endif

STDCLASS (VFrame)
STDCLASS (VScroll)
typedef enum
{
    Horizontal = SB_HORZ,
    Vertical = SB_VERT
} VScrollType;
```

Listing A-63
Continued.

```cpp
class _CLASSTYPE VScroll
{

public:

    VScroll(VFrameRef parent, VScrollType scrollType=Vertical,
            int high=0, int low=0, int page=0, int units=0);
    ~VScroll();
    virtual void Create();
    virtual void Hide();
    void SetRange(int newHigh, int newLow, int newPage,
                  int units=1);
    void ScrollTo(int newPos);
    int  GetUnitSize(void) const { return unit_size; }
    int  GetPos(void) const { return current_pos; }
    int  GetHighRange(void) const { return high_range; }
    int  GetLowRange(void)  const { return low_range; }
    int  GetPageSize(void)  const { return page_size; }
    Boolean operator () (VEventRef);

protected:

    virtual Boolean ScrollAction(VEventRef event);

private:

    VFrameRef parent;
    Boolean   created;
    int low_range;
    int high_range;
    int current_pos;
    int page_size;
    int unit_size;
    VScrollType scroll_type;


};

#endif;
```

Listing A-64
VSCROLL.CPP

```cpp
/* ----------------------------------------------------------------
    vscroll.cpp

         Implementation of the VScroll class.
    Copyright (C) 1992, by Jeff Mackay

------------------------------------------------------------- */
```

```c
#pragma hdrfile "vista.sym"
#include <vista.h>
#pragma hdrstop
#include <vscroll.h>
#include <vwindow.h>

VScroll::VScroll(VFrameRef window, VScrollType type, int high,
                 int low, int page, int units)
        : parent(window)
{
    scroll_type = type;
    low_range   = low;
    high_range  = high;
    current_pos = 0;
    unit_size   = units;
    page_size   = page;
}

VScroll::VScroll(void)
{
    if (IsWindow(parent))
        Hide();
}

void VScroll::Create(void)
{
    SetScrollRange(parent, scroll_type, low_range,
                   high_range, FALSE);
}

void VScroll::Hide(void)
{
    SetScrollRange(parent, scroll_type, 0, 0, TRUE);
}


Boolean VScroll::operator()(VEventRef event)
{
    return ScrollAction(event);
}

void VScroll::SetRange(int newLow, int newHigh, int newPage, int
newUnits)
{
    Boolean redraw;

    if (newLow != low_range)
    {
        low_range = newLow;
        redraw = True;
    }
```

Listing A-64
Continued.

```
        if (newHigh != high_range)
        {
                high_range = newHigh;
                redraw = True;
        }

    if (newUnits != unit_size)
    {
        unit_size = newUnits;
        redraw = True;
    }

    page_size = newPage;

    if (redraw)
            SetScrollRange(parent, scroll_type, low_range, high_range,
TRUE);
}

Boolean VScroll::ScrollAction(VEventRef event)
{
        int newPos = current_pos;

        switch(event.GetWParam())
        {
                case SB_LINEUP:
                        newPos—;
                        break;

                case SB_LINEDOWN:
                        newPo++;
                        break;

                case SB_PAGEUP:
                        newPos -= page_size;
                        break;

                case SB_PAGEDOWN:
                        newPos += page_size;
                        break;

                case SB_BOTTOM:
                        newPos = low_range;
                        break;

                case SB_TOP:
                        newPos = high_range;
                        break;
                case SB_THUMBPOSITION:
                case SB_THUMBTRACK:
                        newPos = LOWORD(event.GetLParam());
                        break;
```

```
            }
            if (newPos != current_pos)
            {
                    ScrollTo(newPos);
            }
            return True;

}

void VScroll::ScrollTo(int newPos)
{
    // make sure pos is within range
        newPos = min(high_range, newPos);
        newPos = max(low_range, newPos);
        if (newPos == current_pos)
                return;

        current_pos = newPos;
        SetScrollPos(parent, scroll_type, current_pos, TRUE);
}
```

```
/*-------------------------------------------------------------
  vstatus.h

                Error status values for the Vista library
                Also includes the VASSERT macro and supporting
            function

  Copyright (c) 1992, by Jeff Mackay

------------------------------------------------------------ */

#ifndef _VSTATUS_H
#define _VSTATUS_H

typedef enum {
                V_SUCCESS = 0,
                V_FAILURE,
                V_NOAPPLYET,
                V_APPCANTCPY,
                V_APPNOWND,
                V_WINCANTREG,
                V_WINCANTCRE,
                V_WINNOWINDOW,
                V_WININVCHILD,
                V_BADPROCCALL,
                V_NOOLDCLASS,
                V_TIMERCANTSET,
```

Listing A-65
VSTATUS.H

Listing A-65
Continued.

```
                    V_ALLOCFAIL,
                    V_CLIPOPEN,
                    V_LASTVISTAERROR,
                    V_USERERROR,
                    // insert your status values here
                    V_LASTUSERERROR
} VStatus;

#ifdef NDEBUG
#define VASSERT(x) ((void)0)
#else
#define VASSERT(x) ((x) ? (void)0 : (void) __VAssertFailed( \
                                         "Assertion failed: ", #x, \
__FILE__, __LINE__))
#endif

inline void __VAssertFailed(char *s1, char *s2, char *file, int line)
{
    char buffer[256];
#ifndef __DLL__
    ostrstream msg(buffer, sizeof(buffer));
    msg << "( " << s2 << " )\n"
        << " file: " << file << " line: " << line << ends;
#else
    wsprintf(buffer, "condition: (%s)\nfile: %s, line: %s", s2, file, line);
#endif
    MessageBox(NULL, buffer, s1, MB_TASKMODAL | MB_OK);
}

#endif
```

Listing A-66
VSTRING.H

```
/* ---------------------------------------------------------
    VString.h

        A simple string class

   Copyright (c) Jeff Mackay, 1992

--------------------------------------------------------- */
#ifndef _VSTRING_H
#define _VSTRING_H

#ifndef _VISTA_H
#include <vista.h>
#endif

#ifndef _VALLOC_H
```

```c
#include <valloc.h>
#endif

#include <string.h>

#ifndef __DLL__
#include <iostream.h>
#endif

STDCLASS(VString);

class VString
{

public:
    // constructors
        VString();
        VString(const charPtr);
        VString(const VStringRef);
    VString(int allocate);

    // destructor
        VString();

    // overloaded operators
        void *operator new(size_t size);
    void operator  delete(void *obj);
        VStringRef operator=(const charPtr);
        VStringRef operator=(const VStringRef s)
        { return VString::operator =(s.ptr); }

    VStringRef operator+=(const charPtr s)
        { Append(s); return *this; }
    VStringRef operator+=(const VStringRef s)
        { return VString::operator +=(s.ptr); }

        TCHAR FAR &operator[](int i);
        operator charPtr() const;

    // accessors
    int Length(void) const { return len; }
    int Allocated(void) const { return allocated; }
    charPtr Buffer(void) { return ptr; }

    // modifiers
    void Truncate(int pos=0);
    void ResetLength(void);
    // friend operators
        friend int operator==(const VStringRef x,
                                              const VStringRef y);
```

Listing A-66
Continued.

```cpp
        friend int operator!=(const VStringRef x,
                                            const VStringRef y);
        friend VStringRef operator +(VStringRef s1,
                                            VStringRef s2)
       { s1.Append(s2.ptr); return s2; }
        friend VStringRef operator +(VStringRef s1,
                                            charPtr s2)
       { s1.Append(s2); return s1; }
    protected:
        void Copy(const charPtr s);
        void CopyInPlace(const charPtr s);
        void Append(const charPtr s);
        void Allocate(int bytes);
        void Grow(int newBytes);
        void MakeEmpty(void);

        charPtr   ptr;
        int       len;                          // characters
        int       allocated;                    // bytes
        static    VAllocatorPtr allocator;
};

inline TCHAR FAR &VString::operator[](int i)
{
    Grow(i*sizeof(TCHAR));
    return ptr[i];
}

inline VString::operator const charPtr(void) const
{
    return ptr;
}

inline int operator==(const VStringRef x,
                                    const VStringRef y)
{
    if (x.len != y.len)
            return 0;
    else
        if (x.len == 0 || y.len == 0)
            return 0;
        else
            return(lstrcmp(x.ptr,y.ptr)==0);
}

inline int operator!=(const VStringRef x, const VStringRef y)
{
    return !(x == y);
}
```

```cpp
#ifndef _VNULLSTRING_DEFINED
extern VString NullString;
#endif //_VNULLSTRING_DEFINED

#endif //_VSTRING_H


/* ----------------------------------------------------------------
   VString.cpp

        A simple string class

   Copyright (c) Jeff Mackay, 1992

   ---------------------------------------------------------------- */
#ifndef _VSTRING_H
#define _VSTRING_H

#ifndef _VISTA_H
#include <vista.h>
#endif

#ifndef _VALLOC_H
#include <valloc.h>
#endif

#include <string.h>

#ifndef __DLL__
#include <iostream.h>
#endif

STDCLASS(VString);

class VString
{

public:
        VString();
        VString(charCPtr);
        VString(VStringCRef);
    VString(int allocate);
        VString();

        void *operator new(size_t size);
    void operator   delete(void *obj);
        VStringRef operator=(charCPtr);
        VStringRef operator=(VStringCRef s);
    VStringRef operator+=(charCPtr s);
        VStringRef operator+=(VStringCRef s);
        TCHAR FAR &operator[](int i);
```

Listing A-67
VSTRING.CPP

Listing A-67
Continued

```cpp
        operator charPtr() const;

        int Length(void) const { return len; }
    int Allocated(void) const { return allocated; }
    charPtr Buffer(void) { return ptr; }

        void Truncate(int pos=0);
    void ResetLength(void);

    // friend operators
        friend int operator==(VStringCRef x,
                                              VStringCRef y);
        friend int operator!=(VStringCRef x,
                                        VStringCRef y);
        friend VStringRef operator +(VStringRef s1,
                                              VStringCRef s2);
        friend VStringRef operator +(VStringRef s1,
                                              charCPtr s2);

    protected:
        void Copy(charCPtr s);
        void CopyInPlace(charCPtr s);
        void Append(charCPtr s);
        void Allocate(int bytes);
        void Grow(int newBytes);
        void MakeEmpty(void);

        charPtr   ptr;
        int       len;                          // characters
    int       allocated;                 // bytes
        static    VAllocatorPtr allocator;

};

inline VStringRef VString::operator=(VStringCRef s)
{
        return VString::operator =(s.ptr);
}

inline VStringRef VString::operator+=(charCPtr s)
{
        Append(s); return *this;
}

inline VStringRef VString::operator+=(VStringCRef s)
{
        return VString::operator +=(s.ptr);
}

inline TCHAR FAR &VString::operator[](int i)
{
```

```
        Grow(i*sizeof(TCHAR));
        return ptr[i];
}

inline VString::operator charPtr(void) const
{
    return ptr;
}

inline int operator==(VStringCRef x,
                                    VStringCRef y)
{
        if (x.len != y.len)
                return 0;
        else
                if (x.len == 0 || y.len == 0)
            return 0;
        else
                    return(lstrcmp(x.ptr,y.ptr)==0);
}
inline int operator!=(VStringCRef x, VStringCRef y)
{
    return !(x == y);
}

inline VStringRef operator +(VStringRef s1, VStringCRef s2)
{
        s1.Append(s2.ptr);
        return s1;
}

inline VStringRef operator +(VStringRef s1, charCPtr s2)
{
        s1.Append(s2);
        return s1;
}


#ifndef _VNULLSTRING_DEFINED
extern VString NullString;
#endif //_VNULLSTRING_DEFINED

#endif //_VSTRING_H



/* ----------------------------------------------------------------  Listing A-68
        vtext.h                                                       VTEXT.H

        Implementation of the VText class.
```

Listing A-68
Continued.

```
                Copyright (C) 1992, by Jeff Mackay
---------------------------------------------------------------- */

#ifndef _VTEXT_H
#define _VTEXT_H

#ifndef _VISTA_H
#include "Vista.h"
#endif

#ifndef _VEDIT_H
#include "VEdit.h"
#endif

STDCLASS(VText);
class _CLASSTYPE VText : public VEditable
{
        public :

                VText(VCompositePtr parent, VStringRef title,
                        int x, int y, int width, int height);
        VText(VCompositePtr parent, int ResourceId);
                virtual int GetActualLength(int start, int end);
                virtual const charPtr ClassName(void) const;
                virtual int GetFirstVisibleLine(void);
                virtual void GetLine(int index, charPtr buffer,
                                                    int bufsize);
                virtual int  GetLineCount(void);
                virtual int  GetLineAt(int start);
                virtual int  GetLinePosition(int index);
                virtual int  GetLineLength(int index);
        virtual void ScrollText(int xAmt, int yAmt);
                virtual charPtr GetTextAt(int start, int end,
                                                charPtr buffer);
};

#endif
```

Listing A-69
VTEXT.CPP

```
/* ----------------------------------------------------------------
            vtext.cpp

                Implementation of the VText class.
        Copyright (C) 1992, by Jeff Mackay

---------------------------------------------------------------- */

#pragma hdrfile "vista.sym"
#include <vista.h>
```

```cpp
#pragma hdrstop
#include <stdlib.h>
#include <vtext.h>
#include <vstring.h>

VText::VText(VCompositePtr parent, VStringRef title,
         int x, int y, int width, int height) :
         VEditable(parent, title, x, y, width, height)
{
    style |= ES_MULTILINE | WS_VSCROLL | WS_HSCROLL;
}

VText::VText(VCompositePtr parent, int resourceId) :
    VEditable(parent, resourceId)
{
    style |= ES_MULTILINE | WS_VSCROLL | WS_HSCROLL;
}

const charPtr VText::ClassName(void) const
{
    return "VText";
}

int VText::GetFirstVisibleLine(void)
{
    return SendMessage(*this, EM_GETFIRSTVISIBLELINE, 0, 0);
}

void VText::GetLine(int index, charPtr buffer,
                                    int bufsize)
{
    int len = GetLineLength(index);
    VASSERT(len <= bufsize-1);
    *(WORD *)buffer = len;
    SendMessage(*this, EM_GETLINE, index,
(LPARAM)(LPSTR)buffer);
    buffer[len]='\0';

}

int VText::GetLineCount(void)
{
    return SendMessage(*this, EM_GETLINECOUNT, 0, 0);
}
int VText::GetLineAt(int start)
{
    return SendMessage(*this, EM_LINEFROMCHAR, start, 0);
}
int VText::GetLinePosition(int index)
{
    return SendMessage(*this, EM_LINEINDEX, index, 0);
```

Listing A-69
Continued.

```cpp
}
int VText::GetLineLength(int index)
{
        return SendMessage(*this, EM_LINELENGTH,
                                GetLinePosition(index), 0);
}

void VText::ScrollText(int xAmt, int yAmt)
{
        SendMessage(*this, EM_LINESCROLL, 0,
                        MAKELONG(yAmt, xAmt));
}

int VText::GetActualLength(int start, int end)
{
        int startLine=GetLineAt(start);
        int endLine=GetLineAt(end);
        int lineCount = max(0, endLine-startLine);
    int actual = abs(end-start) + (lineCount*2);
        return actual;
}

template <class T> inline void swap(T _FAR &a, T _FAR &b)
{
        T c = a;
        a = b;
        b = c;
}

// buffer must be at least GetActualLength()+1 bytes in size
charPtr VText::GetTextAt(int start, int end, charPtr buffer)
{
        int startLine, endLine, curPos=0;

        // handle reverse selections
        if (start > end)
            swap(start,end);

        startLine = GetLineAt(start);
        endLine   = GetLineAt(end);

        for(int i=startLine; i<=endLine; i++)
        {
        // get the current line
                int lineLength = GetLineLength(i);
                char *tempBuf = new char[lineLength+3];
                GetLine(i, tempBuf, lineLength+1);
                int startPos = 0;
        // calculate the starting position
                if (i == startLine)
                {
```

```
                                int lineStart = GetLinePosition(i);
                                startPos = start-lineStart;
            }
                        if (i < endLine)
                        {
                        // copy beginning lines into buffer with newlines
                                _fmemcpy(&buffer[curPos], &tempBuf[startPos],
                                                lineLength);
                                curPos+=lineLength-startPos;
                                buffer[curPos++] = '\r';
                                buffer[curPos++] = '\n';
                        }
                        else
                        {
                // copy last line into buffer
                                int lineStart = max(start,GetLinePosition(i));
                                _fmemcpy(&buffer[curPos], &tempBuf[startPos],
                                                end-lineStart);
                                curPos += end-lineStart;
                        }
        delete tempBuf;
        }
        buffer[curPos]='\0';
        return buffer;
}
```

```
/* ----------------------------------------------------------          Listing A-70
    VTimer.h                                                              VTIMER.H

        Interface for the VTimer class.  Handles Windows
        timers.

    Copyright (C) 1992, by Jeff Mackay

------------------------------------------------------------ */
#ifndef _VTIMER_H
#define _VTIMER_H

#ifndef _VISTA_H
#include <Vista.h>
#endif

STDCLASS(VTimer);

class _CLASSTYPE VTimer
{
private:
```

Listing A-70
Continued.

```
                int         timer_id;
                VWindowPtr  window;
                int         interval;
                Boolean     repeat;
        static  TIMERPROC timer_proc;
        static  int         last_id;

    public:

        VTimer(int value, VWindow *window=NULL,
                    Boolean flag=False);
        VTimer();
        void SetInterval(int value);
        void SetWindow(VWindowPtr win);

        const int GetId(void) const
        {
            return timer_id;
        }

        const int GetInterval(void) const
        {
            return interval;
        }

        const VWindowPtr GetWindow(void) const
        {
            return window;
        }

        int operator <(VTimerRef compare) const
        {
            return (timer_id < compare.timer_id);
        }

        static WORD FAR PASCAL _export
                TimerFunc(HWND, WORD, int, DWORD);
        virtual void Activate(VEventRef event);
};

#endif
```

Listing A-71
VTIMER.CPP

```
/* --------------------------------------------------------
    vtimer.cpp

        Implementation of the VTimer class.

    Copyright (C) 1992, by Jeff Mackay

------------------------------------------------------- */
```

```cpp
#pragma hdrfile "vista.sym"
#include <vista.h>
#pragma hdrstop
#include <vtimer.h>
#include <vappl.h>


const int defaultTimerId = 101;

TIMERPROC VTimer::timer_proc;
int       VTimer::last_id = defaultTimerId;

VTimer::VTimer(int value, VWindowPtr win, Boolean flag) :
        interval(value), window(win), repeat(flag)
{
        if (!timer_proc)
        {
                timer_proc = (TIMERPROC)
                  MakeProcInstance((FARPROC)VTimer::TimerFunc,
GetApplication());
        }
        timer_id = last_id++;
    HWND hwnd;
    if (window)
        hwnd = *window;
    else
        hwnd = 0;
        int status = SetTimer(hwnd, timer_id, interval, timer_proc);
        if (!status)
        {
                timer_id = status;
                GetApplication().SetStatus(V_TIMERCANTSET);
        }
}

VTimer::VTimer(void)
{
        if (!timer_id)
                return;

    HWND hwnd;
    if (window)
        hwnd = *window;
    else
        hwnd = 0;
        KillTimer(hwnd, timer_id);
}

void VTimer::SetWindow(VWindowPtr win)
```

Listing A-71
Continued.

```
{
    UNREFERENCED_PARAMETER(win);
}

void VTimer::SetInterval(int value)
{
    UNREFERENCED_PARAMETER(value);
}

WORD FAR PASCAL _export VTimer::TimerFunc(HWND hwnd,
                                           WORD message,
                                           int timerId,
DWORD time)
{
    UNREFERENCED_PARAMETER(hwnd);
    UNREFERENCED_PARAMETER(message);
    UNREFERENCED_PARAMETER(timerId);
    UNREFERENCED_PARAMETER(time);
    return 0;
}

void VTimer::Activate(VEventRef event)
{
    UNREFERENCED_PARAMETER(event);
}
```

Listing A-72
VTXTFLD.H

```
/* -----------------------------------------------------------------
            vtxtfld.h

               Implementation of the VTextField class.

            Copyright (C) 1992, by Jeff Mackay

   ----------------------------------------------------------- */
#ifndef _VTXTFLD_H
#define _VTXTFLD_H

#ifndef _VEDIT_H
#include <vedit.h>
#endif
class _CLASSTYPE VTextField : public VEditable
{
    protected :

    public :

        VTextField(VCompositePtr parent, VStringRef title,
```

```
                              int x, int y, int width, int height,
                              int size=(-1)) :
                    VEditable(parent, title, x, y, width, height)
                    {
                    }
               VTextField(VCompositePtr parent, int resourceId,
                         int size=(-1)) :
               VEditable(parent, resourceId, size)
               {
               }
               virtual const charPtr ClassName(void) const;

     protected:
          int max_size;
};

#endif
```

Listing A-73
VTXTFLD.CPP

```
/* ----------------------------------------------------------
     vtxtfld.cpp

          Implementation of the VTextField class.

          Copyright (C) 1992, by Jeff Mackay

---------------------------------------------------------- */

#pragma hdrfile "vista.sym"
#include <vista.h>
#pragma hdrstop
#include <vtxtfld.h>
#include <vstring.h>

static VString className("VTextField");

const charPtr VTextField::ClassName(void) const
{
     return className;
}
```

Listing A-74
VWINDOW.H

```
/* ----------------------------------------------------------
   vwindow.h

          VWindow class interface

   Copyright (C) 1992, by Jeff Mackay
---------------------------------------------------------- */
```

Listing A-74
Continued.

```c
#ifndef _VWINDOW_H
#define _VWINDOW_H

#ifndef _VISTA_H
#include <vista.h>
#endif

#ifndef _VDBLLIST_H
#include <vdbllist.h>
#endif

#ifndef _VSTRING_H
#include <vstring.h>
#endif

#ifndef _VDISPTCH_H
#include <vdisptch.h>
#endif

#ifndef _VMENU_H
#include <vmenu.h>
#endif

#ifndef _VSCROLL_H
#include <vscroll.h>
#endif

#ifndef _VAPPL_H
#include <vappl.h>
#endif

STDTYPE(RECT);
STDTYPE(WNDCLASS);
STDTYPE(PAINTSTRUCT);

STDCLASS(VComposite);
STDCLASS(VFrame);
STDCLASS(VFont);
STDCLASS(VColor);

class VDispatcher;

class _CLASSTYPE VWindow
{
public :
        VWindow(VApplRef appl, VCompositePtr par, charPtr caption);
        VWindow(VCompositePtr par, charPtr caption);
        virtual VWindow(void);

        operator HWND(void) const;
```

```cpp
        Boolean operator ()(VEventRef event);
        Boolean operator ()(int id, VEventRef event);

        virtual RECTPtr    GetDimensions(RECTRef rect) const;
        virtual const      charPtr ClassName(void) const;
        virtual VFontRef   GetFont(VFontRef) const;
        virtual VColorRef  GetColor(VColorRef) const;
    virtual Boolean    IsValid(void);
    virtual Boolean    QueryClose(void);
        const charPtr      GetCaption(void) const;
    virtual HINSTANCE GetResourceHandle(void) const;

    virtual void     SetDimensions(RECTRef rect);
        virtual void     Create(void);
        virtual void     InitWinClass(WNDCLASSRef wndClass);
        virtual void     Register(void);
        void             Show(void);
        void             Update(void);
        virtual void     SetColor(VColorRef color);
    virtual void     SetFont(VFontRef font);
    virtual void     SetCaption(charPtr s);
        void             AddAction(VAction action, UINT msgId,
                                                      short ctl=VDEF_CTL_ID,
                                                      short ntfy=VDEF_NOTIFY_ID);
    void             SetRedraw(Boolean value);
    void             Invalidate(RECT _FAR *rect=0);
    virtual Boolean Destroy(Boolean check);

protected :

        HWND                        handle;
        int                         x;
        int                         y;
        int                         width;
        int                         height;
        unsigned long      ex_style;
        unsigned long      style;
        unsigned int       flags;
        unsigned int       state;
        unsigned int       child_id;
        long                        param;
    UINT              menu_or_child;

        VApplRef            appl;
        VCompositePtr   parent;
        Boolean         translate_tabs;
        Boolean             registered;
        Boolean             predefined;
        WNDPROC             old_proc;
```

Listing A-74
Continued.

```
        WNDPROC                 wnd_proc;
        VDispatcher             dispatcher;
    VAcceleratorPtr accel_table;

        virtual void InitActions(void);

        virtual Boolean ActivateAction(VEventRef event);
        virtual Boolean CreateAction(VEventRef event);
        virtual Boolean NCDestroyAction(VEventRef event);
        virtual Boolean SizeAction(VEventRef event);
        virtual Boolean PaintAction(VEventRef event);
        virtual Boolean PaintWindow(HDC hdc, PAINTSTRUCTRef ps);
        virtual LRESULT DefaultProc(VEventRef event);
        void            SetWinPointer(void);
        static VWindowPtr GetWinPointer(HWND hWnd);
        static LRESULT CALLBACK WindowProc(HWND hWnd, UINT id,

WPARAM wParam,

LPARAM lParam);

private:

        VString                 caption;
        static DWORD            prop_name;
        static DWORD            large_prop_name;



};

class VComposite : public VWindow
{

        public:

                VComposite(VApplRef appl, VCompositePtr par,
                                        charPtr caption);
                VComposite(VCompositePtr par, charPtr caption);

                VComposite(void);

        virtual Boolean IsValid(void);
        virtual Boolean QueryClose(void);

                virtual void AddChild(VWindowPtr child);
                virtual void RemoveChild(VWindowPtr child);
                virtual void Create(void);
        virtual void AddCommand(VAction action, short cmdId,
                                short ntfyId=VDEF_NOTIFY_ID);
        VWindowPtr    First(void);
```

```cpp
        VWindowPtr    Next(VWindowPtr child);
        VWindowPtr    Previous(VWindowPtr child);

    protected:
        typedef VDblList<VWindowPtr> ChildArray;
        typedef VDblListIter<VWindowPtr> ChildIterator;
        ChildArray                      children;

        virtual void InitActions(void);
        virtual void CreateChildren(void);

    virtual Boolean CommandAction(VEventRef event);
        virtual Boolean CloseAction(VEventRef event);
    virtual Boolean CreateAction(VEventRef event);
};

inline VComposite::VComposite(VApplRef appl,
                                VCompositePtr par, charPtr caption) :
        VWindow(appl, par, caption), children(0)
{
    style = WS_OVERLAPPEDWINDOW;
}

inline VComposite::VComposite(VCompositePtr par,
                                charPtr caption) :
        VWindow(par, caption), children(0)
{
    style = WS_OVERLAPPEDWINDOW;
}

class VFrame : public VComposite
{
    public:
        VFrame(VApplRef appl, VCompositePtr par,
                                charPtr caption);
        VFrame(VCompositePtr par, charPtr caption);

        VFrame(void);

        const VMenuPtr   GetMenu(void) const;

        virtual VMenuPtr SetMenu(VMenu *newMenu,
                                                    int winPos=0);
        virtual void     Create(void);

    protected:
        VString                 menu_name;
        VMenuPtr                menu;
        VScrollPtr              vert_scroll;
```

Listing A-74
Continued.

```
                    VScrollPtr               horiz_scroll;

                virtual void InitActions(void);

                virtual Boolean HScrollAction(VEventRef event);
                virtual Boolean VScrollAction(VEventRef event);
        virtual Boolean CommandAction(VEventRef event);
                virtual Boolean CreateAction(VEventRef event);
        virtual Boolean DestroyAction(VEventRef event);
        virtual Boolean QueryEndSessionAction(VEventRef event);
        virtual Boolean ExitCommand(VEventRef event);
};


extern VWindowPtr _VCreateWindow;

inline VWindow::operator HWND(void) const
{
        return handle;
}

inline LRESULT VWindow::DefaultProc(VEventRef event)
{
        return DefWindowProc(*this, event.GetId(),
                                        event.GetWParam(),
                                        event.GetLParam());
}

inline HINSTANCE VWindow::GetResourceHandle(void) const
{
        return appl;
}
#endif
```

Listing A-75
VWINDOW.CPP

```
/* -------------------------------------------------------
   VWindow.cpp

        Implementation of the VWindow class.

    Copyright (C) 1992, by Jeff Mackay

   ------------------------------------------------------- */
#pragma hdrfile "vista.sym"
#include <vista.h>
#pragma hdrstop

#include <dos.h>
#include <vwindow.h>
```

```cpp
#include <vappl.h>
#include <vevent.h>

VWindowPtr _VCreateWindow;

static VString className("VWindow");
DWORD   VWindow::prop_name =
                (MAKELONG(GlobalAddAtom("VWinPointer"),0));
DWORD   VWindow::large_prop_name =
                (MAKELONG(GlobalAddAtom("VWinSegment"),0));

VWindow::VWindow(VApplRef app, VCompositePtr par, charPtr capt) :
        appl(app), parent(par)
{
        wnd_proc        = (WNDPROC) MakeProcInstance((FARPROC)
                                        VWindow::WindowProc, appl);
        ex_style        = 0;
        child_id        = 0;
        x = y           = 0;
        width           = 0;
        height          = 0;
        style           = 0;
        state           = 0;
        param           = 0;
    menu_or_child = 0;

    accel_table     = 0;
    translate_tabs  = False;
    predefined      = False;
    registered      = False;
        old_proc        = 0;
        caption         = capt;
        if (parent)
                parent->AddChild(this);
}

VWindow::VWindow(VCompositePtr par, charPtr capt) :
        appl(GetApplication()), parent(par)
{

        wnd_proc        = (WNDPROC) MakeProcInstance((FARPROC)
VWindow::WindowProc,

appl);
        ex_style        = 0;
        child_id        = 0;
        x = y           = 0;
        width           = 0;
        height          = 0;
        style           = 0;
        state           = 0;
```

Listing A-75
Continued.

```
        param        = 0;
    menu_or_child = 0;

    accel_table   = 0;
    translate_tabs = False;
    predefined    = False;
    registered    = False;
        old_proc      = 0;
        caption       = capt;
        handle        = 0;
        if (parent)
                parent->AddChild(this);
}


VWindow::VWindow(void)
{
        if (IsWindow(handle))
        {
#if (sizeof(VWindowPtr) == sizeof(DWORD))
                RemoveProp(handle, (LPSTR) large_prop_name);
#endif
                RemoveProp(handle, (LPSTR) prop_name);
                DestroyWindow(handle);
        }
    if (parent)
        parent->RemoveChild(this);
    FreeProcInstance((FARPROC)wnd_proc);
}


void VWindow::SetWinPointer(void)
{
#if (sizeof(VWindowPtr) == 4)
        SetProp(handle, (LPSTR) prop_name, (HANDLE)FP_OFF(this));
        SetProp(handle, (LPSTR) large_prop_name, (HANDLE)FP_SEG(this));
#else
        SetProp(handle, (LPSTR) prop_name, (HANDLE) this);
#endif

}

VWindowPtr VWindow::GetWinPointer(HWND hWnd)
{
#if (sizeof(VWindowPtr) == 4)
        unsigned ofs = (unsigned)GetProp(hWnd, (LPSTR) prop_name);
        unsigned seg = (unsigned)GetProp(hWnd, (LPSTR) large_prop_name);
        return (VWindowPtr) MK_FP(seg,ofs);
#else
        return (VWindowPtr) GetProp(hWnd, (LPSTR) prop_name);
```

```
#endif
}


void VWindow::Create(void)
{

    if (registered == False)
    {
            Register();
            if (appl.GetStatus() != V_SUCCESS)
                    return;
    }

        VWindowPtr oldCreate   = _VCreateWindow;
        _VCreateWindow = this;
        HWND hwnd;
        if (parent)
                hwnd = *parent;
        else
                hwnd = 0;
        handle = CreateWindowEx(ex_style,
                                                ClassName(),
                                                GetCaption(),
                                                style,
                                                x, y,
                                                width, height,
                                                hwnd,
                                                (HMENU)menu_or_child,
                                                appl,
                                                (LPSTR) param);

        _VCreateWindow = oldCreate;
        if (!handle)
        {
                appl.SetStatus(V_WINCANTCRE);
                return;
        }
}
Boolean VWindow::Destroy(Boolean query)
{
    if (query == True && QueryClose() == False)
        return False;
    else
    {
        DestroyWindow(*this);
        return True;
    }
}

void VWindow::Register(void)
{
```

Listing A-75
Continued.

```
        WNDCLASS wndClass;

    if (GetClassInfo(0, ClassName(), &wndClass) == FALSE)
    {
        if (GetClassInfo(appl, ClassName(), &wndClass) == FALSE)
        {
            InitWinClass(wndClass);
            if (appl.GetStatus())
                return;

            if (!RegisterClass(&wndClass))
            {
                appl.SetStatus(V_WINCANTREG);
            }
        }
    }
    else
    {
        old_proc  =   0;
        predefined = True;
    }

    InitActions();
    registered = True;
}


void VWindow::InitWinClass(WNDCLASSRef wndClass)
{
    wndClass.style                     = CS_HREDRAW | CS_VREDRAW | CS_BYTEALIGNWINDOW;
    wndClass.lpfnWndProc               = VWindow::WindowProc;
    wndClass.cbClsExtra                    = 0;
    wndClass.cbWndExtra        = 0;
    wndClass.hInstance                     = appl;
    wndClass.hIcon                         = LoadIcon(0, IDI_APPLICATION);
    wndClass.hCursor                   = LoadCursor(0, IDC_ARROW);
    wndClass.hbrBackground     = (HBRUSH)(COLOR_WINDOW + 1);
    wndClass.lpszMenuName      = 0;
    wndClass.lpszClassName       = (LPSTR)ClassName();
}


void VWindow::Update(void)
{
    if (!handle)
        appl.SetStatus(V_WINNOWINDOW);
    else
        UpdateWindow(handle);
```

```cpp
}

void VWindow::Show(void)
{
        if (!handle)
                appl.SetStatus(V_WINNOWINDOW);
        else
                ShowWindow(handle, state);
}

const charPtr VWindow::ClassName(void) const
{
        return className;
}

const charPtr VWindow::GetCaption(void) const
{
        return (const VStringRef) caption;
}

void VWindow::SetCaption(charPtr text)
{
    caption = text;
    if (handle)
        SetWindowText(*this, caption);
}

void VWindow::SetDimensions(RECTRef rect)
{
    if (handle)
    {
        MoveWindow(*this, rect.left, rect.top,
                          rect.right-rect.left,
                          rect.bottom-rect.top,
                          True);
    }
    else
    {
        x = rect.left;
        y = rect.top;
        width = rect.right-rect.left;
        height = rect.bottom-rect.top;
    }
}

void VWindow::Invalidate(RECT _FAR *rect)
{
    RECT update;
    if (rect)
```

Listing A-75
Continued.

```cpp
        update = *rect;
    GetDimensions(update);
    InvalidateRect(*this, &update, TRUE);
}

void VWindow::SetRedraw(Boolean state)
{
    SendMessage(*this, WM_SETREDRAW, state, 0);
    if (state == True)
        Invalidate();
}

void VWindow::InitActions(void)
{
    AddAction(&VWindow::ActivateAction,   WM_ACTIVATE);
        AddAction(&VWindow::CreateAction,    WM_CREATE);
        AddAction(&VWindow::NCDestroyAction, WM_NCDESTROY);
    AddAction(&VWindow::PaintAction,      WM_PAINT);
        AddAction(&VWindow::SizeAction,      WM_SIZE);
}



Boolean VWindow::operator()(VEventRef event)
{
        VAction action = dispatcher[event];
        if (!action)
                return False;
        return (this->*action)(event);
}

Boolean VWindow::operator()(int id, VEventRef event)
{
        VAction action = dispatcher[id];
        if (!action)
                return False;
        return (this->*action)(event);
}

Boolean VWindow::ActivateAction(VEventRef event)
{
    if (translate_tabs || accel_table)
    {
        if (event.GetWParam() == WA_INACTIVE)
            appl.SetActiveWindow(0);
        else
            appl.SetActiveWindow(this);
    }
    if (accel_table)
    {
        appl.SetAccelerators(accel_table);
    }
```

```cpp
        return True;
}

Boolean VWindow::CreateAction(VEventRef event)
{
        UNREFERENCED_PARAMETER(event);
        return False;
}

Boolean VWindow::IsValid(void)
{
    return True;
}

Boolean VWindow::QueryClose(void)
{
    return True;
}

Boolean VWindow::NCDestroyAction(VEventRef event)
{
    UNREFERENCED_PARAMETER(event);
    handle = 0;
    return False;    // make sure this message is passed on
}

Boolean VWindow::PaintWindow(HDC hdc, PAINTSTRUCTRef ps)
{
        UNREFERENCED_PARAMETER(hdc);
        UNREFERENCED_PARAMETER(ps);
        return True;
}

Boolean VWindow::PaintAction(VEventRef event)
{
        UNREFERENCED_PARAMETER(event);
        PAINTSTRUCT ps;
        HDC hdc = BeginPaint(*this, &ps);
        Boolean retVal = PaintWindow(hdc, ps);
        EndPaint(*this, &ps);
        return retVal;
}


Boolean VWindow::SizeAction(VEventRef event)
{
        width = LOWORD(event.GetLParam());
        height = HIWORD(event.GetLParam());
        HDC hdc = GetDC(*this);
        DWORD origin = GetWindowOrg(hdc);
        x = LOWORD(origin);
        y = HIWORD(origin);
```

Listing A-75
Continued.

```
            ReleaseDC(*this, hdc);
            return False;
}

RECTPtr VWindow::GetDimensions(RECTRef rect) const
{
        rect.left   = x;
        rect.top    = y;
        rect.right  = width;
        rect.bottom = height;
    return &rect;
}

LRESULT CALLBACK _export VWindow::WindowProc(HWND hWnd,
UINT id,
                                                       WPARAM
wParam, LPARAM lParam)
{
        VWindowPtr window = GetWinPointer(hWnd);
        if (!window)
        {
                window = _VCreateWindow;
                window->handle = hWnd;
                window->SetWinPointer();
        }

        VEvent  event(*window, id, wParam, lParam);
        Boolean filtered = (*window)(event);
        if (!filtered)
                return window->DefaultProc(event);
        else
                return event.GetResponse();
}

VFontRef VWindow::GetFont(VFontRef buff) const
{
        return buff;
}

void VWindow::SetFont(VFontRef)
{
}

VColorRef VWindow::GetColor(VColorRef buff) const
{
        return buff;
}
void VWindow::SetColor(VColorRef)
{
}

void VWindow::AddAction(VAction action, UINT msgId, short
```

```
                                        ctlId,
                                                                        short ntfyId)
{
    dispatcher.AddAction(action, msgId, ctlId, ntfyId);
}
```

Listing A-76
VISTA.MAK

```
#+++++++++++
# VISTA MakeFile - Created by Borland PRJ2MAK utility
#+++++++++++
.AUTODEPEND

.PATH.obj = D:\VISTA\LIB

#               *Translator Definitions*
CC = bcc +VISTA.CFG
TASM = TASM
TLIB = tlib
TLINK = tlink
LIBPATH = D:\BC\LIB;D:\VISTA\LIB
INCLUDEPATH = D:\BC\INCLUDE;D:\VISTA\INCLUDE


#               *Implicit Rules*
.c.obj:
  $(CC) -c {$< }

.cpp.obj:
  $(CC) -c {$< }

#               *List Macros*


LIB_dependencies =  \
 valloc.obj \
 vappl.obj \
 vbutton.obj \
 vcomclr.obj \
 vcomfile.obj \
 vcomfind.obj \
 vcomfont.obj \
 vcompost.obj \
 vcomprnt.obj \
 vcontrol.obj \
 vdbllist.obj \
 vdisptch.obj \
 vdlgbox.obj \
 vedit.obj \
 vevent.obj \
 vframe.obj \
```

Listing A-76
Continued.

```
vgrdev.obj \
vgditool.obj \
vlabel.obj \
vlstbox.obj \
vmdichld.obj \
vmdicli.obj \
vmdifrm.obj \
vmenu.obj \
vmsgbox.obj \
vscroll.obj \
vstring.obj \
vtext.obj \
vtimer.obj \
vtxtfld.obj \
vwindow.obj

#                    *Explicit Rules*
d:\vista\lib\vista.lib: vista.cfg $(LIB_dependencies)
   - del d:\vista\lib\vista.lib
   $(TLIB) $< /C/P512 @&&|
-+d:\vista\lib\valloc.obj &
-+d:\vista\lib\vappl.obj &
-+d:\vista\lib\vbutton.obj &
-+d:\vista\lib\vcomclr.obj &
-+d:\vista\lib\vcomfile.obj &
-+d:\vista\lib\vcomfind.obj &
-+d:\vista\lib\vcomfont.obj &
-+d:\vista\lib\vcompost.obj &
-+d:\vista\lib\vcomprnt.obj &
-+d:\vista\lib\vcontrol.obj &
-+d:\vista\lib\vdbllist.obj &
-+d:\vista\lib\vdisptch.obj &
-+d:\vista\lib\vdlgbox.obj &
-+d:\vista\lib\vedit.obj &
-+d:\vista\lib\vevent.obj &
-+d:\vista\lib\vframe.obj &
-+d:\vista\lib\vgrdev.obj &
-+d:\vista\lib\vgditool.obj &
-+d:\vista\lib\vlabel.obj &
-+d:\vista\lib\vlstbox.obj &
-+d:\vista\lib\vmdichld.obj &
-+d:\vista\lib\vmdicli.obj &
-+d:\vista\lib\vmdifrm.obj &
-+d:\vista\lib\vmenu.obj &
-+d:\vista\lib\vmsgbox.obj &
-+d:\vista\lib\vscroll.obj &
-+d:\vista\lib\vstring.obj &
-+d:\vista\lib\vtext.obj &
-+d:\vista\lib\vtimer.obj &
-+d:\vista\lib\vtxtfld.obj &
-+d:\vista\lib\vwindow.obj,$*.lst
```

```
|
#                  *Individual File Dependencies*
valloc.obj: vista.cfg src\valloc.cpp
        $(CC) -c src\valloc.cpp

vappl.obj: vista.cfg src\vappl.cpp
        $(CC) -c src\vappl.cpp

vbutton.obj: vista.cfg src\vbutton.cpp
        $(CC) -c src\vbutton.cpp

vcomclr.obj: vista.cfg src\vcomclr.cpp
        $(CC) -c src\vcomclr.cpp

vcomfile.obj: vista.cfg src\vcomfile.cpp
        $(CC) -c src\vcomfile.cpp

vcomfind.obj: vista.cfg src\vcomfind.cpp
        $(CC) -c src\vcomfind.cpp

vcomfont.obj: vista.cfg src\vcomfont.cpp
        $(CC) -c src\vcomfont.cpp

vcompost.obj: vista.cfg src\vcompost.cpp
        $(CC) -c src\vcompost.cpp

vcomprnt.obj: vista.cfg src\vcomprnt.cpp
        $(CC) -c src\vcomprnt.cpp

vcontrol.obj: vista.cfg src\vcontrol.cpp
        $(CC) -c src\vcontrol.cpp

vdbllist.obj: vista.cfg src\vdbllist.cpp
        $(CC) -c src\vdbllist.cpp

vdisptch.obj: vista.cfg src\vdisptch.cpp
        $(CC) -c src\vdisptch.cpp

vdlgbox.obj: vista.cfg src\vdlgbox.cpp
        $(CC) -c src\vdlgbox.cpp

vedit.obj: vista.cfg src\vedit.cpp
        $(CC) -c src\vedit.cpp

vevent.obj: vista.cfg src\vevent.cpp
        $(CC) -c src\vevent.cpp
vframe.obj: vista.cfg src\vframe.cpp
        $(CC) -c src\vframe.cpp

vgrdev.obj: vista.cfg src\vgrdev.cpp
        $(CC) -c src\vgrdev.cpp
```

Listing A-76
Continued.

```
vgditool.obj: vista.cfg src\vgditool.cpp
        $(CC) -c src\vgditool.cpp

vlabel.obj: vista.cfg src\vlabel.cpp
        $(CC) -c src\vlabel.cpp

vlstbox.obj: vista.cfg src\vlstbox.cpp
        $(CC) -c src\vlstbox.cpp

vmdichld.obj: vista.cfg src\vmdichld.cpp
        $(CC) -c src\vmdichld.cpp

vmdicli.obj: vista.cfg src\vmdicli.cpp
        $(CC) -c src\vmdicli.cpp

vmdifrm.obj: vista.cfg src\vmdifrm.cpp
        $(CC) -c src\vmdifrm.cpp

vmenu.obj: vista.cfg src\vmenu.cpp
        $(CC) -c src\vmenu.cpp

vmsgbox.obj: vista.cfg src\vmsgbox.cpp
        $(CC) -c src\vmsgbox.cpp

vscroll.obj: vista.cfg src\vscroll.cpp
        $(CC) -c src\vscroll.cpp

vstring.obj: vista.cfg src\vstring.cpp
        $(CC) -c src\vstring.cpp

vtext.obj: vista.cfg src\vtext.cpp
        $(CC) -c src\vtext.cpp

vtimer.obj: vista.cfg src\vtimer.cpp
        $(CC) -c src\vtimer.cpp

vtxtfld.obj: vista.cfg src\vtxtfld.cpp
        $(CC) -c src\vtxtfld.cpp

vwindow.obj: vista.cfg src\vwindow.cpp
        $(CC) -c src\vwindow.cpp

#              *Compiler Configuration File*
vista.cfg: vista.mak
  copy &&|
-R
-ml
-3
-f287
-C
-v
```

```
-d
-W
-vi-
-H=VISTA.SYM
-wpro
-weas
-wpre
-nD:\VISTA\LIB
-I$(INCLUDEPATH)
-L$(LIBPATH)
-P
| vista.cfg
```

Listing A-77
VISTADLL.MAK

```
# Vista DLL MakeFile - created by Borland PRJ2MAK utility
.AUTODEPEND

.PATH.obj = D:\VISTA\LIB

#               *Translator Definitions*
CC = bcc +VISTADLL.CFG
TASM = TASM
TLIB = tlib
TLINK = tlink
LIBPATH = D:\BC\LIB;D:\VISTA\LIB
INCLUDEPATH = D:\BC\INCLUDE;D:\VISTA\INCLUDE


#               *Implicit Rules*
.c.obj:
  $(CC) -c {$< }

.cpp.obj:
  $(CC) -c {$< }

#               *List Macros*


EXE_dependencies =  \
 valloc.obj \
 vappl.obj \
 vcompost.obj \
 vgrdev.obj \
 vdbllist.obj \
 vevent.obj \
 vdisptch.obj \
 vframe.obj \
 vmain.obj \
 vmenu.obj \
```

Listing A-77
Continued

```
          vscroll.obj \
          vstring.obj \
          vwindow.obj

    #                *Explicit Rules*
    d:\vista\lib\vistadll.dll: vistadll.cfg $(EXE_dependencies)
      $(TLINK) /v/x/c/P-/Twd/L$(LIBPATH) @&&|
c0dl.obj+
d:\vista\lib\valloc.obj+
d:\vista\lib\vappl.obj+
d:\vista\lib\vcompost.obj+
d:\vista\lib\vgrdev.obj+
d:\vista\lib\vdbllist.obj+
d:\vista\lib\vevent.obj+
d:\vista\lib\vdisptch.obj+
d:\vista\lib\vframe.obj+
d:\vista\lib\vmain.obj+
d:\vista\lib\vmenu.obj+
d:\vista\lib\vscroll.obj+
d:\vista\lib\vstring.obj+
d:\vista\lib\vwindow.obj
d:\vista\lib\vistadll.dll
                  # no map file
mathwl.lib+
import.lib+
cwl.lib

|
   RC  d:\vista\lib\vistadll.dll
   IMPLIB D:\VISTA\LIB\VISTADLL.LIB D:\VISTA\LIB\VISTADLL.DLL

    #               *Individual File Dependencies*
    valloc.obj: vistadll.cfg src\valloc.cpp
         $(CC) -c src\valloc.cpp

    vappl.obj: vistadll.cfg src\vappl.cpp
         $(CC) -c src\vappl.cpp

    vcompost.obj: vistadll.cfg src\vcompost.cpp
         $(CC) -c src\vcompost.cpp

    vgrdev.obj: vistadll.cfg src\vgrdev.cpp
         $(CC) -c src\vgrdev.cpp

    vdbllist.obj: vistadll.cfg src\vdbllist.cpp
         $(CC) -c src\vdbllist.cpp
    vevent.obj: vistadll.cfg src\vevent.cpp
         $(CC) -c src\vevent.cpp

    vdisptch.obj: vistadll.cfg src\vdisptch.cpp
         $(CC) -c src\vdisptch.cpp
```

```
vframe.obj: vistadll.cfg src\vframe.cpp
        $(CC) -c src\vframe.cpp

vmain.obj: vistadll.cfg src\vmain.cpp
        $(CC) -c src\vmain.cpp

vmenu.obj: vistadll.cfg src\vmenu.cpp
        $(CC) -c src\vmenu.cpp

vscroll.obj: vistadll.cfg src\vscroll.cpp
        $(CC) -c src\vscroll.cpp

vstring.obj: vistadll.cfg src\vstring.cpp
        $(CC) -c src\vstring.cpp

vwindow.obj: vistadll.cfg src\vwindow.cpp
        $(CC) -c src\vwindow.cpp

#                 *Compiler Configuration File*
vistadll.cfg: vistadll.mak
   copy &&|
-R
-ml!
-3
-f287
-C
-v
-WD
-vi-
-H=VISTADLL.SYM
-wpro
-weas
-wpre
-nD:\VISTA\LIB
-I$(INCLUDEPATH)
-L$(LIBPATH)
-D_CLASSDLL
-P
| vistadll.cfg
```

```
/* --------------------------------------------------------
   vclip.h

      Interface for the VClipboard and VClipItem
classes.

   Copyright (C) 1992, by Jeff Mackay

-------------------------------------------------------- */
```

Listing A-78
VCLIP.H

Listing A-78
Continued.

```
#ifndef _VCLIP_H
#define _VCLIP_H

#ifndef _VISTA_H
#include <vista.h>
#endif

STDCLASS(VClipboard);
STDCLASS(VClipItem);

class _CLASSTYPE VClipboard
{
        public:
                VClipboard(VWindowPtr owner, Boolean empty=False);
        VClipboard(void);

                void Open(VWindowPtr owner,  Boolean empty=False);
                void Close(void);
        void Empty(void);
                void SetData(HGLOBAL data, UINT format=CF_TEXT);

                Boolean HasFormat(UINT format);
                HGLOBAL GetData(UINT format=CF_TEXT);

        private:
        static   VClipboardPtr clip;
                Boolean open;
};

class _CLASSTYPE VClipItem
{
        public:
        VClipItem(HGLOBAL copy);
                VClipItem(int size, UINT format=CF_TEXT);
                VClipItem(void);

                void SetContent(voidPtr content);
                void Allocate(void);

                voidPtr GetContent(void);
        int  GetSize(void) const;
        operator HGLOBAL(void) const;
        private:
        int     item_size;
        UINT    format;
        voidPtr content;
                HGLOBAL handle;
                Boolean locked;
};

#endif
```

Listing A-79
VCLIP.CPP

```cpp
/* --------------------------------------------------------
   vclip.cpp

        Interface for the VClipboard class.

   Copyright (C) 1992, by Jeff Mackay

   -------------------------------------------------------- */
#pragma hdrfile "vista.sym"
#include <vista.h>
#pragma hdrstop

#include "vclip.h"

VClipboardPtr VClipboard::clip;

VClipboard::VClipboard(VWindowPtr owner, Boolean empty)
{
        if (clip)
        {
                GetApplication().SetStatus(V_CLIPOPEN);
    }
        clip = this;
        Open(owner, empty);
}

VClipboard::VClipboard(void)
{
    clip = 0;
        Close();
}

void VClipboard::Open(VWindowPtr owner, Boolean empty)
{
        OpenClipboard(*owner);
    open = True;
        if (empty)
        Empty();
}
void VClipboard::Empty(void)
{
        EmptyClipboard();
}


void VClipboard::Close(void)
{
        if (open)
        {
                CloseClipboard();
                open = False;
```

Listing A-79
Continued.

```cpp
    }
}

Boolean VClipboard::HasFormat(UINT format)
{
    return (Boolean)IsClipboardFormatAvailable(format);
}

HGLOBAL VClipboard::GetData(UINT format)
{
    return GetClipboardData(format);
}

void VClipboard::SetData(HGLOBAL data, UINT format)
{
    SetClipboardData(format, data);
}
```

Listing A-80
VCLPITM.CPP

```cpp
/* -------------------------------------------------------------
    vclpitm.cpp

        Interface for the VClipItem class.

    Copyright (C) 1992, by Jeff Mackay

------------------------------------------------------------- */
#pragma hdrfile "vista.sym"
#include <vista.h>
#pragma hdrstop

#include "vclip.h"

VClipItem::VClipItem(HGLOBAL copy)
{
        item_size = 0;
    format    = 0;
        handle    = copy;
    locked    = False;
        content   = 0;
}

VClipItem::VClipItem(int size, UINT fmt)
{
        item_size = size;
    format    = fmt;
        handle    = 0;
    locked    = False;
        content   = 0;
```

```cpp
}

VClipItem::VClipItem(void)
{
        if (locked)
        GlobalUnlock(handle);
}

void VClipItem::Allocate(void)
{
        handle = GlobalAlloc(GHND, item_size);
}


void VClipItem::SetContent(voidPtr item)
{
        if (handle == 0)
                Allocate();
        content = GlobalLock(handle);
        _fmemcpy(content, item, item_size);
        GlobalUnlock(handle);
    content = 0;
}

// the client is responsible for freeing memory
// allocated by GetContent()
voidPtr VClipItem::GetContent(void)
{
        if (!content && handle)
    {
                item_size = GlobalSize(handle);
                voidPtr mem = GlobalLock(handle);
                content = new char[item_size];
                memcpy(content, mem, item_size);
                GlobalUnlock(handle);
        handle = 0;
    }
        return content;
}
VClipItem::operator HGLOBAL(void) const
{
        return handle;
}



/* ----------------------------------------------------------
   vdde.cpp

      Implemenation of DDE support classes
```

Listing A-81
VDDE.H

Listing A-81
Continued.

```
            Copyright (C) 1992, by Jeff Mackay
   -------------------------------------------------------- */

        #ifndef _VDDE_H
        #define _VDDE_H

        #include <ddeml.h>

        #ifndef _VDYNARR_H
        #include <vdynarr.h>
        #endif

        #ifndef _VHANDLE_H
        #include <vhandle.h>
        #endif

        STDCLASS(VDdeObject);
        STDCLASS(VDdeString);

        class _CLASSTYPE VDdeString
        {
                public:
                        VDdeString(charPtr str=0);
                        VDdeString(const VDdeStringCRef);
                        VDdeString(HSZ other);
                operator HSZ(void) const {return handle;}
                        int operator ==(HSZ other) const;
                        int operator ==(VDdeStringCRef other) const;
                        int operator !=(HSZ other) const;
                int operator !=(VDdeStringCRef other) const;
                VDdeStringCRef operator =(VDdeStringCRef copy);
                        VDdeStringCRef operator =(HSZ other);
                        VDdeStringCRef operator =(charPtr str);
                        operator charPtr(void);
                        void Keep(void);
                        void Free(void);

                private:
                static int code_page;
                HSZ handle;
        };

        struct VDdeEvent
        {
                UINT            type;
                UINT            format;
                HCONV           conv;
                HSZ             string1;
```

```cpp
        HSZ             string2;
        HDDEDATA        data_handle;
        DWORD           data1;
    DWORD       data2;
        HDDEDATA        response;
        void SetResponse(HDDEDATA resp) {response = resp;}
    void SetResponse(Boolean resp)  {response = (HDDEDATA)resp;}
        void SetResponse(UINT resp)     {response = (HDDEDATA)resp;}
        HDDEDATA GetResponse() { return response; }
};
STDTYPE(VDdeEvent);

// Use VDdeHandle for data received from DDE
template <class T> class _CLASSTYPE VDdeHandle
        : public VHandle<T, HDDEDATA>
{
        public:
                VDdeHandle(HDDEDATA hdl);
                VDdeHandle(void);
                virtual T FAR *DoLock(void);
                virtual void DoUnlock(void);
                int Size(void) const;

        private:
                DWORD    length;
};

// use VDdeData for data passed to DDE
template <class T> class _CLASSTYPE VDdeData
{
        public:
                VDdeData(VDdeStringCPtr name, T _FAR *obj,
                            DWORD size=0, UINT cf=0);
                VDdeData(T _FAR *obj, DWORD size=0, UINT cf=0);
                void Initialize(VDdeStringCPtr name, DWORD size, UINT cf);
                virtual VDdeData(void);
                void Create(UINT flags=0);
                void SetData(T _FAR *obj, DWORD size=0);
                void SetFormat(UINT fmt);
                operator HDDEDATA(void) const;
                operator T _FAR *(void) const;
                void Destroy(void);
                UINT Format(void) const;
                DWORD Size(void) const;
                VDdeStringPtr Name(void) const;

        protected:
            UINT                clip_format;
                HDDEDATA                handle;
```

Listing A-81
Continued.

```
                    T _FAR               *data;
            DWORD                 data_size;
            VDdeStringPtr   data_name;
};

typedef Boolean (VDdeObject::_FAR *VDdeCallback)(VDdeEventRef);

class _CLASSTYPE VDdeObject
{
        public:
                VDdeObject(void);
                virtual VDdeObject(void);
                operator DWORD(void) const { return id; }
                void SetCallback(VDdeCallback cbk, UINT index);
                VDdeCallback GetCallback(UINT index) const;
                virtual void Initialize(void);
                virtual void Cleanup(void);
                virtual int HandleError(void);

        protected:
                DWORD id;
                PFNCALLBACK callback;
                static HDDEDATA EXPENTRY _export
                        DdeCallback(UINT, UINT, HCONV, HSZ, HSZ, HDDEDATA,
                                        DWORD, DWORD);
                virtual void InitJumpTable(void);
                virtual Boolean ErrorCallback(VDdeEventRef event);
                virtual Boolean DisconnectCallback(VDdeEventRef event);
                virtual Boolean RegisterCallback(VDdeEventRef event);
                virtual Boolean UnregisterCallback(VDdeEventRef event);
                virtual Boolean DefaultCallback(VDdeEventRef event);
};

// returns a reference to the first dde object created
VDdeObjectRef GetDdeInstance(void);

template <class T>
VDdeHandle<T>::VDdeHandle(HDDEDATA hdl)
    : VHandle<T, HDDEDATA>(hdl)
{
}

template <class T> VDdeHandle<T>::VDdeHandle(void)
{
    Unlock();
}

template <class T> T FAR *VDdeHandle<T>::DoLock(void)
{
        return (T FAR *)DdeAccessData(handle, &length);
}
```

```
template <class T> void VDdeHandle<T>::DoUnlock(void)
{
        DdeUnaccessData(handle);
}

template <class T> inline int VDdeHandle<T>::Size(void) const
{
        return length;
}

template <class T>
VDdeData<T>::VDdeData(VDdeStringCPtr name, T _FAR *obj,
                                DWORD size, UINT cf)
        : data(obj)
{
    Initialize(name, size, cf);
        if (obj)
        Create();
}

template <class T>
VDdeData<T>::VDdeData(T _FAR *obj, DWORD size, UINT cf)
        : data(obj)
{
        Initialize(0, size, cf);
        if (obj)
        Create();
}
template <class T>
void VDdeData<T>::Initialize(VDdeStringCPtr name, DWORD size,
UINT cf)
{
        if (name == 0)
                data_name = 0;
        else
                data_name = new VDdeString(*name);
        clip_format = (cf == 0) ? CF_TEXT : cf;
        data_size = (size == 0) ? sizeof(T) : size;
}

template <class T>
VDdeData<T>::VDdeData(void)
{
        if (data_name)
                delete data_name;
}

template <class T>
void VDdeData<T>::Create(UINT flags=0)
{
        VASSERT(data != 0 && data_size != 0);
    HSZ name;
```

```cpp
            if (data_name != 0)
                    name = *data_name;
            else
            name = 0;
            handle = DdeCreateDataHandle(GetDdeInstance(),
                                    data, data_size, 0,
                                        name, clip_format, flags);
    VASSERT(handle != 0);
}

template <class T>
void VDdeData<T>::SetData(T _FAR *obj, DWORD size=0)
{
        data = obj;
    data_size = size;
}

template <class T>
inline void VDdeData<T>::SetFormat(UINT fmt)
{
    clip_format = fmt;
}

template <class T>
inline VDdeData<T>::operator HDDEDATA(void) const
{
        return handle;
}

template <class T>
inline VDdeData<T>::operator T _FAR *(void) const
{
        return data;
}

template <class T>
void VDdeData<T>::Destroy(void)
{
    DdeFreeDataHandle(handle);
}


template <class T>
UINT VDdeData<T>::Format(void) const
{
    return clip_format;
}

template <class T>
DWORD VDdeData<T>::Size(void) const
{
        return data_size;
```

```cpp
}

template <class T>
inline VDdeStringPtr VDdeData<T>::Name(void) const
{
    return data_name;
}


#endif



/*-----------------------------------------------------------      Listing A-82
    vdde.cpp                                                         VDDE.CPP

    Implementation of the VDdeObject class.

    Copyright (C) 1992, by Jeff Mackay

------------------------------------------------------------ */
#pragma hdrfile "vista.sym"
#include <vista.h>
#pragma hdrstop

#include <vdde.h>
#include <vmsgbox.h>
#include <iostream.h>

static VDdeObjectPtr object;
static VDdeCallback callbacks[16];



VDdeObjectRef GetDdeInstance(void)
{
        VASSERT(object != 0);
    return *object;
}


VDdeObject::VDdeObject(void)
{
        object = this;
        id = 0;
        callback = (PFNCALLBACK)
                MakeProcInstance((FARPROC)&VDdeObject::DdeCallback,
                                                GetApplication());
        memset(callbacks, 0, sizeof(callbacks));
}

VDdeObject::VDdeObject(void)
```

Listing A-82
Continued.

```
        {
                object = 0;
                if (callback)
                        FreeProcInstance((FARPROC)callback);
        }

        void VDdeObject::Initialize(void)
        {
                InitJumpTable();
        }

        void VDdeObject::Cleanup(void)
        {
                // placeholder
        }

        int VDdeObject::HandleError(void)
        {
                int status = DdeGetLastError(id);
                char buffer[64];
                wsprintf(buffer, "Encountered DDEML error: 0x%xh", status);
                VErrorBox errorBox(0, buffer);
                return errorBox.Execute();
        }

        void VDdeObject::InitJumpTable(void)
        {
                SetCallback(&VDdeObject::ErrorCallback,
                                XTYP_ERROR);
                SetCallback(&VDdeObject::DisconnectCallback,
                                XTYP_DISCONNECT);
                SetCallback(&VDdeObject::RegisterCallback,
                                XTYP_REGISTER);
                SetCallback(&VDdeObject::UnregisterCallback,
                                XTYP_UNREGISTER);

        }

        void VDdeObject::SetCallback(VDdeCallback callback, UINT index)
        {
                callbacks[LOBYTE(index) >> XTYP_SHIFT] = callback;
        }

        VDdeCallback VDdeObject::GetCallback(UINT index) const
        {
                return callbacks[LOBYTE(index) >> XTYP_SHIFT];
        }

        Boolean VDdeObject::DisconnectCallback(VDdeEventRef)
        {
            return False;
```

```
}

Boolean VDdeObject::ErrorCallback(VDdeEventRef)
{
    return False;
}

Boolean VDdeObject::RegisterCallback(VDdeEventRef)
{
    return False;
}

Boolean VDdeObject::UnregisterCallback(VDdeEventRef)
{
    return False;
}

Boolean VDdeObject::DefaultCallback(VDdeEventRef)
{
    return False;
}

HDDEDATA EXPENTRY _export
VDdeObject::DdeCallback(UINT typ, UINT fmt, HCONV conv,
                                HSZ hsz1, HSZ hsz2,HDDEDATA data,
                                DWORD p1, DWORD p2)
{
        VDdeEvent event;
        event.type = typ; event.format = fmt;
        event.conv = conv; event.string1 = hsz1;
        event.string2 = hsz2; event.data_handle = data;
        event.data1 = p1, event.data2 = p2;
        event.response = 0;
        VDdeObjectRef obj = GetDdeInstance();
    VDdeCallback callback;
        if ((callback = obj.GetCallback(typ)) != 0)
            (obj.*callback)(event);
        return (HDDEDATA) event.response;
}
```

```
/* --------------------------------------------------------
   vddeclnt.h

        Interface for the VDdeClient class.

   Copyright (C) 1992, by Jeff Mackay

   -------------------------------------------------------- */
```

Listing A-83
VDDECLNT.H

Listing A-83
Continued.

```
#ifndef _VDDECLNT_H
#define _VDDECLNT_H

#ifndef _VDDE_H
#include "vdde.h"
#endif


STDCLASS(VDdeConv);
class _CLASSTYPE VDdeConv
{

public:
    VDdeConv(DWORD value = 1000);
        VDdeConv(VDdeStringCRef service, VDdeStringCRef topic,
                        DWORD time=1000);
        VDdeConv(VDdeConvCRef copy);
        VDdeConv(HCONV copy);
        VDdeConvCRef operator =(VDdeConvCRef copy);
    VDdeConvCRef operator =(HCONV copy);
        VDdeConv(void);
    operator HCONV(void) const { return handle; }
        Boolean Connect(VDdeStringCRef service,
                                    VDdeStringCRef topic);
        void Disconnect(void);
        HCONV GetHandle(void) { return handle; }
        void SetTimeout(DWORD value) { timeout = value; }
        DWORD Timeout(void) const { return timeout; }
        DWORD GetXactId(void) const { return xact_status; }
    void ResetId(void) { xact_status = 0; }
        HDDEDATA Request(VDdeStringCRef item,
                                            UINT clip_format=CF_TEXT);
        Boolean StartAdvise(VDdeStringCRef item,
                                            UINT clip_format=CF_TEXT,
                        Boolean NeedData=True);
        Boolean StopAdvise(VDdeStringCRef item);
        HDDEDATA Execute(charCPtr command);
        HDDEDATA Poke(VDdeStringCRef item, voidPtr data,
                                    int data_size);
    HDDEDATA Poke(VDdeStringCRef item, HDDEDATA data);
        void Abandon(void);
        static VDdeConvPtr GetObject(HCONV conv, DWORD id);
protected:
    void SetAsynchData(void);
        HCONV handle;
    DWORD  timeout;
        DWORD xact_status;
};

STDCLASS(VDdeConvList);
class _CLASSTYPE VDdeConvList
```

```cpp
    {
    public:
            VDdeConvList(VDdeStringCRef service, VDdeStringCRef topic);
        VDdeConvList(void);
            VDdeConvList(void);
            VDdeConvList(VDdeConvListCRef copy);
            VDdeConvListCRef operator =(VDdeConvListCRef copy);
        VDdeConvListCRef operator =(HCONVLIST handle);
            operator HCONVLIST(void) const { return handle; }
            Boolean Connect(VDdeStringCRef service,
                                        VDdeStringCRef topic);
            void Disconnect(void);
            VDdeConvCRef First(void);
            VDdeConvCRef Next(void);
            HCONVLIST GetHandle(void) { return handle; }
    private:
            HCONVLIST handle;
            VDdeConv  last_conv;
    };

    STDCLASS(VDdeClient)
    class _CLASSTYPE VDdeClient : public VDdeObject
    {
            public:
                    VDdeClient(UINT flags=0);
                    VDdeClient(void);
                    virtual void Initialize(void);
                    virtual void Cleanup(void);

            protected:
            UINT client_flags;
            virtual void InitJumpTable(void);
                    virtual void AdvDataCallback(VDdeEventRef event);
                    virtual void CompleteCallback(VDdeEventRef event);
    };

    #endif



    /* ----------------------------------------------------------
       vddeclnt.cpp

            Implementation of the VDdeClient class

       Copyright (C) 1992, by Jeff Mackay

       ------------------------------------------------------ */
    #pragma hdrfile "vista.sym"
```

Listing A-84
VDDECLNT.CPP

Listing A-84
Continued.

```cpp
#include <vista.h>
#pragma hdrstop
#include <vddclnt.h>

VDdeClient::VDdeClient(UINT flags)
{
        client_flags = flags;
}

void VDdeClient::Initialize(void)
{
        VDdeObject::Initialize();
        if (client_flags == 0)
        client_flags = APPCMD_CLIENTONLY;
        UINT status = DdeInitialize(&id,
                                        &VDdeObject::DdeCallback,
                                    client_flags|APPCLASS_STANDARD,
0);
        if (status != DMLERR_NO_ERROR)
                HandleError();
}

void VDdeClient::Cleanup(void)
{
        DdeUninitialize(*this);
        VDdeObject::Cleanup();
}

void VDdeClient::InitJumpTable(void)
{
    VDdeObject::InitJumpTable();
        SetCallback((VDdeCallback)&VDdeClient::AdvDataCallback,
                                XTYP_ADVDATA);

SetCallback((VDdeCallback)&VDdeClient::CompleteCallback,
                                XTYP_XACT_COMPLETE);
}

VDdeClient::VDdeClient(void)
{
}

void VDdeClient::AdvDataCallback(VDdeEventRef)
{
}

void VDdeClient::CompleteCallback(VDdeEventRef)
{
}
```

```cpp
/* -------------------------------------------------------------
    vddeconv.cpp

        Implementation of the VDdeConv and VDdeConvList classes.

    Copyright (C) 1992, by Jeff Mackay
   ------------------------------------------------------------- */
#pragma hdrfile "vista.sym"
#include <vista.h>
#pragma hdrstop

#include <vddeclnt.h>

VDdeConv::VDdeConv(DWORD value)
{
        xact_status = 0;
        handle = 0;
    timeout = value;
}

VDdeConv::VDdeConv(VDdeStringCRef service, VDdeStringCRef topic,
                                    DWORD value)
{
    handle = 0;
        xact_status = 0;
    timeout = value;
        Connect(service, topic);
}

VDdeConv::VDdeConv(VDdeConvCRef copy)
{
        handle = copy.handle;
}

VDdeConv::VDdeConv(HCONV copy)
{
        handle = copy;
}

VDdeConvCRef VDdeConv::operator =(VDdeConvCRef copy)
{
        handle = copy.handle;
    return *this;
}

VDdeConvCRef VDdeConv::operator =(HCONV copy)
{
        handle = copy;
    return *this;
}

Boolean VDdeConv::Connect(VDdeStringCRef service,
```

Listing A-85
Continued.

```
                                              VDdeStringCRef topic)
{
        handle = DdeConnect(GetDdeInstance(), service, topic, 0);
    if (handle != 0)
        return True;
    else
        return False;
}

void VDdeConv::Disconnect(void)
{
        if (handle == 0)
                return;

        if (DdeDisconnect(handle) != DMLERR_NO_ERROR)
        GetDdeInstance().HandleError();
}

VDdeConv::VDdeConv(void)
{
        Disconnect();
        handle = 0;
}

HDDEDATA VDdeConv::Request(VDdeStringCRef item, UINT clip_format)
{
        VASSERT((HSZ)item != 0);

        if (timeout == TIMEOUT_ASYNC)
        VASSERT(xact_status == 0);
        HDDEDATA result = DdeClientTransaction(0, 0, handle, item,
                                                        clip_format,
XTYP_REQUEST,
                                                                timeout,
&xact_status);
        SetAsynchData();
    return result;
}

Boolean VDdeConv::StartAdvise(VDdeStringCRef item, UINT clip_format,
                        Boolean NeedData)
{
        VASSERT((HSZ)item != 0);
        UINT xact_type = XTYP_ADVSTART | XTYPF_ACKREQ;
        if (NeedData == False)
        xact_type |= XTYPF_NODATA;
        HDDEDATA result = DdeClientTransaction(0, 0, handle, item,
                                                        clip_format,
xact_type,
                                                                timeout,
&xact_status);
    SetAsynchData();
```

```cpp
            if (result == 0)
                    return False;
            else
            return True;
}
Boolean VDdeConv::StopAdvise(VDdeStringCRef item)
{
        VASSERT((HSZ)item != 0);
        HDDEDATA result = DdeClientTransaction(0, 0, handle, item,
                                                                0, XTYP_ADVSTOP,
timeout, &xact_status);
    SetAsynchData();
        if (result == 0)
                return False;
        else
        return True;
}

HDDEDATA VDdeConv::Execute(charCPtr command)
{
    VASSERT(command != 0);
        HDDEDATA result = DdeClientTransaction((voidPtr)command,
                                                    strlen(command), handle, 0,
CF_TEXT, XTYP_EXECUTE,
timeout, &xact_status);
        SetAsynchData();
        return result;
}

HDDEDATA VDdeConv::Poke(VDdeStringCRef item, voidPtr data, int data_size)
{
    VASSERT((HSZ)item != 0);
        HDDEDATA result = DdeClientTransaction(data, data_size, handle, item,
                                                        0, XTYP_POKE,
                                                        timeout,
&xact_status);
        SetAsynchData();
        return result;
}

HDDEDATA VDdeConv::Poke(VDdeStringCRef item, HDDEDATA data)
{
    VASSERT((HSZ)item != 0);
       HDDEDATA result = DdeClientTransaction((LPVOID)data, -1, handle, item,
                                                    0, XTYP_POKE,
                            timeout, &xact_status);
        SetAsynchData();
```

Listing A-85
Continued.

```cpp
        return result;
}

void VDdeConv::SetAsynchData(void)
{
        if (timeout == TIMEOUT_ASYNC)
        {
        VASSERT(xact_status != 0);
        DdeSetUserHandle(handle, xact_status, (DWORD)this);
    }
}

void VDdeConv::Abandon(void)
{
    VASSERT(xact_status != 0);
        DdeAbandonTransaction(GetDdeInstance(), handle, xact_status);
}

VDdeConvPtr VDdeConv::GetObject(HCONV conv, DWORD id)
{
        CONVINFO info;
    info.cb = sizeof(info);
        int result = DdeQueryConvInfo(conv, id, &info);
        if (result == 0)
        return 0;
        else
                return (VDdeConvPtr)info.hUser;
}

/*-----------------------------------------------------------------
VDdeConvList member functions
------------------------------------------------------------------ */
VDdeConvList::VDdeConvList(void)
{
        handle = 0;
}

VDdeConvList::VDdeConvList(VDdeConvListCRef copy)
{
        handle = copy.handle;
    last_conv = copy.last_conv;
}

VDdeConvListCRef VDdeConvList::operator =(VDdeConvListCRef copy)
{
        handle = copy.handle;
        last_conv = copy.last_conv;
        return *this;
}

VDdeConvList::VDdeConvList(VDdeStringCRef service,
```

```cpp
                                             VDdeStringCRef topic)
{
        handle = 0;
        Connect(service,topic);
}

Boolean VDdeConvList::Connect(VDdeStringCRef service,
                                             VDdeStringCRef topic)
{
        handle = DdeConnectList(GetDdeInstance(), service, topic,
                                             handle, 0);
    if (handle != 0)
        return True;
    else
        return False;
}

void VDdeConvList::Disconnect(void)
{
        if (handle && !DdeDisconnectList(handle))
        GetDdeInstance().HandleError();
}

VDdeConvList::VDdeConvList(void)
{
}

VDdeConvCRef VDdeConvList::First(void)
{
        last_conv = (HCONV)0;
    return Next();
}

VDdeConvCRef VDdeConvList::Next(void)
{
        last_conv = DdeQueryNextServer(handle, last_conv);
        return last_conv;
}

/* ------------------------------------------------------
    vddeserv.h

        Interface for the VDdeServer class.

    Copyright (C) 1992, by Jeff Mackay

    ------------------------------------------------------ */

#ifndef _VDDESERV_H
```

Listing A-86
VDDESERV.H

Listing A-86
Continued.

```c
#define _VDDESERV_H

#ifndef _VISTA_H
#include <vista.h>
#endif

#ifndef _VDDE_H
#include "vdde.h"
#endif

STDCLASS(VDdeServer);
STDCLASS(VDdeTopic);
STDCLASS(VDdeService);

class _CLASSTYPE VDdeTopic
{
    public:
        VDdeString name;
        VDynArray<VDdeString> items;
        VDdeTopic(void) {}
    VDdeTopic(VDdeStringCRef nm) : name(nm) {}
        int operator ==(VDdeTopicCRef other)
            {return name == other.name;}
        int operator ==(VDdeStringCRef other)
            {return name == other;}
        void AddItem(VDdeStringCRef nm)
        {
        items.Add(nm);
}
        VDdeTopicRef operator =(VDdeStringCRef nm)
            {
                name = nm;
                return *this;
    }
        VDdeTopicRef operator =(VDdeTopicCRef other)
            {
                name = other.name;
                items = other.items;
        return *this;
            }
        VDdeStringRef operator[](int ndx)
            { return items[ndx]; }
        int ItemCount(void) const
        {
            return items.Members();
    }
};

class _CLASSTYPE VDdeService
{
    public:
        VDdeString name;
```

```cpp
        VDynArray<VDdeTopic> topics;
        int operator ==(VDdeServiceCRef svc)
                { return name == svc.name; }
        int operator ==(VDdeStringCRef str)
    { return name == str; }

        VDdeServiceRef operator =(VDdeServiceCRef other)
        {
                name = other.name;
                topics = other.topics;
    return *this;
}

        VDdeServiceRef operator =(VDdeStringCRef nm)
        {
                name = nm;
                return *this;
        }

        VDdeTopicRef operator [](int ndx)
        {
                return topics[ndx];
        }

        void AddTopic(VDdeTopicCRef topic)
        {
        topics.Add(topic);
        }

        int TopicCount(void) const
        {
                return topics.Members();
        }
    }
};


class _CLASSTYPE VDdeServer : public VDdeObject
{
        public:
                VDdeServer(UINT flags=0);
                virtual VDdeServer(void);
                virtual void Initialize(void);
                virtual void Cleanup(void);
                virtual void Register(VDdeStringCRef svcName);
                virtual void Register(void)
                        { Register(service.name); }
                virtual void Unregister(void);

        protected:
        UINT serv_flags;
                virtual Boolean AdvRequestCallback(VDdeEventRef);
                virtual Boolean AdvStartCallback(VDdeEventRef);
```

Appendix **491**

Listing A-86
Continued.

```cpp
            virtual Boolean AdvStopCallback(VDdeEventRef);
            virtual Boolean ConnectCallback(VDdeEventRef);
    virtual Boolean ConfirmCallback(VDdeEventRef);
            virtual Boolean ExecuteCallback(VDdeEventRef);
            virtual Boolean PokeCallback(VDdeEventRef);
            virtual Boolean RequestCallback(VDdeEventRef);
            virtual Boolean WildcardCallback(VDdeEventRef);

            // system item support
            virtual charPtr SystemTopics(void);
            virtual charPtr SystemSysItems(void);
            virtual charPtr SystemFormats(void);
            virtual charPtr SystemStatus(void);
            virtual charPtr SystemHelp(void);
    virtual charPtr SystemItemList(void);
            virtual void InitJumpTable(void);

            VDdeService service;
            Boolean registered;
    };

    #endif
```

Listing A-87
VDDESERV.CPP

```cpp
/* ---------------------------------------------------------------
    vddeserv.cpp

            Implementation of the VDdeServer class

    Copyright (C) 1992, by Jeff Mackay

--------------------------------------------------------------- */
#pragma hdrfile "vista.sym"
#include <vista.h>
#pragma hdrstop

#include <vddeserv.h>

static Boolean newSysTopic = True;
static VDdeTopic sysTopic;

VDdeServer::VDdeServer(UINT flags)
{
    serv_flags = flags;
    registered = False;
    if (newSysTopic)
    {
        newSysTopic = False;
        sysTopic.name = VDdeString(SZDDESYS_TOPIC);

sysTopic.AddItem(VDdeString(SZDDESYS_ITEM_TOPICS));
```

```cpp
                    sysTopic.AddItem(VDdeString(SZDDESYS_ITEM_SYSITEMS));
                    sysTopic.AddItem(VDdeString(SZDDESYS_ITEM_STATUS));
                    sysTopic.AddItem(VDdeString(SZDDESYS_ITEM_FORMATS));
                    sysTopic.AddItem(VDdeString(SZDDESYS_ITEM_HELP));
                    sysTopic.AddItem(VDdeString(SZDDE_ITEM_ITEMLIST));
    }
        service.AddTopic(sysTopic);
}

void VDdeServer::Initialize(void)
{
        VDdeObject::Initialize();
        if (DdeInitialize(&id, callback,
                                serv_flags | APPCMD_FILTERINITS, 0L))
        HandleError();
        Register();
}

void VDdeServer::Register(VDdeStringCRef svcName)
{
        service.name = svcName;
        if (!DdeNameService(*this, service.name,
                                                0, DNS_REGISTER))
                HandleError();
    else
                registered = True;
}

void VDdeServer::Unregister(void)
{
        if (registered)
        {
        if (!DdeNameService(*this, service.name, 0,
                                                    DNS_UNREGISTER))
                    HandleError();
                else
                registered = False;
    }
}

void VDdeServer::Cleanup(void)
{
    // Unregister();
        DdeUninitialize(id);
        VDdeObject::Cleanup();
}


void VDdeServer::InitJumpTable(void)
{
    VDdeObject::InitJumpTable();
```

Listing A-87
Continued.

```
    SetCallback((VDdeCallback)&VDdeServer::AdvRequestCallback,
                            XTYP_ADVREQ);

    SetCallback((VDdeCallback)&VDdeServer::AdvStartCallback,
                            XTYP_ADVSTART);

    SetCallback((VDdeCallback)&VDdeServer::AdvStopCallback,
                            XTYP_ADVSTOP);

    SetCallback((VDdeCallback)&VDdeServer::ConnectCallback,
                            XTYP_CONNECT);

    SetCallback((VDdeCallback)&VDdeServer::ConfirmCallback,
                            XTYP_CONNECT_CONFIRM);

    SetCallback((VDdeCallback)&VDdeServer::ExecuteCallback,
                            XTYP_EXECUTE);

    SetCallback((VDdeCallback)&VDdeServer::RequestCallback,
                    XTYP_REQUEST);

    SetCallback((VDdeCallback)&VDdeServer::PokeCallback,
                            XTYP_POKE);

    SetCallback((VDdeCallback)&VDdeServer::WildcardCallback,
                        XTYP_WILDCONNECT);
}

VDdeServer::VDdeServer(void)
{
}

Boolean VDdeServer::AdvRequestCallback(VDdeEventRef)
{
    return True;
}

Boolean VDdeServer::AdvStartCallback(VDdeEventRef)
{
    return True;
}

Boolean VDdeServer::AdvStopCallback(VDdeEventRef)
{
        return True;
}

Boolean VDdeServer::ExecuteCallback(VDdeEventRef)
{
        return True;
}
```

```cpp
Boolean VDdeServer::ConnectCallback(VDdeEventRef event)
{
        if (VDdeString(event.string2) == service.name)
        {
        VDdeString topic(event.string1);
                for (int i=0; i<service.topics.arraySize(); i++)
                {
                        if (service[i].name == 0)
                                break;

                        if (topic == service[i].name)
        {
                                event.SetResponse(True);
                break;
        }

        }
        }
        else
        {
                if (VDdeString(event.string1) == VDdeString(SZDDESYS_TOPIC))
                {
                        event.SetResponse(True);
                }
        }
        return (Boolean)event.GetResponse();
}

Boolean VDdeServer::ConfirmCallback(VDdeEventRef)
{
    return True;
}

Boolean VDdeServer::PokeCallback(VDdeEventRef)
{
    return True;
}

Boolean VDdeServer::RequestCallback(VDdeEventRef)
{
        if (VDdeString(event.string1) == sysTopic.name)
        {
                charPtr str;
        VDdeString topic(event.string2);
                if (topic == sysTopic[0])
        {
                        str = SystemTopics();
                        delete str;
        }
                else if (topic == sysTopic[1])
                str = SystemSysItems();
                else if (topic == sysTopic[2])
```

Listing A-87
Continued.

```
                            str = SystemFormats();
                    else if (topic == sysTopic[3])
                        str = SystemStatus();
                    else if (topic == sysTopic[4])
                            str = SystemHelp();
                    else if (topic == sysTopic[5])
        {
                            str = SystemItemList();
                        delete str;
        }
                    VDdeData<char> data_obj(str, lstrlen(str));
                    event.SetResponse(data_obj);

        }
            UNREFERENCED_PARAMETER(event);
        return True;
}

charPtr VDdeServer::SystemTopics(void)
{
        VString topicString;
        int topicCount;

        if (topicCount == 0)
                return 0;

        VDdeString str = service.topics[0].name;
        charPtr tempStr = str;
    delete tempStr;
        for(int i=1; i<topicCount; i++)
        {
                str = service.topics[i].name;
        tempStr = str;
        topicString = topicString + "\t" + tempStr;
        delete tempStr;
        }
        return topicString;
}

charPtr VDdeServer::SystemItemList(void)
{
        return 0;
}
charPtr VDdeServer::SystemSysItems(void)
{
        return(

"SysItems\tTopics\tStatus\tFormats\tHelp\tTopicItemList");
}

charPtr VDdeServer::SystemFormats(void)
{
        return("TEXT");
```

```cpp
}

charPtr VDdeServer::SystemStatus(void)
{
        return("Ready");
}

charPtr VDdeServer::SystemHelp(void)
{
        return("No help available");
}

Boolean VDdeServer::WildcardCallback(VDdeEventRef event)
{
        if (VDdeString(event.string2) != service.name &&
               event.string1 != 0)
                        return False;

        int topicCount = service.TopicCount();
        HSZPAIR *pair = new HSZPAIR[topicCount+1];
        VASSERT(pair);
    int i,j;
        for (i=0,j=0; i < topicCount; i++)
        {
                if (event.string1 == 0 ||
                    VDdeString(event.string1) == service[i].name)
                {
                        pair[i].hszSvc = service.name;
                        pair[j++].hszTopic   = service[i].name;
                }
        }
        pair[j].hszTopic = 0;
        pair[j].hszTopic = 0;

        VDdeData<HSZPAIR> data_obj(pair, j*sizeof(HSZPAIR));
        event.SetResponse(data_obj);
    return True;
}
```

Listing A-88
VDDESTR.CPP

```cpp
/* ---------------------------------------------------------
   vddestr.cpp

        Implementation of the VDdeString class

   Copyright (C) 1992, by Jeff Mackay
   --------------------------------------------------- */

#pragma hdrfile "vista.sym"
#include <vista.h>
#pragma hdrstop
```

Listing A-88
Continued.

```cpp
#include <vdde.h>
int VDdeString::code_page;

VDdeString::VDdeString(charPtr str)
{
    if (!code_page)
    code_page = GetKBCodePage();
    if (str)
    {
        handle =
DdeCreateStringHandle(GetDdeInstance(),
str, code_page);
        VASSERT (handle != 0);
    }
    else
    {
        handle = 0;
    }
}

VDdeString::VDdeString(const VDdeStringCRef copy)
{
    if (!code_page)
    code_page = GetKBCodePage();
    handle = copy.handle;
}

VDdeString::VDdeString(HSZ other)
{
    if (!code_page)
    code_page = GetKBCodePage();
    handle = other;
}

int VDdeString::operator ==(HSZ other) const
{
    int result;
    if (handle != other)
    {
        result = (DdeCmpStringHandles(handle, other)
== 0);
    }
    else
    {
        result = True;
    }
    return result;
}

int VDdeString::operator ==(VDdeStringCRef other) const
```

```cpp
{
        return (*this == other.handle);
}

int VDdeString::operator !=(VDdeStringCRef other) const
{
        return !(*this == other);
}

int VDdeString::operator !=(HSZ other) const
{
        return !(*this == other);
}

VDdeStringCRef VDdeString::operator =(VDdeStringCRef copy)
{
        handle = copy.handle;
    return *this;
}

VDdeStringCRef VDdeString::operator =(HSZ other)
{
        handle = other;
    return *this;
}

VDdeStringCRef VDdeString::operator =(charPtr str)
{
        handle = DdeCreateStringHandle(GetDdeInstance(),
                                                                str,
code_page);
        VASSERT(handle != 0);
    return *this;
}


// client must delete the returned pointer
VDdeString::operator charPtr(void)
{
        int length = DdeQueryString(GetDdeInstance(),
                                                        handle, 0, 0, code_page);
        charPtr buffer = new char[length];
        DdeQueryString(GetDdeInstance(),
                                handle, buffer, length, code_page);
    return buffer;
}

void VDdeString::Keep(void)
{
        DdeKeepStringHandle(GetDdeInstance(), handle);
}
```

Listing A-88
Continued.
```
void VDdeString::Free(void)
{
        DdeFreeStringHandle(GetDdeInstance(), handle);
}
```

Listing A-89
VOLECDOC.CPP
```
/* -----------------------------------------------------------
    volecdoc.cpp

        Implementation of the VOleClientDoc class

    Copyright (C) 1992, by Jeff Mackay
    ----------------------------------------------------------- */

#pragma hdrfile "vista.sym"
#include <vista.h>
#pragma hdrstop

#include <voleclnt.h>

static char oleProtocol[] = "StdFileEditing";

VOleClientDoc::VOleClientDoc(charCPtr name, VWindowPtr own)
    : VOleClient(own)
{
        handle    = 0;
        doc_name  = name;
        obj_count = 0;
    registered = False;
    dirty      = True;
        if (owner == 0)
                owner  = GetApplication().GetMainWindow();
}

LPOLEOBJECT VOleClientDoc::First(void)
{
    return Next(0);
}

LPOLEOBJECT VOleClientDoc::Next(LPOLEOBJECT obj)
{
        LPOLEOBJECT objVar = obj;
        SetStatus(OleEnumObjects(handle, &objVar));
    return objVar;
}

charPtr VOleClientDoc::NewObjectName(charPtr buff)
{
        if (buff == 0)
                buff = new char[256];
```

```
        char name[128];
            wsprintf(buff, "%d", obj_count);
        return buff;
}

charPtr VOleClientDoc::QueryName(charPtr buff)
{
        if (buff == 0)
                return doc_name;
        else
    {
                lstrcpy(buff, doc_name);
                return buff;
    }
}

void VOleClientDoc::Register(charCPtr className, charCPtr docName)
{
        SetStatus(OleRegisterClientDoc(className, docName, 0,
                                                            &handle));
        if (GetStatus() == OLE_OK)
        registered = True;
}

void VOleClientDoc::Rename(charCPtr docName)
{
        SetStatus(OleRenameClientDoc(handle, docName));
}

void VOleClientDoc::Revoke(void)
{
        if (registered)
        {
            registered = False;
                SetStatus(OleRevokeClientDoc(handle));
    }
}
void VOleClientDoc::Saved(void)
{
    SetStatus(OleSavedClientDoc(handle));
        dirty = False;
}

Boolean VOleClientDoc::CanPaste(OLEOPT_RENDER opt,
OLECLIPFORMAT fmt)
{
        OLESTATUS stat =
                OleQueryCreateFromClip(oleProtocol, opt, fmt);
    return (stat == OLE_OK) ? True : False;

}
```

Appendix **501**

Listing A-89
Continued.

```
Boolean VOleClientDoc::CanPasteLink(OLEOPT_RENDER opt,
        OLECLIPFORMAT fmt)
{
        OLESTATUS stat =
                OleQueryLinkFromClip(oleProtocol, opt, fmt);
    return (Boolean)(stat == OLE_OK);
}

VOleClientObjPtr VOleClientDoc::NewObject(void)
{
        return 0;
}

VOleClientObjPtr VOleClientDoc::Create(charPtr className,
        charPtr objName, OLEOPT_RENDER opt, OLECLIPFORMAT fmt)
{
    Boolean delName = False;
    if (objName == 0)
        {
        delName = True;
            objName = NewObjectName();
    }

        VOleClientObjPtr obj = NewObject();
        obj->Wait(OleCreate(oleProtocol, obj, className,
                *this, objName, &obj->handle, opt, fmt), obj);
        if (delName)
                delete objName;
        return obj;
}

VOleClientObjPtr VOleClientDoc::Invisible(charPtr className,
        charPtr objName, OLEOPT_RENDER opt, OLECLIPFORMAT fmt)
{
    Boolean delName = False;
    if (objName == 0)
        {
        delName = True;
            objName = NewObjectName();
    }

        VOleClientObjPtr obj = NewObject();
        obj->Wait(OleCreate(oleProtocol, obj, className,
                *this, objName, &obj->handle, opt, fmt), obj);
        if (delName)
                delete objName;
        return obj;
}

VOleClientObjPtr VOleClientDoc::FromClip(charPtr objName,
```

```cpp
                                        OLEOPT_RENDER opt, OLECLIPFORMAT fmt)
{
        Boolean delName = False;
        if (objName == 0)
        {
                delName = True;
                objName = NewObjectName();
        }

        VOleClientObjPtr obj = NewObject();
        obj->Wait(OleCreateFromClip(oleProtocol, obj, *this,
                        objName, &obj->handle, opt, fmt), obj);
        if (delName)
                delete objName;
    return obj;
}

VOleClientObjPtr VOleClientDoc::FromFile(charPtr fileName,
                charPtr className, charPtr objName, OLEOPT_RENDER opt,
                OLECLIPFORMAT fmt)
{
        Boolean delName = False;
        if (objName == 0)
        {
                delName = True;
                objName = NewObjectName();
        }

        VOleClientObjPtr obj = NewObject();
        obj->Wait(OleCreateFromFile(oleProtocol, obj, className,
                fileName, *this, objName, &obj->handle, opt, fmt),
obj);
        if (delName)
                delete objName;
    return obj;
}
VOleClientObjPtr VOleClientDoc::FromTemplate(charPtr fileName,
                charPtr className, charPtr objName, OLEOPT_RENDER opt,
                OLECLIPFORMAT fmt)
{
        Boolean delName = False;
        if (objName == 0)
        {
                delName = True;
                objName = NewObjectName();
        }

        VOleClientObjPtr obj = NewObject();
        obj->Wait(OleCreateFromFile(oleProtocol, obj, className,
                fileName, *this, objName, &obj->handle, opt, fmt), obj);
        if (delName)
                delete objName;
```

Listing A-89
Continued.

```
        return obj;
}

VOleClientObjPtr VOleClientDoc::LinkFromClip(charPtr objName,
            OLEOPT_RENDER opt, OLECLIPFORMAT fmt)
{
        Boolean delName = False;
        if (objName == 0)
        {
                delName = True;
                objName = NewObjectName();
        }

        VOleClientObjPtr obj = NewObject();
        obj->Wait(OleCreateFromClip(oleProtocol, obj, *this,
                            objName, &obj->handle, opt, fmt), obj);
        if (delName)
                delete objName;
    return obj;
}

VOleClientObjPtr VOleClientDoc::LinkFromFile(charPtr fileName,
            charPtr className, charPtr objName,
            OLEOPT_RENDER opt, OLECLIPFORMAT fmt)
{
        Boolean delName = False;
        if (objName == 0)
        {
                delName = True;
                objName = NewObjectName();
        }

        VOleClientObjPtr obj = NewObject();
        obj->Wait(OleCreateFromFile(oleProtocol, obj, className,
                    fileName, *this, objName, &obj->handle,
                    opt, fmt), obj);
        if (delName)
                delete objName;
    return obj;
}
```

Listing A-90
VOLECLNT.H

```
/* ------------------------------------------------------------
    voleclnt.h

        Interface for the VOleClient and supporting classes.

    Copyright (C) 1992, by Jeff Mackay
   ----------------------------------------------------------- */
```

```c
#ifndef _VOLECLNT_H
#define _VOLECLNT_H

#ifndef __OLE_H
#include <ole.h>
#endif

#ifndef _VOLEERR_H
#include "voleerr.h"
#endif

#ifndef _VGRDEV_H
#include <vgrdev.h>
#endif

STDCLASS(VOleClientObj);
STDCLASS(VOleClientDoc);
STDCLASS(VOleClient);
STDCLASS(VOleStream);

class _CLASSTYPE VOleClient : public OLECLIENT
{
        public:
                VOleClient(VWindowPtr win=0);
                VOleClient(void);
                void SetStatus(OLESTATUS value) { status = value; }
                OLESTATUS GetStatus(void) { return status; }
                virtual void Wait(OLESTATUS, VOleClientObjPtr);
                VWindowPtr GetOwner(void) { return owner; }
                void SetOwner(VWindowPtr win) { owner = win; }

        protected:
                OLESTATUS                status;
                VWindowPtr               owner;
                virtual int  Callback(OLE_NOTIFICATION, LPOLEOBJECT);
                virtual void ChangedCallback(LPOLEOBJECT);
                 virtual void ClosedCallback(LPOLEOBJECT);
                  virtual Boolean QueryPaintCallback(LPOLEOBJECT);
                   virtual Boolean QueryRetryCallback(LPOLEOBJECT);
                    virtual void ReleaseCallback(LPOLEOBJECT);
                     virtual void SavedCallback(LPOLEOBJECT);
                      virtual void RenamedCallback(LPOLEOBJECT);
                friend class VOleClientImp;

        private:
                static OLECLIENTVTBL     vtbl;
                static int               ref_count;
};

class _CLASSTYPE VOleClientDoc : public VOleClient
{
        public:
```

Listing A-90
Continued.

```cpp
        VOleClientDoc(charCPtr name, VWindowPtr own=0);
        operator LHCLIENTDOC(void) { return handle; }
        LPOLEOBJECT First(void);
        LPOLEOBJECT Next(LPOLEOBJECT);
        Boolean    IsDirty(void) const { return dirty; }
        Boolean CanPaste(OLEOPT_RENDER opt=olerender_draw,
                 OLECLIPFORMAT=CF_METAFILEPICT);
        Boolean CanPasteLink(OLEOPT_RENDER opt=olerender_draw,
                 OLECLIPFORMAT=CF_METAFILEPICT);
        charPtr QueryName(charPtr=0);
        charPtr NewObjectName(charPtr=0);
        VOleClientObjPtr Create(charPtr className,
                        charPtr objName=0,
                        OLEOPT_RENDER opt=olerender_draw,
                        OLECLIPFORMAT=CF_METAFILEPICT);
        VOleClientObjPtr FromClip(charPtr objName=0,
                        OLEOPT_RENDER opt=olerender_draw,
                        OLECLIPFORMAT=CF_METAFILEPICT);
        VOleClientObjPtr Invisible(charPtr className,
                        charPtr objName=0,
                        OLEOPT_RENDER opt=olerender_draw,
                        OLECLIPFORMAT=CF_METAFILEPICT);
        VOleClientObjPtr FromFile(charPtr fileName,
                       charPtr className,
                          charPtr objName=0,
                          OLEOPT_RENDER opt=olerender_draw,
                          OLECLIPFORMAT=CF_METAFILEPICT);
        VOleClientObjPtr FromTemplate(charPtr fileName,
                       charPtr className,
                          charPtr objName=0,
                          OLEOPT_RENDER opt=olerender_draw,
                          OLECLIPFORMAT=CF_METAFILEPICT);
        VOleClientObjPtr LinkFromClip(charPtr objName=0,
                          OLEOPT_RENDER opt=olerender_draw,
                          OLECLIPFORMAT=CF_METAFILEPICT);
        VOleClientObjPtr LinkFromFile(charPtr fileName,
                       charPtr className,
                          charPtr objName=0,
                          OLEOPT_RENDER opt=olerender_draw,
                          OLECLIPFORMAT=CF_METAFILEPICT);
        virtual VOleClientObjPtr NewObject(void);
        void AddObject(void) { ++obj_count; }
        void Register(charCPtr className, charCPtr docName);
        void Rename(charCPtr docName);
        void Revoke(void);
        void Saved(void);

protected:
        int             obj_count;
        LHCLIENTDOC     handle;
```

```cpp
              Boolean       registered;
              Boolean       dirty;
              VString        doc_name;
};

class _CLASSTYPE VOleClientObj : public VOleClient
{
        public:
              VOleClientObj(void);
              VOleClientObj(VOleClientDocPtr par, LPOLEOBJECT=0);
              VOleClientObj(VOleClientDocPtr par, VWindowPtr own,
                            LPOLEOBJECT=0);
              VOleClientObj(VOleClientObjRef copy);

              VOleClientObjRef operator =(VOleClientObjRef copy);
              VOleClientObjRef operator =(LPOLEOBJECT obj)
              { handle = obj; return *this; }
              int operator ==(VOleClientObjRef);
              int operator !=(VOleClientObjRef other)
                    { return !(*this == other); }
    operator LPOLEOBJECT(void) { return handle; }
              void SetHandle(LPOLEOBJECT obj) { handle = obj; }

              void Activate(WORD=0, BOOL=TRUE, BOOL=TRUE, RECT FAR *rect=0);
              void Close(void);
              void CopyToClipboard(void);
              void Delete(void);
              void Draw(VDevicePtr win=0, RECT FAR *bRect=0,
                            RECT FAR *wRect=0, VDevicePtr dev=0);
              void Execute(charCPtr);
      void Reconnect(void);
              void Release(void);
              void Rename(charCPtr objName);
      void SetBounds(RECT FAR *rect=0);
              void SetData(OLECLIPFORMAT, HANDLE);
              void SetHostNames(charCPtr clientName,
                                        charCPtr docName=0);
              void Update(void);

              OLECLIPFORMAT First(void);
              OLECLIPFORMAT Next(OLECLIPFORMAT);
      void RequestData(OLECLIPFORMAT);
              void GetData(OLECLIPFORMAT, HANDLE FAR *);
              RECT FAR *QueryBounds(RECT FAR *);
              charPtr QueryName(charPtr buffer=0, UINT FAR *sizePtr=0);
              Boolean QueryOpen(void);
              Boolean QueryOutOfDate(void);
      Boolean QueryProtocol(charPtr protocol);
              DWORD   QuerySize(void);
              LONG    QueryType(void);
              friend class VOleClientDoc;
```

Listing A-90
Continued.

```cpp
            protected:
                    void Init(VOleClientDocPtr par, VWindowPtr own,
                        LPOLEOBJECT hdl);
                    VOleClientDocPtr parent;
                    LPOLEOBJECT      handle;
                VString              obj_name;
        };

        inline void VOleClientObj::Init(VOleClientDocPtr par,
                                     VWindowPtr own, LPOLEOBJECT obj)
        {
                parent = par;
                owner  = own;
            handle = obj;
        }

        class _CLASSTYPE VOleStream : public OLESTREAM
        {
                public:
                        VOleStream(void);
                        VOleStream(void);
                        void SetStatus(OLESTATUS value) { status = value; }
                OLESTATUS GetStatus(void) { return status; }
                        friend class VOleStreamImp;

                protected:
                        virtual DWORD GetCallback(voidPtr buf, DWORD bufSize);
                        virtual DWORD PutCallback(voidCPtr buf, DWORD bufSize);

                private:
                        static OLESTREAMVTBL vtbl;
                static int ref_count;
                        OLESTATUS status;
        };

        #endif
```

Listing A-91
VOLECLNT.CPP

```cpp
/* -----------------------------------------------------------------
    voleclnt.cpp

            Implementation of the VOleClient and associated classes.

    Copyright (C) 1992, by Jeff Mackay
---------------------------------------------------------------- */

#pragma hdrfile "vista.sym"
#include <vista.h>
#pragma hdrstop

#include <voleclnt.h>
```

```
OLECLIENTVTBL VOleClient::vtbl;
int VOleClient::ref_count = 0;
OLESTREAMVTBL VOleStream::vtbl;
int VOleStream::ref_count = 0;


class _CLASSTYPE VOleClientImp
{
        friend class VOleClient;
protected:
        static int CALLBACK _export
        ClientCallback(LPOLECLIENT clnt, OLE_NOTIFICATION notify,
                                        LPOLEOBJECT obj)
        {
                VOleClientPtr client = VOleClientPtr(clnt);
                client->SetStatus(OLE_OK);
            return client->Callback(notify, obj);
        }
};

VOleClient::VOleClient(VWindowPtr win)
{
        owner = win;
        lpvtbl = &vtbl;
        if (++ref_count == 1)
                vtbl.CallBack = &VOleClientImp::ClientCallback;
}

VOleClient::VOleClient(void)
{
        --ref_count;
}

int VOleClient::Callback(OLE_NOTIFICATION notify,
                                                LPOLEOBJECT obj)
{
    int retVal = 0;
        switch(notify)
        {
                case OLE_CHANGED:
                        ChangedCallback(obj);
                        break;

                case OLE_CLOSED:
                        ClosedCallback(obj);
                        break;

                case OLE_QUERY_PAINT:
                        retVal = QueryPaintCallback(obj);
                        break;

                case OLE_QUERY_RETRY:
```

Listing A-91
Continued.

```
                        retVal = QueryRetryCallback(obj);
                        break;
                case OLE_RELEASE:
            ReleaseCallback(obj);
                        break;

                case OLE_RENAMED:
                            RenamedCallback(obj);
                            break;

                case OLE_SAVED:
                            SavedCallback(obj);
                    break;
        }
        return retVal;
}

void VOleClient::ChangedCallback(LPOLEOBJECT)
{
}

void VOleClient::ClosedCallback(LPOLEOBJECT)
{
}

Boolean VOleClient::QueryPaintCallback(LPOLEOBJECT)
{
    return True;
}

Boolean VOleClient::QueryRetryCallback(LPOLEOBJECT)
{
        return True;
}
void VOleClient::ReleaseCallback(LPOLEOBJECT)
{
}

void VOleClient::SavedCallback(LPOLEOBJECT)
{
}

void VOleClient::RenamedCallback(LPOLEOBJECT)
{
}


void VOleClient::Wait(OLESTATUS stat, VOleClientObjPtr obj)
{
        if (stat == OLE_WAIT_FOR_RELEASE ||
                    stat == OLE_WARN_DELETE_DATA)
```

```cpp
        {
            MSG msg;
                while ((status = OleQueryReleaseStatus(*obj)) == OLE_BUSY)
                {
                        if (GetMessage(&msg, 0, 0, 0))
                        {
                                TranslateMessage( &msg );
                                DispatchMessage( &msg );
                        }
                }
                stat = OleQueryReleaseError(*obj);
                if (stat != OLE_OK)
                {
                OLE_RELEASE_METHOD method = OleQueryReleaseMethod(*obj);
                        VOleReportError(stat, method);
                }
        }
}

class _CLASSTYPE VOleStreamImp
{
        friend class VOleStream;

protected:
        static DWORD CALLBACK _export
        Get(LPOLESTREAM strm, void FAR *var, DWORD varSize)
        {
                VOleStreamPtr stream = VOleStreamPtr(strm);
                stream->SetStatus(OLE_OK);
                DWORD bytes = stream->GetCallback(var, varSize);
                if (stream->GetStatus() == OLE_OK)
                        return bytes;
                else
                        return 0;
        }
        static DWORD CALLBACK _export
        Put(LPOLESTREAM strm, OLE_CONST void FAR *var, DWORD varSize)
        {
                VOleStreamPtr stream = VOleStreamPtr(strm);
                stream->SetStatus(OLE_OK);
                DWORD bytes = stream->PutCallback(var, varSize);
            if (stream->GetStatus() == OLE_OK)
                        return bytes;
                else
                        return 0;
        }
};

VOleStream::VOleStream(void)
{
        if (++ref_count == 1)
```

Listing A-91
Continued.

```
            {
                    vtbl.Get = &VOleStreamImp::Get;
                    vtbl.Put = &VOleStreamImp::Put;
            }
    }

    VOleStream::VOleStream(void)
    {
            --ref_count;
    }

    DWORD VOleStream::GetCallback(voidPtr, DWORD)
    {
            return 0;
    }

    DWORD VOleStream::PutCallback(voidCPtr, DWORD)
    {
            return 0;
    }
```

Listing A-92
VOLECOBJ.CPP

```
    /* ----------------------------------------------------------------
       volecobj.cpp

              Implementation of the VOleClientObj class.

       Copyright (C) 1992, by Jeff Mackay
       ---------------------------------------------------------------- */

    #pragma hdrfile "vista.sym"
    #include <vista.h>
    #pragma hdrstop
    #include <vclip.h>
    #include <voleclnt.h>

    #define MAXOLENAMELEN 128


    VOleClientObj::VOleClientObj(void)
    {
            Init(0,0,0);
    }

    VOleClientObj::VOleClientObj(VOleClientDocPtr par, LPOLEOBJECT
    obj)
    {
            Init(par, par->GetOwner(), obj);
    }
```

```cpp
VOleClientObj::VOleClientObj(VOleClientDocPtr par, VWindowPtr own,
                             LPOLEOBJECT obj)
{
        Init(par, own, obj);
}

VOleClientObj::VOleClientObj(VOleClientObjRef copy)
{
        parent = copy.parent;
    owner  = copy.owner;
        SetStatus(OleClone(copy,
                                                &copy,
                                                *copy.parent,
                                                copy.parent->NewObjectName(),
                                                &handle));
}

VOleClientObjRef
VOleClientObj::operator =(VOleClientObjRef copy)
{
        parent = copy.parent;
        owner  = copy.owner;
        SetStatus(OleClone(copy,
                                                &copy,
                                                *copy.parent,
                                                copy.parent->NewObjectName(),
                                                &handle));
    return *this;
}

int VOleClientObj::operator ==(VOleClientObjRef other)
{
        OLESTATUS status = OleEqual(other, *this);
        return (status == OLE_OK);
}
void VOleClientObj::Activate(WORD verb, BOOL show, BOOL focus,
                                                RECT FAR *rect)
{
        VASSERT(owner);
        Wait(OleActivate(*this, verb, show, focus, *owner, rect),
                  this);
}

void VOleClientObj::Close(void)
{
        Wait(OleClose(*this), this);
}

void VOleClientObj::CopyToClipboard(void)
{
```

Listing A-92
Continued.

```
        VASSERT(owner);
        VClipboard clip(owner, True);
        SetStatus(OleCopyToClipboard(*this));
}

void VOleClientObj::Delete(void)
{
        Wait(OleDelete(*this), this);
}

void VOleClientObj::Draw(VDevicePtr dev, RECT FAR *bRect,
                RECT FAR *wRect, VDevicePtr fmt)
{
        VASSERT(owner != 0);
        Boolean delDev = False;

        if (dev == 0)
        {
        delDev = True;
                dev = new VDevice(owner);
        }

        HDC fDev;
        if (fmt)
                fDev = *fmt;
        else
                fDev = 0;

    RECT rect;
        if(bRect == 0)
                owner->GetDimensions(rect);
        else
                rect = *bRect;

        Wait(OleDraw(*this, *dev, &rect, wRect, fDev), this);

        if (delDev)
                delete dev;
}

void VOleClientObj::Execute(charCPtr string)
{
        VASSERT(string != 0);
        HGLOBAL command = GlobalAlloc(GMEM_DDESHARE,
lstrlen(string)+1);
        if (command == 0)
    {
                SetStatus(OLE_ERROR_MEMORY);
                return;
        }

        charPtr cmdString = (charPtr)GlobalLock(command);
```

```c++
        if (cmdString == 0)
        {
        GlobalFree(command);
                SetStatus(OLE_ERROR_MEMORY);
                return;
        }

        lstrcpy(cmdString, string);
        GlobalUnlock(command);

        Wait(OleExecute(*this, command, 0), this);
}
void VOleClientObj::Reconnect(void)
{
        Wait(OleReconnect(*this), this);
}

void VOleClientObj::Release(void)
{
        Wait(OleRelease(*this), this);
}

void VOleClientObj::Rename(charCPtr objName)
{
        Wait(OleRename(*this, objName), this);
}

void VOleClientObj::SetBounds(RECT FAR *rect)
{
        Wait(OleSetBounds(*this, rect), this);
}

void VOleClientObj::SetData(OLECLIPFORMAT format, HANDLE hdl)
{
        Wait(OleSetData(*this, format, hdl), this);
}
void VOleClientObj::SetHostNames(charCPtr clientName,
                                 charCPtr docName)
{
        if (docName == 0)
                docName = parent->QueryName();

        Wait(OleSetHostNames(*this, clientName, docName), this);
}

void VOleClientObj::Update(void)
{
        Wait(OleUpdate(*this), this);
}
```

Listing A-92
Continued.

```
OLECLIPFORMAT VOleClientObj::First(void)
{
        return Next(0);
}

OLECLIPFORMAT VOleClientObj::Next(OLECLIPFORMAT format)
{
        return OleEnumFormats(*this, format);
}

void VOleClientObj::RequestData(OLECLIPFORMAT format)
{
        Wait(OleRequestData(*this, format), this);
}

void VOleClientObj::GetData(OLECLIPFORMAT format, HANDLE FAR *hdlPtr)
{
        Wait(OleGetData(*this, format, hdlPtr), this);
}

RECT FAR *VOleClientObj::QueryBounds(RECT FAR *rect)
{
    VASSERT(rect != 0);
        SetStatus(OleQueryBounds(*this, rect));
    return rect;
}



charPtr VOleClientObj::QueryName(charPtr buffer, UINT FAR *sizePtr)
{
        UINT sizeVar;
    Boolean delBuffer = False;
        if (buffer == 0)
        {
        delBuffer = True;
                buffer = new char[MAXOLENAMELEN];
                sizeVar = MAXOLENAMELEN;
        }
        else
        {
                VASSERT(sizePtr != 0);
        sizeVar = *sizePtr;
        }
        SetStatus(OleQueryName(*this, buffer, &sizeVar));
    *sizePtr = sizeVar;
        if (GetStatus() != OLE_OK)
        {
                if (delBuffer)
                        delete buffer;
        buffer = 0;
```

```cpp
        }
        return buffer;
}

Boolean VOleClientObj::QueryOpen(void)
{
        return (OleQueryOpen(*this) == OLE_OK) ? True : False;
}

Boolean VOleClientObj::QueryOutOfDate(void)
{
        return (OleQueryOutOfDate(*this) == OLE_OK) ? True : False;
}

// warning: this function may modify the OLE object pointer
Boolean VOleClientObj::QueryProtocol(charPtr protocol)
{
        LPVOID newObj = OleQueryProtocol(*this, protocol);
        if (newObj == 0)
                return False;
        else
        {
                handle = (LPOLEOBJECT) newObj;
                return True;
        }
}

DWORD VOleClientObj::QuerySize(void)
{
        DWORD objSize;

        SetStatus(OleQuerySize(*this, &objSize));
    return objSize;
}

LONG VOleClientObj::QueryType(void)
{
        LONG objType;

        SetStatus(OleQueryType(*this, &objType));
    return objType;
}
```

```
/* --------------------------------------------------------
   voledoc.cpp

        Implementation of the VOleDoc class.

   Copyright (C) 1992, by Jeff Mackay
-------------------------------------------------------- */
```

Listing A-93
VOLEDOC.cpp

Listing A-93
Continued.

```c
#pragma hdrfile "vista.sym"
#include <vista.h>
#pragma hdrstop

#include <volesrvr.h>

OLESERVERDOCVTBL VOleDoc::vtbl;
int VOleDoc::ref_count = 0;


class _CLASSTYPE VOleDocImp
{
    friend class VOleDoc;
        static OLESTATUS CALLBACK _export
        Save(LPOLESERVERDOC docStruct)
        {
                VOleDocPtr obj = (VOleDocPtr)docStruct;
                obj->SetStatus(OLE_OK);
        obj->SaveCallback();
                if (obj->GetStatus() != OLE_OK)
                        return OLE_ERROR_GENERIC;
                else
                return OLE_OK;
        }

        static OLESTATUS CALLBACK _export
        Close(LPOLESERVERDOC docStruct)
        {
                VOleDocPtr obj = (VOleDocPtr)docStruct;
                obj->SetStatus(OLE_OK);
                obj->CloseCallback();
            return obj->GetStatus();
        }
        static OLESTATUS CALLBACK _export
        SetHostNames(LPOLESERVERDOC docStruct,
                        OLE_LPCSTR clientName, OLE_LPCSTR
docName)
        {
                VOleDocPtr obj = (VOleDocPtr)docStruct;
                obj->SetStatus(OLE_OK);
                obj->HostNamesCallback(clientName, docName);
            if (obj->GetStatus() != OLE_OK)
                        return OLE_ERROR_GENERIC;
                else
                return OLE_OK;
        }


        static OLESTATUS CALLBACK _export
        SetDocDimensions(LPOLESERVERDOC docStruct,
                        OLE_CONST RECT FAR *rect)
```

```cpp
{
        VOleDocPtr obj = (VOleDocPtr)docStruct;
        obj->SetStatus(OLE_OK);
        obj->SetDimensionCallback(rect);
        return obj->GetStatus();
}

static OLESTATUS CALLBACK _export
GetOleObject(LPOLESERVERDOC docStruct,
                        OLE_LPCSTR itemName,
                        LPOLEOBJECT FAR *objptr,
                        LPOLECLIENT client)
{
        VOleDocPtr obj = (VOleDocPtr)docStruct;
        obj->SetStatus(OLE_OK);
if (itemName == 0 || *itemName == '\0')
                *objptr = obj->GetDocCallback(client);
    else
                *objptr = obj->GetObjectCallback(itemName, client);
        return obj->GetStatus();
}

static OLESTATUS CALLBACK _export
Release(LPOLESERVERDOC docStruct)
{
        VOleDocPtr doc = (VOleDocPtr)docStruct;
        doc->SetStatus(OLE_OK);
        doc->ReleaseCallback();
        return doc->GetStatus();
}

static OLESTATUS CALLBACK _export
SetColorScheme(LPOLESERVERDOC docStruct,
                        OLE_CONST LOGPALETTE FAR *palette)
{
        VOleDocPtr obj = (VOleDocPtr)docStruct;
        obj->SetStatus(OLE_OK);
        obj->SetPaletteCallback(palette);
        if (obj->GetStatus() != OLE_OK)
                return OLE_ERROR_PALETTE;
        else
            return OLE_OK;
}

static OLESTATUS CALLBACK _export
Execute(LPOLESERVERDOC docStruct,
                        HGLOBAL handle)
{
        VOleDocPtr obj = VOleDocPtr(docStruct);
    obj->SetStatus(OLE_OK);
        charCPtr command = (charCPtr) GlobalLock(handle);
```

Listing A-93
Continued.

```
                        if (command == 0)
                                obj->SetStatus(OLE_ERROR_MEMORY);
                        else
                                obj->ExecuteCallback(command);
                        if (handle != 0 && GlobalUnlock(handle) != 0)
                                obj->SetStatus(OLE_ERROR_MEMORY);
                return obj->GetStatus();
        }
};

VOleDoc::VOleDoc(VOleServerRef par, charCPtr docName)
        : parent(par), name(docName), handle(0)
{
    if (++ref_count == 1)
                SetVTable();
    lpvtbl = &vtbl;
        SetStatus(OLE_OK);
        Register();
}

void VOleDoc::SetVTable(void)
{
        vtbl.Save = &VOleDocImp::Save;
        vtbl.Close = &VOleDocImp::Close;
        vtbl.SetHostNames = &VOleDocImp::SetHostNames;
        vtbl.SetDocDimensions = &VOleDocImp::SetDocDimensions;
        vtbl.GetObject = &VOleDocImp::GetOleObject;
        vtbl.Release = &VOleDocImp::Release;
        vtbl.SetColorScheme = &VOleDocImp::SetColorScheme;
        vtbl.Execute = &VOleDocImp::Execute;
}

VOleDoc::VOleDoc(void)
{
    if (--ref_count == 0)
                ReleaseVTable();
}

void VOleDoc::ReleaseVTable(void)
{
}

void VOleDoc::Register(void)
{
        SetStatus(OleRegisterServerDoc(parent, name, this,
&handle));
}

void VOleDoc::Rename(charCPtr newName)
{
        name = newName;
```

```cpp
        SetStatus(OleRenameServerDoc(handle, name));
}

void VOleDoc::Revoke(void)
{
        SetStatus(OleRevokeServerDoc(handle));
}

void VOleDoc::Saved(void)
{
        SetStatus(OleSavedServerDoc(handle));
}

// only called for linked documents
void VOleDoc::SaveCallback(void)
{
}

void VOleDoc::CloseCallback(void)
{
        Revoke();
}

void VOleDoc::HostNamesCallback(charCPtr, charCPtr)
{
}

void VOleDoc::SetDimensionCallback(const RECT FAR *)
{
}

// Must override
VOleObjectPtr VOleDoc::GetObjectCallback(charCPtr,

LPOLECLIENT)
{
        SetStatus(OLE_ERROR_GENERIC);
    return 0;
}

// Must override
VOleObjectPtr VOleDoc::GetDocCallback(LPOLECLIENT)
{
        SetStatus(OLE_ERROR_GENERIC);
        return 0;
}

void VOleDoc::ReleaseCallback(void)
{
        delete this;
}
```

Listing A-93
Continued.

```
void VOleDoc::SetPaletteCallback(const LOGPALETTE FAR *newPalette)
{
      palette = *newPalette;
}

// Override if necessary
void VOleDoc::ExecuteCallback(charCPtr)
{
        SetStatus(OLE_ERROR_COMMAND);
}
```

Listing A-94
VOLEERR.H

```
/* -----------------------------------------------------------------
   voleerr.h

        Error reporting for OLE error codes.  Use for either clients
        or servers.  Also includes debugging functions.

   Copyright (C) 1992, by Jeff Mackay

   ----------------------------------------------------------------- */

#ifndef _VOLEERR_H
#define _VOLEERR_H

#ifndef _VISTA_H
#include <vista.h>
#endif

#ifndef _VMSGBOX_H
#include <vmsgbox.h>
#endif

// don't use this function from a callback: it uses a messagebox.
int VOleReportError(OLESTATUS status,
                                    OLE_RELEASE_METHOD
meth=OLE_NONE);


// to trace your functions, place an OLE_TRACE statement as the
first
// statement in the function

#ifndef NDEBUG
#define OLE_TRACE(msg) VOleTracer tracer(msg);

#ifndef __IOSTREAM_H
```

```cpp
#include <iostream.h>
#endif

// vOleTraceFlags controls the amount of information dumped to
// stdout.

#define VTRACE_NONE    0x00
#define VTRACE_ENTRY   0x01
#define VTRACE_EXIT    0x02
#define VTRACE_DEFAULT (VTRACE_ENTRY|VTRACE_EXIT)

extern int vOleTraceFlags;


// the VOleTracer class traces entry into and exit from OLE functions.
// to use it, call the _InitEasyWin() function from your program's
// WinMain.
class VOleTracer
{
        public:
                VOleTracer(charPtr msg) : message(msg)
                {
                if (vOleTraceFlags & VTRACE_ENTRY)
                        cout << "Enter: " << message << endl;
                }

                VOleTracer()
                {
                if (vOleTraceFlags & VTRACE_EXIT)
                                cout << "Exit: " << message << endl;
                }

        private:
        charPtr message;
};

#else
#define OLE_TRACE(msg) ((void)0)
#endif


#endif




/* ------------------------------------------------------------
   voleerr.cpp

        Error reporting for OLE error codes.  Use for either clients
        or servers.  Also includes debugging functions.
   Copyright (C) 1992, by Jeff Mackay
```

Listing A-95
VOLEERR.CPP

Listing A-95
Continued.

```c
/* ----------------------------------------------------------- */
#pragma hdrfile "vista.sym"
#include <vista.h>
#pragma hdrstop

#include <voleerr.h>

int vOleTraceFlags = VTRACE_DEFAULT;

static charPtr ErrorString(OLESTATUS status)
{
    switch(status)
    {
        case OLE_OK:
            return "OLE_OK";
        case OLE_WAIT_FOR_RELEASE:
            return "OLE_WAIT_FOR_RELEASE";
        case OLE_BUSY:
            return "OLE_BUSY";
        case OLE_ERROR_PROTECT_ONLY:
            return "OLE_ERROR_PROTECT_ONLY";
        case OLE_ERROR_MEMORY:
            return "OLE_ERROR_MEMORY";
        case OLE_ERROR_STREAM:
            return "OLE_ERROR_STREAM";
        case OLE_ERROR_STATIC:
            return "OLE_ERROR_STATIC";
        case OLE_ERROR_BLANK:
            return "OLE_ERROR_BLANK";
        case OLE_ERROR_DRAW:
            return "OLE_ERROR_DRAW";
        case OLE_ERROR_METAFILE:
            return "OLE_ERROR_METAFILE";
        case OLE_ERROR_ABORT:
            return "OLE_ERROR_ABORT";
        case OLE_ERROR_CLIPBOARD:
            return "OLE_ERROR_CLIPBOARD";
        case OLE_ERROR_FORMAT:
            return "OLE_ERROR_FORMAT";
        case OLE_ERROR_OBJECT:
            return "OLE_ERROR_OBJECT";
        case OLE_ERROR_OPTION:
            return "OLE_ERROR_OPTION";
        case OLE_ERROR_PROTOCOL:
            return "OLE_ERROR_PROTOCOL";
        case OLE_ERROR_ADDRESS:
            return "OLE_ERROR_ADDRESS";
        case OLE_ERROR_NOT_EQUAL:
            return "OLE_ERROR_NOT_EQUAL";
        case OLE_ERROR_HANDLE:
            return "OLE_ERROR_HANDLE";
```

```
        case OLE_ERROR_GENERIC:
                return "OLE_ERROR_GENERIC";
        case OLE_ERROR_CLASS:
                return "OLE_ERROR_CLASS";
        case OLE_ERROR_SYNTAX:
                return "OLE_ERROR_SYNTAX";
        case OLE_ERROR_DATATYPE:
                return "OLE_ERROR_DATATYPE";
        case OLE_ERROR_PALETTE:
                return "OLE_ERROR_PALETTE";
        case OLE_ERROR_NOT_LINK:
                return "OLE_ERROR_NOT_LINK";
        case OLE_ERROR_NOT_EMPTY:
                return "OLE_ERROR_NOT_EMPTY";
        case OLE_ERROR_SIZE:
                return "OLE_ERROR_SIZE";
        case OLE_ERROR_DRIVE:
                return "OLE_ERROR_DRIVE";
        case OLE_ERROR_NETWORK:
                return "OLE_ERROR_NETWORK";
        case OLE_ERROR_NAME:
                return "OLE_ERROR_NAME";
        case OLE_ERROR_TEMPLATE:
                return "OLE_ERROR_TEMPLATE";
        case OLE_ERROR_NEW:
                return "OLE_ERROR_NEW";
        case OLE_ERROR_EDIT:
                return "OLE_ERROR_EDIT";
        case OLE_ERROR_OPEN:
                return "OLE_ERROR_OPEN";
        case OLE_ERROR_NOT_OPEN:
                return "OLE_ERROR_NOT_OPEN";
        case OLE_ERROR_LAUNCH:
                return "OLE_ERROR_LAUNCH";
        case OLE_ERROR_COMM:
                return "OLE_ERROR_COMM";
        case OLE_ERROR_TERMINATE:
                return "OLE_ERROR_TERMINATE";
        case OLE_ERROR_COMMAND:
                return "OLE_ERROR_COMMAND";
        case OLE_ERROR_SHOW:
                return "OLE_ERROR_SHOW";
        case OLE_ERROR_DOVERB:
                return "OLE_ERROR_DOVERB";
        case OLE_ERROR_ADVISE_NATIVE:
                return "OLE_ERROR_ADVISE_NATIVE";
        case OLE_ERROR_ADVISE_PICT:
                return "OLE_ERROR_ADVISE_PICT";
        case OLE_ERROR_ADVISE_RENAME:
                return "OLE_ERROR_ADVISE_RENAME";
        case OLE_ERROR_POKE_NATIVE:
                return "OLE_ERROR_POKE_NATIVE";
```

Listing A-95
Continued.

```
                case OLE_ERROR_REQUEST_NATIVE:
                        return "OLE_ERROR_REQUEST_NATIVE";
                case OLE_ERROR_REQUEST_PICT:
                        return "OLE_ERROR_REQUEST_PICT";
                case OLE_ERROR_SERVER_BLOCKED:
                        return "OLE_ERROR_SERVER_BLOCKED";
                case OLE_ERROR_REGISTRATION:
                        return "OLE_ERROR_REGISTRATION";
                case OLE_ERROR_ALREADY_REGISTERED:
                        return "OLE_ERROR_ALREADY_REGISTERED";
                case OLE_ERROR_TASK:
                        return "OLE_ERROR_TASK";
                case OLE_ERROR_OUTOFDATE:
                        return "OLE_ERROR_OUTOFDATE";
                case OLE_ERROR_CANT_UPDATE_CLIENT:
                        return "OLE_ERROR_CANT_UPDATE_CLIENT";
                case OLE_ERROR_UPDATE:
                        return "OLE_ERROR_UPDATE";
                case OLE_ERROR_SETDATA_FORMAT:
                        return "OLE_ERROR_SETDATA_FORMAT";
                case OLE_ERROR_STATIC_FROM_OTHER_OS:
                        return "OLE_ERROR_STATIC_FROM_OTHER_OS";
                case OLE_WARN_DELETE_DATA:
                        return "OLE_WARN_DELETE_DATA";
                default:
                        return "OLE_UNKNOWN_STATUS";
        }
}

charPtr ErrorMethod(OLE_RELEASE_METHOD method)
{
        switch(method)
        {
                case OLE_DELETE:
                        return "OLE_DELETE";
                case OLE_LNKPASTE:
                        return "OLE_LNKPASTE";
                case OLE_EMBPASTE:
                        return "OLE_EMBPASTE";
                case OLE_SHOW:
                        return "OLE_SHOW";
                case OLE_RUN:
                        return "OLE_RUN";
                case OLE_ACTIVATE:
                        return "OLE_ACTIVATE";
                case OLE_UPDATE:
                        return "OLE_UPDATE";
                case OLE_CLOSE:
                        return "OLE_CLOSE";
                case OLE_RECONNECT:
                        return "OLE_RECONNECT";
```

```
                    case OLE_SETUPDATEOPTIONS:
                            return "OLE_SETUPDATEOPTIONS";
                    case OLE_SERVERUNLAUNCH:
                            return "OLE_SERVERUNLAUNCH";
                    case OLE_LOADFROMSTREAM:
                            return "OLE_LOADFROMSTREAM";
                    case OLE_SETDATA:
                            return "OLE_SETDATA";
                    case OLE_REQUESTDATA:
                            return "OLE_REQUESTDATA";
                    case OLE_OTHER:
                            return "OLE_OTHER";
                    case OLE_CREATE:
                            return "OLE_CREATE";
                    case OLE_CREATEFROMTEMPLATE:
                            return "OLE_CREATEFROMTEMPLATE";
                    case OLE_CREATELINKFROMFILE:
                            return "OLE_CREATELINKFROMFILE";
                    case OLE_COPYFROMLNK:
                            return "OLE_COPYFROMLNK";
                    case OLE_CREATEFROMFILE:
                            return "OLE_CREATEFROMFILE";
                    default:
                    return "OLE_UNKNOWN_FUNCTION";
        }
}

int VOleReportError(OLESTATUS status, OLE_RELEASE_METHOD method)
{
        if (status == OLE_OK)
                return IDOK;

        char buffer[128];
    if (method != OLE_NONE)
                wsprintf(buffer,
                  "OLE Error: %s ( 0x%x ).\nFunction: %s.  Continue?",
                    ErrorString(status), status, ErrorMethod(method));
        else
                wsprintf(buffer,
                        "OLE Error: %s (0x%x ).\nContinue?",
            ErrorString(status), status);
        VErrorBox errorBox(0, buffer);
        int retVal = errorBox.Execute();
        if (retVal == IDABORT)
                PostQuitMessage(status);
    return retVal;
}
```

Listing A-96
VOLEOBJ.CPP

```cpp
/* -----------------------------------------------------------
   voleobj.cpp

        Implementation of the VOleObject class.

   Copyright (C) 1992, by Jeff Mackay
   ----------------------------------------------------------- */

#pragma hdrfile "vista.sym"
#include <vista.h>
#pragma hdrstop

#include <volesrvr.h>

int VOleObject::ref_count = 0;
OLEOBJECTVTBL VOleObject::vtbl;

// VOleObjImp: provides the OLE interface for the VOleObject class
class _CLASSTYPE VOleObjImp
{
        friend class VOleObject;

        static LPVOID CALLBACK _export
        QueryProtocol(LPOLEOBJECT obj, OLE_LPCSTR protocol)
        {
                VOleObjectPtr object = (VOleObjectPtr)obj;
                if (object->QueryProtocolCallback(protocol))
                        return obj;
                else
                        return 0;
        }
        static OLESTATUS CALLBACK _export
        Release(LPOLEOBJECT obj)
        {
                VOleObjectPtr object = (VOleObjectPtr)obj;
                object->SetStatus(OLE_OK);
                object->ReleaseCallback();
            return object->GetStatus();
        }

        static OLESTATUS CALLBACK _export
        Show(LPOLEOBJECT obj, BOOL takeFocus)
        {
                VOleObjectPtr object = (VOleObjectPtr)obj;
                object->SetStatus(OLE_OK);
                object->ShowCallback(takeFocus);
                return object->GetStatus();
        }

        static OLESTATUS CALLBACK _export
        DoVerb(LPOLEOBJECT obj, UINT verb, BOOL show,
```

```
        BOOL takeFocus)
{
        VOleObjectPtr object = (VOleObjectPtr)obj;
        object->SetStatus(OLE_OK);
object->DoVerbCallback(verb, show, takeFocus);
        return object->GetStatus();
}

static OLESTATUS CALLBACK _export
GetData(LPOLEOBJECT obj, OLECLIPFORMAT format, HANDLE FAR *data)
{
        VOleObjectPtr object = (VOleObjectPtr)obj;
        object->SetStatus(OLE_OK);
        *data = object->GetDataCallback(format);
     return object->GetStatus();
}

static OLESTATUS CALLBACK _export
SetData(LPOLEOBJECT obj, OLECLIPFORMAT format, HANDLE handle)
{
        VOleObjectPtr object = (VOleObjectPtr)obj;
        object->SetStatus(OLE_OK);
        voidCPtr data = GlobalLock(handle);
        if (data)
        {
                object->SetDataCallback(format, data);
                if (GlobalUnlock(handle) > 0)
                        object->SetStatus(OLE_ERROR_MEMORY);
        }
        else
        {
                object->SetStatus(OLE_ERROR_MEMORY);
        }
     return object->GetStatus();
}

static OLESTATUS CALLBACK _export
SetTargetDevice(LPOLEOBJECT obj, HGLOBAL handle)
{
        VOleObjectPtr object = (VOleObjectPtr)obj;
        object->SetStatus(OLE_OK);
        OLETARGETDEVICECPtr dev;
        if (handle)
        {
                dev = (OLETARGETDEVICECPtr)GlobalLock(handle);
                if (!dev)
                        return OLE_ERROR_MEMORY;
        }
        else
                dev = 0;
        object->SetDevCallback(dev);
```

Listing A-96
Continued.

```cpp
                if (handle && GlobalUnlock(handle) != 0)
                        object->SetStatus(OLE_ERROR_MEMORY);
            return object->GetStatus();
            }

            static OLESTATUS CALLBACK _export
            SetBounds(LPOLEOBJECT obj, OLE_CONST RECT FAR *rect)
            {
                    VOleObjectPtr object = (VOleObjectPtr)obj;
                    object->SetStatus(OLE_OK);
                    object->SetBoundsCallback(rect);
                return object->GetStatus();
            }

            static OLECLIPFORMAT CALLBACK _export
            EnumFormats(LPOLEOBJECT obj, OLECLIPFORMAT format)
            {
                    VOleObjectPtr object = (VOleObjectPtr)obj;
                    return object->EnumFormatsCallback(format);
            }

            static OLESTATUS CALLBACK _export
            SetColorScheme(LPOLEOBJECT obj, OLE_CONST LOGPALETTE FAR
    *palette)
            {
                    VOleObjectPtr object = (VOleObjectPtr)obj;
                    object->SetStatus(OLE_OK);
            object->SetColorCallback(palette);
                    return object->GetStatus();
            }
};

VOleObject::VOleObject(VOleDocRef par, charCPtr name, LPOLECLIENT
cli)
    : parent(par), client(cli), obj_name(name)
{
    if (++ref_count == 1)
                SetVTable();
    lpvtbl = &vtbl;
}


VOleObject::VOleObject(void)
{
        if (--ref_count == 0)
                ReleaseVTable();
}

void VOleObject::ReleaseVTable(void)
{
```

```cpp
}

void VOleObject::SetVTable(void)
{
        vtbl.QueryProtocol = &VOleObjImp::QueryProtocol;
        vtbl.Release = &VOleObjImp::Release;
        vtbl.Show = &VOleObjImp::Show;
        vtbl.DoVerb = &VOleObjImp::DoVerb;
        vtbl.GetData = &VOleObjImp::GetData;
        vtbl.SetData = &VOleObjImp::SetData;
        vtbl.SetTargetDevice = &VOleObjImp::SetTargetDevice;
        vtbl.SetBounds = &VOleObjImp::SetBounds;
        vtbl.EnumFormats = &VOleObjImp::EnumFormats;
        vtbl.SetColorScheme = &VOleObjImp::SetColorScheme;
}

void VOleObject::NotifyClient(OLE_NOTIFICATION message)
{
        VASSERT(client != 0);

        (*client->lpvtbl->CallBack)(client, message, (LPOLEOBJECT)this);
}

// Callback functions:


// override only to allow additional protocols, or restrict
// StdExecute
Boolean VOleObject::QueryProtocolCallback(charCPtr protocol)
{
    if (_fstricmp(protocol, "StdFileEditing") == 0)
                return True;
        else if (_fstricmp(protocol, "StdExecute") == 0)
                return True;
        else
        return False;
}

void VOleObject::ReleaseCallback(void)
{
        delete this;
}

void VOleObject::ShowCallback(BOOL)
{
}

void VOleObject::DoVerbCallback(UINT verb, BOOL show, BOOL focus)
{
        if (verb == 0 && show)
                ShowCallback(focus);
```

Listing A-96
Continued.

```
}
HGLOBAL VOleObject::GetDataCallback(OLECLIPFORMAT format)
{
        if (format == VOleServer::native)
                return GetNative();
        else if (format == CF_METAFILEPICT)
        {
                VFileDevice dev;
                // dev << palette;
                Draw(dev);
                HMETAFILE hmf = dev.Close();
                HMETAFILE handle = (HMETAFILE) GlobalAlloc(GMEM_DDESHARE,
sizeof(METAFILEPICT));
                if (handle == 0)
                        return 0;

                LPMETAFILEPICT pict = (LPMETAFILEPICT)GlobalLock(handle);
                pict->mm = MM_ANISOTROPIC;
                pict->hMF = hmf;
                pict->xExt = rect.bottom - rect.top;
                pict->yExt = rect.right - rect.left;
                GlobalUnlock((HGLOBAL)handle);
                return (HGLOBAL)handle;
        }
        else
                return 0;
}

void VOleObject::SetDataCallback(OLECLIPFORMAT, voidCPtr)
{
}
void VOleObject::SetDevCallback(OLETARGETDEVICECPtr)
{
}

void VOleObject::SetBoundsCallback(const RECT FAR *bounds)
{
        rect = *bounds;
}

OLECLIPFORMAT VOleObject::EnumFormatsCallback(OLECLIPFORMAT format)
{
        VASSERT(formats && format_count);
        int index = 0;
        if (format != 0)
        {
                while(formats[index++] != format)
                        ;
        }
```

```
        return formats[index];
}

void VOleObject::SetColorCallback(const LOGPALETTE FAR *newPalette)
{
        palette = *newPalette;
}

HGLOBAL VOleObject::GetNative(void)
{
        return 0;
}

void VOleObject::Draw(VDeviceRef)
{
}
```

Listing A-97
VOLESRVR.H

```
/* ----------------------------------------------------------------
    volesrvr.h

        Implementation of the VOleServer and associated classes.

    Copyright (C) 1992, by Jeff Mackay
-------------------------------------------------------------------- */
#ifndef _VOLESRVR_H
#define _VOLESRVR_H

#ifndef __OLE_H
#include <ole.h>
#endif
#ifndef _GRDEV_H
#include <vgrdev.h>
#endif

#ifndef _GDITOOL_H
#include <vgditool.h>
#endif

STDTYPE(OLETARGETDEVICE);
STDCLASS(VOleClient);
STDCLASS(VOleServer);
STDCLASS(VOleDoc);
STDCLASS(VOleObject);

class _CLASSTYPE VOleServer : public OLESERVER
{
        public:
                static WORD native;
```

Listing A-97
Continued.

```cpp
            static WORD object_link;
            static WORD owner_link;
            VOleServer(charCPtr className=0);
    VOleServer(void);
    charCPtr GetClassName(void);
            operator LHSERVER(void) { return handle; }
            virtual void Register(charCPtr className,
                    OLE_SERVER_USE servUse=OLE_SERVER_MULTI);
    virtual void RegisterFormats(void);
    virtual void Revoke(void);
            virtual void Block(void);
            virtual Boolean Unblock(void);
    virtual void AddServer(void);
            OLESTATUS GetStatus(void) { return status; }
            void SetStatus(OLESTATUS value) { status = value; }
            void SetEmbedded(Boolean value) { embedded = value; }
            Boolean IsEmbedded(void) const { return embedded; }

    protected:
            virtual VOleDocPtr NewDocument(charCPtr) = 0;
            virtual VOleDocPtr OpenCallback(charCPtr);
            virtual VOleDocPtr CreateCallback(charCPtr, charCPtr);
            virtual VOleDocPtr CreateFromTemplateCallback(charCPtr,
                                                          charCPtr,
    charCPtr);
            virtual VOleDocPtr EditCallback(charCPtr, charCPtr);
            virtual void ExitCallback(void);
            virtual void ReleaseCallback(void);
            virtual void ExecuteCallback(charCPtr);
    Boolean         terminating;
            LHSERVER        handle;
            OLESTATUS       status;
            VString         class_name;
    private:
    friend class VOleServerImp;
            void SetVTable(void);
    void ReleaseVTable(void);
            static OLESERVERVTBL vtbl;
            static int ref_count;
    Boolean embedded;
};


class _CLASSTYPE VOleDoc : public OLESERVERDOC
{
    public:
            VOleDoc(VOleServerRef par, charCPtr docName);
    VOleDoc(void);
            OLESTATUS GetStatus(void) { return status; }
            void SetStatus(OLESTATUS value) { status = value; }
            virtual void Register(void);
```

```cpp
        virtual void Revoke(void);
        virtual void Rename(charCPtr);
    virtual void Saved(void);
        VOleServerRef GetParent(void) const { return parent; }
    // callbacks
    protected:
    VPalette palette;
        VOleServerRef           parent;
        VString                 name;

        virtual void SaveCallback(void);
        virtual void CloseCallback(void);
        virtual void HostNamesCallback(charCPtr, charCPtr);
        virtual void SetDimensionCallback(const RECT FAR *);
        virtual VOleObjectPtr GetObjectCallback(charCPtr,
LPOLECLIENT);
        virtual VOleObjectPtr GetDocCallback(LPOLECLIENT);
        virtual void ReleaseCallback(void);
        virtual void SetPaletteCallback(const LOGPALETTE FAR *);
        virtual void ExecuteCallback(charCPtr);

    private:
        friend class VOleDocImp;
            void SetVTable(void);
        void ReleaseVTable(void);

            LHSERVERDOC             handle;
        static int          ref_count;
            static OLESERVERDOCVTBL vtbl;
            OLESTATUS               status;
};

class _CLASSTYPE VOleObject : public OLEOBJECT
{
        public:
            VOleObject(VOleDocRef par, charCPtr name, LPOLECLIENT cli);
    VOleObject(void);
            void SetStatus(OLESTATUS stat) { status = stat; }
    OLESTATUS GetStatus(void) { return status; }
            void NotifyClient(OLE_NOTIFICATION message);
            VOleDocRef GetParent(void) const { return parent; }
        protected:
            RECT rect;
            VPalette palette;
            UINT *formats;
            int format_count;
            VOleDocRef     parent;
            VString        obj_name;

            virtual Boolean QueryProtocolCallback(charCPtr);
```

Listing A-97
Continued.

```cpp
            virtual void ReleaseCallback(void);
                virtual void ShowCallback(BOOL);
                virtual void DoVerbCallback(UINT, BOOL, BOOL);
                virtual HGLOBAL GetDataCallback(OLECLIPFORMAT);
                virtual void SetDataCallback(OLECLIPFORMAT, voidCPtr);
                virtual void SetDevCallback(OLETARGETDEVICECPtr dev);
                virtual void SetBoundsCallback(const RECT FAR *);
                virtual OLECLIPFORMAT EnumFormatsCallback(OLECLIPFORMAT);
                virtual void SetColorCallback(const LOGPALETTE FAR *);
                virtual void Draw(VDeviceRef dev);
            virtual HGLOBAL GetNative(void);

            private:
            friend class VOleObjImp;
                void SetVTable(void);
                void ReleaseVTable(void);

                static OLEOBJECTVTBL vtbl;
                static int ref_count;
                LPOLECLIENT    client;
                OLESTATUS      status;
        };

        #endif
```

Listing A-98
VOLESRVR.CPP

```cpp
/* ---------------------------------------------------------------
    volesrvr.cpp

        Implementation of the VOleObject class.

    Copyright (C) 1992, by Jeff Mackay
   ------------------------------------------------------------ */

#pragma hdrfile "vista.sym"
#include <vista.h>
#pragma hdrstop

#include <volesrvr.h>

int VOleServer::ref_count = 0;
OLESERVERVTBL VOleServer::vtbl;
WORD VOleServer::owner_link;
WORD VOleServer::object_link;
WORD VOleServer::native;


class _CLASSTYPE VOleServerImp
{
```

```cpp
        friend class VOleServer;

        static OLESTATUS CALLBACK _export
        Open(LPOLESERVER srv, LHSERVERDOC,
             OLE_LPCSTR name, LPOLESERVERDOC FAR *doc)
        {
                VOleServerPtr server = (VOleServerPtr)srv;
                server->SetStatus(OLE_OK);
                *doc = server->OpenCallback(name);
                return server->GetStatus();
        }

        static OLESTATUS  CALLBACK _export
        Create(LPOLESERVER srv, LHSERVERDOC,
               OLE_LPCSTR className, OLE_LPCSTR docName,
               LPOLESERVERDOC FAR *doc)
        {
                VOleServerPtr server = (VOleServerPtr)srv;
                server->SetStatus(OLE_OK);
                *doc = server->CreateCallback(className, docName);
                if (server->GetStatus() != OLE_OK)
                        return OLE_ERROR_NEW;
                else
                        return OLE_OK;
        }

        static OLESTATUS CALLBACK _export
        CreateFromTemplate(LPOLESERVER srv,
                                           LHSERVERDOC, OLE_LPCSTR className,
                                           OLE_LPCSTR tempName,
                                           OLE_LPCSTR permName,
                                           LPOLESERVERDOC FAR *doc)
        {
                VOleServerPtr server = (VOleServerPtr)srv;
                server->SetStatus(OLE_OK);
                *doc = server->CreateFromTemplateCallback(className,
                                       tempName, permName);
                if (server->GetStatus() != OLE_OK)
                        return OLE_ERROR_TEMPLATE;
                else
                        return OLE_OK;
        }

        static OLESTATUS CALLBACK _export
        Edit(LPOLESERVER srv, LHSERVERDOC,
             OLE_LPCSTR className, OLE_LPCSTR docName,
             LPOLESERVERDOC FAR *doc)
        {
                VOleServerPtr server = (VOleServerPtr)srv;
                server->SetStatus(OLE_OK);
```

Listing A-98
Continued.

```cpp
                *doc = server->EditCallback(className, docName);
                if (server->GetStatus() != OLE_OK)
                        return OLE_ERROR_EDIT;
                else
                        return OLE_OK;
        }

        static OLESTATUS CALLBACK _export
        Exit(LPOLESERVER srv)
        {
                VOleServerPtr server = (VOleServerPtr)srv;
                server->SetStatus(OLE_OK);
                server->ExitCallback();
                if (server->GetStatus() != OLE_OK)
                        return OLE_ERROR_GENERIC;
                else
                        return OLE_OK;
        }

        static OLESTATUS CALLBACK _export
        Release(LPOLESERVER srv)
        {
                VOleServerPtr server = (VOleServerPtr)srv;
                server->SetStatus(OLE_OK);
                server->ReleaseCallback();
                if (server->GetStatus() != OLE_OK)
                        return OLE_ERROR_GENERIC;
                else
                        return OLE_OK;
        }

        static OLESTATUS CALLBACK _export
        Execute(LPOLESERVER srv, HGLOBAL handle)
        {
                VOleServerPtr server = (VOleServerPtr)srv;
                server->SetStatus(OLE_OK);
                charCPtr command = (charCPtr)GlobalLock(handle);
                if (command == 0)
                server->SetStatus(OLE_ERROR_MEMORY);
                else
                        server->ExecuteCallback(command);
                if (command != 0 && GlobalUnlock(handle) != 0)
                        server->SetStatus(OLE_ERROR_MEMORY);
            return server->GetStatus();
        }
};

VOleServer::VOleServer(charCPtr className)
{
    terminating = False;
```

```cpp
        embedded = False;
        if (++ref_count == 1)
        {
                RegisterFormats();
                SetVTable();
        }
    lpvtbl = &vtbl;
        SetStatus(OLE_OK);
        class_name = className;
}
void VOleServer::RegisterFormats(void)
{
    object_link = RegisterClipboardFormat("ObjectLink");
        owner_link  = RegisterClipboardFormat("OwnerLink");
    native      = RegisterClipboardFormat("Native");
}
void VOleServer::SetVTable(void)
{
        vtbl.Open = &VOleServerImp::Open;
        vtbl.Create = &VOleServerImp::Create;
        vtbl.CreateFromTemplate = &VOleServerImp::CreateFromTemplate;
        vtbl.Edit = &VOleServerImp::Edit;
        vtbl.Exit = &VOleServerImp::Exit;
        vtbl.Release = &VOleServerImp::Release;
        vtbl.Execute = &VOleServerImp::Execute;
}

VOleServer::VOleServer(void)
{
        if (--ref_count == 0)
                ReleaseVTable();
}
void VOleServer::ReleaseVTable(void)
{
}

void VOleServer::AddServer(void)
{
        // add the server to the registration database...
}

void VOleServer::Register(charCPtr name, OLE_SERVER_USE use)
{
        SetStatus(OLE_ERROR_CLASS);
    for(int i=0; i<2 && status != OLE_OK; i++)
    {
                SetStatus(OleRegisterServer(name, this, &handle,
                        GetApplication(), use));
                if (GetStatus() == OLE_ERROR_CLASS)
```

Listing A-98
Continued

```
                        {
                                        AddServer();
                                        if (GetStatus() != OLE_OK)
                                                break;
                        }
            class_name = name;
    }

    void VOleServer::Revoke(void)
    {
            if (!terminating)
            {
                    terminating = True;
                        SetStatus(OleRevokeServer(handle));
            }
    }

    void VOleServer::Block(void)
    {
            SetStatus(OleBlockServer(handle));
    }

    Boolean VOleServer::Unblock(void)
    {
            BOOL flag;
            SetStatus(OleUnblockServer(handle, &flag));
        return (flag) ? True : False;
    }


    VOleDocPtr VOleServer::OpenCallback(charCPtr docName)
    {

            return CreateCallback(class_name, docName);
    }

    VOleDocPtr VOleServer::CreateCallback(charCPtr className,
    charCPtr docName)
    {
            LPSTR name = class_name;
            if (_fstricmp(name, className) == 0)
                    return NewDocument(docName);
            else
            {
            SetStatus(OLE_ERROR_GENERIC);
                    return 0;
            }
    }

    VOleDocPtr VOleServer::CreateFromTemplateCallback(charCPtr
    className,
```

```cpp
                                            charCPtr docName,
charCPtr)
{
    return CreateCallback(className, docName);
}

VOleDocPtr VOleServer::EditCallback(charCPtr className, charCPtr
docName)
{
        return CreateCallback(className, docName);
}

void VOleServer::ExitCallback(void)
{
        Revoke();
}

void VOleServer::ReleaseCallback(void)
{
        Revoke();
        PostQuitMessage(0);
}

void VOleServer::ExecuteCallback(charCPtr)
{
}
```

Bibliography

Booch, Grady. 1990. *Object-Oriented Design with Applications*. Benjamin/Cummings.

Borland, International. 1991. *Windows API Guide, Volume 1-3*. Scotts Valley, Ca.: Borland, International.

Borland, International. 1991-1992. *Borland C++ User's Guide*. Scotts Valley, Ca.: Borland, International.

Borland, International. 1991-1992. *Borland C++ Programmer's Guide*, Scotts Valley, Ca.: Borland International.

Clark, Jeffrey D. 1992. *Windows Programmer's Guide To OLE/DDE*. Carmel, IN.: SAMS.

Coad, Peter & Yourdon, Edward. 1991. *Object-Oriented Design*. Englewood Cliffs, NJ.: Yourdon Press.

Coad, Peter and Yourdon, Edward. 1991-1992. *Object-Oriented Analysis*. Second Edition. Englewood Cliffs, NJ.: Yourdon Press.

Coplien, James O. 1992. *Advanced C++ Programming Styles and Idioms*. Reading, Ma.: Addison-Wesley.

Cox, Brad J. 1987. *Object-Oriented Programming: An Evolutionary Approach.* Reading, Ma.: Addison-Wesley.

Dewhurst, Stephen C. and Stark, Kathy T. 1989. *Programming in C^{++}.* Englewood Cliffs, NJ.: Prentice Hall.

Durant, David, Carlson, Geta, and Yao, Paul. 1987. *Programmer's Guide to Windows.* Second Edition. San Francisco, Ca.: Sybex.

Eckel, Bruce. 1990. *Using C^{++}.* New York, NY.: Osborne McGraw-Hill.

Faison, Ted. 1992. *Borland C^{++} 3.1 Object-Oriented Programming, Second Edition.* Carmel, IN.: SAMS.

Lippman, Stanley. 1989. *C^{++} Primer.* Reading, Ma.: Addison-Wesley.

Microsoft Corporation. 1992. *Microsoft Win32 Software Development Kit for Windows NT: Programmer's Reference.* Redmond, Wa.: Microsoft Corporation.

Microsoft Corporation. 1992. *Object Linking and Embedding Programmer's Reference.* Redmond, Wa.: Microsoft Corporation.

Norton, Peter, and Yao, Paul L. 1992. *Borland C^{++} Programming for Windows: Version 3.0.* New York, NY.: Bantam Books.

Petzold, Charles. 1991. *Programming Windows.* Second Edition. Redmond, Wa.: Microsoft Press.

Rumbaugh, J., Blaha, W., Premerlani, W., Eddy, F., Lorensen, W. 1990. *Object-Oriented Modeling and Design.* Englewood Cliffs, NJ.: Prentice-Hall.

Shlaer, S. and Mellor, S., *Object-Oriented Systems Analysis.* Englewood Cliffs, NJ.: Prentice-Hall.

Smith, Jerry D. 1990. *Reusability and Software Construction: C and C^{++}.* New York, NY.: John Wiley & Sons.

Stroustrup, Bjarne. 1991. *The C^{++} Programming Language*, Second Edition. Reading, MA.:Addison-Wesley.

Wilton, Richard. 1991. *Microsoft Windows 3 Developer's Workshop.* Redmond Wa.: Microsoft Press.

Index

<< operator, 203
>> operator, 81-82

A

Abandon function, 263
AboutCommand function, 98
accelerators, 109-113
action methods, creating, 26-27
AddCommand function, 98
address book, 142-150
AddTopic function, 254
AdviseDataCallback function, 263
AdviseRequest function, 255
AdvRequestCallback function, 256
AdvStartCallback function, 255
AdvStopCallback function, 256
AlphaTextField function, 150
application frameworks, 7-8
  Vista, 8-11
application programming interface (API), 4-5
applications
  address book, 142-150
  clipboard, 240-246
  communicating between multiple, 231
  DOS, 13
  launching with MDI, 170-176
  Windows, 13-29
applications class, 8-9, 25-26, 39-53
  cast operator, 45-46
  implementation, 43
  initialization, 44-45
  interface, 40
  maintaining configuration data, 46-47
  member access control, 44
  program cleanup, 45
  retrieving information, 46
ArrangeCommand function, 161

B

Borland C++
  converting Windows programs, 8
  creating resource scripts, 33-35
  creating source files, 32-33
  debugging programs, 36-38
  developing a Windows program, 31-36
  dynamic memory allocation operators, 219-222
  features, 5-6
  help files, 35
  module definition files, 35
  object-oriented programming and, 5-8
  project manager, 36
  Resource Workshop editors, 34-35
Brooch, Grady, 2

C

C programming language
  C++ (*see* Borland C++)
  moving programs to Vista, 87-88, 113, 153, 194-195
CascadeCommand function, 160-161
cast operators, 45
ChangedCallback function, 293
character-level validation, 150-151
child windows
  control objects, 135-153
  MDI, 155-162
  swapping menus, 163-169
class libraries, 6-7
classes (*see* specific class names)
ClassName function, 152
client-server architecture (*see* dynamic link library; object-linking and embedding)
clipboard, 238-246
  OLE formats, 281-282
CloseAllCommand function, 161
CloseCommand function, 161
Coad, Peter, 71
coding, 22 (*see also* source code)
CommandAction function, 169
communications
  asynchronous/synchronous, 261
  clipboard, 238-246
  dynamic data exchange (DDE), 247-265
  object linking and embedding (OLE), 265-295
  Windows interprocess, 237
communicator class, 11
CompleteCallback function, 262
configuration data, maintaining, 46-47
ConnectCallback function, 254
constants, 6
control objects
  child window, 135-153
  custom, 151-152
CopyObject function, 292
Create function, 291
CreateAction function, 60-61, 74, 103
CreateMdiChild function, 162

D

data types, 22-23
  error checking, 5
  LPSTR, 21
data validation
  character-level, 150-151
  field-level, 151
DDE management library (DDEML), 247-251
  client-server architecture, 248
  conversations/transactions, 250-251
  data objects, 250
  identifying DDE data, 249
  string management, 249-250
debugging, 36-38
  OLE applications, 294-295
  Turbo Debugger for Windows (TDW), 36-37
  WInspector, 37-38
DeferDrawing function, 103
delete operator, 219-224
DestroyMdiChild function, 162
device class, 200-210
dialog independence, 141
DisconnectCallback function, 253, 254
DOS, applications, 13
DoubleClickAction function, 179
DragAcceptFiles function, 176
DragQueryFile function, 177
Draw function, 282, 293
DrawOn function, 78
DropFileAction function, 177
dynamic data exchange (DDE), 4, 247-265
  Vista classes, 251-255, 251
dynamic link library (DLL), 231-236
  exporting/importing functions, 233-234
  LibMain/WEP, 232-233
  object requirements, 234-235
  Windows/NT, 233

E

editing
  Borland C++ source files, 32-33
  Resource Workshop and, 34-35
EnableDrawing function, 103
ErrorCallback function, 252-253
errors

boxes, 117
debugging, 36-38, 294-295
  system, 252-253
  unrecoverable application (UAE), 22
events, 4
  mouse, 62-64
Execute function, 262
ExitCommand function, 98
exporting, functions, 233-234
ExtractIcon function, 177

F

field-level validation, 151
FileBuffer class, 79-82
files
  help, 35
  module definition, 35
FileView class, 70-75
  managing the printer, 127-129
  MDI interface, 179-194
FontCommand function, 130
FromClip function, 291
functions, overloading, 6

G

GetCallback function, 294
GetClassName function, 178
GetData function, 238
GetDocCallback function, 281
GetNative function, 283
GetObject function, 262
GetObjectCallback function, 281
GetRecord function, 224
GetWindowPlacement function, 46
GetWinPointer function, 68
global window messages, 152-153
GlobalFree function, 213
GlobalLock function, 213, 228
GlobalMsgAction function, 153
GlobalUnlock function, 228
graphical device interface (GDI), 2-3, 27-28, 197-210
  device context, 198-199
  functions, 199-200
  Vista graphics objects, 200-210
  Win32 improvements, 199-200
graphics class, 10, 27, 200-208
graphics objects, 200-210
  high-level, 204-208
  printing, 208-210

H

help files, 35
HostNamesCallback function, 281
HScrollAction function, 82

I

icons, managing, 177-179
importing, functions, 233-234
InitWinClass function, 178
InsertCommand function, 291

L

LaunchWindow class, 176
LibMain function, 232-233
library, Vista, 297-539
local descriptor table, 215
LocalAlloc function, 221
LocalFree function, 213
LocalLock function, 213, 221
LocalUnlock function, 228
long pointer to string (LPSTR), 21

M

malloc function, 219
MDI class, 156-195
  child windows, 155-162, 193
  drag-and-drop applications, 176-177
  file view, 179-194
  moving programs from C to Vista, 194-195
  object dependencies, 169-170
  program manager icon, 177-179
  strings, 194
  swapping menus, 163-169
  unconventional windows, 170-180
MdiActivateAction function, 168
member access control, 44
memory
  386-enhanced mode, 215-216, 229
  discardable segments, 212
  movable segments, 213
  protected mode, 214
  real mode, 213
  shared segments, 212
  standard mode, 214-215
  Win32 architecture, 219
  Windows 3.x architecture, 212
  Windows operating modes and, 212-218

memory management, 211-231
  dynamic link libraries (DLLs), 231-236
  overloading pointer dereferences, 227-228
  program organization, 216-218
  template class, 225-227
  test program, 220-221
  VAllocator class, 221-224
  VHandle class, 224-225
  Windows allocation functions, 218
  with objects, 219-231
menus
  accelerators, 109-113
  adding to a window object, 97
  cascading, 91-93
  creating dynamic, 98-104
  drag-and-drop applications, 176-177
  floating pop-up, 103-109
  pop-up, 93
  pull-down, 90-91
  reacting to user commands, 97-98
  swapping in MDI program, 163-169
  Vista objects, 94-98
  Windows, 89-109
message class, 115-117
  error boxes, 117
  information boxes, 117
  warning boxes, 116-117
messages, 4
  communicating with, 52
  dispatching, 68-69
  global window, 152-153
  message loop and, 20
  Vista processing, 52-53
  Windows processing, 49-52
MinMaxAction function, 62
module definition file, 35
monitors, color screens, 130-131
mouse events, 62-64
MouseAction function, 62-64
multiple document interface (MDI), 3-4, 155-195 (*see also* MDI class)

N

naming conventions
  far addresses, 21
  Hungarian notation, 22
  Vista, 29

Windows, 21-22
new operator, 219-224
NewChildAction function, 159
NewObject function, 292
NewPage function, 209
NT LibMain function, 233

O

object linking and embedding (OLE), 4, 265-295
  activating/editing objects, 294
  classes, 273
  client applications, 271-273, 284-294
  creating Vista server document objects, 281
  creating Vista server objects, 281
  debugging applications, 294-295
  definition, 269-270
  drawing objects, 293-294
  event dispatching, 273-274
  managing client objects, 292-293
  managing OLE objects, 282-284
  object/clipboard formats, 281-282
  reasons to use, 267-269
  registering OLE applications, 284-285
  server applications, 270-271, 274-284
  Vista client object, 292
  Vista container document, 290-292
  Vista stream object, 294
object-oriented programming, 1-11
  C++ and, 5-8
  definition, 2
  extensions, 6
  Windows and, 2-5
OldClassName function, 152
OpenCommand function, 193
operators
  <<, 203
  >>, 81-82
  cast, 45-46
  delete, 219-224
  dynamic memory allocation, 219-222
  new, 219-224
  overloading, 6, 45-56

P

PaintAction function, 61, 74, 178,

199, 293
Paste function, 291
Poke function, 262
PostAdvise function, 255
PrintCommand function, 127-129
printers and printing
  fonts, 130
  graphics objects, 208-210
  managing with FileView, 127-129
PrintSetupCommand function, 128-129
PrintTo function, 209
ProgramIcon class, 177-179
programming (*see also* source code)
  building programs, 31-38
  memory organization, 216-218
  object-oriented, 1-11
  project manager, building programs with, 36
PutCallback function, 294

Q

QueryDragIcon function, 179

R

Realize function, 203
rectangle function, 208
reentrancy, 140
RegisterCallback function, 253
RegisterMessage function, 133
RegisterWindowMessage function, 153
ReleaseCapture function, 64
remote procedure call (RPC), 269
Request function, 261-262
RequestCallback function, 255
Resize function, 77
resource scripts, creating, 33-35
Resource Workshop, editors, 34-35

S

SavedCallback function, 293
screens, color, 130-131
scrolling, Vista, 82-87
ScrollWindow function, 83
SearchAction function, 133
SearchCommand function, 132, 134
searching, VFindDialog class, 132-134
SelectObject function, 203

servers (*see* object linking and embedding; VDdeServer class)
SetBuffer function, 75
SetCapture function, 64
SetData function, 238
SetMapMode function, 283
SetMenu function, 168
SetNative function, 283
SetPixel function, 207
SetResponse function, 254
SetWinPointer function, 68
ShiftVertical function, 83
ShowCallback function, 282
Simonyi, Charles, 22
SizeAction function, 61, 74
smart pointer class, (*see* VHandle class)
source code
  ACCELMNU.CPP, 110-112
  ACCELMNU.RC, 112
  ADDRC.H, 149
  ADDRESS.CPP, 142-147
  ADDRESS.RD, 147-149
  DDECLNT.CPP, 263-265
  DDESERV.CPP, 258-259
  DLGWIND.H, 33-34
  DYNMENU.CPP, 99-103
  EDITOR.CPP, 240-245
  EDITOR.H, 245, 246
  EDITOR.RC, 245, 246
  FILEVIEW.CPP, 119
  FILEBUF.CPP, 79-81
  FILEVIEW.CPP, 183-187
  FILEVIEW.CPP, 188-193
  FILEVIEW.CPP, 72-73
  FILEVIEW.H, 84-87
  FVRC.H, 118-119
  LNCHICON.CP, 172-174
  LNCHICON.H, 175
  MDI.CPP, 157-158
  MDI.RC, 157
  MDILNCH.RC, 170-172
  MDIMENU.CPP, 163-166
  MDIMENU.RC, 166-167
  MDIVIEW.CPP, 181-182
  MEMTEST.CPP, 220-221
  MSGWIND.CPP, 55-59
  OLECLNT.CPP, 285-290
  OLECLNT.H, 290
  OLECLNT.RC, 290
  OLERVR.CPP, 275-279
  OLERVR.H, 279-280
  OLESRVR.RC, 280
  POPMENU.CPP, 103-108
  PRINTEX.CPP, 205-207
  SIMPLEMNU.H, 97
  SIMPLMNU.CPP, 94-96
  SIMPLMNU.RC, 96
  SIZER.CPP, 40-43
  VALLOC.CPP, 298-299
  VALLOC.H, 297-298
  VALLOC.H, 299-302
  VAPPL.CPP, 302-305
  VAPPL.H, 299-302
  VARRAY.H, 305-308
  VBITMAP.H, 308-309
  VBUTTON.CPP, 310-312
  VBUTTON.H, 309-310
  VCHECK.H, 312-314
  VCLIP.CPP, 470-471
  VCLIP.H, 469-470
  VCLPITM.CPP, 472-473
  VCOMCLR.CPP, 315-316
  VCOMCLR.H, 314-315
  VCOMFILE.CPP, 318-322
  VCOMFILE.H, 316-318
  VCOMFIND.CPP, 323-325
  VCOMFIND.H, 322-323
  VCOMFONT.CPP, 326-327
  VCOMFONT.H, 325-326
  VCOMMON.H, 327-328
  VCOMPOST.CPP, 328-331
  VCOMPRNT.CPP, 332-334
  VCOMPRNT.H, 331-332
  VCONTROL.CPP, 336-339
  VCONTROL.H, 334-336
  VDATADLG.H, 339-340
  VDBLLIST.CPP, 347-348
  VDBLLIST.CPP, 350-354
  VDBLLIST.H, 340-347
  VDDE.CPP, 479-481
  VDDE.H, 473-479
  VDDECLNT.CPP, 483-484
  VDDECLNT.H, 481-483
  VDDECONV.CPP, 485-489
  VDDESERV.CPP, 492-497
  VDDESERV.H, 489-492
  VDDESTR.CPP, 497-500
  VDISPTCH.CPP, 350-353
  VDISPTCH.H, 348-350
  VDLGBOX.CPP, 356-361
  VDYNARRAY.H, 361-362
  VEDIT.CPP, 364-367
  VEDIT.H, 362-364
  VEVENT.CPP, 370-371
  VEVENT.H, 367-370
  VFRAME.CPP, 371-374
  VGDITOOL.CPP, 383-384
  VGDITOOL.H, 374-383
  VGRDEV.CPP, 389-391
  VGRDEV.H, 385-389
  VGROBJ.CPP, 393
  VGROBJ.H, 391-393
  VHANDLE.H, 226-227, 393-395
  VICON.H, 395-397
  VIEWER.CPP, 75-77
  VISTA.H, 397-399
  VISTA.MAK, 463-467
  VISTADLG.CPP, 120-126
  VISTADLL.MAK, 463-467
  VISTARC.H, 399-400
  VLABEL.CPP, 401-402
  VLABEL.H, 400-401
  VLIST.H, 402-405
  VLSTBOX.CPP, 407-410
  VLSTBOX.H, 402-405
  VMAIN.CPP, 410
  VMDICHILD.CPP, 412-414
  VMDICHILD.H, 410-412
  VMDICLI.CPP, 414-415
  VMDIFRM.CPP, 416-420
  VMDIFRM.H, 415-416
  VMENU.CPP, 423-427
  VMENU.H, 420-423
  VMSGBOX.CPP, 429-430
  VMSGBOX.H, 427-429
  VOLECDOC.CPP, 500-504
  VOLECLNT.CPP, 508-512
  VOLECLNT.H, 504-508
  VOLECOBJ.CPP, 512-517
  VOLEDOC.CPP, 517-522
  VOLEERR.CPP, 523-527
  VOLEERR.H, 522-523
  VOLEOBJ.CPP, 536-541
  VOLEOBJ.H, 528-533
  VOLESRVR.H, 533-536
  VRADBTN.H, 430-431
  VSCROLL.CPP, 432-435
  VSCROLL.H, 431-432
  VSTATUS.H, 435-436

VSTRING.CPP, 439-441
VSTRING.H, 436-439
VTEXT.CPP, 442-445
VTEXT.H, 441-442
VTIMER.CPP, 446-448
VTIMER.H, 445-446
VTXTFLD.CPP, 449
VTXTFLD.H, 448-449
VWINDOW.CPP, 454-463
VWINDOW.H, 449-454
WINAPP, 14-16
WINVISTA.CPP, 23-25
StartAdvise function, 263
StartPage function, 209
strings, 194
　DDE management, 249-250
Stroustrup, Bjarne, 2
subclassing, 152
subsegment allocation, 221
superclassing, 152
SysCommandAction function, 178

T

template class, 225-227
TextLine class, 79-82
threads, reentrancy, 140
TileCommand function, 159, 161
Turbo Debugger for Windows (TDW), 36-37
　WInspector, 37-38

U

Unrealize function, 209
Unrecoverable application error (UAE), 22
UnregisterCallback function, 253

V

VAllocator class, 9, 221-224
VAppl class, 9, 36-46, 70
VArc class, 10
variables, 5-6, 87
VArray class, 9, 225
VBrush class, 10
VButton class, 9
VCheckBox class, 9
VClipboard class, 11, 238-239
VClipItem class, 239-240
VColorDialog class, 10, 130-131
VComboBox class, 9

VComposite class, 70, 115
VControl class, 9, 135-136
　custom controls library, 151-152
　data validation with, 150-151
　global window messages, 152-153
　subclassing, 152
　superclassing, 152
VData dialog class, 138-141
VDblList class, 9
VDdeClient class, 11, 260-265
　example program, 263-265
VDdeConv class, 260-265
　advise data callbacks, 263
　transaction complete callbacks, 262-263
VDdeData class, 263
VDdeHandle class, 263
　VDdeObject class, 252-253
　callback methods, 252
　disconnect callbacks, 253
　registration callbacks, 253
　system errors, 252-253
VDdeServer class, 11, 253-259
　connection management callbacks, 254-255
　data management callbacks, 255-259
　example program, 258-259
　execute callbacks, 257
　request/advise callbacks, 255-256
　support objects/operations, 257
　unsolicited callbacks, 257
VDdeString class, 263
VDevice class, 10
VDialog class, 10, 115, 126-127, 130-150
　attaching data objects to, 137-150
　Windows, 117-127
VDispatcher class, 59-60, 68-69
VDisplayDevice class, 10, 200-201
VDynArray class, 9
VEditable class, 10
VEvent class, 9, 48-64
　initializing dispatcher, 59-60
　initializing window, 60-61
　painting window, 61-62
　portability, 53-55
　Win32 modification, 54-55
　Windows messages, 48-53
VFileDevice class, 201

VFileDialog class, 10, 126-127
VFindDialog class, 132-134
VFont class, 10, 130
VFrame class, 70, 193
　Vista, 82
VGlobal class, 9, 224-225, 228
VGlobalHandle class, 263
VGraphicsText class, 10
VHandle class, 9, 224-225
　extending, 228-231
　overloading pointer dereferences, 227-228
viewer class, 75-78
virtual tables, 270
Vista, 8-11
　action methods, 26-27
　classes (*see* specific class names)
　library, 297-539
　message processing, 52-53
　moving C programs to, 87-88, 113, 153, 194-195
　naming conventions, 29
　scrolling, 82-87
　windows application, 23-25
VLabel class, 9
VLine class, 10
VList class, 9, 225
VListBox class, 9
VLocal class, 9, 228
VLocalHandle class, 263
VMdiChild class, 10, 162-169
VMdiClient class, 156
VMdiFrame class, 156, 160-162, 170-176
VMdiParent class, 10
VMemoryDevice class, 10, 201
VMenu class, 10
　creating dynamic menus, 98-104
　Vista, 94-98
VOleClient class, 11
VOleClientDoc class, 291, 292
VOleClientObj class, 292
VOleServer class, 11
VOleStream class, 294
VPaintDevice class, 200
VPen class, 10
VPoint class, 207-208
VPopupMenu class, 10
VPrintDialog class, 10, 127-129
VPrinterDevice class, 10, 201, 208-210

VPushbutton class, 9
VRadioButton class, 9
VRectangle class, 10
VScrollAction function, 82
VScrollbar class, 10
VShape class, 10, 205-207
VString class, 9
VSystemMenu class, 10
VText class, 10
VTextField class, 10
VTool class, 10, 202-204
VWindows class, 9-10, 19-21, 26, 65-70
  procedure, 65-70

W

WildCardCallback function, 254
window objects, 65-88
  adding a menu to, 97
Windows
  applications, 13-29
  converting programs to C++, 8
  creating/displaying windows, 19
  data types, 22-23
  graphics and, 197-210
  interprocess communication, 237
  memory, 212
  memory allocation functions, 218
  naming conventions, 21-22
  program development cycle, 31-36
  program initialization, 18
  WinApp in C, 14-17
Windows exit procedure (WEP) function, 232
WinExec function, 179
WinMain function, 17-18
WinVistaAppl class, 40
WriteBuffer function, 138, 140

Y

Yourdon, Edward, 71

About the author

Jeff Mackay is a Senior Software Engineer for KASEWORKS, Inc., a leading developer of Microsoft Windows and OS/2 Presentation Manager client-server development tools. With almost 10 years of programming under his belt, Jeff's user interface experience includes OS/2 Presentation Manager, Microsoft Windows and Windows NT, and the X Window System using DECWindows, OSF/Motif, and the Andrew Toolkit. Jeff is a member of the Association for Computing Machinery (ACM) and the Computer-Human Interaction Special Group (SIGCHI). Jeff has also provided consulting services for several companies, including IBM and Digital Equipment Corporation.

Order Form for Readers Requiring Two 5.25" Disks

This Windcrest/McGraw-Hill software product is also available on two 5.25"/360K disks. If you need the software in 5.25" format, simply follow these instructions:

- Complete the order form below. Be sure to include the exact title of the Windcrest/McGraw-Hill book for which you are requesting a replacement disk.

- Make check or money order made payable to *Glossbrenner's Choice*. The cost is $7.00 ($10.00 for shipments outside the U.S.) to cover media, postage, and handling. Pennsylvania residents, please add 6% sales tax.

- Foreign orders: please send an international money order or a check drawn on a bank with a U.S. clearing branch. We cannot accept foreign checks.

- Mail order form and payment to:

    Glossbrenner's Choice
    Attn: Windcrest/McGraw-Hill Disk Replacement
    699 River Road
    Yardley, PA 19067-1965

Your disks will be shipped via First Class Mail. Please allow one to two weeks for delivery.

..................................✂..................................

Windcrest/McGraw-Hill Disk Replacement

Please send me replacement disks in 5.25"/360K format for the following Windcrest/McGraw-Hill book:

Book Title _____

Name _____

Address _____

City/State/ZIP _____

If you need help with the enclosed disk . . .

The enclosed 3½-inch diskette should contain the following files:

CHAP10.LIB	CHAP5.LIB	FILE1.LIS	LIB.LIB
CHAP11.LIB	CHAP6.LIB	INCLUDE.LIB	MAIN.LIB
CHAP12.LIB	CHAP7.LIB	INSTALL.EX$	README.TXT
CHAP2.LIB	CHAP8.LIB	INSTALL.LGO	SETUP.EXE
CHAP4.LIB	CHAP0.LIB	INSTALL.INS	SRC.LIB

The Vista Application Framework and sample applications were built using Windows 3.1 and Borland C++ 3.1.

To install the source code and sample programs, copy the files onto your hard drive, then run Windows. Select Run... from the File menu. Run SETUP.EXE in the directory to which you just copied the companion diskette files. This program will create the necessary directories and copy the files to your drive.

Before building the sample applications, you'll need to build the Vista library. Load the VISTA.PRJ project file into BCW, update the include and library directories to reflect the locations of Borland C++ and the Vista library on your machine. Then, select Build All from the Compile menu in BCW.

To build sample applications, load the sample's project file into BCW and update the directories. Then, select Build All to make the application.

See the README.TXT file on the disk for additional information.